MediaWriting

MediaWriting

Print, Broadcast, and
Public Relations

Third Edition

W. Richard Whitaker

Janet E. Ramsey

Ronald D. Smith

Routledge
Taylor & Francis Group

NEW YORK AND LONDON

First edition published 2000
by Addison Wesley Longman

Second edition published 2004
by Lawrence Erlbaum Associates

This edition published 2009
by Routledge
270 Madison Ave, New York, NY 10016

Simultaneously published in the UK
by Routledge
2 Park Square, Milton Park, Abingdon, Oxon OX14 4RN

Routledge is an imprint of the Taylor & Francis Group, an informa business

Typeset in Times New Roman PS and Helvetica by
Florence Production Ltd, Stoodleigh, Devon
Printed and bound in the United States of America on acid-free paper by
Edwards Brothers, Inc.

Library of Congress Cataloging in Publication Data
Whitaker, Wayne R., 1940–.
 Mediawriting: print, broadcast, and public relations/by W. Richard Whitaker,
 Janet E. Ramsey, and Ronald D. Smith.—3rd ed.
  p. cm.
  Includes bibliographical references and index.
 1. Mass media—Authorship. 2. Broadcast journalism—Authorship.
 3. Public relations—Authorship. 4. Journalism—Authorship.
 I. Ramsey, Janet E. II. Smith, Ronald D., 1948–. III. Title.
 P96.A86W48 2008
 808′.066302—dc22   2008010584

ISBN10: 0–8058–6295–1 (pbk)
ISBN10: 0–203–88670–4 (ebk)

ISBN13: 978–0–8058–6295–9 (pbk)
ISBN13: 978–0–203–88670–0 (ebk)

Brief Contents

Contents

Preface

Introduction to *MediaWriting*

About *MediaWriting*

When the first edition of *MediaWriting* was conceptualized in the mid-1990s, industry predictions were that media were coming together in "convergence," spurred by the increasingly interrelated technologies of computer, telephone, and TV. Specialization by media, it was said, was on its way out. Print and broadcast journalists and public relations practitioners would not be merely reporters and writers but would increasingly be in the information-processing business that would require overlapping skills. The president of America Online was quoted in *Broadcasting* magazine as noting that media companies were positioning themselves to take advantage of a synergy of print and video and interactive technologies and, even before the AOL–Time Warner merger, that future media companies would be those that successfully combined the three.

Those optimistic predictions were slightly off, of course. The full impact of convergence has been battered by the collapse of the dot.coms and the subsequent decline in stock values across media properties. On the other hand, hundreds of newspapers have introduced an online presence, many with real-time streaming audio and video. The *Chicago Tribune* and WGN radio and television have a convergent news operation, as does the *Tampa Tribune* and a local TV station. The *Philadelphia Inquirer*, the *Philadelphia Daily News*, three regional newspapers, a local television outlet and 50 radio stations have teamed up in an interactive Web site. Gannett, the nation's largest newspaper publishing chain, has aggressively moved to mesh print, television and information venues. The pattern is replicated in many other markets around the country, where broadcast and print reporters prepare copy for each other's medium. Radio stations, which a few years earlier introduced streaming audio of their programming, now offer streaming video of their DJs doing their programs. Many corporations and non-profit organizations have taken advantage of the opportunities presented by computer technology to provide newsworthy information directly to their publics, bypassing traditional journalistic gatekeepers.

Instead of being merely writers and reporters, print and broadcast journalists and public relations practitioners increasingly find themselves in the business of information processing and dissemination. Tomorrow's news writers will need to be able to write a piece of newspaper copy designed to be read and then converted to a broadcast script that can be heard or with visuals that can be seen. Internet writing requires a mix of print and broadcast writing skills, as well as graphic elements, to make Web-based news interesting to read. Public relations practitioners need to possess the ability to produce news releases in print and broadcast versions for external media, as information for internal organizational media, or for the organization's Web site.

Although traditional daily and weekly newspaper, radio, and television jobs are still available, competition for them has increased. Newspaper readership percentages have been on a downward spiral for years and, although online newspapers are attracting readers, the number of daily newspapers continues to decline. Most local radio stations have abandoned news and television produces news for increasingly fragmented audiences.

Career options in this new media environment, however, have expanded dramatically for those with interchangeable writing skills. Today's media writers can begin careers in a variety of magazine genres and newsletters and the Internet is providing expanded opportunities. Traditional agency and corporate public relations has expanded to non-profit organizations, and advertising continues to be the economic backbone supporting the media. Predictions are that in less than 20 years, media writers will be independent contractors, coming together as part of specialized teams, working on a specific project, then leaving to start another. Today's media freelancer is already working in this way.

MediaWriting is designed for those who will venture into this new multimedia environment. The textbook explores linkages between print, broadcast, and public relations writing styles; outlines the nature of good writing; and synthesizes and integrates professional skills and concepts. Although the subject matter is still divided into print, broadcast, and public relations sections—because each writing form has a distinct style—the textbook pulls these three elements together so that at the end of a semester or term you will have a grasp of the basic principles of media writing.

We not only explain the "hows" of media writing but also the "whys" by discussing the theoretical aspects of communication. This book examines legal and ethical issues, analyzes what makes news and how it is written and reported, how radio and TV stations operate, and the role of the public relations practitioner in today's media environment. With concentrated effort on your part, you'll possess the skills to go on to more specialized writing courses.

MediaWriting seeks to develop professional attitudes and skills that reporters, broadcasters, and public relations professionals need. One objective of the book is to provide beginning newswriting students with a primer that fosters development of the talents needed for a summer job or internship at a small daily or weekly newspaper, at a small or medium-market radio or television station, or in public relations.

MediaWriting's Features

MediaWriting is an introductory, hands-on writing textbook for students preparing for all professional areas of communication and is designed for instructors who want to be writing coaches and mentors as well as teachers. *MediaWriting* is full of real-world examples and exercises, giving students progressive writing activities amid an environment for developing research and interviewing skills. Unlike other textbooks, which talk about writing and the differences among the three writing styles, *MediaWriting* synthesizes and integrates the three concepts, weaving in basic principles of Internet writing and reporting. From a basis in writing news and features for print media, it moves on to writing for broadcast news media. Finally, it introduces students to public relations writing in print, broadcast, and digital media and provides a primer on advertising and copywriting.

New to This Edition

When the first edition of *MediaWriting* went to press, the Internet was still only one step above an exotic toy and the browser of choice was Mosaic. Now the Internet is *the* essential communication tool for print and broadcast journalists, public relations professionals, and for those in a new category: online blogs doing their own brand of reporting. This third edition reflects these changes, with increased attention to computer-assisted reporting and preparation of copy for online. All of the chapters have been reviewed and many have been extensively rewritten to reflect the changes that have taken place in this dynamic, ever-changing profession. New to this edition is a separate chapter on advertising.

Since the first edition, there has been the tragedy of September 11, 2001, which has changed the way news is reported and how information is accessible to journalists. There have also been embarrassing scandals involving reporters from flagship newspapers who have either plagiarized or made up quotes and stories. Because the authors feel it is important to inculcate prospective communicators into the highest standards of the professions, we moved law and ethics into the second chapter position, giving the subject the importance we believe it deserves.

The textbook carries a number of features that we hope readers will find helpful:

- Chapters open with a set of objectives outlining the concepts to be covered.
- Explanatory "How To" boxes aid in understanding and retaining main themes.
- Additional practical exercises bring to life concepts and writing principles.
- Interspersed throughout the book are updated "It Happened to Me" vignettes from the authors' personal experiences.
- For those who prefer specific citations, notes are included in chapters in which we have drawn directly from other sources.
- Suggested readings highlight biographies and books available to expand the scope and definition of professionalism.
- We tried to follow our own advice and make the text "read" well using conversational sentences that are easy to follow, with information and tips to become a successful media writer.

Supplement

An *Instructor's Manual/Test Bank* that contains questions for class discussion, quizzes for each chapter, and authors' discussions of the various exercises is available to adopters.

About the Authors

The authors, all members of the faculty of the Department of Communication at Buffalo State College, bring varied academic and professional talents to this writing project.

W. Richard Whitaker, emeritus professor of journalism and broadcasting, has broad experience in TV news as a reporter, cameraman and producer, and in newspaper work as a reporter and desk editor. A Navy Reserve public affairs officer for 20 years, he was also a consultant and associate producer for a family-owned film and video production company. He taught at the college and university level for 39 years, serving as a department chair for 11 of those years. Whitaker has published articles in *Journalism Quarterly*, *Journalism History*, *Middle East Review*, *Oral History Review*, and *Northwest Ohio Quarterly*, and has written Navy-related articles for a variety of publications including *Curator*, for museum directors, and *U.S. Navy Medicine*. He has written bibliographic entries for *The Encyclopedia of New York State*, *History of the Mass Media in the United States*, and the *Biographical Dictionary of American Journalism*. He holds a B.A. in radio–TV news from San Jose State College, an M.S. in journalism from the University of Oregon School of Journalism, and a Ph.D. in mass communication from Ohio University.

Janet E. Ramsey, a State University of New York (SUNY) Distinguished Service Professor and Dean Emerita, has served as chair of the Communication Department and associate vice president for undergraduate education at Buffalo State College. A professor of journalism, she has 35 years of teaching experience in both the secondary school and university levels. She has published a textbook for college students, *Feature and Magazine Article Writing*; written articles in the *Dictionary of Literary Biography*: *American Magazine Journalists*, and *Journalism Educator*; and done research on Susan Sontag for the *Columbia Dictionary of Quotations.* She has also presented papers on Chaucer, the literary figure of her doctoral studies. Ramsey has been a fellow of the American Press Institute and of the Poynter Institute for Media Studies, and she served as president of the Buffalo Chapter of the Society of Professional Journalists. She has done public relations writing for Buffalo State College and served as chair of its College Senate for three years. She holds an undergraduate degree from Ohio State University in secondary English education, an M.A. in English from SUNY College at Fredonia, and a Ph.D. in medieval literature from SUNY Buffalo.

Ronald D. Smith, professor of public communication and chair of the Department of Communication at Buffalo State College, teaches undergraduate and graduate courses in public relations strategy, writing, case studies, research and related areas. He has worked as a public relations manager and consultant, newspaper reporter and editor, and as a Navy journalist during the Vietnam War. He has written two other textbooks: *Becoming a Public Relations Writer* and *Strategic Planning for Public Relations*, both in their third editions, and has published in the *Journal of Public Relations Research* and in *Sage 21st Century Reference Series: Communication*. Smith is also project director for the American Indian Policy and Media Initiative at Buffalo State and co-editor of the Initiative's 2007 book, *Shoot the Indian: Media, Misperception and Native Truth*. An accredited member of the Public Relations Society of America, he has served as chapter president and district chair and has been honored as Practitioner of the Year. Smith's degrees include a B.S. in English education from Lock Haven University of Pennsylvania and an M.S. in public relations from Syracuse University.

Other Contributors

Several of our Buffalo State College colleagues reviewed our manuscript and suggested or provided content. Our thanks to Joe Marren (news, new technology), Janet Kaye (law, feature writing), Bill Raffel (law, broadcast news), Tom McCray (radio production), and Paul DeWald (television production). Our appreciation too to Monica Wilson, news director of WBEN News Radio in Buffalo, N.Y., for her update on radio news and new technology.

Some Words on Writing

Like all writing, media writing requires discipline because it's hard work. It's also fun and rewarding. A newspaper reporter goes out and covers the news, then comes back and writes a story with his or her byline under the headline. With a constant 24-hours-a-day/seven-days-a-week deadline, Internet reporters face the same challenge that wire-service reporters did a half-century ago. TV correspondents report from the scene with their name superimposed on the screen, and radio journalists often have the challenge of working on even tighter deadlines. Public relations practitioners interact with their journalist counterparts to help in reporting the news, then similarly do interviews and research news stories for use in either internal publications or external news releases. Whichever field you choose, it's a great way to make a living!

The professions are very competitive, however: For every job for which you'll be applying, at least 15 other equally or more talented people want the same position (and the professionals who have read this statement say that's optimistic!). You have to be good to make it. As a prospective communication professional, you need to develop curiosity about the world around you, a broad knowledge base, creativity, attention to detail, and respect for accuracy, objectivity and fairness. You also have to acquire solid writing skills and a passion for words: Communicators are "wordsmiths," people who respect language and have learned its usage. Only when you have developed these characteristics of a language and information specialist will you be able to effectively interpret the world to other people. *MediaWriting* is designed to help you build the necessary foundation to do just that.

W. Richard Whitaker
Janet E. Ramsey
Ronald D. Smith

1

Communication Theory
and News Values

Chapter Objectives

- To describe the challenges facing media writers today
- To summarize media theories and their impact on the communication process
- To discuss the role of media writers in their organizations and in society
- To interpret the elements of newsworthiness as they apply to news judgment
- To evaluate newspeople's and audiences' perceptions of the reporting process

---

Changes in Media Writing

In 1929, when gunmen for mobster Al Capone mowed down members of a rival Chicago gang in what became known as the St. Valentine's Day Massacre, the story became a national media event reported mainly by newspapers. Radio news was in its infancy; newsreels would not be able to produce and distribute a report to movie theaters for several more years, and then not until days after a major event; and TV was still only a laboratory experiment. Public relations was primarily about publicity—at times even involved in keeping stories *out* of the press. Weekly general-circulation magazines offered some news, but they mostly carried features, short literary stories and advertisements. Back then, only newspapers and the wire services that provided copy for papers around the country were capable of thoroughly reporting the story. Media writing was defined as *newspaper* journalism.

In April 2007 a student at Virginia Tech University gunned down more than 30 people before taking his own life as police closed in. Within a short time, satellite trucks clogged roads of the bucolic countryside and television began transmitting the ongoing drama live to millions of viewers around the country, and around the world. Radio also provided coverage;

print and online reporters wrote reams of copy; and bloggers joined the media mix. Public-information specialists from federal, state and local law enforcement agencies interpreted events, as did legal experts and psychiatric consultants hired by cable and traditional TV networks. Although the coverage was still identifiable as "reporting," the technology and the immediacy of the coverage reflected a media writing environment far different from what had existed nearly 80 years before.

Media writing is more than a matter of gathering facts and putting words together. Writers must work within the opportunities and limits provided by the technology, societal values, the communications process, demands of the media business and needs of the audience. This chapter provides a foundation for learning media writing by exploring the context in which print, broadcast and Internet journalists and public relations professionals write.

Media Writing as Mass Communication

Mass communication is a powerful force in modern society. Radio, television, newspapers, magazines, film, public relations and advertising, as well as blogs and the Internet, all shape the manner in which we react to the world around us.

Over the years, various communication theories have been developed about the role of the mass media in society. It can be theorized that media writing has changed, not only because of the immediacy and intensity made possible by today's portable communication technology, but by the demands of the 24/7 news cycle. Communication theories have implications for you as a media writer because they attempt to explain what people pay attention to and why, and how messages become lost or distorted despite communicators' best efforts.

The Purpose of Communication

One of the early communication researchers, Harold Lasswell, identified three functions of the mass media: (1) surveillance of the environment, (2) correlation of the parts of society in responding to that environment (explaining to various publics what the news and information being transmitted means to them), and (3) transmission of the cultural heritage from one generation to the next.[1] Another prominent researcher, Wilbur Schramm, said that in order for media messages to be successful, they must be designed and delivered in ways that gain attention, using language commonly understood by communicator and audience, and that the message must arouse needs and present ways to meet them.[2]

Although those propositions were first offered more than 50 years ago, they remain a valid description of the task facing today's media writers. A reporter's job is to look around and see what is happening, and then communicate what he or she deems important to the reading, listening and viewing public. Clarity in presenting the message is extremely important: If the audience doesn't understand what is being communicated, it will turn away from or misinterpret the message.

Communication Challenges

Increasingly, media messages have become part of the babble of background sound and activities. Nowadays it is rare for people to *only* read a newspaper or *only* watch TV or *only* have a conversation. Often they do one or more while engaged in other activities without paying attention to the background the various mass media provide.

In many respects, Canadian communication theorist Marshall McLuhan was right when he said, "The medium is the message," meaning that societies have always been more influenced by the form of communication than by its content. Long before CNN and satellite TV, McLuhan envisioned an electronic "global village" of shared experiences and information, a holistic environment shattering the isolated "linear" bonds that print communication fostered. McLuhan said that society had entered a new age in which our world and surroundings were changing rapidly, especially due to television, which was responsible for "reshaping and restructuring patterns of social interdependence and every aspect of our personal life." This new world of electronic information media involves all of us all at once, McLuhan said. Information pours upon us instantaneously and continuously: as soon as we acquire information, it is rapidly replaced by still newer information.[3] The accuracy of McLuhan's observations 40 years ago about the power of TV has been compounded by the rise of the Internet and the World Wide Web (WWW).

Ironically, with all of the various information resources available today, people often read superficially or listen with only one ear to a TV report. This inattention contributes to what is known as **perceptual distortion**, the tendency to introduce inaccuracies in perceiving what the writer or announcer said. A cardinal rule of newswriting is that what the communicator sends by way of a message is less important than what the audience receives and perceives. Often, these two are quite different.

One reason why people of different ages, genders, races or religions sometimes receive the same information but take from it different meanings is addressed by the theory of **denotative** and **connotative** meanings. Communication research recognizes denotative and connotative meanings of words and symbols, which complicate the communication process. People attach denotative labels (standard, descriptive names) to things, concepts, and ideas but they also put their own connotations (interpretations of meaning or value) on those same things, concepts, and ideas based on their experiences, attitudes, opinions, and beliefs. For instance, the denotative meaning of a "No Smoking" sign outside your classroom building is that no smoking is permitted inside. Even that simple message has connotations. If a student has trouble making it through a 50-minute class without a cigarette, he or she might feel that "they" are abridging personal rights by prohibiting smoking. A nonsmoker, on the other hand, might interpret the sign as protecting the health of students and faculty.

Another source of message distortion is audience reaction to **cognitive dissonance**.[4] The theory of cognitive dissonance says that people can tolerate only so much emotional upset and, when information we receive is different from that which we accept or with which we are comfortable, our mind seeks a balance by rejecting or modifying the dissonant information. An example is when a news report is so emotionally jarring that people set up internal psychological defenses to deal with the message.

Finally, two types of communication interference, called **noise**,[5] are present in the process of message transmission: **physical noise** and **semantic noise**. Physical noise is anything that distorts the reception of the message—background sounds that drown out a speaker, static, or similar problems. In theory, it can be corrected. Semantic noise is confusion caused by using words or phrases that the audience cannot understand or might misinterpret. Although semantic noise is harder to deal with, effective media writing can eliminate most of its associated problems.

Media Research and Theory

Media research shows audiences are very interactive.[6] Although many people think TV audiences are composed of mindless "couch potatoes," only a small proportion of viewers fall into that category. More typical is the "channel surfer," who zips through cable-system offerings—a type of behavior that also shows up in online media use. Several theories have been developed to explain differences and similarities in media habits. All are directly applicable to media writers because they explain how people receive and distort media messages.

Individual Differences Theory

According to the theory of **individual differences**, people are unique in the way they approach media messages. Individual demographics and experiences shape audience perceptions of communicators and their transmissions. Therefore, the credibility of sources and the way issues-oriented messages are viewed can change from person to person.

Social Categories Theory

While audiences possess individual traits that determine responses to messages, **social categories** theory maintains that people who share similar demographic characteristics will respond similarly to a message. Research has shown, for instance, that women interpret a television news report differently than men. Women (a social category) tend to remember feature news and pay attention to visual background detail, while men (another social category) tend to remember factual detail at the expense of the other.[7]

Social Influence

Often, social categories can be particularly strong when they involve members of a close-knit group, even though the group may have a diversified membership. The theory of **social influence** states that members of a group can construct an artificial reality for themselves, strong enough even to reject appealing mass-media messages or portrayals.[8] Young members of a close-knit religious fellowship who do not drink, for example, will not change their behavior no matter how appealing the beer commercial—with all those suntanned people frolicking on the beach and drinking lots of beer with nary a bathroom in sight—because of the social ostracism that would follow.

Selective Processes

Because so many media voices compete for attention, people's media behaviors are influenced by the so-called **selective processes**: selective attention or exposure, selective perception, selective retention, and even selective recall. The selective processes theory contends that although exposure to some media messages may be accidental, for the most part audience members choose whether to pay attention. Because it is impossible to read, hear and see everything in our mass media environment, people selectively expose themselves to messages they feel will be of interest or help to them, and interpret them according to their biases. Then, because it is impossible to remember everything, only information that seems important is retained. What is retained, some scholars insist, is subject to the distortion of selective recall. Events or facts are remembered or subconsciously altered in a way that reinforces beliefs and attitudes or staves off cognitive dissonance.[9]

Stereotypes

A filtering process takes place as readers, listeners, and viewers interpret facts, statements, and events. Audiences rely on **stereotypes**, the mental images people use as a simplified representation of reality. According to newspaper columnist Walter Lippmann, who first wrote about stereotypes in 1921, "Whatever we believe to be a true picture, we treat as if it were the environment itself, for the real environment is altogether too big, too complex and too fleeting for direct acquaintance." Gradually, we develop a mental picture of the world that seems true to us, then respond to this pseudo-environment as though it were true.[10] Although stereotypes can impede information flow, audiences—as well as news organizations—have long used them in stories about race, gender, age, politics or international relations.

Wants and Needs Gratification

In explaining basic audience behavior, the theory of **wants and needs gratification** maintains that an audience will not pay attention to a media message unless the message or the medium fulfills some perceived want or need. According to the theory, all media behavior is based on the expectation of reward.[11] Even collapsing on the couch at the end of the day "just to watch some TV" is a form of the wants and needs theory in operation. So is watching a "slice-and-dice" horror film with friends in order to be part of the group, even though you may not care for that film genre.

Opinion Leaders

Years ago, researchers identified what became known as the **two-step flow of communication**, in which media messages travel to influential community members known as **opinion leaders**, who then explain the significance of the messages to those who look to them for guidance.[12] For example, labor leaders are opinion leaders for union members; respected business leaders are opinion leaders for residents of a town. Opinion leaders also may be influential people in medicine, education or the clergy. This theory has since been expanded to a multi-step flow of mediated communication, with multiple opinion leaders providing various levels of influence and interpretation in a dynamic process between receiver and sources.[13] Individuals may also bypass opinion leaders entirely, creating their own interpretation of events and ideas relayed by the media. Thus, instead of creating messages for a relatively homogeneous audience, today's media writers must consider a diverse audience, with each member having distinct interests and insisting that individual demands be met.

Narcotizing Dysfunction

Members of audiences sometimes remain unmoved by media messages. For example, although the amount of political information and advertisements has increased, political participation continues to decline. Research has identified a phenomenon known as the **narcotizing dysfunction**, which is often seen among people who pay close attention to news and public affairs issues without acting on that knowledge.[14] These well-informed people choose not to vote or take part in community government because overexposure to messages makes them seem confusing and contradictory. Thus, these members of the audience do not make decisions, even though they are relatively well informed.

Cultivation

Media research has concluded that many people's values and worldviews are related to their media exposure. For heavy viewers of news, public affairs and talk shows, those programs become their version of reality and topics discussed on the programs become important. Local news broadcasts are particularly effective in cultivating certain perceptions of reality. Likewise, those who view violent TV programs may cultivate that view of the environment as reality—"the city is a dangerous place"—or accept similar stereotypes. **Cultivation** theory, then, postulates that mass media, especially television, "cultivate" a perception of reality. People who consume the mass media extensively share those views more than mild or moderate media users.[15]

Acculturation

News professionals are not immune to being influenced by what they do. The theory of **acculturation** suggests that news reporters adopt the attitudes and behaviors of those they cover. Police reporters, for instance, at times are stronger supporters of law and order than many police officers. Political reporters may take on the views of people about whom they report, which is why the networks periodically shift White House, State Department and Pentagon correspondents to different beats. In those examples, news people have become socialized into adopting the mindset of their environment—often without their conscious knowledge—and they pass those values on to the audience.

Spiral of Silence

Not everyone buys into the values and world view expressed by the mass media. The **spiral of silence** theory says that fear of isolation or separation from those around them prevents people from expressing their opinions when they perceive themselves to be in the minority.[16] As more people with out-of-the-mainstream views withdraw from public debate, the majority appears even stronger. Because the media combine to present a common view of the world and imply that it is accepted by most people, those who disagree with the media's perception often remain silent for fear of being considered out of step. Instead, those minority views are expressed only when legitimized by the media. Spiral of silence theory also explains the hostility many people feel toward the news media. People who do not agree with the thrust or bias of a news report may believe they are in the minority or powerless to effect change. If so, they may internalize their resentment rather than speak out.

Implications for Media Writers

What does all this theory mean in practice for the media writer? It is a reminder that communication is not simple and carries no guarantee of success. What the media most commonly do is reinforce opinions, attitudes and beliefs, and maintain the status quo.[17] For the most part, audiences will reject or ignore messages that run counter to already-held opinions, attitudes and beliefs, even if they are carried by the powerful media.

Some attitude modification is possible through the mass media, however, an effect often seen when public opinion polls record a decline in "undecided" respondents in favor of one position or another. The mass media also can serve as powerful educational mechanisms in the diffusion of new ideas or the creation of new attitudes in novel or changing circumstances.[18]

The challenge to the media writer, then, is to write and report stories in a way that avoids creating cognitive dissonance and slips through the selective process filters to be retained because the stories appeal to some want or need felt by members of the audience. Such writing is not always easy.

The Media Business

Like many other businesses—and journalism, broadcast news and public relations are businesses, make no mistake about that—the field has its maxims and sayings. One of them is attributed to Wilbur Storey, editor of the *Chicago Times* during the late nineteenth century, who said the role of the newspaper was "to print the news and raise hell." His contemporary, Charles A. Dana of the *New York Sun*, said newspapering consisted of buying newsprint at two cents a pound and selling it for 10 cents a pound. About 80 years after Storey and Dana, broadcast journalist Edward R. Murrow told his colleagues that television was a mixture of information, entertainment, and sales and that when the three were gathered together under one tent, the dust never settled.[19]

Public relations began with communication efforts of organizations to generate positive public opinion. Edward Bernays, one of the original thinkers in the field, broke new ground in the early 1920s when he helped create what was to become the public relations profession. He defined public relations as the process of "crystallizing public opinion," which involved the "engineering of consent" based on Thomas Jefferson's principle that in a democratic society, everything depends on the consent of the public.[20]

All these quotes reflect a tension that remains in the communication business to this day. The organizational structure, management and newsroom operations reflect the at times conflicting dynamics of serving the public and making money. Although all three media formats share news values and the need for solid writing skills, they differ in their treatment of the news message. Print can go in depth on non-visual stories that broadcasting would never cover. Broadcasters are interested in sound bites and visuals that may not lend themselves to print treatment. Editorial decisions are dictated by both the medium and the economic necessity of drawing and keeping an audience.

Roles Within the Media

As a beginning journalist, broadcaster or public relations practitioner, you will find realities far different from the idealistic concepts lectured about in colleges and universities. To print or broadcast the news, the businesses that run newspapers, radio, and television have to make money; public relations practitioners also must be sensitive to the well-being of their businesses or organizations when they deal with reporters.

Gatekeeping

Communication theory recognizes people called **gatekeepers**, those who open and shut the gates of communication, thereby determining what an audience sees, hears, and reads.[21] Individual newspaper beat reporters and editors are gatekeepers; they decide which stories will be covered, whether the coverage appears in print, and, if so, how it is reported. Radio and television news directors, assignment editors, program producers, and field reporters perform a similar gatekeeping function, as do those who determine a radio station's playlist for the week or a TV station's late-movie offerings. Newsletter gatekeepers include the editor and contributors. Public relations practitioners are also gatekeepers, controlling the flow of information from their organizations as well as access to their sources.

As the information environment has become more complex, the number of gatekeepers has soared. Their decisions are generally based upon news values, with some attention both to what will be effective in the competition for readers, listeners and viewers and how the information will impact those audiences.

Agenda Setting

An important element of the news professional's job is **agenda setting**. Agenda-setting theory holds that the mass media determine what is important by starting newscasts with a particular story or printing it on page one. When news gatekeepers no longer consider an item to be of importance, it is allowed to slip off the public agenda. Although agenda-setting theory concedes the primacy of the media's role in determining which events are important, it concludes that media outlets only tell audiences what to think about, not what to think.[22] Public relations practitioners have learned to be attentive to the topics being covered in the media, because it presents an opportunity for their organization to address a topic that is on the media agenda. A high-profile celebrity who goes public with an admission of depression may provide the news peg for a mental health clinic to give media interviews on how to identify and deal with the condition.

Framing

While agenda setting deals with the perceived newsworthiness of an issue, **framing** focuses on the presentation of the story. Seen often in coverage of political news or social issues, the theory attempts to explain how the news media frame a story. Is a political candidate "ahead," "surging" or "falling behind"? Is there an inherent "good guy" in the story? Whose version of events gets top billing? Which version becomes the standard against which other points of view are measured? Framing provides for a rhetorical context for the text, involving the use of metaphor, story-telling, myths, legends, jargon, word choice, and other narrative elements, including "spin." For example, the report on repeat drunk driving might be framed in several ways: criminal recidivism, police incompetence, lenient judges, or the power of addiction. If agenda setting tells audiences what to think about, framing theory suggests that the media influence how the audience thinks about an issue. [23]

Issue Attention Cycle

A related theory, the **issue attention cycle**, says that the news media and public ignore a serious problem for years, then for some reason they suddenly notice it, declare it a crisis and concoct a solution. When they realize the problem will be costly and not easily fixed, they grow angry, then bored, and finally resume ignoring the problem.[24]

Status Conferral

This theory says that, because of their influential nature, the mass media confer status and legitimacy on people, organizations and ideas.[25] Thus, if a person appears on TV as an expert on an issue, that appearance enhances his or her reputation. After all, if people were not important, according to the theory, they wouldn't appear on television, because TV doesn't have time for unimportant issues, ideas or people. The status conferral theory implies that reporters need to be careful in covering news about groups. When choosing sources to quote, it is important to ensure that the source or organization is indeed legitimate and representative.

Specialization

Traditionally, the mass media have provided a sense of broader community, reflecting who and what Americans are as people, while also influencing social trends and traditions. In recent years, however, newspapers and news reports have become as fractionalized as the audiences they serve. Reporters are often assigned specialized beats beyond the traditional ones of police, courts, and city or county government. Sports, business, the environment, entertainment, lifestyles, and religion are staples of what is defined as news, and many newspapers have created special-interest pages catering to seniors, youth or ethnic groups within a community.

Theories of the Press

The way in which news is covered in American society reflects two important press theories: **libertarianism** and **social responsibility**.[26] Historically, when printing by movable type developed in the latter half of fifteenth-century Europe, authoritarian governments sought to control this new and expanding form of communication. Printers were licensed and expected to support and advance the ruler's policies, and criticism of the political system or those in power was not tolerated. The press was regulated by government guidelines, restrictive press laws, censorship, and by the granting of printing licenses only to those deemed politically reliable.

Libertarianism

Although the authoritarian system still exists under some repressive governments, authoritarian press theory gave way in the eighteenth and nineteenth centuries in the United States and parts of Western Europe to a libertarian concept, based on the philosophy of rationalism and natural rights. **Libertarianism** relies on a "marketplace of ideas," in which anyone with a viewpoint has the right to publish it without prior government approval. Although the purpose of the press is to inform, entertain, and sell goods, its primary responsibilities are to help discover truth, be a "watchdog" for society, and provide a check on government.

Crucial to the American media system is the First Amendment to the Constitution, a logical extension of libertarian theory, which says, "Congress shall make no law . . . abridging the freedom of speech, or of the press." Because of the First Amendment, which basically affirms an individual's right to speak his or her mind, the mass media are permitted wide latitude in what they can report and relatively narrow constraints are placed on what is actionable in court. There have been restrictions on the press, of course, throughout U.S. history: Abolitionist newspapers were barred from the Southern mails during the 1830s, President Lincoln briefly shut down two Northern newspapers critical of his Civil War policies, and sedition acts were passed during World War I. Some press coverage was restricted during World War II, and information flow has been tightened as part of the war on terrorism since September 11, 2001. For the most part, however, any action related to content has come after publication.

Social Responsibility

While libertarianism says that anyone with the economic means to be heard is entitled to a voice in the marketplace of ideas, by the early twentieth century access to the marketplace was being choked off by increased costs and consolidation of ownership. Not everyone who wanted to could afford to start or own a newspaper. Libertarianism thus began to break down. To counter this negative impact caused by market forces, the concept of **social responsibility** developed in the 1940s and 1950s. Social responsibility promoted the proposition that because all voices could no longer be represented in the marketplace of ideas, the media had a responsibility to ensure that all viewpoints were expressed and that conflict was to be elevated to a plane of discussion. If the media did not voluntarily assume this role, the theory said, it might be necessary for some governmental or other agency to see that they did so.

The notion of social responsibility reached its high point in the 1960s as an activist Federal Communications Commission (FCC) threatened and cajoled the radio and television industry in an attempt to elevate American broadcast standards and the U.S. Supreme Court began to pay more attention to media issues.

Broadcast Regulation

Since the earliest days of radio, government has exercised limited intervention through regulation and court decisions based upon the **doctrine of scarcity**, which considers the physical limits to the amount of space available on the electromagnetic spectrum for broadcasting. According to this doctrine, the airwaves belong to the people and broadcast station owners are merely temporary custodians of the frequencies licensed to them. Under the terms of the **1934**

Box 1.1

It Happened to Me: Theoretically Speaking

As a general-assignment TV news reporter, I daily encountered applications of communication theory. One expectation by our assignment editor was that the station's reporters would be alert for visual breaking news stories such as fires, accidents, and crime (*the surveillance function of mass media*), although I kept in mind that my video could not be too graphic (*thereby causing cognitive dissonance*). I covered courts and county government, which involved explaining the proceedings and issues to viewers (*the correlation function*), although I knew I had to keep those explanations brief to maintain viewer interest (*wants and needs gratification*).

On occasion, I would have the pleasure of interviewing noted artists, musical performers and actors for the newscast (*transmission of the social heritage*). In covering election campaigns, I had to be careful about maintaining balance when reporting about a candidate I liked or with whose positions I agreed (*acculturation*). In deciding whether to cover minor-party candidates (*agenda setting*), I had to weigh how viable they seemed, because if they appeared on the newscast, their views would be deemed more credible simply because they appeared on television (*status conferral*).

I routinely interviewed the mayor and other influential people within the community (*opinion leaders*), although I knew that whatever I reported would be filtered through the bias of the viewers (*stereotypes, individual differences*). At times, I would have to "sell" a story to the news producer (*gatekeeper*) because, like other reporters, I had a strong sense that a variety of viewpoints should be heard and that I had an implicit obligation to make that happen (*social responsibility*).

Theory is an abstract? No, not really. — *WRW*

Communications Act, broadcasters are expected to operate in the "public interest, convenience and necessity"—a broad standard open to interpretation, but one that reflects the fact that the FCC cannot censor programming.

There is little regulation of print media because, in theory, anyone can start a newspaper, newsletter or magazine. Radio and TV stations, however, do not enjoy the same First Amendment rights as their print counterparts. The Communications Act prohibits profanity and obscenity, and gives political candidates equal-time access to broadcast stations. There was a seldom-used right of rebuttal against personal attack and, for nearly 40 years, broadcasters had to abide by provisions of a **Fairness Doctrine** that encouraged them to undertake a balanced examination of controversial issues of public importance. The FCC allowed the Fairness Doctrine to lapse in the deregulatory climate of the 1980s, its rationale being that the increase of voices in the broadcast marketplace made it unnecessary for the government to mandate "fairness." The FCC also took the position that the Fairness Doctrine unnecessarily restricted the journalistic freedom of broadcasters and actually inhibited airing controversial issues of importance or presenting unorthodox or unpopular viewpoints.

Further Deregulation

With the passage of the **Telecommunications Act of 1996**, Congress further diluted the social responsibility requirements for broadcasting. The law brought cable TV under the same federal rules that govern telephones, radio, and television, but it allowed regional telephone companies, long-distance carriers, and cable systems to enter each other's markets. The FCC recently eliminated cross-ownership restrictions and allowed greater total penetration by media conglomerates. The emphasis is increasingly on economics, not public service, a change in philosophy that will affect media writers in any of the communication professions because, increasingly, what is communicated is that which sells. With the emphasis on deregulation and minimal governmental intervention, the United States seems to have returned to a libertarian–capitalist system, with the goal of reaching the largest possible audience at a maximum profit (increasingly with a minimum of staffing).

During this consolidation a diffusion of new technologies has put publishing and broadcasting in the hands of the ordinary person, potentially mitigating this return to a marketplace-driven communication system. Desktop publishing, electronic mail, digital video, fiber optics, camcorders, satellite transmission and, of course, blogs, MySpace, YouTube, the Internet and World Wide Web, along with an array of other technological advances, have the potential to turn traditional publishing and network giants into mere voices in the crowd.

Social responsibility concepts remain important to many journalists, however, who jealously guard the freedom of speech and press provisions of the First Amendment to the Constitution. If Americans were to lose those freedoms, it is argued, it would be the first step toward losing all of our political liberties. Thus, speech and publication remain protected, even if they are at times offensive.

What Makes News?

Charles Dana, editor of the *New York Sun* during the late nineteenth century, is credited with the axiom, "If man bites dog, that's news." News is an outstanding deviation from the norm, something that doesn't ordinarily happen. Another definition applies the theory of wants and needs gratification, saying that news is a combination of what audiences need to know and want to know. However news is defined, whether it involves "hard" breaking news or "soft" feature stories, it has certain characteristics, known as the criteria of news value, or the **news pegs** on which the story is "hung." They include timeliness, proximity to the audience, prominence of those involved, consequence, conflict, suspense, human interest, novelty, and progress. The more characteristics present in an event, the more it is newsworthy.

Timeliness

By any standard, especially in this era of instantaneous satellite communication and today's 24/7 news cycle, timeliness—or immediacy—is the most important criterion of news value. News is change, something that has just occurred; what happened a few days ago is history. Few events of major significance can be defined as news if they fail to meet the standard of timeliness. However, an event that occurred some time ago can still meet the timeliness standard if the news of it was just revealed. When in doubt about how to lead a story, go for timeliness: Tell what is happening *now*.

Proximity

We are all interested in what is going on around us; therefore, proximity is an important news element. Proximity means giving the local angle, telling about an event near the readers, listeners or viewers, and explaining how closely it touches their lives. Harry Tammen and Fred Bonfils, editors of the *Denver Post* in the early twentieth century, said that the news value of a dog fight on the street in front of their newspaper office was worth two European archduke assassinations. Local news is also important because people like to see their names in print for the positive things they do or say.

Prominence

"Names make news." When it comes to prominent people, whether the president of the United States or a famous movie or rock star, virtually anything he or she does or says is deemed newsworthy. If a prominent person missteps, like it or not, his or her transgression makes page one and is dissected on the cable talk shows. If an average person does the same thing, it might not make the news at all.

Consequence

The more people affected, generally the greater is the news value. Proposed changes in Social Security benefits might not be newsworthy in many regions of the country, but in Florida and Arizona—states with a large percentage of retired people—that story will have an impact. News writers, editors, and producers need to know local demographics and understand what is important to their audience.

Conflict

Whether or not we like it, conflict is a universal news value, the most common examples being sporting events, political contests, wars, and revolutions. Whether it's team against team, nation against nation, or men and women against the natural elements, conflict sells newspapers and draws broadcast audiences.

Suspense

Related to conflict is the news peg of suspense. Following an explosion in a coal mine, hours or days may go by while rescue workers look for survivors or bring out additional bodies. A search for an escaped convict, the tracking of a kidnapper, the journey of a damaged aircraft attempting to land—all are examples of suspense stories in which audiences have an interest.

Human Interest

People like to read about other people, which is why much of the news lends itself to feature treatment that emphasizes human nature. Features are often characterized by their human-interest elements: the creation of emotional responses such as happiness, sadness, anger, sympathy, hate, love, envy or humor.

Novelty

An unusual or strange aspect will help lift a story out of the ordinary. If an ordinary man jumps out of an ordinary airplane with an ordinary parachute and makes an ordinary landing, the event has no news value. But if the man has only one leg, his jump is newsworthy, just as it is if the parachute fails to open properly but he lands safely. In public relations, writers look for an unusual element because it might determine whether or not the media use the story.

Progress

The most upbeat news and feature stories are often about people accomplishing goals and making their communities better places in which to live or work. Progress stories that involve local business and industry improving life for their community or customers are naturals for public relations and are the staple of small- and medium-market television and smaller newspapers.

Changing Definitions of News

In the view of many members of the public, the media seem to use yet another definition: "If it's good news, that's bad news; if it's bad news, that's good news!" Part of the public's hostility toward the news media arises from the sense that journalists glorify social misfits and ignore the accomplishments of average people who lead ordinary lives and stay out of trouble. Whether audiences really want to know some of what today passes for "news" is open to question.

Box 1.2
It Happened to Me: Should We Show That?

The call from our TV station's answering service came shortly before 4 a.m. A car had been struck by a train as its driver was trying to make it through a railway crossing. The locomotive carried the vehicle 300 yards along the tracks before stopping. The driver, a young woman in her early 20s, died instantly.

When I arrived at the scene, rescue workers were still trying to extract the victim. I got some wide shots of the area, scenes of sheriff's deputies talking among themselves and on the radio to other units. Finally, they had the wreckage cut away so that they could remove the body. I stood back from the scene, then framed my camera shot so that most of the action was blocked by two deputies who were helping. My frame showed a leg at an odd angle and an arm dangling lifelessly. I wasn't sure we would even use that graphic of a scene.

As I finished shooting, I was suddenly confronted by an angry deputy coroner and we were soon shouting at each other. A nearby sheriff's deputy stepped between us and told the coroner to go take care of what he needed to do. He then turned to me. "What was that all about?" he asked. I explained that the coroner had accused me of shooting graphic video just for the purpose of entertaining other news reporters at the station. I found the charge so repugnant, I became angry in turn.

We used the sequence, by the way. I asked the news director, the assignment editor, and the chief photographer to look at the scene. Each of them felt that it was well composed and not unduly graphic. Sometimes you need to report or show unpleasant detail. The important thing is to think about why you are doing so and what it will accomplish. —*WRW*

If you become a news reporter, you will see many things that the public doesn't need or wouldn't want to see. Your job is not to titillate the audience or appeal to their base instincts while pursuing ratings points or circulation numbers. The job at times involves discretion about what not to show or say.

Faced with a proliferation of alternative media outlets, newspapers have felt it necessary to become more reader-oriented in order to retain their share of a fragmenting audience. Broadcast reporters find the competition even more intense. Increasingly, news is becoming more featurized and user-oriented—more of what people appear to want, rather than what the newspaper editor or broadcast-news director thinks they need.

A study conducted by the Project for Excellence in Journalism, which measured changes in news content during a 20-year period, seems to confirm this observation. In 1977, more than half of all stories (52 percent) were basically straight news accounts of what had happened. By 1997, that figure had fallen to less than one in three stories (32 percent), with those stories tending to have a more mediated or thematic approach. The emphasis was on people, human interest, and "news you can use." The study also found a new emphasis on scandal, the bizarre, and fear about the future. In 1977, stories with a traditional news emphasis dominated stories with a feature or scandal by a two-to-one margin. By 1997, that order was essentially reversed. Stories about government and foreign affairs dropped, but the number of stories about celebrities, entertainment, and celebrity crime tripled. The trend continues.

Network newscasts, the study found, moved toward consumer and health news. Like other media, the greatest shift in emphasis was toward coverage of scandal, followed by human interest and quality of life stories. There was a substantial decline in straight news stories or in-depth analyses or updates. Prime time network news magazines, which have replaced documentaries on network television, have all but abandoned traditional topics such as government, social welfare, education, and economics in favor of celebrities, sensational crime, lifestyles, and news-you-can-use. News magazines once concentrated on the coverage of ideas. The Project for Excellence in Journalism study found that only eight percent of the stories concerned the combined areas of education, economics, foreign affairs, the military, national security, politics or social welfare issues. Instead, celebrity profiles and crime were the most popular categories of stories, followed closely by stories about consumer news, health and medicine, and law and justice.

The print news magazines *Time* and *Newsweek* have seen broad shifts in emphasis, the most notable being a decline in coverage of ideas. In 1977, nearly one in five cover stories concerned policies or ideas; by 1987, the number had fallen to one in 20 covers, where it remains. *Time* and *Newsweek* most often have cover stories in the area of consumer and health news and celebrity entertainment, and even serious topics are often presented through a Hollywood prism. In 1977, political or international figures represented nearly one in three of all *Time* and *Newsweek* covers. By 1997, that number had fallen by more than 60 percent to one in 10 covers. Covers that sold the story with celebrities, a sexy man or woman, or an image story about sex, doubled between 1977 and 1997. Front page newspaper trends during the same 20-year period saw shifts in emphasis similar to network TV, although not to the same extent because newspaper front pages remained oriented primarily around traditional news categories.[27] There is no indication those patterns have changed. A recent study noted, "audience news interests and preferences have remained surprisingly static" over the past two decades.[28]

A more recent survey by the Project for Excellence in Journalism noted that fewer resources are being put into newsgathering because revenues are down sharply in the traditional media. According to the study, more newspaper reporters are being turned from specialists back into generalists; most local radio stations have virtually no reporters in the field; and fewer local TV news stories feature correspondents. On television, the range of topics is narrowing even more to crime and accidents, plus weather, traffic and sports. Any Internet sites that have tried to produce original news content have struggled financially; those that are thriving rely almost entirely on the work of others. Among blogs, only five percent of their content is what journalists would call reporting. [29]

Public Perceptions of News and News People

If recent polls are any indication, many people don't like what "The Media" tell them and are increasingly dissatisfied with the quality of news and information they receive. The major criticisms of journalism over the years have been that it is superficial and unduly negative, values appearance over substance, appeals to emotion and celebrity worship, and has moved increasingly to being a forum for conflict rather than conciliation. Critics say that journalism sets the political agenda instead of allowing the campaign dynamic to play itself out, hinders solutions to social problems, and pays inordinate attention to society's dysfunctionals.

Journalists are perceived to at times engage in unseemly behavior, reflect a pack or herd mentality, and some are viewed as seeking celebrity status for themselves while covering the famous or infamous. They are said to be arrogant, abrasive and cynical, an out-of-touch elite not necessarily knowledgeable about what they report. There also is a lingering suspicion that journalists bring their own political or social agenda into news reports. That accusation, by the way, may be inherent in the role of reporter. Kansas editor William Allen White said nearly a hundred years ago that journalism should "comfort the afflicted and afflict the comfortable."

What is troubling is that those attitudes continue to be reflected in measurable numbers. A survey conducted by the Pew Center for People and the Press[30] found that not only did respondents question reporters' fairness, they had doubts about their patriotism as well. While those surveyed rejected the notion of propagandizing the war on terror, with 68 percent saying it is best if news coverage is neutral, 40 percent said the press is too critical of America and 30 percent said it hurts democracy. Sixty percent saw the press as politically biased; only 21 percent of those surveyed said they felt the press dealt fairly with all sides of an issue. Respondents also said that news organizations care more about attracting the biggest audience (75 percent) than in keeping the public informed (19 percent).

In some respects, the survey results were conflicting. While respondents expressed dissatisfaction with overall aspects of news coverage, most Americans say they like mainstream news outlets. Eighty percent give favorable ratings to their local newspaper, 79 percent rated local TV news and cable news positively, and network television news had a 75 percent approval rating. As the survey's directors wrote in an accompanying commentary, "The public is not rejecting the principles underlying traditional journalism. Rather, it suspects journalists are not living up to these principles."[31]

When people turn on the TV, they see the problems of the world live and in color. No wonder they don't like journalists! Nobody likes the bearers of bad news. Keep in mind,

Box. 1.3

What Citizens Should Expect from the Press

What do we as citizens have a right to expect from journalists? The Committee of Concerned Journalists, "a consortium of journalists, publishers, owners and academics worried about the future of the profession," has studied the common principles of the news profession and offers this consensus about what journalists must offer and what citizens should expect.

1. We should expect, above all, truthfulness:

- The integrity of the reporting should be obvious. The process of verification—how news people made their decisions and why—should be transparent in the work so we can judge the value and fairness of the information for ourselves.

- Stories should make clear the sources of information, the basis of their knowledge, and why the information is believable and relevant. With anonymous sources, as much identifying information as possible should be given so readers can judge the source's reliability and potential biases.

- The story's relevance should be clearly stated.

- Important unanswered questions should be noted.

- If the story raises a point of controversy we should expect follow up.

- Citizens, in turn, have an obligation to approach the news with an open mind and not just a desire that the news reinforce existing opinion.

2. We should expect proof that the journalist's first loyalty is to citizens:

- This means stories should answer our needs as citizens, not just the interests of insiders, or the political or economic system.

- There should be a demonstrated effort to understand and reflect the whole community.

- We should see clear cases in which the news company will put its own financial interests at risk by providing information—through news, reviews, retail, and consumer coverage—that could do it harm.

- We should expect news companies to disclose any synergy, connecting partnerships or conflicts of interest as they relate to a particular story. This includes reporting on a news organization's own lobbying efforts.

3. We should expect journalists to maintain independence from those they cover:

- It should be clear that commentators, columnists and journalists of opinion are serving the citizen debate rather than the narrow interests of a faction or a particular outcome.

- While journalists need not be neutral, we should expect they will not have divided loyalties. If journalists get too close to those they cover it only makes it more difficult for them to understand or convey all sides. Secretly counseling or writing speeches for sources is an example.

- Journalists' work should display evidence of independent thinking—not always criticism of one side and praise of the other.

- We should see ample proof that these commentators have really examined the ideas of both those they agree and disagree with.

4. We have the right to expect that journalists will monitor power and give voice to the voiceless:

- The press should use its watchdog power to uncover things that are important and new and that change community thinking. The news media should not squander this constitutional freedom on sideshow or pseudo scandals that research shows may build an audience.

continued . . .

Box. 1.3

What Citizens Should Expect from the Press . . . *continued*

- The press should monitor all the key centers of power in the community—including but not limited to government.

- We should see clear evidence that journalists have not simply become a tool of investigative agencies.

5. *We have a right to a forum for public criticism and problem solving:*

- News providers should offer several channels for public interaction—be it letters, e-mail, phone contacts, or public forums—including mechanisms for readers and viewers to make story suggestions or raise criticisms.

- News organizations also should give us access to a portion of their space or airtime so that we can converse in our own words with our fellow citizens.

- Over time, we should expect to see a broad representation of views and values reflected in the news coverage—and not just those of the extreme positions that leave no room for compromise or problem solving.

6. *We have a right to expect news that is proportional and relevant:*

- Journalists should be aware of our basic dilemma as citizens: that we have a need for timely and deep knowledge of important issues and trends —but we lack the time and means to access most of this crucial information.

- Thus journalists should use their special access to put the material they gather in a context that will engage our attention and also allow us to see trends and events in proportion to their true significance in our lives.

- News reports should not overstate the true nature of threats to our community such as crime and unusual weather.

- To provide a complete picture, we also should expect journalists to cover those aspects of community life that are functioning well. Our successes should be as apparent as our failures.

- Journalists should balance the public right to know with the personal right to privacy.

www.concernedjournalists.org/node/65
Committee of Concerned Journalists Staff, November 21, 2006.
Used with permission.

however, that journalists, broadcasters, and public relations people are describing reality; they don't cause bad things to happen. Ours is a world of political scandals, drive-by shootings, volcanoes, earthquakes, international bullies, war and terrorism, famine, disease, violence, and a myriad of other problems that crowd out good news. Although at times some searching is necessary, the media report a fair amount of upbeat news. In particular, public relations practitioners help journalists and broadcasters report on the positive side of life: medical breakthroughs, scientific advances, social accomplishments, and personal achievements. Beyond the world of the newsroom, special interest publications and programs focus on self-improvement, education, and wholesome entertainment.

As social institutions and technology become more complex, the media increasingly rely on public relations practitioners to provide information that individual reporters or news organizations lack the capability or expertise to gather. Public relations professionals have meshed their standards with those of the news media to effectively convey organizational messages, and they use similar principles to enhance communication within their organizations.

Reporters Look at Their Profession

Journalists seem to agree with criticism by the public about their profession and the quality of their work. Paralleling findings from earlier studies, journalists in a 2004 survey[32] cited quality concerns such as sensationalistic coverage, accuracy, a lack of depth, relevance and objectivity as the most important problems facing the profession. Credibility was also a concern by a fourth of those surveyed, with print journalists considering it more of a problem than those in broadcasting.

Respondents were divided as to whether their profession is advancing or regressing. Only half of those surveyed said the profession was going in the right direction; even fewer national journalists felt that was the case. Those who felt things were going badly said the press had become too timid and paid too little attention to complex issues; they also expressed concern that the distinction between reporting and commentary was being seriously eroded.

A Question of Balance

Your job in the communication business will be difficult because your "balanced perspective" is going to differ from that of the people you write about or who read, watch, and listen to what you write. That's why understanding the theories explained in this chapter is important. Cognitive dissonance, the selective processes, and the theory of wants and needs gratification conspire to make the media writer's job more difficult. The individual audience member is in control of how the message will be received, and people may not perceive it in ways the writer intended, or like what they read or hear.

For years, journalists have adhered to the concepts of objectivity and fairness: All sides of an issue must be presented neutrally for the readers, viewers or listeners to make up their mind. Although media writers continue to strive for fairness and balance, there's no guarantee that our sources or audience will like us in the future any more than they do now.

Discussion Questions

The following are class discussion questions drawn from Chapter 1:

1. What is meant by media "convergence" and why is it important to print and broadcast journalists, as well as to public relations professionals?

2. Is Lasswell's theory of the surveillance, correlation, and transmission function of the press still valid, more than 50 years after it was first formulated? Explain.

3. Which press theory is "best": libertarian or social responsibility? Why?

4. Look at the definitions of what makes news. Is anything missing? Do these classifications guarantee that what is important will be covered?

5. Define and explain the importance to media writers of two of the following terms: cognitive dissonance, perceptual distortion, individual differences theory, selective processes, stereotypes, wants and needs gratification theory, cultivation, agenda setting, status conferral, issue attention cycle.

6. Surveys show there has been a decline of hard news during the past 30 years. Is that merely evidence of changing priorities on the part of audiences, or are the media contributing to a cultural decline that is reflected in criticisms of the press?

7. What should citizens expect from the press? Are the principles expressed by the Committee of Concerned Journalists valid, or are they increasingly irrelevant in this fast-paced, 24/7 multimedia environment with hundreds of "information distribution portals"?

8. So, why don't people like the media? What can be done about it?

CHAPTER EXERCISES

Exercise 1.1—Media Activities Log

Keep a log of your media activities for a week. Which communication theories do you see in operation in your uses of the various media?

Exercise 1.2—More Regulation?

Should there be increased governmental regulation to enforce the social responsibility theory? In subgroups of the class, analyze how socially responsibly the media covered a specific news event. Discuss your conclusions in class.

Exercise 1.3—News Elements

Clip stories from the newspaper in which the news pegs are timeliness, proximity, prominence, consequence, conflict, suspense, human interest, novelty, and progress. How many were covered on local or national TV news? What differences did you see in how the two outlets covered the same stories? Why would some stories be covered by one but not the other?

Exercise 1.4—Interview with "Keep 'em Out"

Ace newspaper reporter Kent Clarke receives a call from the media-relations director for "Keep 'em Out," a controversial anti-immigration group. It has vigorously pressured Congress to pass restrictive immigration legislation, strongly supports the building of the wall separating the U.S. and Mexico as a means of keeping out unwanted immigrants, and has spearheaded the formation of local armed anti-immigrant posses in the Southwest that some have condemned as vigilantes. Because of its strident views, the organization has had difficulty getting its message out, so the media relations director offers Kent the opportunity to conduct an in-depth interview with the group's national president, who is in town for a speech at your college or university.

For Kent, the situation poses an ethical dilemma. He knows that the FBI has been watching the activities of the organization and running checks on allegations of trafficking in weapons and responsibility for attacks on immigrants, although none of its members have been charged with any wrongdoing, let alone been arrested or convicted. Kent does not agree with the group's positions but he knows that many of his readers do. He is fearful that if he does a balanced, in-depth piece, he's going to legitimize what he feels is a misguided organization, if not one that tacitly supports hate crimes against legal and undocumented immigrants. On the other hand, he knows that many readers disagree with the group's position and that the paper will probably be deluged with calls and e-mails protesting *any* story on the organization. Either way the story is covered, some subscriptions may be canceled and a few influential advertisers might even drop their ads or try to induce others to do the same.

Discuss Kent Clarke's responsibility to his newspaper, to his readership and, more broadly, to what he considers the general welfare. If he does the interview, how should he handle it? If he doesn't do the interview, has he missed an opportunity to open debate on a polarizing issue? What should he do?

Exercise 1.5—Are Generalizations Accurate?

Review the section in this chapter entitled "Changing Definitions of News." Are those generalizations still accurate? If so, what can be done to encourage a shift toward more meaningful traditional "hard" news? Discuss in class.

Exercise 1.6—What Should We Expect?

Review the recommendations of the Committee of Concerned Journalists, "What Citizens Should Expect from the Press." Are those valid points, or have they become unrealistic in today's increasingly competitive 24/7 news environment? Discuss in class.

Suggestions for Further Reading

Kovach, Bill, and Tom Rosensteil. *The Elements of Journalism: What Newspeople Should Know and the Public Should Expect* (New York: Three Rivers Press, 2007).

Lewis, Anthony. *Freedom for the Thought That We Hate: A Biography of the First Amendment* (New York: Basic Books, 2008).

Wicker, Tom. *On the Record: An Insider's Guide to Journalism* (Boston: Bedford/St. Martin's, 2002).

Winburn, Janice, Ed. *Shop Talk and War Stories: Journalists Examine Their Profession* (Boston: Bedford/St. Martin's, 2003).

Notes

1. Harold D. Lasswell. "The Structure and Function of Communication in Society," in *The Communication of Ideas,* Ed. Lyman Bryson (New York: Institute for Religious and Social Studies, 1948), pp. 37–51.

2. Wilbur Schramm. "How Communication Works," in *The Process and Effects of Mass Communication* (Urbana: University of Illinois Press, 1954), pp. 13–17.

3. See Marshall McLuhan and Quenton Fiore, *The Medium Is the Message* (New York: Bantam Books, 1967); and Marshall McLuhan, *Understanding Media: The Extensions of Man* (New York: McGraw-Hill, 1964).

4. This concept was first recognized by Leon A. Festinger in *A Theory of Cognitive Dissonance* (Stanford, Calif.: Stanford University Press, 1957).

5. The principle of noise was identified by Claude Shannon and Warren Weaver in *The Mathematical Theory of Communication* (Urbana: University of Illinois Press, 1949).

6. The theory says that media use is motivated by the needs and goals defined by members of the audience. See Mark Levy and Sven Windahi, "The Concept of Audience Activity," in *Media Gratifications Research: Current Perspectives,* Ed. K.E. Rosengren et al. (Beverly Hills, Calif.: Sage, 1985), p. 110.

7. See W. Richard Whitaker, "A Comparison of Viewer Reaction to Color Versus Black and White Television News," unpublished master's thesis (University of Oregon School of Journalism, 1969).

8. These aspects of influence theory research were best summarized by Melvin DeFleur in *Theories of Mass Communication* (New York: McKay, 1970).

9. The selective processes were identified by Joseph Klapper in *The Effects of Mass Communication* (New York: The Free Press, 1960).

10. Walter Lippmann. *Public Opinion* (New York: Macmillan, 1921).

11. Uses and gratifications theory began with Wilbur Schramm, who said that people weigh the level of reward (gratification) from a media message against how much effort they must make to receive that reward. See Schramm, *The Process and Effects of Mass Communication,* p. 19. Several years later, Elihu Katz suggested that communications researchers begin studying what people do with the media instead of what the media do to people. See Elihu Katz, "Mass Communication Research and the Study of Popular Culture," *Studies in Public Communication* 2 (1959): 1–6.

12. The pioneer study of the two-step flow of communication and the opinion leader function took place in Erie County, Ohio, during the 1940 presidential election. See Paul Lazarsfeld et al., *The People's Choice: How the Voter Makes up His Mind in a Presidential Campaign* (New York: Duell, Sloan and Pearce, 1944); and Elihu Katz, "The Two-Step Flow of Communication," *Public Opinion Quarterly* 21 (1957): 61–78.

13. A complex system representation, the Westley–MacLean model, depicted a process in which communicators send out messages, obtain feedback, and adjust their actions. See Bruce Westley and Malcolm MacLean, "A Conceptual Model for Mass Communication Research," *Journalism Quarterly* 34 (1957): 31–38.

14. See Paul E. Lazarsfeld and Robert K. Merton, "Mass Communication, Popular Taste and Organized Social Action," in Wilbur Schramm, ed., *Mass Communications* (Urbana: University of Illinois Press, 1960), pp. 501–502.

15. Cultivation theory was developed by George Gerbner, who has written a series of articles over the years critical of the effect of television violence on children and television's impact on the general population. See George Gerbner, "The 'Mainstreaming' of America," *Journal of Communication* 30 (1980): 10–29; and George Gerbner et al., "Charting the Mainstream: Television's Contributions to Political Orientations," *Journal of Communication* 32 (1982): 100–127.

16. See Elisabeth Noelle-Neumann, "The Spiral of Silence: A Theory of Public Opinion," *Journal of Communication* 24 (1974): 43–51; and Noelle-Neumann's response to critics, "The Spiral of Silence: A Response," in *Political Communication Yearbook, 1984,* Ed. K.R. Sandersetal. (Carbondale: Southern Illinois University Press, 1985).

17. Joseph Klapper, in *The Effects of Mass Communication* (New York: The Free Press, 1960), said that the primary influence of the media is to reinforce behaviors, providing people with reasons to go on doing what they do.

18. Everett Rogers, in *Diffusion of Innovations* (New York: The Free Press, 1983), noted that mass media have been particularly effective in promoting change in developing countries.

19. Biographies of these journalists make excellent reading. The best biography of Storey is by Justin E. Walsh, *To Print the News and Raise Hell* (Chapel Hill: University of North Carolina Press, 1968). Candace Stone, *Dana and the Sun* (New York: Dodd Mead, 1938), is a readable treatment of Dana and his paper. Ann Sperber, *Murrow: His Life and Times* (New York: Freundlich Books, 1986) has the most thorough treatment of the CBS legend, regarded by many as the best-ever broadcast journalist.

20. See Edward L. Bernays, *Crystallizing Public Opinion* (New York: Boni & Liveright, 1923), and Bernays' memoirs, *Biography of an Idea* (New York: Simon & Schuster, 1965).

21. The term *gatekeeper* was first used by social scientist Kurt Lewin. See David M. White, "The 'Gatekeeper,' a Case Study in the Selection of News," *Journalism Quarterly* 27 (1950): 383–390.

22. Maxwell McCombs and Donald L. Shaw, "The Agenda-Setting Function of Mass Media," *Public Opinion Quarterly* 36 (1972): 176–187.

23. See Erving Goffman, *Frame Analysis: An Essay on the Organization of Experience* (New York: Harper & Row, 1974); D.A. Scheufele (1999). "Framing as a Theory of Media Effects." Journal of Communication 49 (1) 103–122; Gail T. Fairhurst and Robert A. Sarr, *The Art of Framing: Managing the Language of Leadership* (San Francisco: Jossey-Bass, 1996); T.E. Nelson, Z.M. Oxley, and R.A. Clawson (1997), "Toward a Psychology of Framing Effects," *Political Behavior,* 19(3), pp. 221–246; Z. Pan and G.M. Kosicki, "Framing as a Strategic Action in Public Deliberation" in Stephen D. Reese, Oscar H. Gandy, Jr., and August E. Grant, Eds., *Framing Public Life: Perspectives on Media and Our Understanding of the Social World* (Mahwah, N.J.: Lawrence Erlbaum, 2001), pp. 35–66.

24. The theory is that of Anthony Downs of the Brookings Institution, from "Up and Down With Ecology: The 'Issue-Attention Cycle'," *The Public Interest* 28 (1972): 38–50, available on the author's Web site, www.anthonydowns.com.

25. Paul Lazarsfeld and Robert Merton, "Mass Communication, Popular Taste and Organized Social Action," in *The Communication of Ideas,* Ed. Lyman Bryston (New York: Harper and Brothers, 1948). James B. Lemert of the University of Oregon published numerous status conferral studies over the years.

26. From Fred S. Siebert, Theodore Peterson and Wilbur Schramm, *Four Theories of the Press* (Urbana: University of Illinois Press, 1956).

27. "Changing Definitions of News," a 1997 report of the Committee of Concerned Journalists, www.journalism.org.

28. Michael J. Robinson, "Two Decades of American News Preferences," Pew Research Center for the People and the Press, August 22, 2007, http://people-press.org/pubs/574/two-decades-of-american-news-preferences.

29. Project for Excellence in Journalism, *The State of the News Media 2006,* "Overview: Introduction" www.stateofthenewsmedia.com/2006/narrative_overview_intro.asp?cat=1&media=1.

30. "Public More Critical of Press, But Good Will Persists," Report of the Pew Research Center for People and the Press," June 26, 2005, http://people-press.org/reports/display.php3?ReportID=248.

31. Tom Rosenstiel and Bill Kovach, "The Public's Complicated Views of Press Point to Solutions," http://people-press.org/reports/display.php3?PageID=971.

32. "Bottom Line Pressures Now Hurting Coverage, Say Journalists," Report of the Pew Research Center for People and the Press," May 23, 2004, http://people-press.org/reports/display.php3?PageID=825. This survey parallels findings in a 1999 Pew survey, "Striking the Balance: Audience Interests, Business Pressures and Journalists' Values," www.people-press.org/press99rpt.htm. Also see updates in the annual "State of the News Media" by the Project for Excellence in Journalism at www.stateofthemedia.org.

2

Ethical and Legal Issues in Media Writing

Chapter Objectives

- To identify media writers' rights and responsibilities in obtaining information from various sources
- To discuss the value of a professional code of ethics
- To explain elements of the legal definitions of defamation, libel, and invasion of privacy and how they pertain to media writers
- To summarize major cases involving defamation and invasion of privacy and their implications for journalists
- To describe the rights and responsibilities of journalists covering trials and legal proceedings.

Sensationalism Sells

Whether it is the lurid sensationalism of tabloid newspapers at supermarket checkout stands, over-dramatized coverage by mainstream television news programs and cable, or slanted reportage passing for "news" on the Internet, it is easy to find much to criticize about American journalism. In recent years, there have been a number of sensational criminal cases and celebrity-related events, and the media have covered them extensively, often to excess. It's far easier to chronicle movie stars and recording artists going in and out of rehab than to analyze the difficulties of nation-building in the Middle East. Sensationalism that panders to the lowest common denominator invariably sells. It always has; it probably always will.

Interestingly, the public says it doesn't like all the sensationalism. A recent survey by the Pew Research Center for People and the Press found that an overwhelming majority of the public (87 percent) believes celebrity scandals receive too much news coverage. The criticism generally holds across most major demographic and political groups, with virtually no one saying there is too little coverage of this sort of "news."

A majority of those surveyed (54 percent) blamed news organizations for giving these stories so much coverage. But a third (32 percent) say the public is to blame for paying so much attention to them, and another 12 percent say the media and the public are both equally to blame. While television was deemed to be the main culprit, many respondents could not differentiate between cable and network television.[1]

Ironically, one reason for the decline in standards may well be the proliferation of media voices in the traditional marketplace of ideas. The three major television networks found it much easier to be socially responsible 30 years ago when they were essentially splitting the audience three ways. Now, with all the various cable and satellite channels added to the mix, the audience is fragmented and everyone is fighting over increasingly smaller pieces of the pie. Part of the downward shift is due to education and income: Better educated, economically well-off people don't watch many of those programs. With the audience divided into identifiable market-based niches, news programmers find that catering to the lowest common denominator yields the largest share of audience and the most advertiser dollars.

News as Entertainment

Over the years, as was noted in Chapter 1, there has been a shift toward lifestyles, celebrity, entertainment, and celebrity scandal as entertainment at the expense of the more traditional "hard" news stories. Media critic Jeffrey Scheuer[2] says that this is characteristic of what he calls a "sound bite society," one that is

> flooded with images and slogans, bits of information and abbreviated or symbolic messages —a culture of instant but shallow communication. It is not just a culture of gratification and consumption, but one of immediacy and superficiality, in which the very notion of "news" erodes in a tide of formulaic mass entertainment.

It has created, Scheuer said, "a society that thrives on simplicity and disdains complexity."

Because the news media are expensive big businesses, reporters and producers increasingly go with sensational aspects of a story to draw readers and viewers and make a profit for their newspapers and broadcast outlets. Let's face it: Not only does crime news, celebrity stories, dramatic footage of car chases, hostage takings, or extreme weather conditions draw audiences, the stories also are generally exciting to cover and they don't require a lot of preparation, just a live camera at the scene for "reality" TV. But while the sensational is colorful and exciting, it often eclipses "real" news of substance. This is not to say these events did not deserve coverage—just not saturation coverage. More important events occurring around the nation and the world were shunted aside because only so much airtime was available on radio and television and only so many column inches in newspapers and magazines.

A Crisis of Confidence

Part of the problem is the necessity for visuals to feed TV's needs. Because television has been the primary source of information for the past several decades, it sets the agenda for all media. Former *New York Times* managing editor Max Frankel, for instance, once expressed his concern about "the murder, mayhem and medicine that passes for news on local television," which, he said, was "pushing all journalism into trashy territory."[3]

Many critics argue that the dividing line between entertainment and reality has blurred and merged, adversely affecting the quality of news and information. Consider these statistics from a report[4] by the Pew Research Center for the People and the Press:

- The number of Americans who say they enjoy the news continues to decline. In 1995, 54 percent said they enjoyed keeping up with the news a lot. That number fell to 50 percent in 1998 and to 45 percent in 2000.
- More than six in 10 people now watch television news with their remote control in hand. Overall, news consumption remains largely event-driven. Slightly less than half of the public actually follows national news on a regular basis; fully 50 percent tune in only for significant or interesting events.
- Fully 64 percent of Americans say they only follow international events closely when something interesting or important is happening; just 33 percent pay close attention most of the time.
- A substantial portion, 28 percent of the respondents, said they preferred news that focuses on their own concerns and interests rather than general news information. This group is less educated, male and young.
- Crime, health, sports, community news, and religion are followed most closely by Americans. News about political figures and Washington events continues to rank low on the public's list of news stories.

Influence of the Bottom Line

One aspect of sensationalism is **checkbook journalism**, the practice of paying for stories that people formerly gave freely out of a desire for publicity or to share information. The payment of standard talent fees is not considered unethical, nor is a network program's picking up the expenses of a guest whose appearance will enhance the show. What is troubling is a person selling his or her story to the highest bidder or arranging with several tabloid-TV programs to air sleaze and gossip, especially if those people are witnesses in a trial or legal proceeding. This type of coverage detracts from important happenings and constricts the voices present in the media's marketplace of ideas. If a publication or program can outspend everyone else, soon it will be the only voice left—or else everyone will imitate what it does. How is the public good served by having only one voice or one message?

There has been an unmistakable intrusion of commercial interests into newsroom decisions. In a 2000 study[5] of 300 journalists, four in 10 said they had avoided newsworthy stories or softened the tone to benefit the interests of their news organizations. Many in broadcast media admitted that newsworthy stories were often or sometimes avoided because of a lack of audience appeal or they were regarded as too complicated for the average person. More than a third of respondents said news that would hurt the interests of a news organization often or sometimes went unreported. Slightly fewer said the same about stories that could adversely affect advertisers.

Local reporters said they faced more pressure than did major market journalists. Half the investigative reporters in the sample said newsworthy stories were often or sometimes ignored because they conflicted with a news organization's economic interests, and six in 10 said they believed corporate owners exert at least a fair amount of influence on which stories to cover.

Business pressure is hurting the quality of news coverage, then, because to reach wider audiences, remain competitive in a 24-hour news cycle, and sell more advertising to make more profit—the ultimate measure of the "bottom line" to stockholders—the media increasingly sensationalize stories and pay too little attention to complex news events. This trend leads to an erosion of confidence by the public, which is reflected in a further loss of audience. Thus, the downward spiral: The media become more sensational to compensate for diminishing, fragmenting audiences, which leads to further audience erosion and loss of confidence.

Recent corporate mergers in the mass communication industry raise concerns that reporters will be confronted by what has been called **journalistic incest** when covering their corporate parents and their related holdings. How independent can a broadcast or print journalist be when working on a story detrimental to corporate interests? If nothing else, such reportage will lead viewers and readers to second-guess news judgments, suspect hidden agendas, or raise questions about journalistic credibility.[6]

Robert McChesney of the University of Illinois, who has studied the impact of media consolidation, states the problem more bluntly: "The preponderance of U.S. mass communication is controlled by less than two dozen enormous profit-maximizing corporations, which receive much of their income from advertising placed largely by other corporations."[7] One result is that newsroom managers increasingly find their pay, and even their job survival, tied to profits and meeting shareholder expectations.[8] Media critic Jeffrey Scheuer says this situation results "in a lack of diversity, self-censorship, and other troubling conflicts and compromises between news values and commercial interests."[9]

At times, the print and broadcasting media speak with one voice, when all of them—the *New York Times*, *Washington Post*, and TV networks—cover the same story the same way. This phenomenon is known as **herd** or **pack journalism**, where other media outlets adopt the agenda set by the leaders. Smaller papers, bureaus, and broadcasters have trouble avoiding this practice. What reporter would tell his or her editor that the *New York Times* or the networks are following the wrong trail and that the editor's paper or station should do something different? Increasingly, too, reporters seem to be covering more sensational trivia at the expense of important news. When those stories draw readers and viewers, news producers are hard-pressed to argue that other things should take precedence.

Public relations has been accused of being overly concerned with image or "spin control," even charged at times with downright misrepresentation. Thus, for seemingly good reasons, politicians and a large segment of the public are angry at "The Media." That anger is unfortunate because most of those who work diligently in print, broadcasting and public relations have high personal and ethical values and take seriously their responsibilities in the information process.

What all this means to those aspiring to careers in print, broadcast or online journalism or public relations is that economic realities are constraints that must be faced on a daily basis. The challenge is to provide meaningful news and information for audiences despite those pressures.

Role of the News Media

Consider the role of the print or broadcast reporter, who often has the unenviable task of going into a conflict-ridden situation to determine what is and is not true, of identifying the good guys and the bad guys. When making such judgment calls, a reporter is likely to alienate at least half the participants. If the news story says the majority of those involved are wrong, or if the reported facts leave that impression, then the reporter has made almost everyone angry. That's when the charges begin to fly about media bias.

For example, photographs and headlines can cause problems because of their juxtaposition with other stories or because they have been altered in some manner, especially with new video and computer technology. Tampering with a photograph can cause a crisis of public confidence, even if a lawsuit does not result. A Reuter's freelancer was fired after it was found that he digitally altered pictures of Israeli air strikes in Lebanon to make the damage appear worse than it was. Even the prestigious *National Geographic* opened itself to criticism when it moved one of Egypt's Great Pyramids to create better photo composition on its cover.

Journalists, of course, are not perfect; they do make mistakes and can be biased. However, most mistakes are inadvertent, not deliberate. Often, people being covered cause part of the problem: If they don't tell reporters something that they should know, then the story is incomplete, like a jigsaw puzzle put together without all the pieces. Sometimes people lie to reporters or at least give the truth a good deal of elasticity. Other times, people are honest, but their honesty reflects bigotry or hostility that shows up in the news report. When it does, the public frequently concludes that reporters are distorting the truth. Also, it's human nature to view it as distortion when reporters write an unflattering or critical story about someone or something we approve. Conversely, it's hard-hitting, interpretative reporting when we agree with a reporter's perspective. Actually, a greater danger may be that reporters become co-opted by the people they cover, a process called acculturation, defined in Chapter 1 as the tendency of reporters to identify with and take on the belief system of those they cover.

An Ideal Media Role

Although reporters should maintain the traditional "watchdog" role with news sources, reporters and sources should be respectful rather than argumentative adversaries. A novice reporter would be well advised to presume good will and openness on the part of those being covered, unless the news source has acted differently. Too many reporters approach all news sources with a

---

Box 2.1

It Happened to Me: General Orders Favorable Coverage

How many times has a public official claimed to have been misquoted, only to have his or her words played back? The official's next response is, "Well, that was taken out of context."

I was once assigned to conduct a TV interview with a retired general who had become a controversial right-wing political figure. The ground rules that the general demanded were absolute: He would give our station a four-minute or longer statement about his upcoming lecture that evening, and we were to run it uncut, unedited on the 6 o'clock news. No agreement, no interview.

I protested that we couldn't go that long. He said he couldn't make his point in less time. That was

the trouble with "The Media," he told me, we took things out of context because of artificially imposed time constraints. Our station was not a common carrier, I explained; we never agree to run things uncut, unedited. He countered that we would distort his words and that we were obviously out to get him and others who spoke out with his version of the truth.

I didn't agree to his terms and didn't do the interview. He raked our station over the coals in his speech that night and, for the next month, the news staff and station management heard from his angry supporters about the incident and how unfair we had been. Sometimes you can't win!—*WRW*

---

level of distrust perhaps appropriate for politicians and industrial polluters but inappropriate for people in less combative environments.

This philosophy of "reporter as attack dog" makes its way into local news reporting as well, generating a lot of unnecessary hostility between news sources and inexperienced reporters who are following a stereotype. A reporter doesn't have to approach with cynicism the opening of a soup kitchen or the start of a new karate class at the YMCA. Unfortunately, the Hollywood image of reporters as tough-as-nails investigators sometimes prevents journalists from realizing that something that looks good on the surface also may be good deep inside.

Professional Ethics

The major professional communication organizations each have their own code of ethical standards. Newspaper organizations were among the first, with the Canons of Journalism adopted by the American Society of Newspaper Editors in 1923, in part as a response to the sensationalist tabloid excesses of the Jazz Journalism era of the 1920s. Today, the Society of Professional Journalists Code of Ethics reflects similar high-minded sentiments. The preamble says that the duty of journalists is to serve the truth and that agencies of mass communication are carriers of public discussion and information, responsible for distributing news and enlightened opinion to serve the general welfare. Journalists, the code says, must be free of obligation to any interest other than the public's right to know the truth. News reports must be objective, free of opinion or bias, and represent all sides of an issue. Journalists are to show respect for the dignity, privacy, rights, and well-being of people encountered while gathering and presenting news.

Similar sentiments and language appear in the Code of Broadcast News Ethics of the Radio–Television News Directors Association. It says that the responsibility of broadcast journalists is to gather and report information of importance and interest accurately, honestly, and impartially. Sensationalism is to be rejected and listeners and viewers are not to be misled or deceived. Broadcast reporters are to avoid conflict of interest, respect the right to a fair trial, and be concerned about the dignity, privacy, and well-being of people with whom they interact.

The vast majority of public relations professionals, like print and broadcast journalists, have high ethical standards reflecting a commitment to truth, accuracy, and a concern for the public well-being. Many public relations practitioners are members of professional organizations such as the Public Relations Society of America (PRSA) or the International Association of Business Communicators (IABC). These organizations have codes of ethics dealing specifically with matters relating to news and journalism. The PRSA code, for example, identifies basic professional values such as advocacy and giving a voice in the marketplace of ideas, honesty in communicating with accuracy and truth, expertise and responsible use of research and information, providing objective counsel, loyalty to clients while serving the public good, and fairness in dealing with clients and media while supporting the free flow of information within a democratic society. IABC members pledge to practice honest, candid, and timely communication, foster the free flow of essential information in accordance with the public interest, disseminate accurate information, and promptly correct any erroneous communication.

The code of the Canadian Public Relations Society similarly binds members to the highest standards of honesty, accuracy and truth, and requires members to avoid disseminating false or misleading information. The code of the International Public Relations Association pledges the following:

> A member shall conduct his or her professional activities with respect to the public interest and for the dignity of the individual. A member shall not engage in practice that tends to corrupt the integrity of channels of public communication, or intentionally disseminate false or misleading information. A member shall at all times seek to give a faithful representation of the organization that he or she serves.

It is commonly understood that many public relations practitioners are advocates for someone or something. Most difficulties arise when those they represent stray from truth or objectivity. Then, it is up to the public relations professional to deal with the consequences. At times, often due to privacy statutes, the spokesperson is constrained by specific directions *not* to provide certain information, even when reporters can clearly see that he or she knows the answers to their questions. Under those conditions, everyone appears tainted.

Despite the challenges, you should enter the communication business with high ethical standards and stick to them. Yes, ethical decisions sometimes are not obvious and clear-cut, and trade-offs must be made. However, if you get into a situation where you are constantly asked to compromise your values of fairness and objectivity, find work someplace else. To go against your own ethical standards takes an emotional toll; it's not worth destroying the best in you.

Legal Pitfalls

The remainder of this chapter provides an overview of legal challenges facing journalists, broadcasters, and public relations practitioners. To deepen your understanding of the law and the difficulties that reporters face, consider taking a law and ethics course, even if it's not a requirement of your communication program. If you are already working in the field and have no previous exposure to media law, make it a point to enroll in a law course at a nearby college or university or at least acquire a good communication law textbook and become familiar with its provisions.[10]

Reporters and broadcasters have no constitutional rights of access to crime or disaster scenes when the general public is excluded. Although courts have struck down some rules barring or limiting access of reporters,[11] the U.S. Supreme Court ruled in 1999 that law enforcement officers who invite journalists to go with them on raids subject to a search warrant violate the Fourth Amendment right to privacy of those being raided. Media representatives are permitted at the scene of breaking news events, but journalists can be arrested for refusing the order of police or fire officials to leave the scene of accidents, fires or disasters. There is even less latitude regarding reporters' access to what are termed "quasi-public" facilities such as military bases and nuclear power plants.

The Supreme Court has ruled that the First Amendment does not protect news *gathering* to the same degree it guarantees the *publication* of most truthful, lawfully acquired information. The public does not have a right to information under the First Amendment, the court has ruled, and the public's right to know can be balanced against at-times conflicting social needs. Generally, the media may record or take photographs of what is seen, said, and heard in public and semipublic places, but harassment or overzealous surveillance is not permitted.

Libel and Defamation

Defamation involves a fault (negligence or recklessness of some type), and compensation for defamation is based on the amount of harm a jury determines was done. Reporters get into the most legal trouble over **libel**, defined as a false, defamatory (damaging to one's reputation) statement published or broadcast to a third party that holds someone up to public hatred, contempt or ridicule and, in the case of a business, causes monetary damages. Libel was traditionally defined as printed defamation and slander as spoken defamation, but the courts have held broadcasters subject to libel law because broadcasting reaches a mass audience.

During World War II, a popular slogan warned shipyard workers, "Loose lips sink ships." This message was an appeal to be careful and avoid talking with strangers, who might be spies, about shipyard work or the movements of ships. Reporters should have their own version of this adage: "Sloppy reporting causes libel suits." It is easy to slip and make a mistake that will cost your organization thousands of dollars, and possibly ruin your career as well. What makes matters difficult is that each state is free to enact its own libel statutes, subject to First Amendment constraints. Because each state's laws differ, media writers need to be familiar with the nuances of libel law where they work.

The "Chilling Effect" of Lawsuits

The threat of libel action can exert what has been called a **chilling effect** on news coverage: Reporters become more cautious about what they print or broadcast because they or their news organizations are fearful of big-money lawsuits. Damages sought are often in the millions of dollars. In one instance, ABC News retracted a report saying tobacco companies "spiked" cigarettes with nicotine after Philip Morris and R. J. Reynolds Co. filed a $10 billion lawsuit against the network. In its settlement with the cigarette companies, ABC apologized twice in prime time and paid the plaintiffs' legal expenses, estimated at $15 million to $17 million.[12] Small- to medium-sized newspapers and broadcast outlets have become wary because the cost for them of defending against a libel suit can run into the hundreds of thousands of dollars. The fact that more than two thirds of verdicts against news organizations are reversed on appeal is of small consolation.

Because of the difficulty in successfully litigating libel suits, plaintiffs often look for other ways to obtain a favorable judgment. ABC was ordered to pay the Food Lion supermarket chain $5.5 million in punitive damages after two reporters with concealed cameras produced an exposé accusing several of the chain's stores of selling tainted meat and poultry. The facts of the story were not at issue. Instead, the jury awarded damages based upon the reporting methods, having determined that the network committed fraud, trespass and breach of loyalty—in part for the way in which the two producers misrepresented themselves to get jobs as clerks at the food chain. While a U.S. district court judge reduced the punitive damage award to $315,000 and an appeals court cut the amount to only $2, the case tied up the network in years of costly litigation.[13]

One can only speculate about how many of the recent corporate scandals were suspected by national media long before they burst into public view but weren't reported because tips and hunches wouldn't be enough to satisfy a libel jury. It seems reasonable to assume that the threat posed by big-money lawsuits has deterred smaller market broadcast outlets and newspapers from pursuing undercover investigative pieces and controversial news stories that cannot be completely verified, or from doing stories about actions that can be interpreted in various ways.

The chilling effect means that the public does not get the news and information it should have. Instead, the fear of being sued, or of not being backed by news organizations when stories are questionable, has effectively pulled the teeth from the media watchdog.

Allegations in News Stories

"The news stories that generate the most claims of injury to reputation," the Associated Press says in its libel primer, "result from publication of charges of crime, immorality, incompetence or inefficiency." Although truth is generally an absolute defense against a libel suit and those bringing the action are obligated to prove falsity, the Associated Press warns that there is no substitute for accuracy. There might be legal challenges even when statements made by someone else have been accurately reported. Court verdicts have gone to plaintiffs (those bringing the suit) because the story was misleading or implied that the plaintiffs had done something illegal, even though the facts of the story were substantially correct.

Libel actions have been filed over allegations of incompetence, unethical practices, and improper credentials. Businesses may sue if news accounts allege that they cheat, sell shoddy merchandise, take advantage of their customers or fail to perform promised services. Even falsely reporting that a business or financial institution is in trouble provides grounds for a lawsuit to be filed if it can be shown that the organization lost money as a result.

Box 2.2

Building a Case for Defamation

Our police reporter covered a story about four lumber yard salesmen who were falsifying invoices and having thousands of dollars' worth of building materials diverted to one salesman's garage, to be sold at a discount. I shot video of the garage; it looked like a small building supply outlet!

The next twist in the case came with the arrest of the firm's bookkeeper who, one of the salesmen told police, was the mastermind. We ran the story on the 6 o'clock news, the 11 o'clock news and probably the noon broadcast the next day to go with video shot during his arraignment. Police said that he did it and logic said there had to be a mastermind. That it is libelous to wrongfully report that someone committed a crime, or is accused of committing one, did not seem to occur to any of us.

A few days later, our police reporter returned to the newsroom, visibly upset. "The bookkeeper didn't do it," he said. "The one salesman confessed to police that he made it all up because the bookkeeper wouldn't go along with them." We collectively said something the FCC wouldn't like us to say on the air. Our reporter nodded, then went into the news director's office and closed the door to give him the bad news. We heard the news director shouting and occasionally we picked out questions like "How could

this happen?" and "Why weren't you more careful?" Then he and the reporter went to see the station manager, who probably yelled at both of them and asked the same questions.

The bookkeeper's lawyer called the station's lawyer. They reached an unusual settlement: Because we had devoted four minutes and 47 seconds to reporting that the bookkeeper did it, we would give the bookkeeper four minutes and 47 seconds to respond, telling what it was like to be accused of a crime he didn't commit. In a moving interview, he described the agony of seeing the doubt in the eyes of his own family when he declared his innocence, of the crank and obscene phone calls in the middle of the night, and of being shunned by acquaintances and members of his church.

How much libel was involved? Perhaps not much. Because the man had been booked, charged and arraigned, we had a right to report his arrest. However, we went overboard in reporting some of the details of his alleged masterminding and, worse, we got the story wrong. All of us in the newsroom realized how easy it is to make a mistake that would cost the station a lot of money and someone his or her reputation.

—WRW

Falsely reporting that a person engages in sexual activity that deviates from the norm is defamatory; it is libelous to falsely say that someone has AIDS or suffers from sexually transmitted diseases. People wrongly accused of being communists or communist sympathizers have successfully sued for libel, as have those who were falsely reported as belonging to a discredited organization or one considered a threat to national security. To falsely report that someone has engaged in embezzlement, theft or financial wrongdoing is libelous. Inexperienced reporters often use the term *allegedly* or *it is alleged* in reporting crime news. The word gives *no* protection against a libel action, however, any more than covering phrases such as *police say, it is reported* or *it is rumored*.

Even typographical errors can cause lawsuits. For instance, a news report will say a criminal defendant was "acquitted" or "found innocent" instead of using the phrase "not guilty" because if the word *not* is accidentally dropped from the headline or copy, the statement becomes defamatory. Middle initials must be accurate; if names are used without middle initials, a libel suit may result if two people in town have the same first and last names. Associated Press cautions that petty criminals sometimes give the name of a famous person—often a former athlete—in hopes of getting a lenient sentence. To falsely report that name would libel the famous person.

Identification   To bring a successful libel action, plaintiffs must prove that they are identified or identifiable in the defamatory material. The *Associated Press Stylebook* warns writers that if the description—physical or otherwise—readily identifies people to those in their immediate area, the story has, in effect, named them. Media writers should also be careful when describing someone as part of a group. Although the courts have ruled that protection against defamation does not apply to large groups, there may be problems, especially in a smaller community. If, for instance, police say they are investigating a prostitution ring and an arts major at the local college is believed to be the ringleader, the reputation of every arts major at the college has been called into question.

Privilege   Reporters are generally given what is called **qualified privilege** (legal protection from prosecution for defamatory statements) in reporting what public officials say, particularly while covering official proceedings, and in disclosing the contents of most public records. This protection does not extend to errors committed in reporting or demonstrable malice toward people involved.

Elected public officials have **absolute privilege** and are immune from libel action against statements they make while on the floor of a legislative body. The concept of absolute privilege also gives the media protection when someone consents to a defamatory publication or when defamatory speeches by political candidates are broadcast.

Thus, the media can usually publish or broadcast anything said in a legislative or official public hearing, even defamatory charges. Experience has shown, however, that it is a good tactic to offer the person who has been defamed an opportunity to respond to the report. The potential to present his or her side dilutes the argument that the media treated the person unfairly.

Public and Private Figures

Courts have always made a distinction between public and private figures. A **public figure** is either a person of widespread fame or notoriety, with celebrity or special prominence in society, or a public official, elected to public office or appointed to a position and responsible for public policy. Public figures generally have far less recourse to the libel courts than do private citizens, especially if the contested material reflects upon the performance of their official duties. Even personal lives and activities have traditionally been given less protection if those individuals have willingly put themselves in the public spotlight.

Box 2.3

Major Public-Figure Libel Cases

In several rulings beginning in the 1960s, the U.S. Supreme Court has ruled that to collect libel damages, a public figure must not only show that the publication or broadcast was false, but that the defendant engaged in falsity, reckless disregard for the truth, and malice:

- *New York Times v. Sullivan*: This case involved a city commissioner in Montgomery, Ala., who was awarded $500,000 in damages from a suit against the *New York Times* for an ad published in 1960 during the civil rights struggle. The Supreme Court, in reversing lower-court holdings, ruled that public figures could succeed in a libel suit only if actual malice—that the statement was published with knowledge of its falsity or with reckless disregard of the truth—could be shown on the part of the media organization.

- *Associated Press v. Walker*: The Associated Press inaccurately reported the activities of retired Maj. Gen. Edwin Walker during a chaotic integration protest at the University of Mississippi in 1962. In reversing an award of $500,000 by a Texas court, the Supreme Court ruled that only an extreme departure from ordinary standards of journalistic investigation would be grounds for awarding damages, thus expanding protection for the press in reporting breaking news.

- *Herbert v. Lando*: This 1979 case said there was no infringement of a reporter's First Amendment rights for the defense to inquire what journalists, editors, and producers were thinking as a story was written and produced.

- *Sharon v. Time*: In this case, a jury held that Ariel Sharon, while Israeli defense minister, had been libeled by *Time* magazine in a 1982 story about massacres at two Palestinian refugee camps in Lebanon. Because malice could not be proven, however, Sharon's $50 million lawsuit was denied under the *Sullivan* guidelines. A subsequent libel action against *Time* by a former Greek prime minister was filed in London courts because English libel law is less restrictive than in the United States.

- *Westmoreland v. CBS*: A *60 Minutes* report accused William Westmoreland, former commanding general in Vietnam, of knowingly providing false battlefield information to civilian policymakers in Washington. The 1985 trial lasted nearly eight weeks before both sides agreed to a settlement; each claimed to have made its point. Westmoreland did not receive any damages, his $4 million in legal fees bankrupted a conservative think tank backing his suit, and the trial was also costly for CBS.

A **private figure**, in contrast, is someone who is neither a famous person nor a public official. In libel suits, private figures are held to an easier standard, having to prove only that the reporter failed to act with reasonable care in determining whether a story was true or false. The process of defining who is a private figure is still evolving and presents a gray area in communication law. The law recognizes **limited purpose public figures**, people who are public figures only in matters of public controversy in which they voluntarily participate. They must prove actual malice only in situations involving their voluntary participation; they are treated as private persons in other matters.

Although the courts have provided the media more latitude in reporting matters of public concern, they have also permitted plaintiffs' attorneys to ask questions such as why a particular interview was used or what motivated a reporter to approach the story in the manner in which he or she did. The courts have even ruled that reporters' notes and video out-takes (video that was shot but not used on the newscast) can be subpoenaed as evidence. The reporter who refuses to obey a court order and give the plaintiff critical information in a libel suit faces contempt of court charges with a possible fine or jail sentence. But, in a few cases, where a reporter has failed to reveal a source for a libelous story, the court has ruled as a matter of law that no sources for the story exist. This effectively strips away the libel defense because, in effect, the judge is saying the reporter made up the story. While not a common occurrence, it is a potentially frightening one.

Fair Comment

The media often comment about matters of public importance or interest, especially in reviews of public performances or those who offer their services to the public. The courts have traditionally permitted fair comment as long as factual material is truthful and opinions are stated without malice or prospect of gain. Determining "truth" is often difficult, however; reviewers generally mix fact and opinion. Lawsuits may result, for instance, if an unfair negative review forced the premature closing of a play or if the loss of business following a bad write-up forces a restaurant to close. In theory, those who present themselves to the public implicitly agree to accept public comment (a role traditionally given to the media), but because some have sued anyway, media writers should exercise caution.

Most libel cases involve newspapers or broadcast media, but news releases and other public relations vehicles are not immune from charges of defamation. Public relations practitioners, because they are not as likely to run into the same type of situations as are news reporters, should probably be more concerned about copyright violations and trademark infringements than traditional libel and privacy law problems. Sometimes there are instances of what is known as **misappropriation**: taking what belongs to someone else and using it unfairly for monetary gain. An example is the use, without permission, of look-alikes or sound-alikes of famous people or celebrities. Owners of business trademarks are particularly sensitive, insisting that their marks be capitalized and used as proper nouns or adjectives so that trademarked names do not lose their proprietary value by assuming generic meanings. A good first check for such problems is to consult the *Associated Press Stylebook* for usage guidance.

Privacy

One complaint of readers and viewers is that the media violate personal privacy, whether with exposés of politicians' sexual peccadilloes from years before or intrusions on the space of celebrities and private individuals. An American Society of Newspaper Editors survey found that more than half of the respondents said that the press has no right to invade the privacy of politicians. The public places a high value on protecting the privacy of people in situations that journalists consider "news." In fact, some surveys have shown people believe that journalists are willing to hurt people just to publish a story.[14]

The Supreme Court has interpreted the Constitution as offering privacy protection to private citizens, and lawsuits in this area focus on the issue of whether a person has been singled out for attention without his or her consent. State laws vary but, in general, they protect people from being exposed against their will to the glare of publicity. The media are prevented from revealing private facts about people, especially when the information is personal and not of legitimate public concern. Protection extends to a person's finances, sexuality and health, unless it can be shown that such information is newsworthy.

One of the most sensitive issues in publication is the identification of sex-crime victims, still considered confidential information in some states or jurisdictions. Other problem areas concern the debate over whether information should be published about convicted sex offenders being released from prison into a community, and whether television should broadcast pictures of "deadbeat dads" or men who have been arrested for soliciting prostitutes.

Faced with invasion-of-privacy charges, the media can defend themselves by showing that either the person gave consent or the information is newsworthy and thus belongs in the public sphere. Explicit consent refers to signed or taped releases. The courts presume implicit consent when it is apparent that a person willingly exposed himself or herself to publicity, such as by posing for a photograph or participating in a public rally. The courts generally consider on-the-spot news reporting as permissible, although follow-up reporting is not necessarily exempt.

Like reporters, public relations practitioners are concerned with privacy issues. They also face problems in preparing material for internal media and in providing information to external news media. Such was the case of the public relations director for a company under investigation for mismanaging a government contract. Allegation had been made by a "whistle-blower," a former company employee, who told the district attorney that the company had handled the contract illegally. The public relations director could not point out that the former employee may have had a grievance against the company or that he had made similar allegations against a prior employer. By law, the director could only verify the accuser's name, job title and dates of employment. She was criticized by reporters and fellow employees for sitting on information about the case—which, of course, she was—because the law prevented her from doing otherwise.

Avoiding Libel Suits

If a potentially libelous statement is published or broadcast, and the statement is drawn to the attention of the reporter by a person who believes he or she has been libeled, the reporter

---

Box 2.4
The Peril of Naming Names

Shortly before our 6 o'clock newscast, there was a gang-related scuffle and a youth was shot. Our sports editor, still in the newsroom, thought he would do us a favor and batted out a story that came from a police department source. The police had arrested a 17-year-old boy in the shooting, he said, and gave a name. We ran it on the newscast: "This just in—police have arrested a 17-year-old in connection with the shooting reported at the beginning of this newscast, identified as . . ."

When we got back to the newsroom after the telecast, the phone rang. It was our police informant. "Hey," he said, "you guys still on the air?" The person who took the call said we weren't, then paled. The 17-year-old, whom we had named, had not been arrested. He was not a suspect. He was just being questioned as a witness—and only briefly at that.

To publish that someone was arrested (taken into legal custody) if that person is not booked (finger-printed, photographed at a police station, and charged with a crime) is libelous.

The attorney for the boy's family called shortly after 8 p.m. We lucked out. The family agreed to a compromise: We would run a correction at the beginning, in the middle, and at the end of the 11 o'clock newscast, stating that the youth was in no way involved. The correction would also be run in the 6 o'clock news the next day. In addition to the fact that we shouldn't have used his name because he was a juvenile, the incident shows that sloppy reporting can get you in a whole lot of trouble!

—WRW

---

should *never* try to solve the problem alone. The reporter should not admit guilt but rather take the matter to the editor or news director. (The worst your boss can do is fire you!) Often, people who have been libeled merely want to clear their name. In that case, the reporter and editor, generally in concert with the attorney for the paper or station, can work out a compromise to resolve the difficulty. Some studies have shown that many people who are libeled do not initially plan to sue and do so only when they are treated curtly or rudely while trying to get the errors corrected.

Free Press—Fair Trial

Among its implicit provisions, the **First Amendment** to the Constitution protects a journalist's right to report news about criminal cases. The **Sixth Amendment** provides a defendant's right to a speedy, fair and impartial public trial. Often, the two amendments have collided. Which is better for society: to have full disclosure through reporting, even though it may taint prospective jurors, or to limit the scope of criminal justice proceedings to better ensure that an innocent person is not wrongly convicted?

Media involvement in sensational murder cases is not new in the United States. In the 1890s, Lizzie Borden of Fall River, Mass., was acquitted in the hatchet murder of her father and stepmother, in part because of a sympathetic climate generated by maudlin and sentimental newspaper stories about her. New York City tabloid newspaper coverage of the lurid details of the turn-of-the-century trial of Harry Thaw, who killed famed architect Stanford White—

his wife's former lover—prompted President Theodore Roosevelt to ask for censorship, and Canada made it a crime to print accounts of the Thaw trial. The *New York Daily News* caused controversy in the 1920s—and broke circulation-sales records—when it published a full front-page picture of convicted murderer Ruth Snyder receiving a fatal jolt of current in the Sing Sing Prison electric chair. The trial of Bruno Hauptmann, accused in the kidnapping and murder of the infant son of aviation hero Charles Lindbergh, became a media circus in the mid-1930s. Photographers were so unruly that the American Bar Association later enacted Canon 35 of its Code of Standards, effectively keeping cameras out of courtrooms for the next 30 years.

Cameras in the Courtroom

In the 1960s, two cases seemed to portend that cameras would stay out of courtrooms. One of the most sensational murder trials before the O.J. Simpson case was that of Sam Sheppard in 1954. He told police a "bushy haired intruder," not he, had killed his pregnant wife. Local newspapers jumped on the story with sensational pretrial publicity, and one editorial demanded that police "stop stalling" and charge Sheppard with the murder. During the trial, which drew national attention and coverage, the judge exercised little control over the disruptive media in the courtroom. After Sheppard had served 11 years in prison, the Supreme Court reversed his conviction on grounds that he did not receive a fair trial because of prejudicial publicity and a circus-like atmosphere. The case was retried and Sheppard was acquitted, but he died shortly thereafter.

The Supreme Court also reversed the fraud conviction of Texas grain dealer Billie Sol Estes, a case made noteworthy because he was a protégé of then-Vice President Lyndon Johnson. The court said that the mere presence of television cameras in the courtroom during pretrial motions and his trial violated his Sixth Amendment rights. The court's ruling caused state courts, which had begun to permit television coverage, to rethink their position. Many terminated TV access to courtrooms, especially in sensational cases, to avoid a reversal based on the *Estes* decision.

The Supreme Court ruled in *Florida v. Chandler* in 1981 that the Constitution does not prohibit states from experimenting with cameras in courts, as long as the defendant's right to a fair trial is not affected. The change from earlier rulings was based upon advances in technology. At the time of *Estes*, noisy cameras required bright lights and cables. *Chandler* involved pooled video operating in a natural light. Cameras eventually came into courtrooms in most states, although they are not permitted in federal courts. Some jurisdictions restrict televised trial coverage; others allow it with the permission of the judge or defendants.

The executive director of the Reporters Committee for Freedom of the Press at the time of the O.J. Simpson murder case, Jane Kirtley, made the following strong appeal for cameras in the courtroom:

> A camera in the courtroom is the logical extension of the First Amendment right of the media,
> the public's surrogate, to attend a criminal trial. It provides a more accurate version of court
> proceedings than a third-person account can ever hope to do. A fixed, silent camera in the

courtroom commits no excesses, but instead neutralizes inaccurate and sensational reports based on out-of-court interviews. It doesn't intimidate witnesses or jurors, but helps keep them alert and mindful of their sacred mission. Nor does a camera cause flamboyant behavior on the part of lawyers, judges or witnesses. It simply records and exposes it to public scrutiny when it occurs. [15]

The New Hampshire Supreme Court has ruled that cameras in the courtroom should be the state standard. "The use of cameras by the electronic media is merely an extension of the reporting function of the more traditional arms of the press," the decision declared. Judges should limit electronic media coverage only if there is a "substantial likelihood" of harmful consequences, and only when no other practical alternative is available. The ruling came after the judge in a murder case said the defendant's right to a fair trial would be infringed by cameras. After the defendant pleaded guilty, the *Boston Globe*, a television station and the New Hampshire Association of Broadcasters challenged the ban.[16]

There is always debate about whether publicity prevents a fair trial. None of the convictions of the Watergate defendants were overturned in the 1970s, even though their actions were the subject of massive publicity during congressional hearings on the matter. The conviction of newspaper heiress Patty Hearst on bank robbery charges in a case that drew national and, at times, sympathetic media coverage, was not overturned, nor were cases with other celebrated defendants. In fact, experience has shown that a defendant can be acquitted by an unsequestered jury despite massive unfavorable media attention to the case.

Some judges, prosecutors and attorneys remain unconvinced, however. Prosecution and defense attorneys argued against live television coverage in the trial of two men accused of multiple sniper shootings in the Washington, D.C. area several years ago, saying that it would potentially affect how witnesses testified and their conduct in court, and could potentially taint jurors in other jurisdictions where the accused face charges. The judge ruled that electronic coverage could intimidate witnesses, affect testimony, cause counsel to behave differently, and make it difficult for jurors to follow the court's instructions.[17]

Judges and the Media

Although judges have the authority to control the behavior of the press within the courtroom— the judge in the O.J. Simpson murder trial once ordered two reporters expelled for continually talking—courts generally cannot prohibit news media from publishing any details they legally uncover about a case. In an effort to restrict the spread of information about pretrial motions— generally concerning evidence, a defendant's mental condition or whether to try a juvenile offender as an adult—judges have sought to close proceedings to the public. The Supreme Court ruled, however, that courts can be closed for only the most compelling of reasons, after alternatives have been considered and only for as long as necessary.

The Supreme Court, in a series of decisions, upheld the right of the news media—a segment of the public—to attend trials and judicial proceedings. In a 1976 ruling, *Nebraska Press Assn. v. Stuart*, it held that any order barring the press from publishing information about a case violated the First Amendment. Trial courts got around this ban by imposing prior restraint on court officers and law enforcement personnel, prohibiting them from making out-of-court statements to the news media or limiting information about a case to minimize the possibility of prejudicial publicity (called a **gag order** by reporters). News media can also be prohibited from interviewing jurors about deliberations after the trial has concluded. The courts have reasoned that these restrictions are less onerous than outright censorship, but the net effect is the same: The flow of news and information to the public is restricted and, some argue, making this a significant threat to the First Amendment rights of the press.[18]

Voluntary Press—Bar Guidelines

Over the years, the U.S. Justice Department, the American Bar Association and various press–bar advisory panels have issued guidelines about information that reporters should not use in stories. Journalists are asked to restrict reports about confessions, prior criminal records, results of tests conducted during investigations, rumor or hearsay about a defendant's habits or lifestyle, speculation about potential witnesses, evidence or testimony, speculation by officials, and any sensational or inflammatory statements. The rationale is that unsubstantiated allegations often surface but are never introduced in court as evidence—as happened before the O.J. Simpson case went to trial in 1995 and during the Oklahoma City federal building bombing case. If the news media report those allegations, it is argued, potential jurors may find them difficult to disregard, even if the allegations are not introduced during the trial.

The effectiveness of these and similar guidelines is debatable, of course. With the proliferation of media channels in recent years, not to mention the impact of the Internet on news dissemination, it is increasingly difficult for mainstream media to avoid publishing some of the same material as the sensationalist tabloids or questionable online sources. In the O.J. Simpson trial, as in later sensational cases, the *New York Times* and TV networks were printing and airing some of the tabloid allegations, whether or not their truth could be verified. Once again, the economics of the media marketplace increasingly dictates that media outlets will go with sensational aspects of a case to draw audiences. Such sensationalism is not conducive to following guidelines to ensure a fair trial.

Police and the Media

The criminal justice system is often part of an elaborate ritual, and unless a news reporter is aware of the dynamics involved, justice may not be served. Law officers, as well as defense and prosecuting attorneys, use the news media to present their cases to the public, despite judicial admonitions to the contrary. Believing they have cracked an important case, police may attempt to manipulate public opinion to pressure prosecutors into moving for an indictment or to reassure a jittery public. Defense attorneys will attempt to create doubt about evidence or witnesses or make a bid for sympathy for the defendant. Prosecuting attorneys try to create pressure for high bail or maximum charges.

A new form of prejudicial publicity takes advantage of television's need for visuals in covering the arrest on fraud charges of CEOs of now-bankrupt companies. Instead of permitting those charged to quietly turn themselves in, the usual practice, federal officers staged early morning raids, quickly hustling the handcuffed accused past a throng of news reporters. This

---

Box 2.5

It Happened to Me: "Hold that story!"

There had been a particularly vicious homicide. A preteen girl had been abducted and her body, with more than 40 stab wounds, was found in the hills above the city. Police were making a major effort to find the killer before he possibly struck again. I was standing in the corridor of the detective bureau shortly before my paper's deadline, waiting to speak to the chief of detectives to update my earlier story. I heard the chief talking with two other detectives. A truck matching the description of the kidnap vehicle had been spotted, and officers had a partial license plate.

The chief said to get out an all points bulletin but to do so during shift changes, without using the police radio, in case the killer had the capability to monitor frequencies. As the three of them came out into the corridor, they saw me. The chief swore softly.

"You know, if you get this into the late edition, the radio station and the television will use it and it's gonna blow any chance we have of getting this SOB,"

he said. I nodded. The same thought had crossed my mind. I had already envisioned the banner headline on the late edition—"Partial Plate on Killer's Truck"—with my byline below it. But I also wanted to see the killer caught, and I didn't want our paper to be blamed for his getting away. I needed to make a snap decision because (in those pre-cell phone days) I couldn't call my editor.

"How much time do you need?" I asked. The chief said they were already running a check of possible plates and he would like to wait until late in the evening before word got out to the public. "O.K.," I said. "But on the condition you give it to us first." The chief nodded. I had mixed feelings when I opened the next morning's edition and saw the headline of what should have been my story with someone else's byline.

They caught the killer a couple of days later, by the way.—*WRW*

---

staged event, called a "perp walk" ("perp" is the abbreviation for *perpetrator*), is usually reserved for more heinous criminal defendants. In this case, however, the government wanted to send a signal that it was going to be tough on corporate crime in order to restore confidence in the nation's business system. Another objective was to stop the slide in the stock market. In one case, the tactic worked. On the day the top executives of cable giant Adelphia were arrested and paraded before news cameras, the stock market jumped nearly 500 points!

On the other hand, in many jurisdictions, police, courts and media have agreed on voluntary cooperative measures to reduce conflict and minimize harmful pretrial publicity. Most working reporters would say that police generally arrest the right person for a crime and innocent people are seldom convicted. But there *are* cases when the wrong person is picked up or found guilty. However infrequent those cases might be, reporters need to remember that under the American justice system, the accused is considered innocent until proven guilty in a court of law.

Reporters should write stories with a presumption of innocence and should never allow themselves to identify with police, prosecution or defense. Journalists should report the news with as little sensationalism and speculation as possible. They should treat the defendant impartially and the victim, or the family of a victim, with consideration, making every effort to avoid "victimizing the victim" by unnecessary, intrusive or insensitive coverage.

Access to Information

Although reporters try to stay out of the criminal justice process, sometimes they are dragged into legal proceedings because of interviews they conducted, videotapes they made or photographs they shot. The U.S. Supreme Court has ruled that judges can order reporters to turn over notes or names of sources in criminal proceedings. This ruling collides head on with journalists' perceptions of themselves as professionals who are duty-bound not to share such information. Reporters argue that they are not agents of law enforcement and that their ability to report news about crime and corruption often depends on promises of confidentiality.

The Reporters Committee for Freedom of the Press, in an effort to deal with the problem, has released a detailed compendium of reporter's privilege in every state and federal circuit to help journalists quash subpoenas for their work product and testimony. The guide, compiled by lawyers who handle subpoena cases in their jurisdictions, contains summaries of the law and practical advice on fighting subpoenas through trial and appellate courts. The Reporters Committee said that it developed the project because of the number of subpoenas served on journalists nationwide.[19]

Jeopardy of source confidentiality was one of the side issues in that $10 billion suit filed by Philip Morris against ABC. The cigarette company subpoenaed the expense reports of the story's producer and reporter, including specifics such as pick-up and drop-off points for taxi rides, in an effort to retrace the journalists' steps and reveal primary sources for the story. Such tactics mean that reporters need to exercise more care and that would-be whistle-blowers, not only those in the tobacco industry, will be more cautious about giving out damaging information about organizations—even if such information *ought* to be in the public domain.

In an unusual twist, a Minnesota public relations consultant was awarded $200,000 from newspapers in St. Paul and Minneapolis after his name was published, even though reporters had pledged confidentiality. The consultant gave reporters negative information about an opposing candidate. Editors overruled the reporters and said the public was entitled to know from where the 11th-hour information had come. The consultant was fired and he sued. The case, *Cohen v. Cowles Media Co.,* which went through several reversals, was decided by the Supreme Court, which said that the First Amendment gives no protection to journalists who reveal the names of sources who were promised confidentiality.

Reporters and Their Sources

Law enforcement officials contend that journalists have a civic duty to cooperate with the courts and provide evidence against criminal suspects. The Supreme Court, in the *Stanford Daily* case in 1971, upheld the use of search warrants by law enforcement authorities to make unannounced searches of newsrooms for journalists' notes and photographs. While the search warrant was not widely used, predictable excesses in some jurisdictions led to modification of the policy. The **Privacy Protection Act of 1980** restricts the use of warrants to exceptional circumstances to seize information in the possession of public communicators. State and federal statutes encourage the use of subpoenas rather than search warrants, but they are still used by local police or prosecutors.

After several reporters were jailed for contempt of court in the early 1970s when they refused to name news sources, 32 states and the District of Columbia enacted **shield laws** for reporters, which protect them from being forced during legal proceedings to reveal their news sources. Reporters in most of those states are not required to disclose sources or notes to the prosecution, to the defense or to parties in a civil suit without compelling reason. Even states without shield laws have legal decisions recognizing a reporter's privilege.

A reporter's immunity from testimony is often argued on a case-by-case basis. Although shield laws preclude "fishing expeditions" on the part of prosecutors, they do not give iron-clad protection. For instance, many states do not protect reporters' notes, audiotapes or other materials, which may be subpoenaed as evidence. Generally, reporters' rights groups encourage newspeople to be familiar with the provisions of their state's shield laws and how they are interpreted by the courts in order to avoid facing unexpected penalties.

There is no federal shield law, although the office of the attorney general has in the past adopted guidelines designed to limit the use of subpoenas served on journalists following the 1972 *Branzburg v. Hayes* ruling by the Supreme Court that said reporters have no right under the First Amendment to refuse to answer questions from a grand jury. But the legal landscape appears to have changed following the leaking in 2005 of the name of a CIA agent in apparent retaliation for her husband's essay in the *New York Times* questioning the accuracy of weapons intelligence prior to the beginning of the Iraq War.

When the name was published, the federal prosecutor subpoenaed journalists who worked on the story and one, Judith Miller of the *New York Times*, was jailed for 85 days for refusing to divulge news sources with whom she talked for a story she didn't write. A federal appeals court had also ordered a *Time* magazine reporter jailed for refusing to cooperate with the prosecutor. Potentially ruinous fines, stayed on appeal, were levied against the magazine and the newspaper. The former chief of staff of Vice President Cheney was later convicted of lying to federal investigators after several well-known journalists were called by the prosecution to refute his version of events.

Federal prosecutors pressured two reporters from the *San Francisco Chronicle* to name a source who provided them with grand jury information about the use of steroids in baseball. A freelance photographer was jailed for months for refusing to turn over to federal prosecutors a videotape of an anarchist protest in which a police officer suffered a fractured skull. While there are gray areas in all the cases, the erosion of reporters' rights to maintain confidential sources at the federal level could filter down to the state and local level. If so, it would be a development that could only serve to restrict the flow of information necessary for democracy to thrive.[20]

Freedom of Information Act

One of the difficulties in obtaining government records has always been locating documents and convincing the holding agency to release them. All states and the federal government have adopted statutes mandating access to many government documents. While some lower courts seal records, official court documents have long been open for inspection and copying by the public and the news media, although the Supreme Court has not specifically declared a constitutional right to inspect or copy materials.

For a number of years, federal records were closed to public scrutiny, until Congress passed the federal **Freedom of Information Act (FOIA)** in 1966, with expanded versions in 1974, 1986, and 1996. FOIA made many documents—some of them embarrassing to the government—accessible to journalists. The FOIA is limited in that it applies only to federal executive branch agencies, not to Congress, the courts, the president's immediate staff, or state and local governments.

The FOIA requires federal agencies to provide any citizen or foreign national residing in the United States access to records of all cabinet and independent agencies, regulatory commissions, and government-owned corporations that do not fit one of nine exempt categories: national security, confidential business information, law enforcement reports and records, banking documents, oil and gas data, agency rules and practices, statutory exemptions by Congress, personnel and medical records, and invasions of privacy.[21]

Records are defined as documents, papers, reports, and letters in the government's possession, including films, photographs, sound recordings, computer tapes, and electronic databases. The **Government Printing Office Electronic Information Access Enhancement Act of 1996** provides Internet access to GPO documents, and the **Electronic Freedom of Information Act of 1996** directs government agencies to make electronic records stored on computer disk, CD-ROM, and the Internet available to news reporters.

The law sets time limits for responding to FOIA requests, although it is often not met. A tremendous backlog of requests—more than a million requests are filed each year—has caused reporters to routinely complain that bureaucrats drag their feet in releasing information. FOIA officers counter that they cannot respond quickly because Congress and the executive branch have not been willing to allocate money for adequate staffing.

Anyone can seek personal information through the Freedom of Information Act. To obtain such information, first contact the public information officer or the FOIA officer of the federal agency holding the desired information. The information usually can be obtained through an informal request. If this effort is not successful, file a written request to the person listed by the agency in the *Federal Register* as the FOIA contact. Agencies are required to explain their FOIA procedures, provide indexes of available information, set reasonable fees for duplication of materials, and maintain reading rooms to assist in locating information. The FOIA allows recovery of court costs by requesters who, in the process of seeking records, file lawsuits and win their cases.

Limits to Freedom of Information

In the wake of the events of September 11, 2001, federal FOIA officers have been directed by the attorney general to give strong consideration to exemptions before releasing information and to ask if there is a "sound legal basis" for withholding information from requestors. Even before the terrorist attacks, the government rarely viewed exemptions for privacy or business information as discretionary, and agencies had increasingly been withholding information on named individuals as a matter of course. The automatic use of exemptions for internal records such as staff recommendations and policy draft comments is back, and federal agencies have been ordered to withhold "sensitive but unclassified information" for national security reasons, even when the FOIA exception for national security does not apply. The Homeland Security Act provides criminal penalties for people who disclose "critical infrastructure" information that businesses want kept secret, and makes that information automatically exempt from the FOIA.[22]

Reporters often feel stymied because they have to know exactly which document they are searching for before they can request its release. Journalists also complain that the FOIA is ineffective because, they say, agencies interpret exemptions broadly and employ procedural ploys to block access or delay release of information until it is no longer newsworthy. When documents finally arrive, they often contain large blacked-out portions. A beginning newswriter might want to avoid this thicket. There is usually more than one way to obtain information, generally by developing good sources of information so that FOIA requests are not needed. Most newswriters have enough to do every day without getting involved in a time-consuming struggle with a governmental agency.

Open Records, Open Meetings

State laws give access to state, county, and municipal government records, although access through common law (unwritten laws or statutes, based upon custom and precedent) places two main restrictions:

- Records are limited to those with a legal interest in the records. The media and public are not *entitled* to them under those terms.
- A public record is not subject to disclosure unless it is required to be kept.

Likewise, the First Amendment and common law do not provide the media with access to meetings of federal, state or governmental bodies. This limitation has led to enactment of federal and state **sunshine laws** requiring that executive agencies meet in public, although exemptions to that requirement are similar to FOIA exemptions for federal agencies.

Once again, because the law has changed considerably over the years, reporters and public relations practitioners need to keep track of the legal regulations in the state where they work.[23] It also seems practical to develop and cultivate sources in order to work out potential problems in advance before lawsuits are filed and relationships are unnecessarily strained.

Broadcast Regulation

Broadcasters have fewer First Amendment rights than print journalists. Although the government cannot tell newspapers and magazines what or what not to print, radio and TV stations—licensed by the government—are expected to provide a balanced presentation of diverse views on matters of public concern.

Broadcast regulation by Congress is based on a **doctrine of scarcity**, which presumes there are more applicants for broadcast licenses than space available on the electromagnetic spectrum, which is the range of wavelengths or frequencies of electromagnetic radiation that includes radio and television broadcast bands. The Radio Act of 1927 defined the concept of the broadcast medium as a quasi-public utility expected to meet the needs of the audience. The **Communications Act of 1934**, amended over the years, was the basic broadcast law under which American radio and TV operated for more than 60 years. In the words of the 1927 and 1934 acts, broadcasters are required to operate "in the public interest, convenience, and necessity." A five-member Federal Communications Commission acts as a legislative body to make rules governing broadcasting and as a judicial authority with the power to levy fines and even revoke licenses. The regulatory authority of the FCC has grown to include traditional broadcasting, cable, telephone systems, and various new electronic media-related technologies being developed. The Supreme Court ruled in 1994 in *Turner Broadcasting v. FCC* that cable operators—because there are more channels and it is a subscription service—have greater First Amendment rights than broadcasters, but not as much as print.

Although the Telecommunications Act of 1996 made major deregulatory changes in the structure of the broadcast industry, radio and TV still face numerous regulations. For example, broadcasters must keep obscene, indecent or profane language off the airwaves and limit the airing of "indecent" programs. Those who do not are fined, often considerably. Section 315 of the Communications Act requires broadcasters to provide **equal time** opportunities to legally qualified candidates for public office at the lowest rate and in equivalent time blocks. Bona fide newscasts, news interviews and news documentaries are exempt from the equal time provisions, as is on-the-spot coverage of news events. Although not required, broadcasters are expected to provide airtime for political candidates.

News has long been of interest to regulators. In 1949, for instance, an FCC report on editorializing said that broadcast licensees had an obligation to present the news accurately and warned broadcasters not to distort newscasts. Although the FCC has refused to closely regulate news, it has said it will intervene if broadcasters mislead viewers and listeners by intentionally slanting or staging news or intentionally misrepresenting events or interviews through editing. In the distant past, the FCC refused to renew licenses because of news distortion.

The FCC's **personal attack rule**, which said broadcasters must offer reply time if the honesty, character or integrity of a group or individual is attacked during discussion of a controversial issue of public importance, was rescinded in 2000 at the direction of the Federal Court of Appeals in Washington. The FCC was also directed to drop the **editorial reply** requirement that broadcasters must provide notification for any editorials—specific statements of station policy—that oppose a candidate or endorse an opponent. Notification is not required in commentary—observations by members of the news staff or station clearly labeled as opinion.

Although the FCC can fine radio stations airing programs with indecent language, it has permitted some latitude regarding the language in news programs. The FCC may levy a fine of up to $25,000 for licensees who broadcast hoaxes about crime or catastrophe deemed harmful to the public. The FCC warned stations not to frighten audiences following CBS's 1938 broadcast of "War of the Worlds," a radio drama that panicked thousands of people, who heard on the radio that Martians had landed in New Jersey.

What the Profession Should Be

There have been some highly publicized cases of reporters at prestigious publications making up interviews, lifting descriptions from other papers and passing them off as their own work, or letting freelancers and researchers do most of the reporting without being given credit. In no uncertain terms, this is unacceptable! Journalism deals in truth. The authors do not think it is an overstatement to say that the mission of reporting the news is a sacred trust.

Ideally, journalism should be the eyes and ears of readers, listeners, and viewers: informing the public, acting as a watchdog over government, business and industry, facilitating democracy, and serving as a medium of socialization. News stories should be reported with accuracy, fairness, and lack of bias. Journalists should avoid rumor and sensational reporting, keep a social distance from those they cover, and maintain a professional, mutually respectful adversarial relationship with newsmakers, especially political figures.

Perhaps the issue comes back to each reporter living up to his or her personal standards and code of ethics. Each specialty covered in this book—print, broadcast and public relations— has a set of ethical codes subscribed to by professionals. Practitioners in each field should become familiar with these guidelines and develop their own sense of appropriate conduct and responsible professional behavior. Ultimately, ethical standards are only as good as those individuals who are reporting, writing, editing, and broadcasting the news or engaging in public relations.

Discussion Questions

The following are class discussion questions drawn from Chapter 2:

1. What is the ideal relationship between news reporters and sources? Why?

2. News reporters and public relations practitioners subscribe to codes of ethics. Why? Why at times do some appear to violate the standards of those codes?

3. Why do we need libel laws? Shouldn't the "marketplace of ideas" provide enough of an opportunity for truth to emerge? Explain.

4. The "chilling effect" of threatened lawsuits "means the public does not get the news and information it should have." But should that be the role of the media? Should the press instigate exposés or just report the news? Explain your answer.

5. Analyze the conflict between the First and Sixth Amendments. Is there any way to resolve the legitimate differences between the media and the courts without sacrificing media freedom or a fair trial for the accused?

6. Should there be shield laws for journalists? Analyze the pros and cons.

7. What is the Freedom of Information Act and why is it important to journalists and the public they serve?

8. Given the number of cable channels on the air, is the "Doctrine of Scarcity," which justifies governmental regulation of broadcasting, still valid? Explain.

9. "Each reporter [should live] up to his or her personal standards and code of ethics." But is that enough in this increasingly economics-driven media environment? Explain your answer.

CHAPTER EXERCISES

Exercise 2.1—Freewriting

 Freewrite (do nonstructured writing in which you put down your thoughts) for five minutes on the following topic, and then discuss this issue in class: From what you already know and without studying further, what do you think the balance should be between personal privacy and the public's right to know?

Exercise 2.2—Telephone Interview

 Conduct a telephone interview with a professional writer or photographer involved in print journalism, broadcast journalism or public relations. Ask this writer or photographer to tell you about a situation in which he or she had to confront the issue of privacy or defamation. How did the person handle the situation? What did he or she learn in the process? In retrospect, how might the situation have been handled better? Summarize your interview in a memo to your instructor.

Exercise 2.3—Newsletter Editing

 You are editing the newsletter for Burlington–Fitzsimmons, a refrigeration company with 700 employees at four different locations. One of your staff writers turned in the following item for the next issue. Underline any problem areas you find in this article, then write a memo to your staff writer explaining any parts that carry legal risks.

> Bill Hernden of the shipping department has been nominated for Volunteer of the Year by the Morningside Preschool Program, where his daughter, Alicia, is enrolled. Bill's ex-wife is a teacher's assistant with the Morningside program.
>
> Bill, who works on the night shift, has been with Burlington–Fitzsimmons for more than six months. He has just received his first performance evaluation and received a "Satisfactory-Plus" rating, which shows that he is a quick learner and a good worker.
>
> B–F personnel director Ariel Lee said she is pleased that community-minded people such as Bill are working for this company. She noted that Bill is a member of the board of directors of EAR, a community rehabilitation group formerly known as Ex-Offenders Against Recidivism.
>
> Bill is also a volunteer peer counselor at the Alternative Men's Health Center in neighboring Proximity County, according to a co-worker. The health center is part of a

statewide system of clinics that have been active in fighting the spread of AIDS within high-risk populations.

Before coming to work for Burlington–Fitzsimmons, Bill worked as a bartender at the Hard Body Dance Club.

■

Exercise 2.4—Sheriff's Guidelines

 You are working as a communication specialist for the county sheriff's department. Part of your job is to help officers use the news media to help them report on newsworthy cases and generate public support for law enforcement issues. The sheriff has asked you to help draft departmental policies on what information should be given to the news media.

List the pros and cons of providing identities of people in the following situations:

- arrested clients of prostitutes

- arrested prostitutes

- child abusers released from prison

- parents failing to pay child support

- rape victims

- underage drinking offenders

- victims of child abuse

■

Notes

1. "Public Blames Media for Too Much Celebrity Coverage," "Cable and Network TV Worst Offenders," a report of the Pew Research Center for People and the Press, Aug. 2, 2007, at http://people-press.org/reports/display.php3?ReportID=346.
2. Jeffrey Scheuer. *The Sound Bite Society: Television and the American Mind* (New York: Four Walls Eight Windows, 1999), pp. 8, 10.
3. Max Frankel. *New York Times Magazine*, January 18, 1998, from www.journalism.org/Frankel column.html.
4. "Internet Sapping Broadcast News Audience: The Changing Media Landscape," a Pew Research Center for the People and the Press report, June 11, 2000, at www.people-press.org/media00sec1htm, p. 5.
5. "Self-Censorship: How Often and Why," a survey of journalists in association with *Columbia Journalism Review*, a report of the Pew Research Center for the People and the Press, April 30, 2000, at www.people-press.org/jour00rpt.htm, pp. 1–3.

6. For a discussion of corporate interrelationships and news coverage, see Marc Gunther, "All in the Family," *American Journalism Review*, October 1995, p. 38. The problem hasn't abated over the years.

7. Robert McChesney. *Corporate America and the Threat to Democracy* (New York: Seven Stories Press, 1997), pp. 6–7, quoted in Scheuer, *Sound Bite Society*, p. 41.

8. Cynthia Gorney. *The Business of News: A Challenge for Journalism's Next Generation* (New York: Carnegie Corporation of New York, 2002), p. 4.

9. Scheuer, Jeffrey. *Sound Bite Society*, pp. 41–42. See also Robert McChesney, *Rich Media, Poor Democracy: Communications Politics in Dubious Times* (New York: New Press, 2000).

10. Recommended texts include Ken R. Middleton, William Lee, and Bill F. Chamberlin, *The Law of Public Communication* (Boston: Allyn & Bacon, 2007); T. Barton Carter, Marc A. Franklin, and Jay B. Wright, *The First Amendment and the Fourth Estate* (Egan, Minn.: Foundation Press, 2004); Dwight L. Teeter, Jr. and Bill Loving, *Law of Mass Communications: Freedom and Control of Print and Broadcast Media*, 11th ed. (Egan, Minn.: Foundation Press, 2004); and Don R. Pember and Clay Calvert, *Mass Media Law*, 15th ed. (New York: McGraw-Hill, 2007/2008). See also "Covering Crime and Justice: A guide for Journalists," written by members of the organization Criminal Justice Journalists, reporters who cover crime and the courts, at www.justicejournalism.org/crimeguide.

11. The original limiting decision was *Branzburg v. Hayes* in 1972. The Supreme Court held in *Richmond Newspapers Inc. v. Virginia* (1980) that reporters act as agents for the public and, thus, access by journalists to information about government promotes the discussion of public affairs. The Court noted in *Globe Newspaper Co. v. Superior Court* (1982) that because publishing news relies on a reporter's ability to gather information, restrictions on the right to gather news impedes the right to publish, thus abridging First Amendment press freedoms. See the summary provided by the Reporters Committee for Freedom of the Press, "Access to Places: Do You Have a Right to Gather News?" at www.rcfp.org/places/doyouhavearighttogathernews.html.

12. See Reese Cleghorn, "Cigarette Settlement Shames ABC," *American Journalism Review*, October 1995, pp. 8–9, and Wayne Overbeck, *Major Principles of Media Law* (Belmont, Calif.: Wadsworth, 2003), pp. 107–108.

13. The case was *Food Lion v. Capital Cities/ABC*. See Overbeck, *Major Principles*, p. 107.

14. Christine D. Urban. *Examining our Credibility: Perspectives of the Public and the Press* (Reston, Va.: American Society of Newspaper Editors, 1998), pp. 6, 65.

15. Jane Kirtley. "Forget O.J.: Cameras Belong in Court," *American Journalism Review*, October 1995, p. 66.

16. "Courtrooms Should Be Presumed Open to Cameras, Court Rules," December 16, 2002, from the Web site of the Reporters Committee for Freedom of the Press, www.rcfp.org/news/2002/1216petiti.html.

17. See Josh White, "Judge Bars TV Cameras From Trial of Sniper Suspect," December 12, 2002, *Washington Post online*, www.washingtonpost.com/wp-dyn/articles/A445992002Dec12.html; "Judge Bars Cameras From Trial in Sniper Case," *New York Times*, December 13, 2002, p. A-27; and "Sniper Suspect's Trial Will Not Be Televised," December 12, 2002, from the Web site of the Reporters Committee for Freedom of the Press, www.rcfp.org/news/2002/1212virgin.html.

18. Ashley Gauthier, "Gag Orders and the Effect on News Gathering," from the Web site of the Reporters Committee for Freedom of the Press, www.rcfp.org/secretjustice/gagorders/effect.html.

19. The guide is available at www.rcfp.org/privilege/. The "Introduction" provides a theoretical and historical background to the issue of sources and subpoenas. A User's Guide covers each state and federal circuit. Sections are arranged according to a standard outline, making it easy to compare the law in various states.

20. See Adam Liptak, "After Libby Trial, New Era for Government and Press," *New York Times*, March 8, 2007, p. A-14, and Howard Kurtz, *Washington Post*, "Jailed Man is a Videographer and a Blogger, But is He a Journalist?" March 8, 2007, C-01, WashingtonPost.com.

21. The *Associated Press Stylebook* contains a summary of FOIA provisions and strategies for obtaining documents and the Web site of the Reporters Committee for Freedom of the Press has a primer on "How to Use the Federal FOI Act" at www.refp.org/foiact/index.html.

22. See "Freedom of Information" in *Homefront Confidential: How the War on Terrorism Affects Access to Information and the Public's Right to Know*, by the Reporters Committee for Freedom of the Press, www.rcfp.org/homefrontconfidential/. It is updated annually on the anniversary of the 9/11 attacks. The RCFP also publishes "Behind the Homefront," described as "a daily chronicle of homeland security news affecting the news media and the public's right to know," at www.rcfp.org/behindthehomefront/.

23. The Reporters Committee has published an "Open Government Guide," a state-by-state reference to open records and meetings laws. It is available at www.rcfp.org/ogg/index.php.

3

Basics of Writing
and Editing

Chapter Objectives

- To stress the importance of using standard conventions of the English language
- To explain construction of simple and understandable messages
- To enhance writing through the use of meaningful language
- To avoid biased language

Writing Effectively

Effective writers have an enthusiasm, even a passion, for words. Just as musicians coordinate the sounds of instruments and voices to create captivating music, just as artists let beautiful pictures emerge from many different colors and shapes, so too do writers weave words into exquisite patterns of ideas. Media writers in particular seek to inform and sometimes to motivate and persuade. To accomplish this goal, they use simple everyday words in original combinations to create rich understandings and new insights for their readers.

As a media writer, your aim should be to use words not to impress but rather to express. That is, don't write to show off (indeed, writing that draws attention to itself is probably more showy than effective). Rather, try to create expressive writing that gives pleasure to your readers by helping them absorb information, gain insight, and explore ideas. Good media writers use language to present sophisticated information and ideas so that casual readers can understand and appreciate them.

Good writers are sufficiently comfortable with the conventions of English that they can concentrate not so much on following rules but rather on developing patterns of effective communication with audiences. This chapter presents principles and guidelines rather than rules.

Obeying the basic rules of writing does not guarantee good writing, though it does point the way toward acceptable writing. By first reflecting on these principles and then refining your writing through the various exercises presented in this chapter, you can develop your effectiveness as a writer beyond mere acceptability. With practice, you can become a highly competent, even skilled writer.

You probably already have achieved a basic competency in the correct use of the English language. Before you read the remainder of this chapter, assess your writing skills by taking the diagnostic test in Exercise 3.1. When you have completed the test, ask your instructor to review the answers in class. If you correctly identified all or most of the errors, congratulations. The test is difficult. Did you do better on the word usage section or on the punctuation section? If you had some troublesome areas, concentrate on them as you study this chapter. The suggested readings at the end of this chapter are other books that can help you improve your writing skills.

The basics of effective writing detailed in this chapter fall into four categories of principles: (1) standard usage, which creates a common bond between writer and reader; (2) simple language, which allows readers to understand the writer; (3) meaningful language, through which the writer can communicate the subtlety of his or her ideas; and (4) inclusive language that avoids bias and giving offense. Following are basic principles in each category.

Principles of Standard Usage

Writers communicate clearly with their audience by following the principles of **syntax**, the branch of grammar dealing with the arrangement and relationship of words in sentences.

1. Use Technically Accurate Language

The ultimate rule is to write so the reader can understand the intended meaning. To accomplish this goal, writers need to observe at least the baseline of technical accuracy by following the canons of grammar, punctuation, and syntax. Use a comprehensive and up-to-date dictionary. The Associated Press recommends Webster's New World Dictionary and, as an even more complete source, Webster's Third New International Dictionary. In addition, adopt a good contemporary grammar reference book.

Follow the standard grammatical conventions of the language, but don't follow them blindly. For example, if a sentence is grammatically accurate but nevertheless sounds stilted or confusing, rewrite the sentence. Writing should not only be correct, it should also read well.

Use correct spelling. Misspelled words signal a careless writer. Journalists and public relations writers cannot afford to have readers (or editors) conclude that they are careless. When the dictionary or your computer's spellchecker lists two acceptable spellings, check the stylebook; one of the alternatives is likely preferred. Turn off the hyphenation tool on your computer.

2. Use the Appropriate Level of Formality

Effective media writers use what has been called "operational English" or "standard English." In the news media, this English is sometimes called "network standard" because it is the measure of appropriate language for broadcasting in every part of the country. Some label it "the language of wider communication" so as not to offend people who use narrower languages. Whatever it is called, this English is the version you will use professionally, the one on which this textbook is based.

English has a rich diversity of forms and formalities, and it ranges from the very formal language of legal documents to the informal conversational style. Editorial or column writers might use a fairly formal style, including words and phrases such as *it is to be noted that . . .* and *according to one's abilities . . . .* Journalists writing straight news stories would not use such formal phrasing, but they would maintain a neutral stance, such as when they report on a survey of college graduates by referring to those polled as *they* rather than *we.* A feature or editorial writer, on the other hand, might feel free to use *you* and *us* and perhaps even sentence fragments in a lighter, more conversational writing style.

A public relations writer preparing a newsletter story or a service article might use an informal and personal style, and an even more conversational tone for a fundraising letter. Meanwhile, an advertising copywriter might prepare an ad full of sentence fragments and pop jargon. English is a language with such diversity that it can accommodate many different styles and purposes.

Here is a comparison of the various aspects of formal and informal language:

Formal Language

- *He, she, they* in reference to readers
- Complete sentences
- Compound sentences with phrases and clauses
- Complex sentences with frequent use of modifying phrases and clauses
- Passive voice
- No slang and/or colloquialisms
- Straight news articles and news releases, backgrounders, position statements and editorials

Informal Language

- *You* in reference to readers
- Single words, phrases and fragments
- Simple sentences in conversational order (subject, verb, object)
- Dashes and ellipses for incomplete or interrupted thoughts
- Active voice
- Contractions, slang and/or colloquialisms
- Feature articles, some columns, newsletter articles, brochures, advertising copy, and broadcast scripts

You also should try to write in a form appropriate for the audience. English has many cultural dialects, such as those associated with New England, the Deep South, Louisiana's Cajun region, and the Pennsylvania Dutch country, as well as the English associated with Canada, Australia, and Scotland. Dialects also may be associated with urban hip-hop, down-home country or ValleySpeak. Some dialects are cultural, such as the Spanglish sometimes heard in Hispanic communities.

Although the general advice is to use standard English in writing news stories, dialects occasionally can be appropriate. For example, a print journalist might capture with quotations the folksy allure of an Appalachian speaker. A broadcaster might make judicious use of street slang when interviewing a community advocate in an inner city. Sometimes a public relations writer or advertising copywriter might use a particular dialect when writing for a specific and narrowly defined audience. The general guideline when writing in a particular dialect is to write, if not from experience, then at least from research. Write in a way that does not overplay the dialect or demean the people who lay personal claim to the language.

3. *Avoid Grammatical Myths*

Accomplished writers understand that some "rules" are not rules at all. For example, the common advice to avoid sentence fragments is good advice, but it is not an absolute. Sentence fragments can enhance readability. Sometimes. Used with care.

Likewise, the supposed ban on splitting infinitives *(to* plus a verb) is a carryover rule from Latin, where it is impossible to split an infinitive because it is a single word. But English separates the word *to* from its verb. An adverb added between the two carries particular emphasis, as in the phrases *to weakly protest* and *to quietly fume.*

Additionally, some words are becoming obsolete whereas others are being added to the language. *Shall* is one of those words that you probably can do without, especially because few people understand the rule for using *shall* instead of *will.* As for new words and novel usages coming into the language, media writers should take a conservative tack and avoid being on the leading edge of language innovation.

Experienced writers know that, on occasion, conventional guidelines for English, the supposed absolutes, may be bent to achieve special effects. The key is to do the bending carefully, infrequently, and with full knowledge of both the rule and the reason for bending it. Writers cannot claim creative license to justify sloppiness or ignorance. Generally, however, it is better to rewrite the sentence to avoid the need to bend the rule in the first place.

4. *Avoid Bulky Sentences*

With any type of sentence, writers should strive for simplicity. A good sentence delivers only one thought, and its phrases and clauses work to support the main thought rather than introduce extraneous information. This is especially important when you are writing for the broadcast media, because the audience will not have the opportunity to reread an awkward sentence. Often a sentence is cumbersome because the subject and verb are separated with phrases and/or clauses. It may be appropriate to revise the sentence, perhaps by using the intruding clauses as separate sentences.

5. Make Sure Subjects and Verbs Agree

In its basic form, the principle of subject–verb agreement is simple: A singular noun takes a singular verb and a plural noun takes a plural verb. That's why we write *The truck hits the pedestrian* and *The trucks hit the pedestrian.*

Beyond the basics, the rules sometimes get confusing. For example, collective nouns are words representing individuals working together as one unit; they may involve more than one person but are used in the singular form. In the sentence, *The management is pleased with the union offer*, the collective noun *management* is singular; it refers to a group of people who, precisely because they are acting as a group, do the administrative work of an organization. So, it makes sense to say, *The management is pleased . . .* when referring to the company leadership in general, but *The managers are pleased . . .* when referring to various individual administrators. Other commonly used collective nouns include *jury, team, couple,* and *audience.*

Also, be careful with nouns that, although they end in *s*, are singular in their use: *Public relations is a rewarding career.* Other examples of singular nouns ending in *s* are *athletics, ethics, mathematics,* and *politics.* So you would write *Politics is competitive* and *Ethics is important.* Likewise, take care with Latin-based words, such as *data* and *media*, which already are a plural construction. Write *The media are . . .* rather than *The media is . . . .*

Compound subjects are two or more nouns acting together as the subject of a plural verb. Even if one of the nouns in a compound subject is singular, treat the compound subject as plural: *Both the teacher and her class regret the delay*, even though both subjects (teacher and class) are singular. Of course, if both subjects of a compound subject are plural, the verb also is plural: *The players and the fans want a victory.* Plural verbs also are needed when one subject element is singular and the other is plural, as in *The coach and the owners are in agreement.*

It can be confusing when the compound subject includes both singular and plural elements joined by *or* or *nor*. In that case, the two subjects are not acting together, so use the verb appropriate to the noun closest to it. For example, write *Neither the editor nor the copyeditors were correct* or *Neither the copyeditors nor the editor was correct.* To sound more natural, use the singular noun before the plural.

Pronouns also can be confusing. Singular verbs go with pronouns that have a singular meaning: *anyone, anybody, each, either, everyone, everybody, neither, no one, nobody, someone, somebody.* Plural verbs go with pronouns having a plural meaning: *both, few, many, several.* However, in some situations, the verb is determined by the meaning in context: *all, any, most, none, some.* For example, write *Some of the book was destroyed* (a portion of the book), but *Some of the librarians were late for work* (several people).

6. Make Sure Nouns and Pronouns Agree

The same logic that says singular nouns take singular verbs applies to nouns and their pronouns. For example, in *The school lost its mascot*, the singular pronoun *its* agrees with *the school.* In *The players won their game*, the plural pronoun *their* agrees with *the players.*

With collective nouns, the guideline is to use a singular pronoun when the elements of the collective noun are acting as a unit. For example, write *The board will hold its monthly meeting* and *The team honored its coach.* When elements are acting individually, it is usually best to rewrite the sentence to avoid using the collective noun: *Members of the board* (not simply *The board) argued about where to hold their monthly meeting* or *Members of the team were undecided about how to honor their coach.*

7. Place Words Properly

Keep the meaning of a sentence precise by placing words where they belong, particularly by placing modifiers immediately next to the words they are supposed to modify. Consider the many different meanings that result from the placement of a single word, *only*, in the following sentences:

> *The only editor of the company magazine recently complained about the photographer.*
> (one editor)

> *The editor of the only company magazine recently complained about the photographer.*
> (one magazine)

> *The editor of the company magazine only recently complained about the photographer.*
> (not earlier)

> *The editor of the company magazine recently complained only about the photographer.*
> (not about the writer)

> *The editor of the company magazine recently complained about the only photographer.*
> (one photographer)

Both dangling modifiers with nothing to modify and misplaced modifiers far from what they modify can confuse writers and readers. Good **syntax** (sentence structure) calls for phrases to modify the noun or pronoun that immediately follows them:

> *Going to the store, Beverly met her friend.* (Beverly was going to the store. We don't know where her friend was going.)

> *The newsletter will include a picture about your award next month.* (Is it next month's newsletter or will the award be presented next month?)

Violations of this syntax may be confusing:

> *As a writer, I want your opinion about this piece.* (Who is the writer, you or me? The word *I* following the introduction says it's me.)

> *To pass this course, study is important. (Study* is not trying to pass this course.)

Violations of this syntax sometimes can be amusing:

> *While practicing jump shots, Grandma waited in the bleachers.* (Was Grandma practicing jump shots from the bleachers?)

8. Be Moderate with Adjectives and Adverbs

A principle of media writing—whether for print or broadcast journalism or for many elements of public relations—is to be judicious with adjectives and adverbs. Both are useful in explaining and qualifying; however, both also can be overused by beginning writers, who thus risk losing the objectivity sought by media writers.

Limiting adjectives qualify meanings, as in *The veteran firefighter ran through the side doorway carrying the 3-year-old child.* The limiting adjectives are *veteran, side* and *3-year-old*; notice that each adjective is a factual word. Objective writers frequently use limiting adjectives because they can add rich detail to the story.

Descriptive adjectives also can enliven the basic information, as in *The exhausted firefighter ran through the blazing doorway carrying the terrified child.* The descriptive adjectives are *exhausted*, *blazing*, and *terrified*; they are more subjective than limiting adjectives. Therefore, media writers are careful with descriptive adjectives because they often ask the reader to rely on observations and conclusions of the writer.

For example, it would be a matter of objective fact to report that a building is 30 stories high, but to call it a tall building asks the reader to accept the writer's interpretation of the meaning for the word *tall*. That meaning itself will be influenced by the frame of reference; 30 stories may not be tall for Manhattan, N.Y., but quite tall for Manhattan, Kan.

Adverbs do for verbs what adjectives do for nouns: They provide a degree of nuance or detail, as in *The writer approached the assignment happily.* Or *fearfully.* Or *half-heartedly.* Adverbs can also modify adjectives, such as *breathtakingly beautiful*. Media writers use adverbs even more sparingly than adjectives. Adverbs often result from what the writer observed. Good media writers don't ask readers to accept the writer's conclusions, but they do provide details to allow readers to draw their own conclusions. Descriptive phrases also can serve the same function as adverbs, such as *The writer approached the assignment with eagerness.* The phrase *with eagerness* accomplishes the same meaning as would an adverb: *The writer eagerly approached the assignment.*

Media writers pay careful attention to adjectives and adverbs that reflect comparisons or degrees of intensity. Comparisons should make sense. Writers need to be accurate in using modifiers that are absolute (that is, those that cannot be modified by comparatives or superlatives). Absolutes include *first*, *last*, *only*, and *unique.* Never use a qualifier such as *very* with such words. Remember also that there is no "first annual" anything unless you are writing historically about something that began in the past.

9. Avoid Empty Phrases

Some words are like weeds. They simply take up space, hide the good stuff, and offer nothing of value. Effective writers avoid **empty phrases** such as *it is, there are*, and other forms of the linking verb *to be*:

Wimpy sentence: *There is a university plan to raise tuition.*

Stronger and more informative: *The university plans to raise tuition.*

Weak: *It will be legal for a 20 year old to buy beer when the new law goes into effect.*

Stronger: *A 20 year old may legally buy beer when the new law goes into effect.*

However, *it is* and *there are* occasionally serve a useful purpose. In some constructions, these phrases emphasize the subject of the sentence. For example, *It was my classmate who helped us understand this* gives more attention to the subject than *My classmate helped me understand this.*

10. Keep Elements Parallel

Good writers make sure that items presented in a series are used in parallel fashion. Good writers don't mix elements in a series or switch voice. **Parallel structure** calls for repeating grammatical patterns, such as a series of nouns, verb phrases, infinitives, clauses, and so on. For example, it would clearly be unbalanced to write *The dog learned to fetch, play dead and rolling over.* The final element is not parallel with the first two. Rather, a parallel construction would be *The dog learned to fetch, play dead and roll over.*

Sometimes writers signal that a parallel structure is coming. Common ways to do this are with words like *either, neither, both* and *not only.* The reader knows that two things are being introduced by these signals and that the writer will present them in parallel fashion:

We are interested in either going to the movies or attending a play. (two gerund phrases)

Both when to go and what to see were decisions they left to their dates. (two noun clauses)

My intention is neither to scold nor to intimidate. (two infinitive phrases)

Another way writers signal parallel elements is by introducing a sequence: *First, mix in the milk and egg whites; second, knead the dough; third, bake for two hours.* Or, writers may clearly signal that a series is coming: *This recipe has three steps: mixing in the milk and egg whites, kneading the dough, and baking for two hours.*

Often, parallel structure is accomplished by writing in threes:

I came, I saw, I conquered.

Government of the people, by the people, for the people . . .

Larry, Moe and Curly

Such parallelism has a rhythm that can stir the reader.

Another structure for parallelism is the **turnaround statement**. An example of this is found in President John F. Kennedy's inaugural address: *And so, my fellow Americans: Ask not what your country can do for you—ask what you can do for your country.*

11. Keep Punctuation Simple

Most writing appropriate for the media has fairly simple and standard punctuation. Broadcasting uses fairly simple punctuation, primarily commas and periods, while print not only makes use of those and question marks, hyphens, and quotation marks. Go lightly on dashes and parentheses and be wary about using semicolons, colons, and exclamation points. Punctuation should help the reader (and the speaker) break up sentences and give guidance on how the sentence will sound.

Writers should use punctuation according to standard guidelines rather than whimsy. For example, commas create a pause in a sentence, but they are not used only for when a reader or speaker would pause. They also separate items in a series, separate two independent clauses with a coordinating conjunction, and conclude long introductory phrases and clauses.

Commas　The use of commas with internal clauses is perhaps the most problematic because the comma's use depends on the meaning of the clause. Do not use commas with essential (restrictive) clauses, which provide information crucial to the meaning of the sentence. Here is an example of an essential clause: *The students who failed the exam will have to do an extra term paper.* The clause *who failed the exam* is essential. It tells us that not all the students but only these specific ones must do the term paper. Because it is an essential clause, no commas separate it from the rest of the sentence.

However, use commas with nonessential (nonrestrictive) clauses, which add nice-to-know information. Consider this sentence with a nonessential clause: *Four students, who failed the exam, will have to do an extra term paper.* Here we learn that four specific students must do the paper. The clause is optional because the sentence is complete without it; it suggests that the students doing the paper happen to be those who failed the exam, but no cause–effect relationship is established. Being nonessential, the clause requires commas at both the beginning and the end.

The same can be said about phrases: Essential phrases take no commas. For example, *The girl standing in the yard is my friend* refers to a specific girl, the one standing, not another girl who is sitting on the lawn or walking down the street. The phrase *standing in the yard* is essential to clear meaning, so no commas are used. However, *The girl, standing in the yard, was waiting for the barbecue grill to heat up* gives us nice-to-know information about the girl (she was standing in the yard), but the description is not essential to the clear meaning of the sentence. Therefore, commas are used at the beginning and the end of the phrase.

Also use commas if they keep the reader from misreading an otherwise ambiguous sentence, such as after a long introductory clause or when repeating the same word:

Ambiguous sentence: *After meeting the teacher representatives of the PTA executive committee complained to the superintendent.*

Clearer sentence: *After meeting the teacher, representatives of the PTA complained to the superintendent.* Or perhaps a very different meaning: *After meeting, the teacher representatives of the PTA complained to the superintendent.*

Or consider this sentence: *What I'm asking is, is this the best way to study for the test?* Without the comma, the sentence would be difficult to understand.

Beginning writers sometimes use a comma to connect two independent clauses without a coordinating conjunction. This results in a syntax error called a **comma splice** or **comma fault**

run-on sentence. For example, *The wallpaper is green, the paint is violet* is wrong because the comma is not strong enough to link the two clauses. Here are three ways to correct a comma splice:

1. Use a coordinating conjunction (such as *and, but, however): The wallpaper is green, but the paint is violet.*
2. Use a semicolon: *The wallpaper is green; the paint is violet.*
3. Divide it into two sentences: *The wallpaper is green. The paint is violet.*

Quotation Marks   Because they are used so often in newswriting, quotation marks deserve special mention. Quotation marks are used to enclose direct quotations, separated by a comma (or, if appropriate, by a question mark) from the attribution that follows. When quoting only a partial sentence, do not use a comma to introduce or conclude the quotation. Quotation marks are almost never used in broadcast copy because the listener and viewer can't see them when the copy is read. Chapters 10 and 11 explain how to handle quotes in writing for radio and television.

Journalists also use quotation marks for titles of books, songs, TV shows, and other compositions, but not for titles of magazines or newspapers. Go figure! Better yet, go check out the stylebook.

A few rules apply to using quotation marks with other punctuation. A period or comma always goes before the concluding quotation mark: *"That's a nice story," said Tony, who had just finished reading "Of Mice and Men."* Always.

The position of a question mark depends on what it refers to. If the question mark is part of the quoted material, the question mark precedes the concluding quotation mark: *"Who's Afraid of Virginia Woolf?" is one of my favorite books.* If the entire sentence is a question, the question mark follows the closing quotation mark: *Who wrote "A Tale of Two Cities"?* The same principles apply to exclamation points.

Other Punctuation Marks   Other punctuation marks seem to cause fewer problems, perhaps because writers use them less frequently than commas and quotation marks. Parentheses and pairs of dashes intrude into the sentence with additional information. Colons or dashes introduce lists or quotes.

Writers sometimes use an **ellipsis** (. . .) to let the reader know that something has been taken out of quoted material or that a lengthy quotation is being condensed. However, media writers should avoid using an ellipsis because readers will wonder about what has been deleted.

12. Stick With the Stylebook

When Ralph Waldo Emerson wrote "A foolish consistency is the hobgoblin of little minds," he obviously didn't have a media stylebook in mind. Stylistic consistency is important in media writing, but one of the nice things about writing for the media is that you don't have to memorize everything. Instead, you can turn to the stylebook. The news media have adopted certain language standards to help writers. Become familiar with the most commonly used standard, the *Associated Press Stylebook*. The broadcast media also have specific stylebooks, and some publications have their own in-house stylebooks as well.

Principles of Simple Language

"The first and most important thing of all, at least for writers today, is to strip language clean, to lay it bare down to the bone." Writer Ernest Hemingway gave that advice a half-century ago, but it remains true today. The power of language lies not in overpowering readers, but rather in easing them into a new awareness or a better understanding. Good writing is simple writing. Media writers need to remember that their readers are voluntary readers. People read newspapers and magazines, follow broadcast scripts, and read public relations materials and advertising copy not because they have to but because they want to. And they will want to read only when they are able to understand the writing. Following are a dozen principles relating to the writer's need to write clearly and simply.

1. Think Before You Write, Then Write Logically

Writing often becomes cumbersome because the writer has no clear idea of what he or she wants to say or how it should be said. Before starting the writing process, think about what you want to say and organize your thoughts in a logical order. Clear, readable sentences should follow easily when this step is carried out.

Then, write logically. Avoid colloquialisms that are jarringly inaccurate, such as a newspaper article that confusingly reports that *The two boys went missing* or *The boys were found missing after school.*

2. Write Naturally

Good media writers don't sound as if they are putting on airs or using words they wouldn't normally use. They write the way they talk. Naturally. Your aim should be to write in a way that isn't artificial or strained, yet in a way that is professional, conversational, and not unduly influenced by either jargon or novelty. The best way to develop the naturalness of your writing is to read it out loud. Learn to trust your ear. Listen to determine whether your writing sounds stiff or awkward. If it does, revise it and read it again.

3. Eliminate Unnecessary Words and Phrases

In a meat market, the butcher trims the fat from the meat. Treat your writing the same way: Trim away the fat words and replace them with lean ones. Don't let empty phrases take up space. When you encounter a wordy phrase, look for a simpler way to express the thought. For example, the sentence *The librarian said to cease and desist the unnecessary talking* can be simplified to *The librarian said to end unnecessary talking.*

4. Avoid Redundancies

Redundant words add no meaning to a sentence because another word already has provided the meaning. Redundancy takes up space but offers nothing in return. For example, a writer might say *This was a serious tragedy.* Could a tragedy be anything but serious? The adjective *serious* contributes nothing. Here are other examples:

She grew up in a <u>little</u> village. (A big village would be called a town or a city.)

The committee did some <u>advance</u> planning. (Planning can't be done after the fact.)

The committee will refer <u>back</u> to its minutes. (Referring can't be done ahead.)

He is a <u>former</u> graduate. (He may be a former student, but once a graduate, always a graduate.)

As you can see, each underlined word added <u>absolutely</u> nothing to the sentence. (There's another!) Careful writers should challenge every word they write to make sure it adds to the sentence.

5. Prefer Simple Words

Abjure sesquipedalian, obfuscatory terminology. If you understand this advice, follow it. If you don't know what it means, you're probably better off because you won't be tempted to use unnecessarily fancy words. (Translation: Swear off big, confusing words.) Just keep it simple. Research shows that simpler and more common words make it easier for readers to

---

Box 3.1

Fog Index

The Gunning Readability Formula, also called the Fog Index, is an easy-to-use tool for media writers. It provides a simple way of gauging the level of reading difficulty, a level you can compare to the educational level of your potential audience. The Fog Index is simple to calculate as follows:

1. Select a 100-word passage. For a lengthy piece of writing, select several different 100-word passages and average the Fog Index.

2. Count the number of sentences. If the passage does not end on a sentence break, calculate a percentage of the final sentence in the passage and add it to the sentence count. For example, four or five words into a 15-word sentence is about 30 percent, so add 0.3 to the sentence count for the passage.

3. Divide 100 by the number of sentences. The result is the average sentence length.

4. Count the number of long words in the passage (words of three or more syllables). But do not count words in which *es* or *ed* forms the third and final syllable, hyphenated words like *state-of-the-art*, and compound words like *newspaper*.

5. Add the average sentence length (from Step 3) and the number of long words (from Step 4).

6. Multiply the total from Step 5 by 0.4. The result indicates the approximate grade level of the passage.

People can understand writing that measures lower than their educational achievement. A college graduate, for example, can read something written for high school juniors. General-interest newspapers are written at approximately the eighth-grade level, yet they count among their readers highly educated professionals, as well as people who did not complete high school. Simple writing does not have to be simplistic, and writing at below capacity levels does not have to bore or patronize the reader. Indeed, many complex and sophisticated topics can be presented in ways accessible to virtually all readers.

understand a text. Researchers have found that messages averaging 1½ syllables a word are best for average readers. Some states have adopted a requirement that words in consumer-oriented legal documents such as warranties and contracts average no more than 1½ syllables.

Writers need not fear that simple writing means writing simplistically. Important information and profound ideas still can be presented within that syllable limit. For example, Lincoln's Gettysburg Address averages 1⅓ syllables a word. An accomplished writer knows that the meaning can and must be conveyed without writing over the heads of the readers.

At times writers cannot avoid using big technical words, especially in medical or science writing. Even if multisyllabic words are necessary, writers should use a simpler paraphrase to explain the concept. Otherwise, readers will not read very far.

6. Use Contractions Carefully

Generally, contractions are appropriate for conversational speech and for informal writing, but not for formal writing. Contractions are rare in straight news stories and news releases for print media other than in quoted material, although they are appropriate for the more conversational style found in broadcast copywriting. Contractions generally are not used in other formal writing such as position statements, proclamations, and editorials. However, writers often use contractions in feature stories, broadcast scripts, brochures, and promotional copy.

In addition to being less formal, contractions sometimes are less forceful. For example, *I won't go with you* does not carry the power of *I will not go with you.*

7. Avoid Creating New Words

Business and academic writers sometimes create new words for their own purposes. That process might be legitimate when the writer is dealing with an emerging field within science, for example. But too often the writer is simply seeking a shortcut that can leave the reader confused or alienated.

Two frequent offenders are use of the suffixes *-ify* and *-ize* to create a hybrid between a noun and a verb. Sloppy writers take a perfectly good noun, add the suffix, and create a silly verb-like structure. We end up with awkward sentences such as *Joanne will CD-ROMify the computer network* and *Jon will corporatize the family business.* In some situations, parallel construction is not possible. We can *Latinize* a culture, but can we also *Paraguayify* it or *Kenyanize* it? Ever since the political uproar that began at the Watergate Hotel, some columnists and newswriters have *-gated* other political scandals, giving rise to Irangate, Travelgate, Zippergate, Katrinagate, even Attorneygate in reference to the 2007 scandal involving the fired U.S. attorneys. The Watergate break-in occurred 35 years ago, probably time to retire the *-gate* suffix as an outdated reference to a scandal.

Adding *-ation* to the end of verbs also can lead to awkwardness. These words unfortunately have been used in print: *conscienticization, Frenchification* and *teacherization.*

8. Avoid Foreign Constructions

The English language is rather accepting of words from other languages. *Restaurant, assassin, sushi, amen,* and *chipmunk* all come from other languages (French, Arabic, Japanese, Hebrew, and Algonkian, respectively). Many such words and phrases are commonly used and widely understood and thus are legitimately part of the ever-evolving English language. Avoid foreign-based words and phrases that, even if they are listed in an English dictionary, are not popularly understood, such as *ex post facto* and *a priori*. When you must use foreign words, use quotation marks around them and provide a translation: *The provost ceremoniously proclaimed that the college had been committed to the education of women "ab initio" (a Latin phrase meaning "from the beginning"), pointing out that the first graduating class included 87 women and 15 men.*

9. Avoid Unwanted Rhyme and Alliteration

After you have written something, read it aloud to yourself or have someone read it aloud to you. Listen for **cadence** (the rise and fall of the voice), **meter** (the patterned arrangement and emphasis of syllables) and **tempo** (the pace) of the words. Listen particularly for any **alliteration** (repetition of initial sounds of words) or rhyme (repetition of concluding sounds of words or phrases):

Alliteration: *Sixteen snapdragons circle stately sycamores.*

Rhyme: *Mike Hite might wear bright white for his Friday night fight.*

Occasionally these literary devices are effective, but writing can be awkward if they are used unwittingly.

10. Use Short Sentences

Journalists have special reasons to value brevity in their writing. One is a financial incentive: Words cost money in a newspaper or broadcast medium. The words of a news reporter vie for time and space with income-generating advertising, and the words of one writer compete for precious news space with those of other writers. Similarly, the need for brevity is true for public relations writers preparing news releases or internal copy.

Another prime reason for writing short sentences is that readability studies show they are more easily understood. Research on readability models, such as the Fog Index outlined in Box 3.1, suggests that readers most easily comprehend sentences that average about 16 words. Of course, that is an average. Some sentences will be longer, some shorter. Variety should be considered one of the standards of effective writing.

11. Vary Sentence Structure

Effective writers seek simplicity while avoiding monotony. One way to accomplish this objective is to vary not only the length of sentences but also their structure, eliminating any unintended patterns. Not every sentence should be written in the subject–verb–object pattern. Introduce phrases or clauses and arrange them in different places. Use compound and/or complex sentences, as well as parenthetical expressions. If appropriate, use an occasional single-word sentence or a sentence fragment. If variety is the spice of life, variety in sentence structure makes for lively reading.

12. Prefer Active Voice

The term **voice** describes the relationship between the subject and the verb of a sentence. When we learn a language, we naturally use **active voice**, in which the subject is doing the action, as in *Abdul read the book*. Later, as we learn to vary sentence structure and manipulate our words, we learn how to revise our writing into **passive voice**, in which the action is being done to the subject, as in *The book was read by Abdul*.

One of the most common guidelines for effective writing is to prefer active voice because it is more powerful and more direct than passive voice. Consider the following examples of active and passive voice:

Set 1

Active: *The principal asked the teachers to meet at 3 p.m.*

Passive: *It was requested by the principal that the teachers meet at 3 p.m.* or

The teachers were asked to meet at 3 p.m.

Set 2

Active: *The editor will write her editorial.*

Passive: *The editorial will be written by the editor.*

Box 3.2

When Passive Is Permissible

Despite its usefulness, active voice is not required in every situation. Passive voice exists for a reason, and it offers the following three significant benefits:

1. Passive voice emphasizes the receiver. Sometimes the recipient of an action (the object) is more important than the person or entity that performed it (the subject):

   Emphasis on recipient: *Xeneda Mugamba was hired as the Channel 16 weekend anchor.*

   Emphasis on performer: *Channel 16 has hired Xeneda Mugamba as its weekend anchor.*

2. Passive voice diverts attention from the doer. Occasionally, the writer tactfully wishes to downplay the identity of the person who performed an action:

   More tactful: *Spaghetti sauce was spilled on the guest of honor.*

   Less tactful: *Cynthia spilled spaghetti sauce on the guest of honor.*

3. Passive voice provides the writer with a way to handle missing information. When the subject is unknown or no longer important, the writer could use passive voice:

   Passive: *The room was repainted 15 years ago.*

   Active: *Someone repainted the room 15 years ago.*

Although effective and careful writers seldom use passive voice, when they do so, it is always deliberate. When they encounter passive voice in their writing, they challenge its use and rewrite the sentence into active voice unless the passive voice is clearly more appropriate.

Set 3

Active: *The company reported twice as many absences this year.*

Passive: *Twice as many absences were reported by the company this year.*

Set 4

Active: *Political opponents have criticized Tomasso's benefactors for backing health care reform.*

Passive: *Tomasso's benefactors have been criticized by political opponents for backing health care reform.*

Active voice offers several benefits to the writer: It gets to the point quickly, eliminates unnecessary words, increases readability, provides more specific information, and presents information in a natural order. In the preceding examples, the active voice in Set 2 informs the reader that the editor is a woman, a fact lost in the passive voice. Writers preparing news stories need to be especially careful about using passive voice because it sometimes masks or minimizes information.

Principles of Meaningful Language

"When I use a word," Humpty Dumpty said, in rather a scornful tone, "it means just what I choose it to mean—neither more nor less." "The question is," said Alice, "whether you can make words mean so many different things."

(*Through the Looking-Glass* by Lewis Carroll)

Humpty Dumpty can claim what he likes, but Alice's question is right on the mark. Can writers expect words to mean anything they want them to? Or should writers use words the way readers will best understand them?

A writer's greatest strength is the ability to share meaning and communicate so that readers accurately understand. Shared meaning and accurate understanding require that the writer and the reader apply the same meanings to the words being used.

The following principles are reminders of how to write in ways that are meaningful to readers.

1. Create Word Pictures

Show, don't tell. That is the common advice for news and feature writers, public relations writers, and advertising copywriters. Writing is most powerful when it demonstrates a fact and invites the reader to draw a conclusion, rather than when it interprets the situation for the reader. Effective writers provide concrete information so that readers can properly interpret the situation for themselves.

For example, in the sentence, *The little boy was happy to see his mother*, the reader must trust that the writer witnessed, understood, correctly interpreted and accurately reported a happy encounter between a mother and her child. A more concrete telling of the encounter might be, *The little boy smiled, ran to his mother, and hugged her.* Now readers can see for themselves the happiness of the situation. They can draw their own conclusion, without having to rely on the writer's interpretation.

2. Use Analogies

Suppose a writer is trying to explain the effect of high cholesterol. He likens it to a busy city street with cars double-parked. He reports on a new medicine that works like a tow truck clearing the streets by removing those double-parked cars and allowing traffic to flow at its normal pace. This writer has used an **analogy**—a comparison that uses imagery or familiar terms to explain unfamiliar concepts. Referring to something readers already know about (traffic) helps them understand a complicated situation with which they may not be familiar (cholesterol).

Using analogies requires systematic reasoning. Students are exposed to this reasoning on standardized tests, as in the following example:

Kitten is to cat as
  (a)   beagle is to dog.
  (b)   sparrow is to bird.
  (c)   flock is to duck.
  (d)   fawn is to deer.

Think logically about the relationships. You know that a kitten is a young cat. Compare that relationship with the choices. Is a beagle a young dog? Is a sparrow a young bird? Is a flock a young duck? Is a fawn a young deer? From this reasoning, you know that *d* is the correct answer.

Writers approach analogies from the other end. They suggest the relationships, so they use their imagination to identify parallel relationships that can illuminate meaning.

3. Use the Right Word

Words that at first glance seem alike may have significantly different meanings. Good writers understand those differences and they write accordingly.

For example, accomplished media writers know the difference between *imply* and *infer*, and they don't use *disinterested* when they mean *uninterested.* They write *different from* rather than *different than.* They also know why a car cannot *collide* with a tree, why the 50 states don't *comprise* the United States, and why *titillate* isn't a nasty word. They know not to write about a *voting block* and when to avoid *hopefully.* Accomplished writers know when to say *Jones drowned* and when to say *Jones was drowned*, and they know the difference. They never use *alot* and *irregardless.* And they certainly know the difference between *its* and *it's* and among *there, their* and *they're.*

Accomplished writers also avoid unintentionally using an **oxymoron**, a term that means *sharply dull* in its Greek-language origins. An oxymoron is a combination of self-contradictory words: *thunderous silence, alone together.* (Note that the serious writers do not apply the term to comedic references such as *military intelligence* or *jumbo shrimp*.) In general, media writers avoid using an oxymoron. However, in the right circumstance and in the hands of a skilled writer, the deliberate use of an oxymoron can be both powerful and insightful. Shakespeare used an oxymoron when he wrote about the parting of lovers as "sweet sorrow."

4. Use Precise Descriptions

Effective writers, particularly newswriters, provide concrete and specific information. For example, rather than reporting *The company lost a lot of money last year*, a careful writer will say *The company lost $1.5 million last year.* The reader can interpret whether this is a lot of money from the context of the report.

Likewise, writers avoid words that do not provide specific information to readers. Here's an example of vague words and phrases: *As soon as possible, we should finalize this contract.* When is as soon as possible? And what does finalize mean in this context? To write the contract? To reach agreement on the terms? To sign it?

5. Use Strong Verbs

What a difference a single word can make! Effective writers use words, particularly verbs, that forcefully make the point. Effective writers have learned to be particularly frugal about using forms of *is*, *have*, and *make*. Consider how the following sentences can be made more meaningful by using more precise verbs:

Weak: She has a new car.

Stronger and more specific: She drives a new car. (or leases or owns)

Vague: He went to the store.

More meaningful: He ran to the store. (or walked or drove or jogged or dashed or ambled or hiked)

Weak: "I hate you," she said.

Stronger: "I hate you," she sobbed. (or cried or screamed or muttered or wailed or announced or shouted)

6. Replace Clichés with Original Words

Familiarity breeds contempt, or at least boredom. Clichés are familiar expressions overused to the point that they become weary and stale. When your readers know exactly where you are heading, you've probably used a cliché. Consider these:

Just a drop in the _____.

Few and _____ between.

Right under their _____.

Only time will _____.

Swept under the _____.

Never a dull _____.

Because clichés are predictable, they no longer carry much meaning. When they were original, phrases like *sadder but wiser*, *an apple a day*, and *last but not least* were picturesque turns of phrase—so much so that people used them, and used them, and finally used them up. Today, each phrase has become a cliché, a good thing overdone.

Many clichés today have also lost much of their original meaning, leaving readers both bored and uninformed. Just how long is it before the cows come home? Where is Square One? Perhaps near the mean streets. And what is a bread-and-butter issue? Or is it a nuts-and-bolts issue? Accomplished writers challenge common phrases that carry little meaning, replacing them with their own fresh expressions. In short, avoid clichés like the plague.

7. Avoid Journalese

Newswriters may not read enough of what others have written or perhaps they just get used to their own words. Or maybe they do too much writing while paying too little attention to words. Whatever the case, journalists sometimes fall into a sloppy style of generalities, clichés, jargon, and overwriting. This style even has a name: **journalese**. In the language of journalese, temperatures *soar*. Costs *skyrocket*. Fires *rage* and rivers *rampage*. Projects are *kicked off*. Opponents *weigh in*. Buildings are *slated for demolition* or perhaps they are *tagged*. In journalese, people get a *go-ahead* and projects get a *green light*.

Real people don't talk that way, so it's best to avoid such trite writing. This chapter advises using strong verbs and solid descriptions. Also remember that word choice should be both fresh and accurate.

8. Rewrite Jargon

Jargon is specialized or technical language unfamiliar to average readers. It can be appropriate when writing for people in the know, such as readers of a technical column or a specialized magazine. Print journalists also can use technical language when writing about specialized subjects such as sports and business. But, more often, writers are addressing people who are not highly informed on a given issue, and they must make "in" words and phrases meaningful to lay audiences.

Faced with jargon, effective writers rewrite it using commonly understood words. Sometimes they use the word and then provide an easy-to-understand definition, or they avoid the technical term and simply use a meaningful paraphrase. What the writer should not do is simply put quotation marks around the jargon; it does no good to highlight jargon without providing a definition or paraphrase.

9. Avoid Loaded Words

Consider this proposition: You are 25 pounds over your ideal weight. Would you rather be called *fat* or *full-figured*? How about *plump? Corpulent? Husky? Chunky? Pudgy? Stout?*

Rotund? Big-boned? The word makes a difference, doesn't it? Advertisers go to great lengths to describe their products with terms that do not have negative connotations, which is why manufacturers package queen-sized pantyhose or dresses in size XL–Petite.

Consider other scenarios. Is *nagging* the same as *being persistent?* Is calling someone a *colored woman* the same as referring to her as *a woman of color?* What are the differences among an *indulgent, permissive* or *tolerant* parent? Or between a *casual* and an *aloof* smile?

English has many words with similar definitions but vastly different, even opposing, meanings. Effective writers take great care in choosing words with the appropriate denotation and connotation. For example, *chat, chatter, gibberish, prattle* and *babble* all denote the same thing: a loose and ready flow of inconsequential talk. But each word connotes a slightly different meaning: a light and friendly chat, aimless and rapid chatter, rapid and incoherent gibberish, childish prattle, and unintelligible babble.

In journalistic situations, precision is essential. It matters a great deal—to both reporters and public relations practitioners—whether a news source *declined* to return a phone call, *failed* to, *neglected* to, or *refused* to. There is a mountain of difference among *would not, could not* and simply *did not.* Effective and ethical writers choose the word or phrase that provides the most accurate nuance for the situation.

10. Avoid Pretentious Words and Euphemisms

Pretentious language uses words that are inflated to sound more impressive than the facts warrant. A car dealership advertises *experienced vehicles* or *previously owned vehicles*; bald people are *follicly impaired*; midriff bulge is *personal insulation*; and a government report refers to cows, pigs, and chickens as *grain-consuming animal units*. In the pretentiousness of it all, travel agents become *vacation specialists*, junkyard dealers are *auto recyclers*, and belts are made of *genuine synthetic leather*.

There is no real harm in such language; it can even be humorous. But writers approach this kind of self-important language carefully because it can obscure the real meaning for their readers. Pretentious language slows down readers, makes them work harder to understand the meaning, and risks causing them to become cynical. Pretentious writing can be a particular concern for public relations and advertising writers who, in their attempt to present a positive message, can slip into this style.

Note the difference between pretentious language and **euphemisms** (language deliberately made less precise because the more direct words may be offensive or upsetting). Speaking euphemistically, we express our sorrow that a friend's father *passed on* rather than saying that he died. Although there may be a place for euphemisms in journalistic and public relations writing, be careful in their usage.

11. Write Honestly

A half-century ago, George Orwell coined the term **doublethink** to refer to a system of thought in which the true meaning of reality was distorted to make it more politically and socially acceptable. Writers have drawn from Orwell's idea another word, **doublespeak**, which describes statements that tend to misrepresent reality—especially those made by public officials and organizational spokespersons. Doublespeak takes something negative and tries to make it seem positive. Effective and ethical writers avoid such misleading language.

Regrettably, many examples of doublespeak are associated with the military and other governmental activities. The public is deliberately misled when the military reports civilian deaths as *collateral damage* and *soft targets* and the White House insists that the military invasion of Granada by U.S. paratroopers was not an invasion but only a *predawn vertical insertion*.

Businesses also have engaged in doublespeak, calling budget cuts *advanced downward adjustments* and identifying layoffs as *employee repositioning, proactive downsizing, rightsizing* or *restructuring staff resources*. Or how about this one: It wasn't a layoff, the company merely offered employees *career alternative enhancement programs*. Calling bad loans *nonperforming assets* is more than creative cuteness in language; it deliberately masks the true meaning of the words to minimize the impact of the truth. In most cases, that's called a *lie*.

The nuclear power industry also has invented misleading terms, calling an explosion an *energetic disassembly* and an accident an *abnormal evolution* or a *normal aberration*.

The second Bush White House, meanwhile, added a growing list of examples of doublespeak. Relaxation of forestry restrictions was called *environmental reforms*, prisoners became merely *detainees*, and it was more politically salable to talk about *regime change* than to admit that a plan was designed to topple the head of a sovereign nation. During travels of the president or vice president, the Secret Service ordered local police to confine protesters to *free speech* zones remote from both officials and TV cameras.

The National Council of Teachers of English, through its Committee on Public Doublespeak, has turned the spotlight on individuals and groups committing violence against the integrity of language. In recent years the committee called attention to government reports that, when discussing deforestation projects that strip every tree and bush from hundreds of acres of forest, call the denuded landscapes *temporary meadows*. The committee criticized a Russian report that a driver was not drunk but rather in a *nonsober condition* and it criticized U.S. government reports that called death *failure to thrive*. The committee gave its Doublespeak Award to Reagan White House aide Oliver North for his claim that he was merely *cleaning up the historical record* when he lied to Congress and to the Defense Department for a pattern of *perception management* related to military spending.

The committee also highlighted a Canadian military report that called a helicopter crash a *departure from normal flight*.

The use of doublespeak raises serious ethical issues. The Society of Professional Journalists holds its members to standards of "intelligence, objectivity, accuracy and fairness." Codes of professional standards for public relations practitioners are more specific, calling for honesty, accuracy, truth and avoidance of false or misleading information. Advertising and marketing codes, reinforced by government requirements to protect consumers, also require standards of honesty. All communication professionals are called on to write with honesty and integrity.

Principles of Inclusive Language

Media writers are most effective when their writing uses words and phrases that apply to everyone in their audience, with no unnecessary exclusion. Careful writers, therefore, favor terms that encompass many people.

1. Use Gender-Inclusive Words

Much attention has been given to language that is gender-inclusive, such as *firefighter* instead of *fireman* and *police officer* rather than *policeman.* Writers must also pay attention to how their words reflect physical characteristics (such as age and capacity) and social characteristics (such as ethnicity, cultural background, and lifestyle).

Some people use inclusive language to be politically correct, others use it to be contemporary, still others use it just to be nice. But journalists, public relations writers, and advertisers have a more practical reason: Inclusive language makes writing more effective. No writer can afford to alienate or unwittingly offend people. The reality for media writers is that if even one member of the audience feels excluded from what they are writing, they have created a barrier to communication. Notice the use of the word *feels.* It matters little whether the writer meant to exclude; if any reader feels excluded because of the words used, the writer has failed to communicate effectively.

The problem of biased language often arises when the writer implies that one group sets the standard or tone for all others. Someone who perceives that surgeons usually are men might make special note of a female surgeon. Here is where media writers walk a tightrope. News often is defined in terms of how an event differs from norms and expectations. Because good writing calls for detailed description, it well might be newsworthy that a surgeon is a woman, that the mayor is Hindu, or that the athlete is gay. Accomplished writers present those details in the course of telling their story, without drawing inordinate attention to them. Good writers also refrain from implying that the surgeon's gender, the mayor's religion or the athlete's sexual orientation is that person's major defining characteristic. Following are several guidelines for making your writing more inclusive.

2. Proper Pronouns With Mixed Groups

Until recently, *he* was considered a generic pronoun that could refer to both sexes. This is no longer the case. Writers have several options for avoiding use of the masculine pronoun when referring to groups that include both women and men. Consider this sentence: *The professional artist should take care of his brushes.*

Here are six ways to rewrite the sentence with inclusive language:

1. Use the plural form: *Professional artists should take care of their brushes.* This is probably the easiest and most unobtrusive way to handle the situation.
2. Eliminate the possessive pronoun: *The professional artist should take care of brushes.*
3. Use first or second person: *As professional artists, we should take care of our brushes. As a professional artist, you should take care of your brushes.*
4. Use passive voice: *For the professional artist, great care should be taken with brushes.* Be careful, though, because passive voice can sound awkward.
5. Use double pronouns: *The professional artist should take great care of his or her brushes.* Use double pronouns sparingly, and only when you want to draw attention

to the inclusiveness. In writing for the media, avoid use of some of the hybrid forms that are emerging in business and academic writing, such as s/he and he/she.

6. Use the word one: *As a professional artist, one should take great care of one's brushes.* Use *one* only in formal situations.

3. Avoid Generic Words

Avoid using either masculine or feminine words as generics meant to include both men and women. Replace them with neutral terms. For example, replace words such as *foreman, housewife* and *statesman* with *supervisor, homemaker* and *diplomat*, respectively. Or replace general terms such as *clergyman* with specific terms: *rabbi, priest, imam* or *rector.*

Be careful about using the add-on word *-person.* Some of these words, such as *spokesperson,* are in common use. But other usages can stand out as artificial. You can't replace *fireman* with *fireperson,* nor can you call a *seaman* a *seaperson.* Instead of *newspaper person,* try *journalist* or *reporter.*

Remember that it is appropriate to use specifically masculine or feminine forms when referring to individuals or single-gender groups. Use *congressman* if you are referring to someone who is male, *congresswoman* if you are referring to a female. More generally and for mixed groups, refer to *members of Congress* or *congressional representatives.* Similarly, you may call three males who handle trash *garbage men,* but refer in general to people in the occupation as *garbage haulers* or *refuse collectors* because both men and women do this kind of work.

Be careful. Some words don't work in the feminine form. George may be a *watchman,* but don't call Sally a *watchwoman;* don't call her a *watchperson* either. Better to call both of them *guards* or *security personnel.*

4. Avoid Gender Stereotypes

Use the specific pronoun with words solely linked with one gender or the other: *nun, pro football player, ballerina, sperm donor.* However, be careful with words that presume a link solely with one gender when this linkage is not warranted. Senators and astronauts are not always men; nurses and secretaries are not always women.

Also, avoid archaic feminine forms such as *poetess, priestess, Jewess* and *authoress.* The word *actress* is still used occasionally, although it is becoming more common to hear a woman refer to herself as an *actor.*

Don't use feminine labels in situations for which you would not similarly use masculine labels. For example, don't refer to a *female attorney* or a *woman doctor* unless you also are prepared to mention a *male attorney* or a *man doctor.*

5. Use Parallel Treatment

Politeness and tradition have their places, but writers in public media should not be deferential to women merely because they are women. Instead, treat women and men the same way in similar situations. The sentence, *The movie starred Diesel, Hawke and Miss Ryder* is not parallel because the courtesy title is used only for the last actor.

Newswriters wouldn't generally describe the hairstyle or clothing of a man who is president or prime minister, but such information about the female head of state or a woman who is a political candidate sometimes slips off the fashion pages into news articles. Good writing suggests that we limit ourselves to issues of significance to the story. Writers always have more information than they use, and one of their responsibilities is to sort out relevant information from the irrelevant. Don't identify the spouse of a female candidate unless you would also identify the spouse of her male rival. If a person's age, marital status, sexual lifestyle or some other personal characteristic is relevant, then report it; if it is superfluous, leave it out.

6. Exercise Caution with Race, Religion and Ethnicity

Accomplished writers are cautious about using race and ethnic background, religion, political affiliations and other such personal information to which people may attach great emotional significance.

Handle race according to principles similar to those for dealing with gender. For example, don't refer to a *black senator from Georgia* unless you also would refer to a *white senator from Tennessee.* But first be certain that race is relevant to mention.

Regarding religion, remember that various religious groups place considerable value on their uniqueness. Don't confuse objectively different terms such as *priest* and *minister*; realize that a Baptist deacon is different from a Catholic deacon. Although Latin-rite Roman Catholic priests normally may not marry, be aware that priests in some denominations do (including some Roman Catholic priests in Eastern-rite Churches and even some western Roman Catholic priests with special permission). Make religious references inclusive. For example, *The governor met with representatives of various churches* refers to mainly Christians. Did the meeting also include those who worship at the synagogue, mosque, temple, kiva or longhouse? If so, the sentence would be more accurate if it reported, *The governor met with representatives of various religious groups.*

Writers should realize that their audience will include people who may be offended—perhaps with justification—by a report saying, as if it were significant information, that a robbery suspect is Hispanic, that a hostage taker is a Vietnam veteran, that a Pentecostal preacher is an ex-Episcopalian, or that an alcoholic is of Irish ancestry. Don't exclude such information if it is important to the story. Use it if it is relevant, but use it in a way that does not demean entire groups of people.

With the increasing attention being given to the Middle East and Central Asia, newswriters must be particularly careful with the facts. Distinguish between religion and ethnicity. Ethnically, not all Muslims are Arabs; in fact, most followers of Islam are non-Arab peoples such as Turks, Persians (in Iran), Indonesians, Nigerians, Malaysians, Moroccans, and so on. Religiously, not all Arabs are Muslims. Some are Catholic, Orthodox or Protestant; in the United States, more Arab Americans are Catholic than are Muslim.

7. Be Sensitive in Describing Age

In the past, newspapers routinely reported the age of newsmakers as part of the basic identification. Amid growing concern about personal privacy as well as security, listing a person's age is no longer routine. It probably matters little that the new principal is 35 years old, although it may be significant to know that it is her first or her eighth year as principal.

When choosing words, be careful not to be unwittingly exclusive about age. *Student* refers to a learner of any age and thus is more inclusive than *schoolchild* or *pupil*. Also be particularly wary about using fuzzy words such as *middle age, senior citizen* and *young adult*.

8. Describe Physical Characteristics with Care

If physical condition is a relevant description, use it with great care. Terms of physical capability such as *dumb* or *crippled* no longer carry neutral connotations; instead, consider *unable to speak* or *uses a wheelchair*. Neutral inclusive language often is a matter of putting the focus on the person rather than on the physical characteristic, such as writing *people with handicaps* rather than *handicapped people*, *a man with AIDS* rather than *an AIDS victim*. Likewise, consider the context and connotation for designations of mental or emotional conditions.

Do not refer to normal physical conditions such as advanced age, pregnancy or menopause as though they were illnesses or ailments. These physical conditions are not inherently negative or incapacitating.

9. Avoid Using Offensive Quotes

Accomplished writers don't allow offensive or irrelevant language to enter their stories through quotes. Just as newswriters must justify their own choices, so must they also be able to demonstrate the relevance of information they choose to quote. If it would be irrelevant for the reporter to note the ethnic background of a candidate for public office, it may be equally irrelevant to include that same information in quoted material. However, it also may be a matter of journalistic integrity to give readers a quote that reveals the true feelings, including biases and prejudices, of public officials and other well-known figures.

Professional Writing Style

Clearly, there are many rules and guidelines to help writers. This chapter skimmed the surface with various principles that should remind you of what you already know. Effective media writers make frequent use of writing guidebooks, some of which are listed at the end of this chapter.

While novelists and poets try to develop a personal writing style, media writers instead write without a conspicuous personality. News and public relations writing is good precisely to the extent that it goes beyond individual writing style to display the look and feel of truly professional writing.

Discussion Questions

The following are class discussion questions drawn from Chapter 3:

1.   What are the principles of standard usage?

2.   What are the principles of simple language?

3.   What are the principles of meaningful language?

4.   What are the principles of inclusive language?

CHAPTER EXERCISES

Exercise 3.1—Diagnostic Test

Part One: Usage

Read each sentence and decide whether an error in usage appears in any of the underlined parts of the sentence. If you find an error, write in the blank space the letter corresponding to the underlined word or phrase. If you do not find an error, write the letter *E*.

1.   _____   A <u>pile</u> of <u>newspapers</u> <u>are</u> <u>sitting</u> in the tub.
            A   B   C   D

2.   _____   Everyone <u>is</u> asking <u>themselves</u> if Marshovenko should be elected <u>as</u> the new
                     A   B   C
            lead ballerina with the Uptown Tap and Ballet <u>Troupe</u>.
                                                            D

3.   _____   The <u>oldest</u> twin <u>was</u> selected <u>last</u> week to be the first contestant in a
                  A   B   C
            <u>shoot-the-rapids</u> contest at Niagara Falls.
                  D

4.   _____   <u>Its</u> important that we <u>finish</u> the project this week, <u>because</u> next week I am
            A   B   C
            scheduled to referee a <u>Scrabble</u> tournament.
                                      D

5.   _____   <u>Nobody</u> <u>is</u> more <u>pleased</u> to see him than his own sister, from <u>whom</u> he was
            A   B   C   D
            separated at birth.

6. _____ Everyone <u>was</u> trying hard to obtain for <u>themselves</u> a copy of her <u>latest</u> romance
                            A   B   C
        novel about the charming relationship <u>involving</u> two steel-workers and a duck.
                                                    D

7. _____ Sylvia <u>smells</u> <u>sweetly</u> because she works <u>in the fudge department</u> of a <u>large</u>
                        A   B   C   D
        bakery.

8. _____ There is absolutely no question in <u>anyone's</u> mind that Emilio, Franz and <u>him</u>
                                               A   B
        <u>have been</u> responsible for the <u>team's</u> 2–15 season.
             C   D

9. _____ The <u>operation</u> is expected <u>to be</u> rescheduled <u>as</u> the surgeon is <u>herself</u>
                  A   B   C   D
        recovering from surgery after being tackled by a disgruntled patient.

10. _____ <u>Whom</u> do you expect will be <u>laid off</u> when the president <u>returns</u> from his African
           A   B   C
        safari and finds that the executive suite has been repainted <u>in shades</u> of mauve
                                                                        D
        and chartreuse?

11. _____ <u>There</u> on the wall, <u>displayed discretely</u>, is Maria's graduation certificate from the
           A   B
        Mid-State Truck Driving Institute, <u>where</u> it can be seen by <u>everyone</u> who enters
                                         C   D
        her salon.

12. _____ The <u>sergeant</u> opened the door to the snack room, dramatically <u>lay</u> the basket
                A   B
        on the table, <u>and</u> demanded to know which of the recruits <u>had left</u> a litter of
                            C   D
        kittens in his locker while he was taking a bubble bath.

13. _____ The reporter <u>noticed</u> that <u>either</u> printing charges or postage <u>were</u> left <u>out</u> of the
                            A   B   C   D
        mayor's proposed budget for the city's new dance hall for senior citizens.

14. _____ <u>While</u> standing in line a <u>long</u> time to enter the restaurant with my
          A   B
        <u>girlfriend's cousin</u> and his best friend, Malcolm, <u>my head</u> began to hurt.
                  C   D

15. _____ The editorial staff <u>has</u> <u>steadfastly</u> remained true to <u>their</u> vow to boycott the
                              A   B   C
        employee cafeteria after it was discovered that the cooks were using oil from
        olives imported from a small country <u>which</u> does not allow freedom of the press.
                                                          D

16. ____   <u>If</u> you wish to travel on <u>this</u> holiday excursion flight to Bosnia, 100 pounds <u>are</u>
          A   B   C
the limit allowed for any <u>single</u> piece of baggage.
                                    D

17. ____   The <u>principal</u> told the English department <u>that</u> it was <u>alright</u> to require seniors to
                A   B   C
prove they can read <u>before</u> graduation.
                         D

18. ____   Minerva <u>couldn't</u> hardly stand on her own two feet <u>after</u> the doctor <u>removed</u> the
                  A   B   C
cast from <u>her</u> leg.
            D

19. ____   The statistics books <u>placed on</u> the reserve list in the library <u>numbered</u> between
                               A   B
30 <u>to</u> 40 each semester until the students signed a petition demanding that
 C
their professor use no <u>more than</u> 27 reserve books.
                              D

20. ____   "<u>We'll</u> try to keep that information just <u>between</u> us," the hare told his three <u>furry</u>
              A   B   C
associates as they <u>scurried out</u> of the hollow tree.
                          D

21. ____   Despite <u>having been</u> stripped of his rank <u>over</u> that embarrassing incident with
                    A   B
the pig, <u>Brown's friends</u> continued to call him "<u>Admiral</u>."
               C   D

22. ____   Melodia was both <u>embarrassed</u> and angered when her Volkswagen <u>collided</u>
                           A   B
with the Mercedes-Benz that was parked <u>alongside</u> the narrow country
                                         C
<u>roadway</u> not too far from the bridge over Whirlee Creek.
   D

23. ____   Mitchell announced with a hint of arrogance in her voice <u>that</u>, as far as she <u>was</u>
                                                              A   B
concerned, either of her friends <u>were</u> welcome in her home, despite their
                                      C
suspension from <u>their jobs</u> delivering flowers at the local hospital.
                       D

24. ____ Three students were expelled and <u>two suspended</u> because the <u>principal</u>
                                    A   B
believed they <u>instigated</u> the plot to repaint the school van bright pink, equip it
                C
with a <u>loudspeaker system</u>, and drive it in the Halloween parade.
            D

25. ____ My mother wants me to get the kind of <u>a</u> summer job <u>that</u> pays enough <u>so</u> I can
                                A   B   C
save for college and still not have to borrow from her all summer <u>long</u>.
                                                         D

Part Two: Punctuation

Read each sentence and decide whether an error in punctuation appears at any of the underlined parts of the sentence. If you find an error, write the letter in the blank space. If you do not find an error, write the letter F.

26. ____ It was Sept<u>.</u> <u>1</u> before Johnson finally showed up for any of his
                 A B
classes<u>,</u> tw<u>o</u> weeks after the semester began.
        C   D

27. ____ The anchorman<u>,</u> who had attended a wil<u>d-b</u>oar barbecue right before arriving in
                        A   B
the newsroom, announced on camera<u>,</u> <u>"</u>I think I'm going to be sick<u>"</u> before an
                                               C   D
estimated 157,000 viewers.

28. ____ In a festive<u>,</u> even jubilant<u>_</u>celebration attended by 15 parking<u>-l</u>ot attendants,
                          A   B   C
Uncle Clyde, the owner of the restaurant<u> </u>treated each guest to a lobster dinner.
                                                     D

29. ____ The part<u>y</u> ended with a lengthy tribute to the newl<u>y</u> hired vic<u>e</u> president,
                      A   B   C
remarked Mary Elizabeth<u>,</u> failing to explain why she was late in picking up the
                                D
family's pet beagle at the kennel.

30. ____ "I really support the concept of public television because it takes the high road
in broadcasting the arts<u>,"</u> said Crumle<u>y,</u> "but I fin<u>d</u> that I spend an inordinate
                                    A   B   C
amount of my time watching <u>'South Park'</u>."
                                    D

31. ____   Remembering suddenly, his missing book, Marcel tried to resist the urge
                                        A

        to trudge through the snow back to the restaurant; nevertheless, with much
                                                                B

        effort, he did so, finding the book on a chair by the corner table.
            C   D

32. ____   Poor dental hygiene, an uncompromising sweet tooth and a busy schedule
                                A   B

        combine to exacerbate the condition of his teeth—teeth that even in the best
                                                       C

        of times were a dentist's vision of wealth and prosperity.
                         D

33. ____   "She never wants to see you again," said Stephanie's elder sister,
                                           A

        Suzanne. "Get out of here. Go away. And stay away from her, you
               B   C   D

        miserable freak."

34. ____   Because Molly was hardly more than a child herself, thought Jefferson, this
                                                       A

        14 or 15-year-old girl should not be saddled with the entirety of the family's
        B   C   D

        shopping chores.

35. ____   For the sake of family harmony, Billy said he would work an additional summer
                                           A

        on his grandfather's farm before following his dream to pursue a PhD in
                        B   C   D

        agricultural biology.

36. ____   "It won't be me young lady, who will explain this mess to your grandmother,"
                       A   B   C

        Uncle Jim said sharply to Mary Alice, as she stared blankly at the shattered
                                  D

        wine goblet on the fireplace hearth.

37. ____   A priest, a minister and a rabbi sat in the crowded bleachers, reminiscing
                          A

        about the "good old days" when they got free tickets at the ballpark and
                                    B   C

        complimentary Cokes at the concession stand.
                      D

38. ____ Pacing in the penalty box at the noisy stat<u>e-of-the-art</u> stadiu<u>m wa</u>s an angry
                                                    A   B

    Number 1<u>5, w</u>hose torn jersey proclaimed his nickname, "Bonker<u>s" d</u>emanding
           C   D

    that he be allowed back into the game.

39. ____ Marsha's <u>in your face</u> attitude is getting rather tiring, especially because
                    A

    she maintains such a finel<u>y h</u>oned ability to take offens<u>e a</u>t everything her
                              B   C

    c<u>o-w</u>orkers suggest.
     D

40. ____ The blon<u>d-h</u>aired hun<u>k, w</u>ith the wel<u>l-d</u>efined muscle<u>s a</u>nd the expensive
                  A   B   C   D

    motorcycle was the envy of so many at the beach that day, surrounded as he
    was by seemingly half the girls celebrating Spring Break.

41. ____ I think I read that in the 13t<u>h c</u>entury, the Anasazi left their ancestral cliff homes
                                       A

    at Mesa Verd<u>e, m</u>oving to friendlier surroundings along the Rio Grand<u>e, w</u>here
                B   C

    their descendants, the Pueblo Indian<u>s c</u>ontinue to live today.
                                         D

42. ____ In the upland meado<u>w, w</u>ild flowers clustered near polluted streams, stagnant
                             A

    pond<u>s a</u>nd rock outcropping<u>s, i</u>ronically they attracted the photographer
        B   C

    seeking the contradictio<u>n t</u>hat is so often found in nature.
                            D

43. ____ "Can't we agree among ourselve<u>s," s</u>aid McAaronsdale in a contentious
                                        A

    ton<u>e, "</u>that the time has com<u>e—</u>indeed passed—to put an end to this silly feud
       B   C

    between the history teachers and the lunchroom staf<u>f"?</u>
                                                        D

44. ____ The good public relations write<u>r t</u>ries to be objective <u>(u</u>nbiased) in presenting
                                        A   B

    information<u>, a</u>nd perhaps finds it hardest to be objectiv<u>e w</u>hen dealing with
              C   D

    organizational priorities.

45. ____   Tony Hillerma<u>n, the</u> journalism professo<u>r w</u>ho wrote a series of mystery stories
                      A   B

        set on the Navajo reservatio<u>n, is</u> an excellent example of a write<u>r, w</u>ho does
                                      C   D

        extensive first-hand research that makes his stories both interesting and

        believable.

46. ____   Preparin<u>g as</u> they were for another one of those grueling<u> 1</u>8 <u>m</u>ile hikes
                           A   B C

        tomorrow, the campers had little support for Michael's suggestion that they

        sing song<u>s a</u>round the dying campfire.
                     D

47. ____   "Mr. Asadee," said Jo<u>n, t</u>he waiter, "I think you will like this salad dressing for
                                                A

        three reason<u>s, it</u> tastes heavenly, <u>it's</u> low in fat, and it is re<u>d (s</u>o if you spill it on
                   B   C   D

        your tie it won't show)."

48. ____   Fiberglas<u>s w</u>hich is a stron<u>g, l</u>ight-w<u>e</u>ight plastic, has been used in everything
                           A   B   C

        from auto bumpers to shower curtains, making it trul<u>y a</u> material for all
                                                          D

        occasions.

49. ____   The u<u>p-s</u>tate meeting of student journalists from six area colleges and
                      A

        universities—both public and private institution<u>s—w</u>as, arguabl<u>y, t</u>he
                                                       B   C

        mos<u>t i</u>mportant professional meeting ever held in this area.
          D

50. ____   The taxi driver had to travel fiv<u>e m</u>iles out of his way to pic<u>k u</u>p a fare who then
                                               A   B

        asked to be driven <u>in and around</u> the park as she looked for her boyfriend, who
                                        C

        she suspected of cheating on her with her <u>16-year-old</u> cousin.
                                                             D

Exercise 3.2—Bulky Sentences

Following are examples of sentences that are technically accurate but cumbersome. Revise each. Your objective is to maintain the information while presenting it in a way that is easier to understand.

1. Out in the hallway, the student who was delayed because her bus was late stood, waiting for the courage to interrupt the professor, who was known to publicly humiliate students who arrive late to class, and she was uncertain whether to go into the classroom or simply skip class.

2. The student in the writing class, which is taught by Professor Jefferson, a former city editor with the *Central City Courier*, which has an intensive program for journalism interns, hopes to work on a newspaper after she graduates from college.

3. The candidate for City Council, an advocate of reducing the tax assessment for businesses, is urging her opponents to participate in a public debate on the economic issues facing Middlevale, which has suffered from unemployment rates as high as 25 percent in recent years, brought on by the loss of several businesses that relocated to the suburbs, claiming that the city's tax structure prevents them from earning a fair profit and remaining competitive while suburban businesses receive the same public services while paying lower taxes.

4. Eager to accept the congratulations of Mayor Meredith Sampson-Jones on behalf of her fellow dancers, and apparently a bit nervous about being asked to speak in public, Velma Bryerlee, president of the All-County Jazz Ensemble, which recently returned from a 10-city tour in Nova Scotia, broke her ankle when she tripped going up the steps of the City Hall Auditorium to accept her honor, thereby preventing her from dancing with the ensemble in its upcoming performance at the State Capitol, where the governor will be in attendance.

Exercise 3.3—Subject–Verb Agreement

Circle the correct form of the verb in the following sentences:

1. Nobody care/cares what happens to Jimmy.

2. Several editions of the newsletter was/were illustrated by Bibi Johenger.

3. The media is/are important public relations tools.

4. The alumni was/were very generous.

5. Few of the items on the list was/were available.

6. Each of the items on the list was/were available.

7. All is/are lost.

8. All is/are going to the game.

Exercise 3.4—Noun–Pronoun Agreement

Circle the correct form of the pronoun in the following sentences:

1. The board of directors issued its/their report.

2. The directors issued its/their report.

3. The association leaders met for its/their annual meeting.

4. The association met for its/their annual meeting.

5. The association leadership met for its/their annual meeting.

6. The school board of directors announced its/their agenda.

7. The school directors announced its/their agenda.

8. The school board announced its/their agenda.

9. The football team will welcome its/their new coach.

Exercise 3.5—Wordy Phrases

Rewrite the following sentences to trim wordy phrases. Draw a line through words that can be eliminated, and write in words that express the meaning more succinctly.

1. He paid the bill with a check in the amount of $124.

2. From what your friend has told us, it is our understanding that you wish to purchase a new car.

3. The staff photographer will be beginning soon to update the mug shot file.

4. Our new editor shows a preference for feature stories.

5. We have found that, in a majority of cases, the audience is most interested in the weather report.

6. It is the intention of our company to hire the most experienced candidate.

7. It would be appreciated if you arrive at 9 a.m. for your tour of the newsroom.

8. In view of the fact that we lost our biggest account, we must lay off three employees.

Exercise 3.6 — Unnecessary Words

Draw a line through any words that can be eliminated from the following sentences without losing any significant meaning:

1. It has come to our attention that you have three overdue library books.

2. It is necessary to remember to proofread your writing carefully.

3. At this point in time, the managing editor is ready to hire two new photographers.

4. It has been learned that the station will add two reporters to its news staff.

5. There are six columnists who write for our newspaper.

6. It is an established fact that the building was renovated 16 years ago.

7. The copywriter is preparing material for what is known as a display ad.

8. Walter will not be able to cover his beat this week due to the fact that he is in the hospital. ∎

Exercise 3.7 — Redundancies

Draw a line through any redundant words in the following sentences:

1. The university produced two different versions of the report, giving close scrutiny to new techniques for growing crops in rice paddies.

2. The mayor said it is absolutely necessary to increase tourism for the city of Philadelphia.

3. Whether or not we are absolutely certain about Thelma's skill as an ice skater, we are convinced that she is a very unique personality who will be a positive asset to our team.

4. The general consensus of opinion is that the students should not protest against the curfew.

5. In the final outcome, the board expects to see that foreign auto imports will continue to maintain a positive current trend.

6. Each and every one of our local residents will gather together on Easter Sunday at 3 p.m. in the afternoon.

7. The honest truth is that the candidate must still remain in good standing with the party leaders.

8. A friend of mine who owns his own home said the true facts about the plumbing scandal will probably never be known.

9. At about the same time the paratroopers completely demolished the village, the submarine attack totally destroyed the harbor.

Exercise 3.8—Simple Words

If you are not already familiar with the following words, look up each in a dictionary. Write a simple word or phrase that means the same thing.

- articulate
- subsequently
- commence

- demonstrate
- equitable
- finalize

- prioritize
- succumb
- utilize

Exercise 3.9—Simplifying Sentences

Rewrite each of the following sentences to make it simpler:

1. The directors will hold a meeting at the Fireside Lounge.

2. Professor Sanderson will give a lecture about the issue of free press and fair trial.

3. Jaime was the winner of two theater tickets.

4. The alumni association has made a $25,000 donation to the new sports arena.

Exercise 3.10—Word Pairs

If you are not already familiar with the following words, look up each in a dictionary and write a brief explanation of the difference between the words in each set:

- advise, inform
- advise, advice
- anxious, eager
- complement, supplement

- farther, further
- gantlet, gauntlet
- imply, infer
- invent, create, discover

- complement, compliment
- disease, injury, ailment
- disinterested, uninterested

- less, fewer
- sensual, sensuous

Exercise 3.11 — Clichés

In each of the following sentences, underline the clichés. Then rewrite each sentence by replacing the clichés with original language:

1. Let's run this idea up the flagpole and see who salutes it.

2. After 9 p.m., taxis are few and far between.

3. It is time for journalists and public relations practitioners to bury the hatchet.

4. Get a ballpark estimate of how much it will cost to print the brochure.

5. It's time to bite the bullet and announce the layoffs.

6. John was green with envy when Lee was given the Oxford account.

7. Progress came grinding to a halt when the new managing editor took over.

8. Beyond a shadow of a doubt, this is the worst decision you have ever made.

Exercise 3.12 — Inclusive Language

Rewrite the following sentences as needed to eliminate any biased or exclusive language:

1. "Do something about your son," my neighbor's wife screamed out the back door.

2. According to union rules, policemen must be in proper uniform when they appear in public.

3. The highway gas station is manned at all times of the day and night for the convenience of travelers.

4. Mrs. Ramadera was elected chairman of the League of Women Voters.

5. The new chief of surgery is a woman doctor from Pittsburgh.

6. Five students in the class—three girls and two men—wrote the winning essays on malnutrition.

7. Like many women drivers, Mrs. Jefferson was fearful about driving alone after dark.

8. Michael Axman, who is crippled and confined to a wheelchair, was voted Man of the Year by the Handicapped Workers' League.

9. Maria doesn't have a job; she is just a housewife.

10. Early immigrants to this part of the state included Frenchmen, Germans, Swedes and Scotsmen, as well as some blacks and Indians.

11. A good computer operator must be certain that he or she continually updates their skills.

12. The airline will provide a bonus to every pilot, stewardess and air-traffic control-man.

13. It is tradition that a cabinet member should meet with his staff every Monday morning.

14. The law says policewomen must receive the same pay as policemen.

15. A handicapped child may still be able to feed and clothe himself.

16. Will the men in the audience please turn and shake hands with the ladies?

17. With help, victims of cerebral palsy can live normal lives.

18. The Negro attorney is an expert in common law.

19. The movie theater admits children and old folks for half price.

20. Each first-grader was asked to have his mother pack some fruit for a snack.

21. "Kirk is a real credit to his kind of people," said Mrs. Tomlee, referring to the accountant, Kirk Fitzhubert, who is gay, who received the chairman's congratulations for saving the company more than $2 million. ■

Suggestions for Further Reading

Brooks, Brian S., James Pinson, and Jean G. Wilson, *Working With Words: A Handbook for Media Writers and Editors* (New York: Bedford/St. Martin's Press, 2005).

Gordon, Karen Elizabeth. *The Disheveled Dictionary: A Curious Caper Through Our Sumptuous Lexicon* (Boston: Houghton Mifflin, 2003).

——. *The Deluxe Transitive Vampire: The Ultimate Handbook of Grammar for the Innocent, the Eager, and the Doomed* (New York: Random House, 1993).

——. *The New Well-Tempered Sentence: A Punctuation Handbook for the Innocent, the Eager, and the Doomed* (New York: Random House, 2003).

Jenkins, Evan. *That or Which, and Why: A Usage Guide for Thoughtful Writers and Editors* (New York: Routledge, 2007).

Kessler, Lauren, and Duncan McDonald. *When Words Collide: A Media Writer's Guide to Grammar and Style,* 6th ed. (Belmont, Calif.: Wadsworth, 2003).

Lederer, Richard and Richard Davis. *Sleeping Dogs Don't Lay: Practical Advice for the Grammatically Challenged* (London: Griffin, 2001).

O'Connor, Patricia T. *Words Fail Me: What Everyone Who Writes Should Know About Writing* (San Diego, Calif.: Harcourt Bruce, 1999).

——. *Woe Is I: The Grammarphobe's Guide to Better English in Plain English,* 2nd ed. (New York: Riverheat, 2004).

Truss, Lynne. *Eats, Shoots and Leaves: The Zero Tolerance Approach to Punctuation* (New York: Gotham, 2006).

Walsh, Bill. *Lapsing Into a Comma: A Curmudgeon's Guide to the Many Things That Can Go Wrong in Print—and How to Avoid Them* (New York: McGraw-Hill, 2000).

Zinsser, William. *On Writing Well: The Classic Guide to Writing Nonfiction,* 30th Anniversary Edition (New York: HarperResource, 2006).

4

Basic News Stories

Chapter Objectives

- To explain, according to the standard of newsworthiness, what information should be included in print journalism news articles

- To show how to organize information into an inverted pyramid news story

- To demonstrate how to write a summary lead in appropriate print journalism style

- To present principles of accuracy, brevity, and clarity in writing news stories

- To explain what information is necessary in basic accident, fire, and crime stories

- To tell how chronological narratives can be used in news stories

Determining What is News

News reporting involves decision-making on the part of reporters, editors, and various gatekeepers who are part of the information process. Chapter 1 discusses how media experts decide which events on any given day are worth reporting and what criteria are used to make these decisions: How do they know when a news story will be worthwhile to their readers, viewers, and listeners? How do they select the most significant and satisfying stories from the many possible stories available to them on any given day?

The answer, we said, depends on what people need and want to know. Some stories become newsworthy because they reflect the media's responsibility to inform citizens of a democracy of public events and public policy debates; other stories are newsworthy simply because they are entertaining and unusual. Generally speaking, an event or item of information can be judged newsworthy if it meets the following criteria:

- Timeliness or currency: Is it happening now?
- Proximity: Is it taking place in a location close to media consumers?
- Prominence: Is it about a famous person or place?
- Consequence: Does it have a strong impact on people's lives?
- Suspense: Is it related to conflict and its resolution?
- Human interest: Does it appeal to human emotions?
- Novelty: Does it concern the unusual or strange, the "firsts," "lasts" and "onlys"?
- Progress: Does it give positive or negative information about people and communities achieving or failing to achieve their goals?

The importance of each criterion varies somewhat among the different media. Broadcast and online journalism particularly value timeliness, or the ability to tell a news story quickly. Broadcast newscasts also especially emphasize the aspects of being at the scene; they value novelty, human interest, and conflict because these are particularly dramatic and quickly draw attention to the broadcast. Radio and television journalists are also concerned with keeping that attention, with being sure not to give listeners and viewers a reason to turn off news presentations.

Public relations practitioners, on the other hand, tend to tell stories that emphasize the values of progress or novelty or that focus on human-interest news. As advocates for a company, candidate or cause, they seek to generate positive stories that put their subjects in a good light. Public relations stories emphasize the positive things people have accomplished or experienced, providing a balance to the "bad news" told in print and electronic journalism. Public relations professionals, as well as magazine journalists, have to be concerned about their printed materials being ignored or discarded. Their objective is to connect with readers' lives in a way that will keep readers choosing to read and remembering what they have read.

In print publications as well as in their online counterparts, newspapers emphasize the values of proximity, impact, and prominence. They seek to give readers the local news of interest and to relay significant national stories about events, prominent people, and public policy most significant to their readers' lives. Print journalists take seriously their role as government "watchdogs." They judge news stories for their ability to tell readers about all activities of governmental agencies—from the work of police units to social welfare organizations to the courts and the county libraries—to let citizens know whether governmental work reflects the public's best interest.

Because more words can be printed on a newspaper's pages (or included in links of its online counterpart) than can be said in a 30-minute TV or five-minute radio newscast, print journalists can tell longer stories and choose more stories to tell. They can have a greater breadth to their reporting—telling not only the positive, dramatic stories readers might choose to read, but also the negative, ugly stories readers might need to read but would prefer to avoid— stories that offer information important for readers' participation in the decision-making process of a democracy.

Once readers subscribe to (or buy) the newspaper, they get *all* of it every day: the good news with the bad, human interest articles with business updates, movie reviews with sports stories, editorials with speech coverage articles. Readers tend to buy, read and keep the publication because, *overall*, most of its information is useful, even if a particular article doesn't appeal to them. Print journalism's strength, then, lies in its breadth and depth of information, rather than in its timeliness. Even in their online versions, newspapers can't compete successfully with broadcast media in getting out information quickly and in creating a sense of immediacy, but they can be more effective in providing more detail and depth of information, and more choices of stories and paths to follow.

Print News Stories

This chapter introduces you to how to write news stories suitable for print journalism in newspapers and online. As you learn to write these basic stories, remember that detail and thoroughness are the strengths of print journalism. Print stories are different than stories written for brief broadcast sound bites.

Include as much information in your print stories as you deem relevant to what you're trying to tell readers. Remember, if you have written a longer story than your editors can use in terms of column inches available to them on a particular day, they can always cut sections of your story. Cutting what's there is easier than the opposite case: trying to fill column inches with a story that's not there. When you "write short," editors must find you or someone else to expand on the story or to write another one if they need more words to fill a given number of column inches.

Do not, however, overwrite or provide trivial detail. Exercise news judgment—a sense of a story's newsworthiness—and write all that seems relevant. Your job is to always be sure editors have all the information they will need to effectively edit the story.

At certain times, of course, editors will provide some idea of the preferred story length *before* you report and write the story; follow their guidelines unless some striking new angle to the story develops during the reporting process. In such cases, confer again with your editor. Don't ignore a newsworthy development simply because your editor previously has said the story should be only 10 column inches.

Writing an Inverted Pyramid Story

The trick to good news writing is to exercise news judgment in such a way that you can construct any story in an order that reflects the newsworthiness of the material. What do readers most need to know? That information goes first. What do they secondarily need to know? That information goes next, and so on. The result is a news-judgment process that ends with a story constructed according to the **inverted pyramid structure**. This traditional print journalism style of writing gives the most important information in the first paragraph of the news article, then works down through all subsequent information in order of import-ance, paragraph by paragraph, until the least important information is given in the article's final paragraph.

When stories are written in inverted pyramid style, editors can cut unnecessary paragraphs quickly, from the bottom of the article, if they must readjust column inches of page space at the last minute. More important, the inverted pyramid reveals to readers (and to editors) what you judge to be the most significant, newsworthy aspects of the news event and allows them to grasp quickly what they most need to know.

Indeed, the test of any first paragraph should be a scanning reader's ability to understand the nature of the news. Does the first paragraph contain the essence of the news story? If that paragraph were the only one readers were to read, would they still get the gist of what happened? The first paragraph should give readers the most complete information in as few words as possible.

The Lead Paragraph

A few decades ago, the first paragraph of a news story, called its **lead** (sometimes spelled **lede**), was said to contain as much of the *who, what, when, where, why* and *how* of the news as possible—the so-called **five W's and an H**. Leads were also limited to about 35 words.

Today, leads typically emphasize four of those original five W's—focusing on the who, what, when and where—and may be much shorter than 35 words. They may also be longer, although shorter is usually preferred. Different newspapers have different average lead lengths depending on what appeals to the newspaper's readers. Some papers, such as *New York Times*, prefer longer, more thorough leads; others, like the *USA Today*, use quite short leads.

A lead should be a single sentence, and that single sentence should typically comprise the first paragraph of the news article. The one-sentence lead paragraph should be no more than five typed lines; it is frequently fewer. If your lead turns out to be six lines, rewrite it, unless you can articulate a solid reason for its unusual length.

A lead should be written in the same straightforward way acquaintances use sentences to talk to each other. The lead should not be super-casual or extremely informal, but it should

---

Box 4.1

Two Lengths of Leads

This *New York Times* lead represents a longer, more complex approach to lead writing:

> BERN, Jan. 23—After months of pressure from American Jewish groups, the Swiss Government, leading banks and businesses agreed today to establish a memorial fund for Holocaust victims in what a senior official called "the humanitarian traditions of Switzerland."
>
> (Alan Cowell, *New York Times*)

This *USA Today* lead represents a more succinct approach:

> Taxpayers now can prepare and file taxes on the Internet and get the line-by-line help offered by more expensive retail software.
>
> (Anne Willette, *USA Today*)

be plainspoken and direct. A person delivering certain kinds of news would simply tell you either who did what to whom or what just happened to someone. For example, if that person wanted to tell news about a person you both know, he or she probably would say something like this: *John just got hurt—a mine shaft collapsed on top of him and a number of other people.* If he or she wasn't sure who was injured, the sentence would focus on the event:

> *A mine shaft just collapsed and hurt a number of people.*

Try to write your leads to reflect a similar emphasis on what happened, on what you would say to a group of people if you wanted to get some information to them quickly and completely.

The first words of the lead are the most important words in the entire story. If the story is about someone well known or prominent, then the first words of the lead typically emphasize the person's name:

> *Gov. Politico announced today he would ask the state legislature to enact another tax cut to stimulate the economy.*

If what happened is more important than who did something, the lead should begin with what happened:

> *An Amtrak train derailed this morning outside New York City, killing two commuters and injuring 12 others.*

The first words of the lead sentence rarely give the *where* and *when*. *Where* and *when* words (adverbs) should appear as close as possible to the action word (the verb) and should only begin the lead sentence when the *where* or *when* is unusual or noteworthy: *Midnight tonight marks the beginning of a nationwide strike by auto workers.* (Notice that in the earlier lead about the president, the where is assumed to be Washington, D.C. If the president were making an announcement from a place other than the White House, the location would be specified in a dateline.)

Telling the *how* and *why* of the news story is typically reserved for the second sentence, which is usually also the story's second paragraph. However, like the *where* and *when*, if the *how* and *why* are unusual, the *how* and *why* may begin the story's lead sentence. For example, the *how* and *why* often begin sports stories, because repeating a score after a game's result has been broadcast does not exactly give the news:

> *A missed point-after kick and five penalties in the final quarter led to a 10–6 Miami Dolphins loss Sunday to the Buffalo Bills.*

Summarizing the News

Straightforward leads that present a brief statement of the most important aspects of the news event are called **summary leads** because they succinctly summarize newsworthy information.

Box 4.2

Well-Written Summary Leads

The following are examples of some well-written summary leads:

In a practice becoming commonplace in American hospitals, medical devices are being recycled—from arthroscopic knee-surgery blades to catheters threaded into patients' hearts—and federal regulators are investigating whether this effort to save money is endangering lives.

(Lauren Neergaard, *Associated Press*)

Federal authorities are trying to deport the head of one of Dallas' busiest towing companies, saying he overstayed a tourist visa and became a repeat thief.

(Brooks Egerton, *Dallas Morning News*)

Two months after the disappearance of an 82-year-old New Bedford man who was later found strangled to death in a wooded area, police have arrested a man for allegedly robbing him.

(James A. Duffy, *Boston Globe*)

A Buffalo woman has filed a discrimination complaint against a discount department store, claiming it refused to hire her because her religion bars her from working between sundown Fridays and sundown Saturdays.

(Dan Herbeck, *Buffalo News*)

Summary leads are the most common leads for hard news stories. Typically, summary leads state clearly the significance—the impact—of a news event. For example, *Americans will pay more at the gasoline pump next month, after a bill Congress passed today raises the federal gasoline tax two cents a gallon* emphasizes how readers may be affected.

Rarely does a lead paragraph include the name of an average private citizen. Typically, only famous individuals are identified specifically by name, primarily because such names require no further identification. Most readers know who the president is or the name of the secretary of defense or the prime minister of England. Such well-known people are identified by name and title: *Secretary of State Harold Globetrotter traveled to Cairo today . . .*

Print journalism news stories identify private citizens, unknown to the world at large, by first name, middle initial, and last name, as well as by age and street address or local area (for example, *Miguel Z. Satchell, 23, 55 S. Riverview Road . . .*). Because such identifications are cumbersome, they are usually reserved for the second paragraph of the story. This complete identification is said to be "delayed," so such leads are known as **delayed identification leads** or **blind leads** or **impersonal who leads**. Although the exact label for this type of lead isn't mentioned frequently in the jargon of journalists today, a delayed identification lead is almost constantly in use in newspapers.

Because the specific identification of the private individual is delayed until the second paragraph, the lead includes other identification to help the reader understand what happened, as in the following examples:

A railroad worker was injured when . . .

A high school teacher was charged with misconduct after . . .

A 23-year-old man was hospitalized with multiple bullet wounds following . . .

Of course, a variety of alternative leads can also be used to begin news stories. Alternative feature-like leads (discussed in Chapter 9) are usually followed by what is sometimes called a **nut 'graph**, a paragraph that gets to the kernel of the news story, summarizing its significance to readers. In other words, the true summary lead is delayed until the second or third paragraph.

For example, a news story might begin in a feature-like way by directly addressing the reader: *So, you think you can get away with cheating on your income taxes?* That lead paragraph would then be followed by a nut 'graph saying something like this: *Congress passed the Federal Income Tax Reform Bill today, making it harder for you to cheat on taxes and more likely you'll go to jail if you do.*

Observing Style and Other Technicalities

Lead writing, and story writing as well, should conform to the rules of the *Associated Press Stylebook* or the stylebook prepared by the news organization for which you are writing. Particularly important are the rules regarding addresses, numbers, abbreviations and ages.

Most newspapers observe the following conventions for telling when something takes place:

- Don't use the words *yesterday* and *tomorrow* in news stories because readers have to project forward or back from the paper's dateline to be sure to which date the writer is referring. Stories can use *tonight* or *this morning* and even *today*, although some would argue the word is implicit unless it is said otherwise.
- Use the day of the week for events taking place within a week's time frame and the date (i.e., month and date) for events taking place more than a week before or after the story. Do not use both day and date together (e.g., *Monday, March 1*); the combination is considered redundant.
- Also redundant is the use of *a.m.* or *p.m.* with *this morning* or *this evening*. For example, a story should say *10 a.m.,* not *10 a.m. this morning.*
- Except in obituaries, do not include the year with the month and date, unless referring to a year other than the current one.
- In announcing an upcoming event, the format is *always* time, date or day, then the place. For example, a sentence might conclude with . . . *will be held 11 a.m. Tuesday in Memorial Auditorium.*

Accuracy in all details, even minor ones such as street address numbers, is highly important. The newspaper's credibility depends on its accuracy in small matters as well as large. If you're unsure of something, do not use it. Don't guess or assume. It is never acceptable to include information in the story because it's "probably" true. It would be wrong to assume, for

---

Box 4.3

Leads to Avoid

To stay focused on newsworthy facts, a story's lead should avoid certain pitfalls. One approach to avoid is a no-news lead, one that states the obvious or relates the routine. Instead, the lead should reflect the reporter's effort to uncover some unusual or new aspect of the story, as follows:

Obvious fact: *Today is the first day of winter.*

Unusual elements of obvious story: *Winter began today with record low temperatures and the first snow in December.*

Routine event: *The City Council met at 2 p.m. today.*

New aspects of the routine: *The City Council voted to institute a new garbage collection fee following a five-hour, heated discussion.*

Also avoid general all-purpose phrases that do not give a clear sense of what happened. Instead of broad generalities, you should provide details that tell readers what made the event distinctive, as in the following examples:

Vague: *A 17-year-old high school dropout was arrested today on charges of armed robbery.* (How was this armed robbery unique, distinctive?)

More interesting: *A 17-year-old youth was arrested today after a masked gunman burst into a local veterinary hospital, pointed a gun at the receptionist, and demanded that she give him cash from a change box and a toy poodle waiting to be picked up by its owner.*

Vague: *Several people were injured Tuesday night on State Route 19 in a serious car accident.* (How many people? What kind of injuries? How serious an accident?)

More interesting: *A Boston couple and their 3-year-old son received second-degree burns when their car spun out of control Tuesday night on State Route 19, plunged over an embankment and burst into flames.*

Box 4.4

It Happened to Me: What's in a Name?

I once was reporting a routine story about five people who were to be honored with a Citizen of the Year award by an organization at an upcoming meeting. The director of the organization provided me with the necessary information, including the names of the five honorees. I verified the spelling of each, including one Silvio D'Agostino.

In my report, I named each of the honorees and included a brief sentence about what each had done to earn the award. In D'Agostino's case, I wrote "She has volunteered more than 10 hours each week to coordinate activities of the village's Senior Community Center, which serves about 75 senior citizens each week." After the story appeared, I got a call from Silvio's wife. She good-naturedly informed me that her husband's unusual first name frequently led to confusion. Although she didn't want a printed clarification because her husband had already suffered enough embarrassment, I learned a valuable lesson: Don't guess; always check out anything of which you are not absolutely certain.

—*RDS*

example, that a 16-year-old youth living in Middletown, Ohio, attends Middletown High School. Maybe she does; maybe she doesn't. If you don't know something is so, don't write it. Don't include it in the story.

Remember that the principal goals of journalistic writing are accuracy, brevity, clarity, and—of course—objectivity. In addition, journalistic writing values crisp, sharp and conversation-like sentences that "read" smoothly and naturally.

To achieve brevity, journalists should try to use as few words as possible, but never so few that the meaning of the story is unclear. Forget the literary impulse to use a variety of synonyms; rather, repeat the same words if they represent the same meaning. For example, a story about the city council shouldn't use the substitute words *legislative body, governmental organization*, or *official group* to replace the word *council.* Instead, the story should keep repeating *council* so that the meaning of who is doing what is clear. Of course, also consider whether the word really needs to be used repeatedly.

The Flow of the Text

Transition Words

Transition words require particular care as your text flows from one idea to another. Each transition word must represent exactly the correct relationship between the ideas in your story. Be sure that you are using the precise transition word your meaning dictates. These are some common transition words and the connections they indicate:

- Transitions that link: *also, in addition, moreover, furthermore*
- Transitions that compare: *in the same way, likewise, similarly, as well as*
- Transitions that contrast: *although, but, however, nevertheless, on the other hand, on the contrary*
- Transitions that create emphasis: *clearly, indeed, surely, truly, certainly*
- Transitions that show cause and effect: *as a result, consequently, therefore*
- Transitions that show a relationship in time: *afterward, later, then, while, next, during, since, before*
- Transitions that sum up: *finally, in conclusion, in short, thus, to sum up*

Breaking the Text

News stories should be broken into separate paragraphs whenever the topic slightly changes or the emphasis or meaning shifts. Journalists do not follow the formal expository writing style in which a paragraph has an opening sentence, followed by developmental sentences and a concluding sentence. In print journalism, most paragraphs are a single sentence or two brief sentences because short paragraphs look better when printed in columns. The use of frequent paragraph breaks, with the final sentence filling less than a full line of text, creates more white space in the column, making text look less "gray" and thus less formidable and more approachable to readers.

Another way to break up the gray of printed text on the newspaper page is to use **subheads**, small headlines between paragraph units of the story. Writing the subheads is not usually the job of the reporter but of the copy editor. Nonetheless, it is helpful when you are writing a long story to keep in mind how units of your story could be divided. Within the framework of the inverted pyramid, construct the information as chunks of text, keeping similar ideas together and writing clear transitions from one chunk to the next. When you write the article that way, the copy editor (or you yourself) will have less difficulty seeing where the copy of the text naturally divides and be able to quickly write a subhead for each unit. Because we know that most newspaper readers are scanners, subheads identifying the content of different units of the story give readers another reason to jump in at a later point in the article or to read a story they had overlooked on a previous page.

Opportunities for Graphics

Another way that you, as a writer, can help the overall presentation of the text of your news story in the paper (or online) is to think graphically—that is, to think of the possibility of using information graphics to enhance your story or perhaps to take the place of long units of explanatory text. Graphics that add extra meaning to the story are always welcome, not only for the additional information they provide readers, but also for the color and graphic interest they add to the printed or online page. Sometimes a graphic can take the place of many paragraphs of text.

Don't use an information graphic to avoid writing or, indeed, understanding a complicated issue, but do consider an information graphic if it would explain a complicated subject more clearly to your readers than your text. If it would take five or six paragraphs to explain how the wing of an aircraft is constructed and a graphic would use about the same space and provide a clearer meaning, consult with your editor. Together you may decide to have a graphic constructed.

The opposite case is also true, however. Don't consider a graphic if it would take up more space than it would to write the same information in a sentence or two, particularly if you're using the graphic because it has color and graphic interest—that is, it's a pretty picture—but doesn't offer much information.

Writing for Online Newspapers

Many newspapers now have online versions for which beginning reporters have an opportunity to write. So, a natural question is how online print journalistic writing differs from newspaper writing. One answer is that, basically, it doesn't.

In many ways, online news writing is regular news writing, only more so. That is, the reader is still a scanning reader, but even more online than when reading newspapers. Research tells us that online reading is slower and harder and that online readers don't scroll through longer stories. Rather, they give screens on the Web site a glance, looking for headlines, subheads, highlighted words, bulleted items, pictures, graphics, links—anything that provides information quickly and easily.

The emphasis on speed and ease doesn't mean that the Web site version of the newspaper can't offer the depth that is the essence of print journalism. It means that the depth of that journalism isn't presented in long columns of text, but rather through layers of text with links to other stories, features, opinion pieces, biographical information, informational graphics, maps, audio tapes, sets of pictures, other related Web sites, and so on. Therefore, even more than the newspaper writer, the online writer has to consider other places the story can take the reader, adding the depth that online news can offer.

More than the newspaper writer, the online writer has to "write tight." All the usual advice on writing—short paragraphs, simple sentences, standard subject–verb order, active-voice verbs, reduced adjectives and adverbs—becomes more essential for the online writer trying to keep the story as brief as possible. The online writer always has to think about keeping the story short enough to fit on a single screen (because, studies show, the reader is unlikely to scroll), or at least creating brief units of the story that will fit on a single screen. The advice is to think links, not scrolling. See if you can deepen the story by branching out in all directions (e.g., writing the outbound links into the story text itself) rather than working hierarchically downward (or clustering related links at the end).

The inverted-pyramid structure is still customary and is perhaps even more important than in newspapers, because the online reader is more likely than the newspaper reader to glance only briefly at a story and then, with the click of the mouse, move on. Just as newspaper writing follows the stylebook for consistent news preparation, a reputable stylebook such as the *Associated Press Stylebook* is followed in online journalism to keep the site consistent.

Accuracy is stressed online as well as in newspapers, but perhaps its importance must be stressed more forcibly, because the temptation to compete with other online news sites is so strong. There's always the desire to be the first to get the story online, even to beat out the broadcast outlets.

Yet the credibility of a Web site is not unlike that of a newspaper; it is built over time through being correct in matters small and large. The credibility of a site makes it respected and popular, just as the credibility of a newspaper's pages makes it well reputed. Therefore, it's important not to forget that being first and wrong seldom pays off. It's better to follow "when in doubt, leave it out," even if it means your site is not always the first with (maybe) the latest.

How It's Different

There are a few ways that online writing is different. One is using the "bold" function on your word processor, with the goal of making significant points in the story jump out at the reader. Boldface or color highlight important terms and words in the story. Bulleted lists of information and the creation of subheads within the text when the story is long are other devices used to keep the attention of site visitors.

Remember, too, that people from *anywhere* can be reading your site. Online publications are not limited in locality as are most print newspapers: Your "paper" isn't going to arrive on someone's front porch or at a newsstand, but rather in a room in any home or business in the world. Your online newspaper, for example, may be a way that someone living in a distant location keeps in touch with home or the way that someone thinking about visiting will learn

Box 4.5

Writing for the Web: One Expert's Advice

Here are some tips from someone who's studied and taught online journalism:

Writing for a Web page calls for a hybrid mix of print and broadcast writing skills and presentation, especially with the advent of streaming audio and video and the increased capability of home computers to use that technology. Web copy is non-linear, because visitors do not necessarily follow the story from start to finish. Instead, readers are interactive, expecting to be able to click on Web site links. Thus, the Web story has to be planned in advance, with related sidebars or links with graphics, pictures, transcripts, or other supporting data.

Writing should be similar to that of broadcasting—brisk, crisp and conversational—because research shows most Web site visitors don't take time to read the detail found in a traditional newspaper article. Conversely, the Web allows reporters to go into greater depth on some stories because the news hole is infinite in cyberspace. Just as in traditional journalism, the lead is most important. Because Web users scan pages rapidly to see if the story is of interest, the opening words must be well written, even riveting, in order to capture the reader's attention. Since many readers do not scroll down on a page, the main points must be in the opening paragraphs, which is also an important consideration for attracting the increased number of people who get their news on mobile phones. Once the story has been summarized, the writer can develop subsequent details for those interested in reading on.

Use short, simple conversational sentences made up of short, simple wording. Writers are advised to read their copy aloud. If a sentence seems too complex, start another. Most stories are only between 300 to 400 words. While that seems short, the technology actually forces better copy, making writers cut unnecessary words, contributing to the readability of a story. Punctuation and grammar have to be right. If the mechanics are sloppy, readers will focus on the mistakes rather than the story.

Headlines must summarize the story and grab attention. Web writers suggest a maximum of six words, and short ones at that. Avoid too much detail, confusing words or obscure acronyms. Sub-heads should be inserted every few paragraphs to help readers understand the story's unfolding, especially if a new topic is introduced. Boldface words are another way to break up monotony on a page. Like their print counterparts, Web stories must be visually appealing, not only with headlines and sub-heads, but with bullets and visuals or explanatory graphics.

Graphic devices such as boxes, maps and charts not only make the story more understandable but also provide visual relief from a solid block of copy. Boxes may use bullet points to summarize the main story or make detailed information easier to comprehend. A strong quote can be effective if boxed, although it should not be used adjacent to where the actual quote appears in a story. Maps provide visual depiction, either of the changes in local traffic flow or the location of an earthquake in southwestern China. Data and complicated figures can be made easier to understand by presenting them in a graph or chart.

Internet reporting surpasses both print and broadcasting in that links can be provided to other Web sites. Instead of reading a journalist's analysis of the president's news conference, for instance, visitors can follow a link to the White House Web site and access a transcript of what was said within 20 minutes of the event's conclusion and reach their own conclusions. Timeliness is particularly important. Major ongoing stories have to be updated every few minutes because Web readers now expect news on demand, as it happens, with constant updates. If news isn't fresh, they'll go somewhere else.

This immediacy poses an unforeseen problem for both the Web site and the journalist, however. If the Internet does away with the daily or edition deadline, then reporters, too, have to work 24/7, raising costs, changing traditional work patterns, and probably exacerbating the high rate of burnout already felt by many news professionals. On the other hand, wire services for years have bragged about being on constant deadline, providing timely updates to ongoing stories. The Internet merely offers a larger audience.

Keep in mind that Web writing has the potential creative use of text, audio, video, live action, background sound, graphs, charts, photographs and even animation. The Web's interactivity even allows visitors to participate in a poll, express an opinion or rate a particular story. In many respects, the Web writer becomes an editor who tries to anticipate what the reader wants, and how best it may be provided.

Like any other news stories, Web pieces must be accurate, balanced, and reliably sourced. If not, the writer's credibility suffers and a disservice has been done to the reader. If you conduct interviews by e-mail, tell your readers. Attribute data and information to a Web site, just as you would a human source: *Jon Mare, executive director of Friends of the Sea, said in a statement on the organization's Web site that the oil* spill was *"a catastrophe of unimaginable magnitude that would adversely affect adjacent fishing grounds for years to come."* If you draw on information in a chart compiled by Friends of the Sea showing the economic impact of major oil spills during the past 20 years, attribute your information to the organization's Web site, just as you would be expected to do in citing any other source. Don't merely skim the information from them and other sources, then rewrite without giving credit. That's not being honest with your readers, or fair to the organizations from which the information came.

The writer, Joseph J. Marren Jr., a former managing editor of Business First newspaper, Buffalo, New York, is an associate professor of journalism at Buffalo State College.

---

about your city. As you're writing the news online, be sure that all local references are explained clearly so nonresidents reading the Web site will understand what you're writing about.

Three Basic Hard News Stories

The three most basic hard news stories of print journalism—all of which emphasize *what happened*—are stories about accidents, fires and crime. Although each of the three has distinctive features, all share common characteristics.

For example, common to all three is the inclusion of information about loss of life, considered of paramount importance in any news story. Information about any human death or loss of significant lives should be in the lead—in the *first* paragraph of any news story. A guiding principle in journalism is that loss of human life is always more significant than human injury, and injury is always more significant than loss of property.

Questions to Ask

Accident, fire and crime stories are also similar in that they all require you to keep in mind your role as a watchdog of local, state, and federal governments. If time permits, consider the question of how well the authorities handled their civic responsibilities. If time does not permit you to work much as a watchdog on the initial story, try to address the question of civic responsibility, when appropriate, in follow-up stories.

In a traffic accident story, for example, consider and inquire about road conditions and appropriateness of signage. Should the snow removal crews have been putting salt on the icy roads? Should there have been a stop sign or traffic light at the intersection? Were there unsafe conditions that should have been corrected?

Another issue to consider is the effectiveness of the legal system. Was the driver in a fatal crash a repeat drunk-driver offender whom the courts let off on probation? Did the drivers have licenses? Were the cars registered and, if state law requires, did they have recent safety inspections?

In fire stories, the response time of fire personnel is significant, as is the issue of whether the fire department had adequate equipment. Consider, too, whether the building that burned was in violation of fire codes. Is arson or insurance fraud suspected?

In crime stories, the question of police conduct, as well as police response time, can be significant. Were police justified in any shooting or use of force? Did they arrest individuals for just cause? Did police arrive on the scene in time to prevent violence? Were the criminals repeat offenders the judicial system should not have allowed out on probation?

You can probably think of many additional questions to ask about the behavior and responsibility of public officials that should be answered in fire, accident and crime stories. One of the unwritten codes of conduct in being a news reporter is that you have the responsibility to ask those watchdog questions on behalf of readers, viewers, and listeners. Be constantly alert and keep your eyes and ears open. Pay attention to what is not said or to information not released. Don't accept blindly and casually everything you hear.

Box 4.6

It Happened to Me: Making Change Happen

One of the joys of working in news is to come across an unsafe condition that puts people in jeopardy and to bring enough pressure on responsible officials so that the situation is changed. The *San Jose Mercury-News* once christened a particularly bad 10-mile stretch of four-lane highway south of the city "Blood Alley" following several multiple-fatality head-on crashes. Even then, it took months for the state to make simple changes such as posting reduced speed limit signs and increasing visibility of highway patrol units.

I covered a story once where a speeding car missed a curve on a freeway lane east of San Jose and plowed through a barrier of oleander bushes, colliding head on with another car. Nine people were killed. I went to the location and it was difficult to get enough usable video because the scene was so horrific. One of the highway patrol officers was particularly incensed, profanely denouncing the traffic engineers who designed the stretch of road with such flimsy barriers.

When we ran the story, I cleaned up the officer's statement, and we ended the story with the fact that there was no explanation about why such a dangerous situation was allowed to exist. The next day I did a follow-up, standing amid the broken bushes while traffic whizzed by. I had made some calls but had gotten no answers. Shortly after my piece ran, I got a call from the office of the director of the division of highways. The director was going to be in town the next day and a staffer asked if he could visit our station to do an interview and explain.

The answer was simple, he told me the next day. State traffic regulations called for barrier strips to be constructed when there were 40,000 cars per hour on the average. This section had only 38,000. "You mean," I asked, "that if 2,000 more cars per hour used that stretch of freeway, those nine people wouldn't have died?" I let the question hang. The director paused. "Yes," he said. "I guess you're right."

The state had temporary barricades up before the end of the week! —*WRW*

While remembering the presumption of innocence, you should not naively assume that every public official acts responsibly and appropriately at all times. The majority do, so most of the time everything goes along as it should—and that's *not* news. But when it doesn't, it's your responsibility to uncover that information and report it to the public. Government officials perform their roles as servants of the people. It's your job to see that the public is well served and to alert the public when it is not. You also need to tell people when laws, rules and regulations don't seem to be working the way they were intended to work. Then the public and its civil servants, including politicians, can consider whether these laws, rules and regulations should be changed.

Ethical Considerations

In serving as a watchdog for governments and public officials, journalists also serve the public good; therefore, they need to have high standards for themselves as well as for others. Stories should not suggest misconduct when there has been none, simply to hype the story for publicity's sake. Do not dress up a story to build your reputation as a tough investigative reporter or simply to play "gotcha" with a politician you dislike. Don't use news stories as a way to grind a personal ax about a rule or regulation that you don't happen to believe is a good one.

Disqualify yourself from writing a story in which you are personally involved. Notify your editor of any conflicts of interest so another reporter can be assigned to the story.

Box 4.7

It Happened to Me: Campaign Dilemma

While working as a television reporter, I agreed to shoot some video for a local candidate for the state legislature and to work on his campaign in an advisory capacity. To avoid a conflict of interest and being assigned to any stories dealing with the campaign, I told my news director and assignment editor about what I was doing.

They weren't too happy with me, and after a while I understood why. Not only did I take myself out of the pool of reporters on an already short-staffed station, but there also were other potential ethical conflicts of interest. What would happen, for instance, if "my" candidate's opponent in the race came into the newsroom to do an interview? Should I leak any of his statements or his campaign strategy to "my" candidate? And what would happen if another reporter dug up something negative on "my" candidate? Would I tip off the candidate or let things fall where they may?

Fortunately, I didn't encounter any of these problems. By election day, however, I had vowed to remain apolitical from that time on. By the way, "my" candidate lost. Resoundingly. —*WRW*

Avoiding Libel

Some of the points raised in Chapter 2 bear repeating in the context of news reporting. In writing accident, fire, and crime stories, be especially careful to use language in such a way

Box 4.8

It Happened to Me: My Big Story—the Case of the Missing Murder

Here's an example of what used to be called "shoe-leather reporting." The writer is an award-winning newspaper reporter and a retired professor of journalism.

Having been on the *Kansas City Star* and *Times* crime beat in Kansas City, Kan., for more than a year back in the late 1940s, I'd made a lot of friends—detectives as well as uniformed officers. Thus I had more or less free access to the police department's records, from traffic accidents to homicide.

Making my rounds one evening, I came across a report of an abandoned automobile with some stains on one seat that appeared might be blood. No follow-up had been done, however, because the car's registration holder worked at a chicken slaughter house.

Later, I saw a missing persons report in which the subject had the same name as that of the owner of the abandoned car. The first name was spelled differently, but near enough to the one on the other report to suggest the same person.

Considering that possibility, I went to the chief of detectives and told him the relationship between the two reports raised the specter of murder. Although skeptical, he said he would assign a couple of detectives to pursue the possibility.

With that assurance, and after some telephone calls, I wrote a story that evening that said the unexplained disappearance was being investigated as a possible murder.

The next morning after the story appeared, a woman called the office and asked to speak to the reporter. She told me I should talk with an acquaintance of hers. I did so, at the acquaintance's home. After prolonged questioning, she told me that a son of hers had left a newspaper clip of my news story under her door with a note explaining, "This is why I left town."

With the name of the possible suspect, two detectives and I began trolling the taverns along old Central Avenue in Kansas City, Kan., known to have been frequented by our suspect and his friends.

Showing bartenders and patrons photos of the suspect and the apparent victim, we asked if they'd seen either. If so, we pressed them to tell us when it had been, who they were with. Were the circumstances unusual? Had anyone overheard any conversations? Had our suspect been in the place before? We asked lots of questions.

We exchanged information daily. Eventually, we identified two additional suspects who had apparently fled the city. The story soon began to fall into place.

With a hefty week's pay in his pocket, the missing man had gone to one of Central Avenue's taverns to drink. There he met three younger men, and soon all four were drinking together like old friends. When they were finished, he offered the three a ride home.

Before the drinking bout, he had been grocery shopping and there was a bag of food on the rear seat of the car. As they drove along, the men riding in the back seat took cans of beans and condensed milk out of the grocery bag and beat him on the head until he lost consciousness and took his money. They then drove into rural Wyandotte county and threw his body over a bridge into a creek.

Temporarily recovering consciousness, he attempted to crawl to a nearby lighted farmhouse, but collapsed only several yards from the creek. There his body lay, soon covered by deep snow, until discovered many weeks later after his killers had been arrested and one had confessed.

Someone informed "The Big Story," a popular radio program of that era, about my assistance in solving the murder, and it was dramatized several years later. In recognition of the help that I'd been in solving the case, I received a handsome bronze plaque and an award of $500. An accompanying letter congratulated me for my "outstanding achievement in the field of journalism." I still have the plaque, and I presume I'm still a member of the "Big Story" alumni club of more than three hundred journalists.

John DeMott, Emeritus Professor of Journalism, Memphis State University

that you never commit libel. The first and foremost requirement is to be accurate. If you get the facts straight, most libel problems are avoided.

Always presume innocence until a person is proven guilty. Sometimes the facts will make it clear in your mind beyond a reasonable doubt that criminal behavior occurred. Even so, in terms of the law—and thus in terms of your reporting and writing—a person is not guilty until he or she pleads guilty or is found guilty in a court of law. Charges may be dropped, the case may be plea-bargained, or new information may surface (e.g., the driver involved in an accident may appear to be drunk but actually was driving erratically because of a prescription drug). If any of those changes occur after a news story implied that someone was guilty of criminal behavior (e.g., driving recklessly, setting a building on fire or robbing a bank), you and your paper can be sued for libel.

In crime stories, therefore, it's generally best to describe the incident without using identification of suspects until you are actually writing about the charges or arrests, as in the following example:

Wrong: *Rob Taylor took $175 from the clerk of a . . .*

Right: *A masked robber took $175 from a convenience store clerk at gunpoint . . .*

While arrests can be reported without fear of a libel suit because they are covered by privilege, reports of the arrest should nonetheless use language that does not declare guilt, as follows:

Wrong: *Rob Taylor was arrested for robbing a bank.*

Right: *Rob Taylor was arrested in connection with a bank robbery.*

Wrong: *The driver was arrested for being drunk while driving down the highway.*

Right: *The driver was arrested and charged with driving while intoxicated.*

When you are reporting fire, accident and crime stories, be wary of what witnesses say. Their statements can guide your reporting and help you describe what happened, but they should not be used if they represent idle speculation about behavior that could be criminal. Witnesses may think the driver looked drunk or was speeding, or that the fire was the result of arson, or that the police fired before they had reason to think they would be fired on, but only an official investigation will reveal the legal version of the truth. Until tests and investigations are complete, idle speculation is only that—don't use it, especially if it's libelous.

When victims, witnesses, neighbors, relatives and friends of victims do want to talk to you, however, it is perfectly legitimate to quote what they say in your story (*witnesses said* or *witnesses told police*), as long as what they say is not potentially libelous and they have agreed to be your source—that is, they talked to you knowing you were a reporter. Accounts by witnesses and others can add color and detail to crime, fire and accident stories.

Contradictory accounts are not necessarily a problem. They may be the most honest way of telling the story until an investigation determines what really happened. When TWA Flight 800 crashed into the waters off Long Island a number of years ago, there were differing preliminary accounts from witnesses: the plane caught on fire, appeared to explode, or was shot down by a guided missile. Taken together in all their contradiction, those different versions of what people perceived could be the best version of a confused reality to publish.

Using "Allegedly," "Reportedly," and "Apparently"

Beginning reporters frequently assume that using the word *allegedly* removes the risk of writing something libelous. This belief is only partly correct. The meaning of *allegedly* is "according to legal documents." Used this way, the word indicates that certain legal documents (e.g., arrest reports) exist and the writer is in essence claiming the privilege of those documents. The protection of privilege, however, has nothing to do with using the word *allegedly*; it has to do with the fact that documents exist. So don't use *allegedly* if they don't exist. You often see and hear the phrase used in crime story reports, but it still isn't right.

Similarly, the word *reportedly* indicates the existence of official reports or at least of spoken "reports" or accounts of what happened. Don't use the word unless such reports exist and you have seen or heard them.

For most accident stories, the word *apparently* is more appropriate. It is used frequently to describe events that no one was around to see: *The ironworker apparently lost his footing and fell 30 feet to his death.*

Even if speculation comes from semi-official sources, such as firefighters or police officers, news stories should not suggest that what they say is absolute truth. A more accurate way to report their statements is to say that officials are investigating or pursuing inquiries (those are established truths) or that the possibility of criminal behavior has not been eliminated.

What Must Be Included

Each basic news story requires certain types of information. Accident stories must include a complete account of what happened and precisely where it happened, as well as information about the extent of injuries or death and the exact offense with which any suspect is charged. If someone dies when a traffic accident occurs, then he or she was *killed* in the accident; if that person dies later, at the hospital, then he or she was *fatally injured* in the accident.

Fire stories should include information about who reported the fire, how many fire companies responded to the alarm, the time the fire started, how long it burned, the insurance value of the land and buildings, damages as determined by the investigation, the extent of injuries or death, and whether some people are still missing. The description of the fire should use words precisely, as in the following:

- A *holocaust* is a fire that kills a great number of people.
- A building is never *partially destroyed*; destruction is always complete.
- If the building has been *gutted*, its interior has been destroyed.

Descriptions of the nature of the fire should rely on specific facts rather than the writer's opinion. Thus *flames reached 50 feet* is more precise than *were towering*. Likewise, *The heat melted plastic* tells more than *was intensely hot.*

Crime stories should include information about any weapons used, what goods or money was taken, the value of anything taken, how entry was obtained, who discovered the body (if there was one), the official cause of death, police attempts to pursue the criminals, the status of any ongoing investigation, circumstances of any arrest, identification of anyone arrested, and the exact nature of the charges.

In general, accident, fire and crime stories should report the names, ages, and addresses of victims, arrested suspects, and witnesses. Be sure to gather this information when you're on the scene. Many newspapers have policies about not reporting the names of victims until relatives are notified. Many do not report the names of crime witnesses in order to protect them from retaliation. Sometimes newspapers have special guidelines about how much of the address of a witness to print. Obtain the information, however, and then let your editor make the call on what to use.

Newspapers also are concerned about victimizing the victim—that is, exposing to unwanted publicity someone who has already been victimized by a crime—by revealing that person's name in the paper. Therefore, newspapers frequently withhold the names of rape victims and victims of domestic abuse and violence. Names of minors also are generally not published unless the youths are charged as adults.

As discussed earlier in this book, information about any previous criminal record of a suspect is difficult to handle. Most lawyers believe such information is injurious to the suspect's right to a fair trial; therefore, they won't give it to you and don't want police to either. The same is true for confessions. Suppose, however, that you find evidence of a previous record and/or a confession and believe that your role as a watchdog over the criminal justice system requires you to inform the public. In that case, discuss the issues with your editor. Such decisions are never easy and should be made with full editorial and legal awareness.

Including a Chronological Narrative

Almost all basic hard news stories are told using the inverted-pyramid structure, but many people nonetheless believe that such a story structure can be somewhat confusing and has little appeal to readers. If the story tells readers everything in the first sentence, they ask, why should readers finish the rest of the story? A better way, they believe, is for journalists to be storytellers, relating events chronologically, spinning out narratives that end in satisfying conclusions. Other media people remain stoutly loyal to the inverted pyramid and scorn narrative writing.

Given these differences of opinion, a storytelling narrative *may be* an option, although rarely a necessity. Some news stories can be told chronologically, particularly if they are not the only story about a particular news event and your editor likes more experimental story structures. Traditionally, narrative writing was typically used in feature writing; a news story told chronologically is said to have been given **feature treatment** and is classified as a **news feature**.

Inverted pyramid stories, however, also sometimes have employed narrative writing within an article, telling the story (after the inverted-pyramid lead) as a narrative or interrupting the inverted pyramid story with a narrative segment(s). Typical examples come from stories about sports, accidents or weather disasters. A play-by-play narrative review of the highlights of a basketball game might interrupt a coverage story otherwise written in the inverted pyramid structure. A news story about a complicated traffic accident might give a narrative recounting of the probable chain of events (*Police said the fatal chain reaction began when a car . . .*). A narrative of a hurricane's progress over a particular time period or geographic location might appear within a larger story of the storm's disastrous consequences.

If explaining a news story chronologically makes it more understandable or more comprehensive, you may want to pause in the middle of the inverted pyramid (or at the story's end) to write a brief narrative. This technique can serve the guiding principle of clarity, as well as take advantage of print journalism's ability to cover comprehensively events in depth. However, use the chronological narrative only when it helps readers grasp the information more easily or thoroughly, not just because it makes writing the story easier. Never construct a narrative simply to escape the difficult work of deciding the appropriate inverted-pyramid order for presenting information.

A Worthwhile Effort

The work of creating an inverted pyramid story that reflects the material's newsworthiness is time-consuming. Most often, however, your labor serves your readers well. You reward the public for reading by bringing them timely, useful information that is clearly and coherently organized and presented. You sort out the news and prioritize information so readers can more easily make sense of the world. You also serve as a watchdog, telling readers when their democracy is working for them and when they need to pay attention to their civic responsibilities.

Discussion Questions

The following are class discussion questions drawn from Chapter 4:

1. What are the different ways in which news is defined for print, broadcasting and public relations?

2. How is the inverted pyramid story structured?

3. What elements should be part of the lead?

4. What are the different ways leads may be constructed?

5. What factors determine whether a name is used in a lead or its use is delayed?

6. What are things to avoid in composing leads?

7. How does online writing differ from newspaper writing? How is it the same?

8. What are some basic commonalities among accident, fire and crime stories?

9. How do you avoid libel problems in writing crime stories?

10. Why might a story be written with a chronological, narrative structure instead of the traditional inverted pyramid?

CHAPTER EXERCISES

Exercise 4.1—Improving Leads

Consider the following leads. How could you improve them?

1. The committee met this morning to discuss items of concern to employees.

2. Torrance Lakeman, administrator of County Hospital, announced today that a cardiac care unit would be added next year to the hospital's services.

3. At a morning news conference today, Mayor Michael Bucksin criticized the police department for failing to reduce the incidences of drunk driving.

4. A 12-year-old boy was involved in an accident about 5 p.m. Tuesday, suffering multiple injuries.

5. A variety of holiday festivities will be celebrated in the next two weeks. ∎

Exercise 4.2—Writing Summary Leads

Write one-paragraph summary leads of 35 words maximum for each of the following sets of information:

1. There is a threat of a massive crude oil spill along the length of England's southern coast. The oil is spewing from a wrecked oil tanker, the 42,777-ton *Toxico Queen*. The tanker ran aground on an English Channel mud bank early this morning and now has flames roaring from its ruptured oil tank. The ship ran aground at about 5 a.m. and the fires have been burning for the past three hours. The ship was en route from Saudi Arabia and was due in Hamburg, Germany. The ship is owned by Toxico Oil Corp.

2. FBI agents arrested three men in Phoenix, Arizona, this morning. They were charged with a bank robbery that occurred in [your city] the ninth of last month. The men were charged with taking $31,000 from the Community Center Mall branch of the First

National Bank. In the holdup of the bank, the two men, wearing ski masks and carrying sawed-off shotguns, forced bank employees and customers to lie on the floor while they took money from cash drawers. A driver waited outside during the robbery. The three men who were arrested did not put up a struggle at six this morning when agents entered their plush hotel room in the Expensive Suites Hotel.

3.   There was a single-car automobile accident eastbound on State Route 38 shortly after 5 a.m. today. State highway patrol officer Reggie Reynolds identified the driver of the car as Archie Goodson, 63, 131 Birch Ave. [your city]. His auto struck an overpass abutment at a high rate of speed after he apparently fell asleep at the wheel and drove off the side of the road, the highway patrol report said. Goodson is a night watchman at Davis Auto Supply, 222 Hontel Ave. He was taken to Mercy Hospital, where he is in a critical condition with head and chest injuries, according to hospital spokeswoman Marian T. Greene.

4.   Five-year-old Willie Walters, 248 Linwood Ave., dashed across the street in front of his home when he heard the Clarton District school bus coming about 7:30 this morning. He was struck by a pickup truck driven by Marvin Middlefield, 61, 652 Harwood Place. The boy was taken by ambulance to Children's Hospital, where he was admitted for treatment of a broken leg, cuts, and bruises. Police said Middlefield will not be cited.

5.   The Chamber of Commerce will hold a dinner meeting tonight. They will meet at the Royale Hotel at 7 p.m. Members of the Chamber of Commerce will hear two reports: one on the progress of the organization's membership drive, which is now under way (given by Chamber vice president Maurice Sweeney, 75 Lexington Court), and another, an analysis report of a major study of the local economy conducted by the State Development Committee, headed by Chamber member Vincent T. Brown, 7399 North Windom Road.

Exercise 4.3—More Leads

Write two different leads from the following facts:

Lead A

When: Thursday morning

Where: Erie Canal locks east of Steeple Street

Who: Michael Ratkouski, 44, 457 St. George Boulevard.

What: fell down a 25-foot shaft

Source: county fire officials

Ratkouski, a state inspector, was inspecting construction work inside the locks when he fell down the mine shaft as he was walking through a tunnel. A fire crew and two construction workers rescued him after an hour and a half. Ratkouski was taken to St. Swithin's Hospital. He is listed in fair condition. He might have broken a leg.

Fire Battalion Chief James Harris suffered chest pains during the rescue and will be kept overnight in St. Swithin's Hospital for observation. He is listed in good condition.

Lead B

When: today

Where: At Helmsley Avenue near Clinton Street

Who: Alan Cardigan, 34, 701 Hopkins St.

What: was arrested and charged with obstructing governmental administration, resisting arrest, possession of illegal drugs, tampering with evidence, having a bad tail light, and making an unsafe turn

Source: city police

Cardigan is alleged to have struck Officer Mark Slator when Slator stopped Cardigan for traffic violations. Cardigan, police say, swung open his car door, striking Slator's right arm and causing him to twist his right leg. Then Cardigan drove off. When police caught him, they observed him place cocaine into his mouth. Then he fought with officers.

Lead C

When: yesterday

Where: Lewis Road, Watlass (a small town outside your city), near State Route 91

Who: Calvary Baptist Church

What: high winds blew down two thirds of the new church building

Source: the Rev. Albert Rayside, pastor of the 150-member congregation

Church members began raising church walls and roof trusses two weeks ago; today they are picking up debris. New roof trusses were ordered today. They should arrive in two weeks, and then construction can begin again. The building is fully insured, the Rev. Rayside tells you. No one was injured.

Exercise 4.4—Expanding Your Writing

Write a lead and then a news story based on the following information. When you are finished with the print version, write an online version of the same story for your university's student newspaper Web site.

The Board of Trustees last night, in a meeting at [your] college or university, did these things:

• voted to increase tuition by three percent, effective at the beginning of the next academic year;

• approved a contract to build a new 20,000-seat sports arena at a cost of $63 million, to be funded from state and federal monies and alumni contributions;

• rejected a $1.25 million joint request by the Fine Arts and Design Departments for new photo–video cameras and computers that the departments would have shared.

The meeting was acrimonious. More than 400 people showed up, and the city fire marshal ordered the meeting site moved to Memorial Hall Auditorium on campus. Then an additional 200 people came in after the meeting began. Student government representatives were extremely critical of the tuition-increase proposal. More than 35 people spoke during the 3½ hours of debate about the tuition issue.

Equally controversial was the sports arena proposal. Students, faculty, and community representatives seemed divided on the issue, with 10 speaking for and 11 against.

The decision to reject the Fne Arts and Design equipment requests was met by hoots and catcalls. The meeting, which had begun at 8 p.m., adjourned at 3 a.m. this morning. Members of the board had no comment as they left the building, to the jeers of about 50 students who stayed until the meeting's end.

Exercise 4.5—Writing a Complex Story

Write the lead for a news story from the following facts, then write the entire story. Discuss with the class some of the choices you had to make about which details and quotations to use in the story.

Victim: Eva Marino, 9, 1156 Ellington Place, your city

Current Condition: stable at the Children's Hospital pediatric intensive care unit, with head injuries. Arrested: Edward Gorgonnola, 34, 1525 Hemenway St.; charged with refusing to submit to a police officer and fleeing the scene of the accident.

Narrative

Police were chasing a car they presumed to be stolen. The car, a late-model sedan, struck the victim as she stood on a street corner with her younger sister, then slammed into a fence. The driver got out of the car and ran across a parking lot at the corner of Ruggles Street and Tremont Avenue. A telephone company repair technician grabbed him and held him until police could handcuff him.

The sedan's owner, Tara Cranch, 44, 1152 Upper Falls Blvd., saw her car was missing when she looked out her window at 8 a.m. Three hours later, her brother saw the car on Washington Street and flagged down a police cruiser. The cruiser, according to police, switched on its lights and sirens at Washington Street and Ruggles Street but was three cars back from the stolen car in traffic. The vehicle sped north on Washington and made an illegal left turn onto Melena Cass Boulevard and headed the wrong way against traffic, Officer James Beverly said. The officers in the car stopped chasing the vehicle but tried to keep it in sight. The sedan turned onto Tremont Avenue, fishtailing as it headed south. The car swiped a light pole as it attempted a left turn onto Ruggles Street, lost control and jumped the curb, hitting the girl. The entire chase, which began at 10:47 a.m., lasted about 10 minutes.

Quotes

From the telephone company repairman, Eric Triplett, 34, 768 West Stevens Road: "I heard a crash and then a scream, then saw a man running across the lot. I grabbed him and threw him up against the wall and held him, then gave him to the officer."

From 11-year-old next-door neighbor of the Marino family: "The two girls were just walking along from their uncle's house when the crash occurred. They were always together."

From Odell Owens, 64, 10 Ruggles St., who saw the crash: "The police had the lights and sirens on, but they weren't right behind him. He was driving like a fool, but that doesn't mean he was being chased."

From Barbara Gains, 45, 14 Ruggles St., who was cleaning her car outside and saw the accident: "That poor baby went up in the air 20 feet and fell in a balled knot. The cops should have slowed down. It was just a stolen car. It doesn't make sense."

From a Tremont Avenue resident: "The police were more interested in putting handcuffs on the man than they were of taking care of that child."

Exercise 4.6—*Creating a Story*

As a class, discuss a "what if" story. Begin with the name of a prominent local celebrity. Then have each member of the class add in sequence a detail about what might have occurred in an incident involving him or her.

Evaluate each additional detail in terms of its newsworthiness. How does each new detail change or not change the order of how the story would be told? Discuss what, if writing an online version of the story, you might link this story to—what kind of Web sites, giving what information.

Suggestions for Further Reading

News Reporting

Itule, Bruce D. and Douglas A. Anderson. *News Writing and Reporting for Today's Media*, 6th ed. (Boston: McGraw-Hill, 2003).

Mencher, Melvin. *News Reporting and Writing*, 10th ed. (New York: McGraw Hill, 2005).

Online and New Media

Berkman, Robert I. and Christopher A. Shumway. *Digital Dilemmas: Ethical Issues for Online Media Professionals* (Ames: Iowa State University Press, 2003).

Clark, Roy Peter, and Don Fry. *Coaching Writers: Editors and Reporters Working Together Across Media Platforms* (New York: St. Martin's, 2003).

Craig, Richard. *Online Journalism: Reporting, Writing and Editing for New Media* (Belmont, Calif.: Wadsworth, 2005).

Foust, James C. *Online Journalism: Principles and Practices of News for the Web* (Scottsdale, Ariz.: Holcomb Hathaway, 2005).

Salwen, Michael Brain, Bruce Garrison and Paul D. Driscoll. *Online News and the Public* (Mahwah, N.J.: Lawrence Erlbaum, 2005).

Resources for Writers

Goldstein, Norm, Ed. *The Associated Press Stylebook and Briefing on Media Law* (Cambridge, Mass.: Perseus Books, 2007).

Kessler, Lauren and Duncan McDonald. *When Words Collide: A Media Writer's Guide to Grammar and Style,* 7th ed. (Belmont, Calif.: Wadsworth, 2008).

Anthologies

Colon, Aly, Keith Woods, Christopher Scanlan, Karen Brown, Don Fry and Roy Peter Clark, Eds. *Best Newspaper Writing* (Washington, D.C.: Congressional Quarterly Books, 2005–Present; Chicago:

Bonus Books, 1993–2004; St. Petersburg, Fla.: Poynter Institute, 1979–1992). Published annually since 1979.

Sloan, W. David and Cheryl S. Wray. *Masterpieces of Reporting, Vol. 1* (Northport, Ala.: Vision Press, 1997).

Zinsser, William, et al. *Speaking of Journalism: 12 Writers and Editors Talk About Their Work* (New York: Harper Information, 1994).

5

Interviewing

Chapter Objectives

- To identify the characteristics of a good interviewer
- To describe basic types of interviews and interview subjects
- To explain how to prepare for an interview, including how to select subjects and write appropriate questions
- To explain accepted practices for maintaining control of the content of interview stories and for handling requests to speak off the record
- To give tips on how to conduct an interview, including how to appropriately handle sensitive or difficult interview situations
- To suggest how to end an interview smoothly

The Importance of Interviewing

Whether you become a print, broadcast or online journalist or a public relations practitioner, interviewing will be at the heart of much of what you do. Professional communicators—people who get and give information—need to be experts at talking to people.

They must develop the art of the interview: how to approach or call a person they have never met before, establish rapport, ask intelligent and pertinent questions, and come away with material for stories that their audiences need and want to read, see, and hear. Interviews do not have a "standard" form. Each interview differs, depending on the subject and the circumstances of the story.

Each of the three media—print, broadcast, and public relations—has slightly different objectives for the interviews its practitioners conduct. Print journalists want longer, more detailed quotations useful in substantial stories. Broadcasters prefer brief and emotionally rich sound bites suitable for newscasts. Broadcasters may also sometimes want to do the interview simply to let listeners or viewers know the station is on the scene, keeping up with the story as it happens; what is said in the interview itself may be less important than the interview's offering evidence that the station has been a witness to the news event. Public relations practitioners want positive, encouraging explanations appropriate for company newsletters, annual reports or news releases.

Even within a given medium, interviews vary widely. For instance, an interview for an investigative article about politics appearing in the viewpoints section of the daily newspaper will look and feel quite different from an interview for a celebrity profile appearing in the lifestyles section on Sunday. Interviewing generally involves brainstorming and tracking down sources who have been identified as having important information. Sometimes, however, confirmation of what you have is all you want.

Characteristics of a Good Interviewer

At the most basic level, all interviews are about seeking information. To be a good interviewer, you must *want* to *know* about things. An honest, sincere and heartfelt curiosity is the most valuable asset you can bring to interviewing.

Of course, you should be curious for your own sake, but even more so for the people in your audience or readership. You need to imagine yourself in their place and determine what

---

Box 5.1

The Difference Between Print and Broadcast Interviewing

I was a rookie reporter with the television station, and I got to go along with the sheriff's narcotics detectives who raided a gas station where drugs were being distributed. It was exciting and I got some good video to lead our 11 o'clock news. Nearly a million dollars worth of drugs were seized, so it was a fairly significant story.

When I got back to the narcotics bureau, I wanted to do an interview with the lieutenant heading the raid. The newspaper crime reporter told me to go first. He had a couple of hours before his deadline, and I was pushing our production schedule as it was. I asked the lieutenant the routine questions: How much was seized? ("Not sure yet.") How much cash was confiscated? ("We're still counting.") How did you find out about this supply center? ("We can't say too much because we don't want to compromise our informants, but we've been watching the place for the past

month.") Actually, I got a good minute-and-a-half sound bite that would go well on the late news. I started packing up my gear and the newspaper reporter started with his questions.

I listened and was amazed at the detail he went after: names, ages, and addresses of all those arrested; charges; units that were involved in the raid; where exactly the drugs were stashed; what volume of business they had; and a myriad of other details. I was impressed with the depth of his questioning. I also realized that I hadn't even thought of some of the questions he asked because I was "in TV and we can't go into that much detail." I began to understand, however, that I needed the detail for my own background to report the story, even if I didn't use much of the information. I think I became a better interviewer after that experience.

—WRW

they want to know, what they want you to ask on their behalf. Then you must be gutsy enough to go ahead and ask those questions, clever enough to ask them in a way that will get answers, sensitive enough to listen effectively to the answers, and determined enough to ask even *more* questions, until your—and your audience's—curiosity is satisfied

Obviously, not everyone excels as an interviewer at the beginning of his or her career. Developing interviewing capabilities takes practice. Highly trained journalists with years of experience can still find ways to fine-tune their interviewing skills.

Nevertheless, each interview is a unique experience at a given point in time between two or more people. Therefore, even a first interview can be superb. You may develop a special camaraderie with an interview subject or you may ask just the right question at precisely the moment when the subject is eager to express his or her feelings about a topic. Then, voilà, you have a great interview!

Kinds of Interviews and Subjects

Interviews typically fall into the following three general categories:

- **Factual interviews**: In the relatively neutral atmosphere of this interview, the interviewer is seeking primarily impartial information. These interviews are often done on the telephone.
- **Positive interviews**: The interviewer tries to establish a warm, comfortable atmosphere so the subject will talk candidly and expansively about feelings, beliefs and experiences. These interviews are often done in person.
- **Negative interviews**: The interviewer must struggle in an adversarial way to pull admissions and/or confirmations from an unwilling or hostile subject. These interviews are often done in person or in an "ambush" situation.

Interview subjects also tend typically to fall into two general categories: those who don't like to talk and those who do. Some interview subjects respond to most questions with monosyllabic answers. Convincing them to say anything takes real effort. You can exhaust a set of questions in about 10 minutes and feel as if the interview has gone on for hours. Other interview subjects almost literally can't stop talking. You may have difficulty interjecting your questions or keeping the interview focused on what you want to discuss. Under those conditions, an hour flies by like minutes.

You may not always know beforehand which type of interviewee you will be talking to, so be prepared for both. One way to get a general idea of what to expect is to consider the subject's career choices: A politician or English professor is likely to be a fairly verbal person; a mechanic or bacteriologist will likely be the opposite.

Preparing for an Interview

Whatever the subject's nature, great interviews rarely just happen. Rather, they typically result from substantial efforts on the part of the interviewer. Good interviews "happen" when solid preparation has taken place—after the interviewer has done legwork and homework.

Most important in that preparation is to thoughtfully consider what you want and expect to happen. Such consideration doesn't mean preconceiving the interview to the extent of determining beforehand precisely what will occur, and then refusing to let anything else take place—or worse, refusing to accept information that does not fit your preconceived bias. Rather, it means you should ponder what you want from the interview: Why am I going there? What do I think my subject can offer my readers or viewers or listeners? What kind of article do I intend to write after the interview? How do I expect my subject to react to my presence and my questions?

Choosing Sources and Subjects

In addition to considering what type of interview situation and what sort of person to expect from a single interview, consider the number of interviews you need to do. How many people do you need to interview to find out all you need to know and what do you want to interview each of them for? Not all interview subjects are equal. Some have a higher name recognition or greater credibility; some are witty or blunt; some are tremendously knowledgeable about particular specialized topics; some may not provide any quotable material, but may share good background information or gossip that will lead you to people whom you should interview next.

Remember, too, a subject's accessibility is a consideration, but it shouldn't be the primary one in choosing whom to interview. Don't choose a subject simply because he or she is easy to contact, is a friend of a friend, or is always willing to drop everything and chat for a while. Journalists may frequently consult people with those characteristics, but the value of an interview subject depends on his or her value to the content of the story.

To identify valuable subjects, ask, "Who is the person or people I most need to talk to in order to tell this story in an accurate, balanced and comprehensive way?" Suppose, for example, you are doing a human interest feature on someone whose dog just won best-in-show at a local kennel club event. You might need to speak only to the dog's owner, or perhaps to the sponsor of the show or the judge who selected the winner, or maybe to someone from the dog owner's family. In contrast, if you were doing an investigative series on the use of handguns, you might need to talk to scores of people—from police, lawyers, and judges to victims, gun store owners, criminologists, advocates on all sides of the issue, social workers, and emergency room physicians.

You always want your interview subject to be reliable. The subject should not be using the interview with you to grind a personal ax. Remember that people may want to talk to you to get someone else in trouble, or to get free advertising, or to send you off in a false direction. Their impure motives don't mean you should not interview them, but you should interview them only if you believe they can offer legitimate insights or directions in which to take the story. If so, go ahead and listen to what they say—with the proverbial grain of salt. If sources don't have anything worthwhile to offer, it's a waste of time to talk to them. There's no sense in interviewing someone who's not reliable for material you won't use.

Brainstorming and Making Contacts

Many journalists simply sit down and brainstorm about possible interview subjects. A prioritized list of people develops, and then the journalist starts from the top, phoning or e-mailing to request interviews. After the reporter has gone through the list once, it's time to start from the top again, picking up the people who weren't available the first time.

People have many reasons for refusing to talk to a journalist. They typically have many fears: of being embarrassed, being misquoted or being the focus of unwanted publicity. They also may not want to talk because they are shielding someone they love or are afraid they may reveal how little they know about a topic. They may not like the reputation of your newspaper or broadcast station. They may even, on first impression, dislike your voice or looks or feel they can't trust you.

Certainly, one advantage of being a public relations practitioner rather than a print or broadcast reporter is having access to sources. People within the organization are usually willing to talk to you. They may want the publicity for themselves, their unit of the organization, or the organization as a whole. Or they may have been directed by a superior to cooperate with your public relations interview efforts. In addition, they most likely realize that, as a public relations professional, you are working hard to present the organization and the people connected with it in a positive light. Such in-house interview subjects have little to fear. They may be offered a second interview if the first doesn't go well or be given an opportunity to rephrase a quotation that looks more negative on paper than it seemed in conversation. So it is rarely difficult to schedule an interview with them.

Persuading Reluctant Interview Subjects

In many neutral reporting situations, obtaining the information necessary to write a news story is relatively easy. Public officials or employees are used to reporters asking questions, and most of the time such people are willing to oblige an inquisitive reporter. In contrast, for investigative pieces, obtaining the interview and establishing a trust level with the interview subject can be difficult. Reporters may need to revisit reluctant sources several times to pry information from them.

You, as a beginning reporter, can learn tricks of the trade regarding making contacts from more experienced colleagues and through practice. One "trick" is requesting only a few minutes for an interview; once a subject has agreed to talk, he or she will rarely limit comments to the few minutes initially agreed upon. Another strategy is cultivating the "gatekeeper" who stands between you and the subject—usually a secretary or receptionist. At other times you can catch your potential subject away from the rigors of work or during a lunch hour, when he or she may be more cooperative. Then too, you may be able to convince a reluctant interviewee that the interview is a chance to tell his or her own version of the story. When all else fails, constructing a particularly dynamic and well written request for an interview may convince a prospective subject that you are, indeed, the best person to write the story (and to do the interview for it).

Requesting the Interview

Most of the time, telephone calls are the appropriate method to arrange an interview. The written letter, in-person visit, or e-mail request is used less frequently. Written requests and e-mails can be easily ignored, whereas person-to-person requests have a direct quality that makes them hard to refuse. However, written requests and e-mail may seem more respectful and polite in certain situations, whereas in-person requests can annoy interview subjects if they are offended by the audacity of a reporter just showing up and demanding interview time.

If you do decide to send an e-mail or write a letter, be sure that your request for the interview is brief and clearly indicates who you are and where you intend to publish the article. Indicate how much time you want to do the interview. Don't write a general request that sounds like you either don't have a focus to the interview or haven't yet done any research and want the subject to help you (*Could I interview you on the loss of rain forests?*). Also, don't imply that the subject should sit down and respond to your e-mail by basically writing a treatise about the subject in his or her spare time (*I was wondering if you could give me some information on rain forests and what to do about their loss?*). Writing a response to your e-mail or letter takes much more time than talking about it on the telephone or in person. Be clear that you don't expect to use e-mails or letter-writing as a substitute for the interview; you're simply requesting the time for an interview.

When you call to set up an interview meeting—assuming you're not a public relations practitioner calling someone in-house—be sure to give not only your name but also the name of your media outlet. Be open about the fact that you're doing a story for publication or broadcast. It's a mistake to hide who you are or what you are doing. You do not want to mislead people or betray their trust.

Indicate in your initial phone call or e-mail the type of interview you envision (i.e., how much time it will take) and give a general sense of the topic or angle of the article you are writing or the story you will be broadcasting. This description should leave open the possibility that you may need a second brief opportunity to talk to the subject to double-check details, confirm the article's overall accuracy or obtain a response about questions that arise later. Also indicate when you expect the story to be published or to air.

In attempting to persuade someone to talk to you, you can use psychology in a variety of ways, appealing to the subject's sense of justice ("people have a right to know") or pride ("people won't have a good impression of your honesty if you don't comment") or fairness ("you're the only one who can tell the story properly") or even vanity ("I'd like to quote you as the real expert on this").

If a source refuses to talk to you, persist and offer good reasons why the subject *should* cooperate. If the subject still refuses, quit asking, do some further reporting, then try again and again . . . and again. Persistence is a big part of success in obtaining an interview.

Sometimes people who are initially reluctant to talk may become more willing to do so after other people have gone on record or after you have obtained verification of information through written documents or computer searches. Or the potential interviewee may agree to an interview simply to make you go away. Or he or she may take pity on you for all your hitherto unsuccessful efforts to schedule a conversation. Or the person may just respond to your smile, laugh or attempt at making a joke, and start seeing you as a fellow human being who can be trusted.

Whatever the case, be persistent, while also avoiding any harassing or rude behavior. Ill-mannered actions seldom get a reporter anywhere, and they may make it more difficult for the next reporter. Poor manners can quickly create a negative reputation that can hurt a newsperson's effectiveness.

Conducting Additional Research

For a substantial news story or a feature such as a backgrounder or profile, your preparation before the interview will likely involve a good deal of library or online research and interviewing "around" the subject. Do your homework: Go into the interview knowing as much as possible about the topic and the interview subject. Find out what else about your interviewee has already been published, obtain basic biographical information, and research any alternative topic about which the subject is likely to talk.

There are two reasons for conducting this extensive research. It saves time in the interview itself and it helps you establish credibility with the subject. If you only have 25 minutes with the mayor, you don't want to spend 20 minutes educating yourself about the new parking restrictions policy. Do your homework beforehand so you can ask the mayor not about what the policy is, but about what impact it will have on pre-election public opinion or the city budget for next year, or about whatever aspect of the story the media have not already covered.

Because you want the mayor to be candid and give you good publishable material, create the impression that you know your stuff. Let the mayor know that you already understand all the basics and most of the minor details, as well as the people involved. You're knowledgeable, hardworking, and savvy; you can be trusted because you are not ill informed, lazy or unsophisticated. Interviewees trust interviewers who show that they care about their professional responsibilities and demonstrate it by preparing thoroughly for the interview.

In addition, subjects may be flattered that you thought they were important enough to read about them beforehand. This good will helps make the interview go more smoothly. Pre-interview research may also reveal some unexpected hobby or avocation of the subject or some cause about which he or she is passionate. If you ask about that hobby or interest, you may win instant good will or garner a story with an unusual new angle no one else has presented.

If your interview subject is an author on a book promotion tour, read the reviews of the book and at least scan one or two chapters before the subject arrives. (The preface and the first and final chapters often provide a blueprint of the book's subject and the points an author is trying to make.) Then, warm up your subject for a few moments before the interview by asking about the book or the review. For example, you might say, *"You've recently written a biography about Theodore Roosevelt, and I notice it got a good review in one of the national magazines. What's new about your work?"* This question tells the subject you've done some homework. The subject is probably used to being interviewed, so this icebreaker question has opened a logical way to begin a conversation.

Ground Rules for the Interview

Generally, under no circumstances should you promise that the subject of a journalistic interview will exercise final review or control over the article or broadcast. Do not relinquish the responsibility of doing your job as a reporter and writer. You are the professional expert in the media profession; the interview subject is not.

In public relations interviewing, however, a more collaborative role may be appropriate. A public relations practitioner is working within the organization; interview and story are produced through the collaborative efforts of the organization "team" working with the public relations practitioner, who may negotiate the final version of the story with his or her superiors and other involved parties. (Even in a public relations situation, however, the public relations practitioner should expect to be acknowledged and respected as an expert in interviewing and writing.)

Journalists, on the other hand, are reluctant to make concessions to any interviewees about viewing the finished article before publication or about what may be discussed during the interview. Certainly, media reporters sometimes allow certain topics to be off limits in an interview, but this rarely happens—and then primarily when the interviewee is a celebrity or public official of such stature that the agreement is necessary even to obtain the interview at all.

Sometimes reporters tell potential interviewees the general topic of the questions beforehand, so the news sources can obtain needed information in order for the interview to be productive. At other times, especially in broadcast situations, reporters may share some of the actual questions before the interview, especially if the subject seems particularly shy or inarticulate and would handle the interview better on air with some time to prepare. This preview allows the subject to begin framing answers and makes the actual live interview go more smoothly with fewer pauses. Previewing the questions this way is rare in print journalism, however. Most print journalists believe they get more honest responses when questions are unrehearsed. In typical circumstances, the print or broadcast journalist should maintain basic control of the interview and the story that grows from it. Preparing the news is, after all, their area of training and expertise.

Agreeing to Off-the-Record Status

Sometimes an interview subject says, "Don't quote me on this, but . . ." Journalists categorize the agreements they make with subjects regarding off-limits statements using the following language:

- **Not for attribution**: What is said can be used for publication but not attributed to the subject by name. For example, the source would be indicated as *a White House official* or *a hospital spokesperson*.
- **Off the record**: The material cannot be used in the story at all.
- **Background**: This would be another way of saying the information would be "not for attribution"; the source would be identified only generally—for example, as *a senior company official.*
- **Deep background**: With this type of information, the source would not be identified even generally; it is, in essence, completely off the record. The information is supposed to help the reporter understand the topic and encourage him/her to do further reporting and/or direct the reporter to new sources.

Even if reporters understand those terms, however, their interview subjects usually don't. It is therefore important to clarify what conditions are being agreed on *before* the interview begins.

Why would anyone say anything "off the record" to a reporter? Occasionally, sources want to be whistle-blowers about some wrongdoing but they are fearful of losing their jobs or of dealing with unwanted public attention. They may disclose something only to steer the reporter in the right direction or tip him or her off about something happening, but on the condition that the reporter keep silent until later or until someone else confirms it. Sometimes sources want to speak candidly to prevent the media from reporting something that is wrong or that would endanger or humiliate someone else, particularly by mistake. Other times, a source has his or her own agenda and cynically tries to use a reporter to provoke or damage someone else.

The most important aspect about off-the-record status is that it is agreed on by the reporter and the source *before* the information is discussed. Most journalists believe that if you agree to an off-the-record condition before hearing something, you are honor-bound to observe this commitment to silence. The keeping-silent principle does not apply, however, if an interviewee slips, says something indiscreet, then mutters afterwards something like, "That was off the record, right?" As a reporter, you have no obligation to agree to silence after the fact. If the subject was foolish enough to speak, that indiscretion is not your fault and you have no obligation to help him or her make up for it.

The ethical issue of agreeing to off-the-record status is cloudy, however: If someone told you off the record that someone else was going to set off a bomb in a local elementary school, would you be honor-bound to keep silent because of your before-the-fact promise? Probably not. In deciding whether to honor their promises, journalists generally believe they serve the welfare of the common good first, and the particular welfare of any single individual after.

A drawback of promising off-the-record and not-for-attribution status is that any anonymous source weakens a story. When you can't say who told you something, you are open to the charge that you simply made something up or that your source is not really knowledgeable. Try not to agree to off-the-record status or even hearing background information. Always strive to get your interview subjects to be willing to be identified by name. If a subject won't agree at first, listen to what he or she has to say, then try to get someone else to confirm the information—and then go back after doing more reporting and try to get the subject to go on the record at that time. If you report what is on the record, you and your sources can stand by your stories—the sources, by what they believe they said in the interview; you, by what you believe you heard in the interview.

When you take whistle-blowing information to someone else who might be willing to put his or her name to it, you must be careful not to compromise the identity of the original source. Don't go to someone who can easily figure out who that source must have been.

Using Technology, New and Old

Print journalists must decide whether to take a tape recorder or other taping technology to an interview. (The use of taping is a given in broadcast because subjects must accept the technology as part of agreeing to the interview.) The first consideration for a print journalist is whether a taping technology will make the interview subject uncomfortable or less willing to talk. If it will, many print journalists leave the technology behind.

Tape recorders can provide excellent interview insurance but they should not be used as a substitute for note-taking. There is simply too great a risk that machines will malfunction due to either human or mechanical error. Broadcast journalists obviously also fear equipment malfunction, but in that medium, necessity compels the use of recorders, cameras, and other technical equipment. Their situation is more likely to be reversed, with broadcast reporters using note-taking as insurance for videotape and tape recorder malfunction.

In print, for a short news story written on deadline, consider also whether listening to a playback will be counterproductive in terms of time. Using written notes is faster and more efficient, although the recording can be useful for verifying problematic or lengthy quotations. For a feature story with longer, more detailed quotations (or in public relations writing, where deadlines are less imminent), recording the interview is more likely to be useful because you can take the time to replay the entire interview and reflect on what angle the story might ultimately take.

One suggestion, of course, is for a reporter to use a footage counter or other measuring device. Then, if a good quote is recorded, its approximate location can be noted and easily found when the reporter writes the interview story. This practice is particularly helpful in covering long public meetings.

Most reporters equip themselves with a narrow notebook with flip-over covers. You need to be able to hold the notebook firmly when standing up, and turn its pages quickly, and write on both sides of the paper. Since many interviews and "media opportunities" require you to be on your feet, some reporters prefer to write with a pencil because ballpoint pens can run dry when used to write on an upward angle.

Writing Interview Questions

After thoughtfully considering the objectives of an interview, brainstorming for potential sources, making the telephone calls to set up the interview, and doing preliminary research, you're ready for the last stage of interview preparation: writing the questions. This is a must for beginning interviewers. Seasoned reporters can frame appropriate questions in their heads on the spot, but until you develop skill in wording questions effectively, it's better to plan exactly what you want to say.

However, don't feel that you must be absolutely wedded to the questions you write. They represent the results of planning before the interview how to word questions and in what order to ask them. This activity is a warm-up to the interview; your list of questions is insurance that if the interview stalls or if questions and follow-ups don't immediately come to mind, you'll still have a worthwhile experience.

Distill your questions to a list of keywords that will prompt you during the interview itself. If you're working as a print or audio reporter, put the keywords at the top of the notebook page in the order of their importance or their asking. You might paper-clip them to the front cover of your notebook or devise another system with which you're comfortable. The objective is to be able to look at the keywords during the interview while writing down the subject's responses. Constantly flipping notebook pages while asking questions and writing down the answers can distract the interview subject. Likewise, reviewing the previously written questions can create long silences (and waste time) during the interview.

On-the-scene TV reporters should keep their list of questions in their pocket to review before the interview starts. They should try to commit the questions to memory, since handling cards or notes looks awkward on camera.

Some final advice about question preparation: Be sure to have more questions than you think you will need. Nothing is as embarrassing as requesting a half-hour interview and then asking all your questions in 10 minutes. When preparing the list of keywords, highlight the essential questions and have ready a number of less significant questions in case you need them. Put the questions in priority order, then work through them, keeping an eye on the clock to pace yourself through the questions you most need to ask.

Types of Questions

One reason to write out questions beforehand is that the process forces you to consider the wording of the questions and to determine whether the types of questions are appropriate. Questions generally fall into the following three categories:

- **Closed-ended questions** typically elicit a simple "yes" or "no" response, although a closed-ended question can also be any question an interviewee can answer with one word or phrase:

  Question: *How old are you?*
  Response: *21.*

- **Open-ended questions** require the subject to expand his or her responses and to answer in more than one word:

  What was the most embarrassing moment during your theater career?
  Describe your strategy for winning the marathon.

- **Loaded questions** (sometimes called **biased** or **leading questions**) imply that the questioner has already made up his or her mind about what is the "right" answer:

  You believe the president lied, don't you?

No one type of question is bad or good, but each type should be matched to stories, situations, and subjects.

Closed-ended questions are good for warming up an interviewee because they generally are easier to answer. For example, "*Where did you go to school?*" isn't typically a demanding question and thus can be easily dealt with. Closed-ended questions also are useful for pinning down a subject "*Given all that you just said, will you vote for renewal of the Clean Air Act, Senator?*" The difficulty with closed-ended questions, however, is that they can frequently produce only incomplete or superficial answers, and they can let the subject get away with monosyllabic responses.

Open-ended questions ("*What was the most difficult experience you had during your first year on the job?*"), on the other hand, are good for eliciting expansive answers offering quotable quotations. The drawback is that they allow the subject to choose what to say. As a result, he or she may dwell on irrelevant information or hold back something important—either deliberately or because the importance of the material isn't clear.

The crucial principle is to avoid using a closed-ended question when you want to obtain an open-ended answer. For example, if you want to know what conditions are like in the international space station and you ask an astronaut who has been there, "*Was it hot in the space station?*" you might only get a "yes" response. But if you say, "*Describe conditions in the space station,*" you will likely get a more interesting and useful answer.

Most of the time journalists try to avoid loaded questions that imply what the response will be, but they can use them for certain kinds of investigative interviews. For example, asking the loaded close-ended question, "*Did you embezzle money from the charity fund?*" could generate only the subject's denial. Asking, "*What did you do with the money you took from the charity's fund?*" signals that you already know about his or her guilt, so the subject might move to a different kind of response.

Try, however, to avoid loading questions unconsciously and when you don't intend to, which is especially a problem with adverbial qualifiers, for example,: "*Do you **really** think the new waterfront development plan will work?*" or "*Can you **honestly** say you're not a candidate for senator?*"

Whatever your question, be sure to ask it singly—not in conjunction with another question. For example, "*Where will you go and what will you do when you get there?*" combines two questions. This leaves the subject the choice of which question to answer. Most of the time he or she will choose the safer, more innocuous question. So instead of using double or triple questions, limit each question to a single idea and be prepared to ask *follow-up questions* (sometimes called *secondary questions*). Think of the process as involving several questions coming one right after another, leading in the direction you want to go.

Broadcast Questions

You also may vary the construction of the questions according to the medium in which you are working. Like print, broadcast interviewing has the goal of acquiring information from a news source, but broadcast questions are simpler, more straightforward, more conversational, and sometimes, leading. Broadcast questions often have an open-ended approach, as in the following:

> *You must read a lot of good things about yourself in the paper. What's that like?*

> *How did you react to learning that you were the No. 1 ranked tennis player in the state?*

Broadcast interviews are typically brief news or spot interviews inserted into a radio story or newscast, or are sound bites for television. Especially in radio, however, interviews can also sometimes be live or taped segments that run in their entirety for several minutes or longer. The chief difference between broadcast and print interviewing is that the broadcast reporter is not only gathering information but also editing at the same time. Thus, questions have to be logically structured and sequenced to lead the subject through the story in a way that makes sense to the listener or viewer. A good interview, especially a radio interview, sounds like a smooth-flowing conversation and has many of its same attributes: curiosity, interest in the subject, genuine warmth and a sense of humor, and uncontrived sympathy when appropriate.

Print Questions

In print, readers seldom see and never hear the questions that originally produced what is quoted in the story, so the vocabulary level of the questions is more likely to be matched to the educational level of the interview subject, rather than that of the viewing or listening audience. The print reporter uses language in common with the subject to put him or her at ease and to create a semblance of similarity that suggests the reporter has a sympathetic ear.

The print journalist also is committed to more in-depth, longer stories than the broadcaster, so the print journalist is likely to ask more substantial questions, which suggest that longer responses are required. Print journalists also may ask more open-ended questions, because they are searching for full-sentence, quotable responses. Print reporters can afford to listen to the subject ramble a little if that rambling eventually leads to worthwhile information or especially well-spoken use of language.

Public Relations Questions

In public relations, the situation may require that the interviewer cover certain topics or subject areas and tread carefully in some touchier areas of questioning. For a print or broadcast journalist, the consequences of offending a source are not as great (although it could be a problem if the journalist needs to consult that source again). A public relations practitioner doing internal interviewing, however, may be employed by the person being interviewed or, at least, may work for the same organization. Questions about difficult topics may be met with a superior's rebuff, which the practitioner must either accept or argue reasonably about not accepting. Print or broadcast journalists can be much tougher and hang onto their lines of questioning, badgering subjects if need be; the public relations interviewer cannot. (Broadcast reporters, however, do have to worry about the image their badgering may create with their watching and listening public.)

The public relations interviewer has to be sure in these circumstances not to ask only "fluff" questions that will elicit only "fluff" answers. If such answers were to be used in quotations in subsequent news releases, the reporters and editors reviewing the releases would simply delete the quotations as lightweight material. The public relations interviewer needs to always remember that all quotations used in media writing must have substance and newsworthiness.

Electronic Questions

With all the work entailed in writing interview questions, an obvious query is why not simply e-mail the subject your carefully prepared questions and let him or her write the answers. In some few circumstances, that process actually can work. For example, if you have a source who is difficult to reach, has a tight schedule, or is traveling out of town, you could send an e-mail and the source could reply from an airplane or the office in the quiet after-hours at work. An e-mail response is certainly better than no response at all, and if the subject prefers to write on a computer, it may be even superior to what you would get in person.

However, most sources don't have time to write full responses to electronic questions; their answers will likely be less expansive than if they were asked in person. There also is no opportunity to ask follow-up questions or seek clarification. You can't judge your subject's physical reactions to your questions, nor can you "read" the environment or the subject's character. So an e-mail interview is likely to be weak in many respects.

Nonetheless, a valuable aspect of electronic responses to questions is that they are permanently in writing. You don't have to worry about note-taking. The e-mail or text message indicates the date and time of the questioning, and can serve as evidence of when and how a given question was answered.

Conducting the Interview

When the subject has agreed to be interviewed and you have prepared the questions, you will move to what many people think of as the heart of journalism: conducting the interview. Interviewing is an art, not a science. It applies communication and human relations skills to achieve the delicate balance between eliciting information of interest to the audience and helping the subject talk freely.

Being a Good Listener

During the interview, listen intently to the responses to your prepared questions, then let your natural curiosity lead you to spontaneously follow up on any intriguing statements the person makes. One benefit of planning questions beforehand is that you don't have to think of questions as you're listening; therefore, you can concentrate on what you're hearing. Pay attention to the language your subject uses. Listen for words with heavy connotative meaning. Is the subject subtly putting down someone else by using condemnatory language? Or is he or she revealing a hidden bias? Also listen to the logic of the presentation. Does it make sense or is the interviewee obviously twisting the reasoning to exculpate himself or herself? Can you hear an answer that "squirms" out of being direct and open? Is the subject trying to shift the topic? Taking up air time to avoid answering the question? Or perhaps suggesting some fascinating area of discovery that you hadn't even thought of? Or admitting more than you ever would have believed possible before the interview?

Too often, however, beginning interviewers don't listen. To feel secure, they hold tight to what they've prepared, adhering inflexibly to their list of questions with the result that they don't comprehend what the subject says. No matter what fascinating or offbeat remarks the interviewee makes, it is lost on the reporter. If you let this happen, you may lose many great quotes and potential story angles. Be a good listener and follow up on what appeals to your sense of curiosity!

Warming Up the Subject

For a print or broadcast interview, it is beneficial to warm up the subject with some casual conversation about unrelated topics. When shooting a TV interview, for instance, chat with the subject about the best background and lighting, and ask the subject to sit or stand in a specific place. For a radio interview, place the microphone on a desk or table, and remind the subject not to move in the chair (causing him or her to fade off mike) or rattle paper or make other sounds that will be magnified on tape. Talk about what you're doing when you set voice levels.

Once the subject is settled, thank him or her for taking the time to talk and explain how the interview fits into the larger picture. Then get the subject to talk about something: where he or she is going to have lunch today, what he or she plans to do this weekend. The objective is to have the interviewee forget about the surroundings and concentrate on answering questions.

When interviewing someone in his or her own office or home, look unobtrusively for clues to understanding the person. Diplomas, family photographs, trophies, knickknacks and personal jewelry may provide information to help you talk informally and warm up the subject. Ask some brief casual questions about what you see. Generally, establishing a better rapport with the subject helps readers, viewers or listeners better understand the individual and the way he or she answered the questions.

Personal Conduct During the Interview

In any in-person interview, your demeanor is important. Always act like a professional—and a mannerly professional at that. The image of the smart-talking, sassy, tough reporter is long gone as a reality, except for infrequent hostile investigative reporting situations, which by nature cannot be cordial. Generally, however, interviewers should be courteous, serious, and warm enough to help put their subjects at ease.

Most interviews do require that you be tough and aggressive in certain ways. You must keep the interview focused, returning to the questions you want answered and not allowing the subject to wander off to irrelevant fields. Do not accept a vague answer when your audience deserves a specific one—for example, if the subject digresses, you say "*Yes, Senator, but you still haven't quite answered my question . . .*" You should be firm, but not abrasive. Just because you're the media and have the power to be in-your-face, doesn't mean you should needlessly take advantage of your status.

Be prepared to back off, if a subject becomes emotional or argumentative or otherwise clearly indicates that he or she believes your questions are inappropriate. Without necessarily accepting the subject's belief, pause a moment and think about whether the information is really necessary; if it is, then return to the line of questioning later, but in a slightly different way.

Interviewing in a Professional Manner

Your conduct during any interview is a case of not going too far in any one direction:

- Be polite, but not subservient.
- Be agreeable, but don't let the subject walk all over you.
- Be human: talk about your family, your hobbies, your difficulty in getting tickets to the ball game. But don't express human error in any way that makes you seem unprofessional, such as asking the interviewee for paper to write down your notes.
- Be in control, but not so controlling that you won't follow the subject off in a new story direction if the topic he or she mentions is a compelling one that your readers would appreciate.

Ideally, reporters should ask the questions that members of their audience or readership would ask if they were there. You're not a conduit for channeling whatever the subject wants to communicate but rather the means through which the needs and interests of your audience can be raised and considered.

Establishing Good Communication

Keep the focus on the person being interviewed and try to keep the language flowing. Don't interrupt too often or disagree with the subject just for the sake of argument. Also, don't "help" an interviewee who is searching for the right word.

Keep the source on track. In longer, live radio interviews, not letting sources wander is particularly important. The audience will switch to another station if it sounds as though the conversation is going nowhere.

Effective body language can help establish good communication. Leaning forward indicates agreement or intense interest in what the subject is saying; leaning away indicates relaxation or lack of interest. Nod your head in support, cock your head in disbelief, and raise your eyebrows in astonishment.

While talking and listening during the interview, use your eyes. Television reporters especially should maintain eye contact with the subject. It is also a good way to detect any subtle body-language reactions in the subject, especially when you've asked a tough question.

Use vocal cues as well: Murmur "yeah," "yes," or "huh" in agreement and say "hmm" when you want the subject to continue explaining. Personal interaction with the subject is crucial to the dynamic of the interview. (Of course, if you're interviewing on air, be more subdued and say "yes" rather than "uh-huh.")

Again, learn to use silence effectively; don't rush to fill in a pause just because it makes you uncomfortable. Silence often suggests to the interviewee that you would like more information or you're somewhat skeptical about what he or she just said. If the silence lingers, the subject may fill it with more commentary or explanation.

Your dress during an interview should complement your demeanor. It should be professional and subdued, help the subject feel comfortable and have confidence in you, and let the subject remain the center of attention. If you're interviewing a rock star, you might dress more casually than you would if you were interviewing a bank president. In either case, however, you shouldn't outshine the subject.

News Conferences

A news conference presents problems for journalists because reporters and news organizations are competing with one another and they don't have control over the situation; the source does. Staff people often make arrangements for the conference, and the interviewee or his or her public relations advisers determine when the conference should end. To get the best position, arrive early and have videographers set up in a good camera location, or place a microphone in the most advantageous position (then watch that no one moves or replaces the mike).

Another drawback to news conferences is that the interviewee may ignore some reporters and take questions from people expected to ask soft questions. Under those conditions, a reporter can only listen to what others have asked and structure a news story around what develops.

Even if a reporter does get to ask a question in a news conference, there is usually no opportunity for follow-up. Therefore, it is often necessary to ask two questions together—the main question and a built-in follow-up question.

Asking the Tough Ones

In most one-on-one interviews, the tough questions should come toward the end, when the subject is more comfortable with the interview situation. One technique for asking tough, penetrating questions is to phrase them so they sound as though you're trying to clear up misinformation. For example, if gossip around city hall suggests that something suspicious is going on, you could introduce a question this way:

> *I need to raise one last question. It's based on some things I've been hearing the past few days, and I want to hear your side.*

With this phrasing, you back into the question without being confrontational.

Box 5.2

It Happened to Me: Caught Between a Source and an Editor

At times, the interviewing reporter is caught between source and editor. While working in television news, I was asked by my assignment editor to interview the city's chief of detectives about a particularly vicious homicide that had occurred a few days before—perpetrated, it was charged, by members of a teen gang that the local newspaper was already characterizing as a "rat pack."

The assignment editor was specific in what he wanted: "Make sure you ask the chief why these kids would do something like this, what was it in their background, that kind of stuff." I made the mistake of reminding the editor that the chief had gotten into hot water over statements he had made in previous cases and was unlikely to be receptive to answering. The editor's temper flared. "Ask the question!" he said. "I want to see the question asked on camera, even if he doesn't want to answer it."

The chief gave better answers when he knew what was coming, so I discussed the general questions he would be asked about new breaks in the case, and concluded with a capsule of the assignment editor's question. "I'll answer everything but the last one," the chief said. "You know I can't touch that." I

nodded and started the camera rolling, then took a seat by the detective and began the interview. He gave good answers to most of my questions, so I took a deep breath and asked, "Well, chief, one last question. Why would these kids do something like this? What was it in their background that . . ."

The chief became livid. "%$#@&!" he swore. "I told you not to ask that *&% question! Shut that %$#@ camera off and get out of here and don't come back! I don't wanna see you here anymore!" The camera continued rolling until I got up to shut it off.

"You're lucky we like you, chief, or we might just run that on the 6 o'clock news," I said, hoping the smart-aleck reply wouldn't provoke a new round of shouting. "C'mon. You know I had to ask that. That's what people want to know."

The chief replied profanely that he didn't care and asked why was I taking so long to get out of his office and his sight forever. I spent another five minutes calming him down; he could close off vital news sources if he wanted to, but that would be in no one's interest. "C'mon," I said, "I'll even buy coffee this morning."

—WRW

The tough questions belong at the end of the interview, however, because if you start with them, you'll put the subject on the defensive and the interview might not amount to much, or even end early.

During a broadcast interview, if the subject hasn't answered a tough question on your second try, you might let "dead air" take over. Just look at the interviewee and wait; many people can't bear the silence and begin talking, often giving the desired details at that point. The risk for reporters is that some interviewees may consider the silence to be the end of the interview, thereby finding a way to avoid further questions.

Another tough but necessary part of a journalist's job is interviewing people in tragic situations. In those cases, be prepared to respect someone's grief or embarrassment, allowing that person a few moments to calm down. If a person has consented to do an on-camera interview, for example, the reporter and videographer may have to deal sensitively with the situation, turning off the camera and reassuring the subject, "That's all right. If you need a few moments to compose yourself, we can wait." A beginning reporter's nightmare is interviewing someone who has just endured a traumatic loss or the death of a loved one, but people are often willing to talk about the ordeal they have suffered or the person they have lost. For them, the interview is a way of expressing their emotions and processing their grief.

Note-Taking

Taking notes should not interfere with communication. If you're a print journalist, try to develop a personal shorthand system to avoid wasting time writing down nonessentials. Also, learn to take notes selectively. As you listen, you'll hear some things that are quotable and some things that are not. There's no need to write down word for word all the material conveyed. Rather, be sure to get the accurate meaning of the information given you and, when you do hear something quotable, make an extra effort to write those words verbatim.

For print journalists, it isn't unprofessional to say to an interviewee, "Hold on a second. You said that so well that I want to be sure I've got it all down." Nor is it wrong to read back some wording for verification. When you don't understand something the subject has said, it's usually better to restate the information in your own words—letting the subject correct what's wrong with your understanding—rather than saying, "I'm not sure I understand. Could you explain that again?"

Some sources, especially those in technical fields, become testy with reporters who don't understand everything they do. Remember, there's no such thing as a dumb question (except something you should already have researched), although there are occasionally dumb answers. If you don't know something an interviewee is talking about, ask for an explanation. Chances are, many listeners and viewers won't know it either. Unless the interview is live, you can reshoot or rerecord after the source has explained in a sentence or two the concept that the audience may not understand.

Try to make your note-taking as unobtrusive as possible, writing as little as you can and still be able to accurately recapture the material later. Then, as soon as the interview is over, go somewhere for a few quiet minutes and flesh out your notes. Fill in the blank places with what you remember and identify the memorable sentences and phrases that you have captured entirely word for word.

Wrapping Up

Interviews often wind down toward the end. A reporter can tell when that time is coming because the important or controversial questions have already been asked and answered.

For print journalists, it's generally a good idea to signal to the interviewee in some way that you have what you need and are almost finished asking questions. Some interviewers verbally signal the conclusion of the interview, saying something like, "Well, I just have one or two more questions to ask." Other reporters simply stop writing so vigorously; others ask a **wrap-up** or **clearinghouse** question, something like "*Is there anything I haven't asked you about that my readers should know?*" or "*So what has all this experience meant to you?*" The point is to avoid abruptly slapping the notebook closed and jumping out of the chair or walking away.

Some broadcast interviewers believe that after the camera or mike has been turned off and the lights are out, it's a good idea to wrap up any loose ends and check details. Another good way to end is to informally make sure of name spellings. (Some reporters, on the other hand, like to check name spellings at the beginning of the interview to warm up the interviewee.)

Before leaving an interview, thank the subject for his or her time. Suggest that you may need to double-check with him or her again before going to press or on the air. If you will be frequently using the same person as a source, you might call later to ask the source what he or she thought of the story. Although the interviewee's criticism or praise might not be especially valid or require much attention, the reaction to your work may provide insight for sharpening your interviewing and writing skills.

Improving Interviewing Skills

You can practice interviewing virtually anywhere, anytime. Whereas some parts of interviewing require actually working on a news story—calling sources, setting up appointments, persuading reluctant subjects to talk—other parts don't require an actual news story situation for you to practice. For example, you can ask questions, listen to the answers and then ask questions again with people around you: friends, teachers, family members, coworkers and leisure-time partners or team members. Just practice concentrating on what you can learn from your personal interaction with other people, rather than on what *you* will share. Listen to others, focus on them; don't talk about yourself. With this mindset, you can "hold interviews" all day every day.

Good interviewers are made, not born. Interviewing is an art, a skill developed with practice. You have to work at it to do it right. But when you do, you'll be amazed at what people will tell you, if only you ask.

Discussion Questions

The following are discussion questions drawn from Chapter 5:

1. What are some of the characteristics of a good interviewer?

2. What are the three main types of interviews and the two main classes of interviewees?

3. How do you decide whom to interview?

4. How do in-house public relations interviews differ from mainstream journalistic interviews?

5. How can you get a reluctant interview subject to talk to you?

6. Why is research important prior to an interview?

7. Why is it important for the journalist to control an interview?

8. Differentiate between *off the record* and *not for attribution*. When are they used? Are there any drawbacks to their use?

9. Distinguish between open-ended, closed-ended and loaded questions. When is it appropriate to use each type?

10. Explain the broad differences in style, content and purpose between interview questions for print, broadcast and public relations.

11. How important is personal interaction between interviewer and subject? How can this interaction be enhanced?

CHAPTER EXERCISES

Exercise 5.1 — Choosing Interview Subjects

Identify five people you might want to interview in each of the following scenarios:

- A local college student is invited to play lead violin with the largest philharmonic orchestra in your state.

- An area family is adopting its fourth deaf child.

- An elderly man is in a coma after being robbed and tied up in his home for five days.

- A 30-year-old suspect is arrested in the previous scenario.

Exercise 5.2 — Asking for an Interview

For each of the following news sources, identify three reasons why the news source should agree to an interview (the reasons should be benefits to the news source, not the media or the reporter):

- mayoral candidate accused of misusing campaign funds

- man whose wife is undergoing emergency surgery after being hit by a car operated by a drunken driver

- undocumented immigrant fleeing political oppression in his homeland

- police officer who doesn't like "the media" investigating a series of rapes in a college community

Exercise 5.3—*Asking Questions*

Select an interviewee from Exercise 5.2. Write 10 questions you might ask this person that call for comments or significant opinion responses rather than facts.

Exercise 5.4—*Questions for the Governor*

The governor is coming to town and you have press credentials from the college newspaper to cover the news conference. Develop six questions to ask during the session on one topic or issue. Revise those six questions into two that would generate similar information for a broadcast interview. Explain your rationale.

Exercise 5.5—*Loaded Questions*

The following questions are loaded with a sense of the journalist's personal opinion or expectation about the answer. Explain what each question reveals about the journalist's beliefs regarding the person being interviewed or the topic being discussed.

- Are conditions on the city's East Side really as bad as the media say they are?

- From farm boy to big-city attorney—isn't that quite a difference?

- Are you this stubborn in arguing about everything?

- Has your life always been so well ordered?

- What is it *really* like in California? (New York City?) (the South?) (the Midwest?)

Exercise 5.6—Marine Interview

The following questions were developed by students for an interview with a U.S. Marine who had recently returned from Iraq.

Part 1: The students thought all the questions they were asking were open-ended but several could be answered with a "yes" or "no." Identify those which are not open-ended.

Part 2: Rewrite the closed-ended questions as open-ended ones that can elicit the desired information.

- Did you feel proud to be an American?
- What's the best thing about being home?
- What were the attitudes of the people there toward Americans?
- Were there bad things that went on that the media didn't cover?
- Describe how fighting in the war affected you.
- Did you think this war was necessary?
- What will you miss about being in the Marine Corps?
- Do you feel the conflict has benefited the Iraqi people?
- Did you think the fighting would go on for as long as it did?
- What things that you did made you most proud?

Exercise 5.7—New President

A new president has arrived on campus and you have been assigned to conduct an interview. Write a set of six questions for each of the following articles. Be sure that the questions you prepare are different for each story. Also be sure that each set of questions reflects what the reader of that publication would want to know about the new college president. Write a combination of open-ended and closed-ended questions, composing no more than two closed-ended questions for each set of questions. Ask each question separately; don't combine questions.

- a story to be published in the faculty/staff newsletter
- a story to be published in the campus student newspaper
- a story to be published in the alumni magazine of the college where the president received a bachelor's degree
- a live interview to be conducted on the campus radio station
- a taped interview to be edited into a fundraising tape for major financial donors

Suggestions for Further Reading

Adams, Sally. *Interviewing for Journalists* (New York: Routledge, 2001).

Brady, John. *The Craft of Interviewing* (New York: Random House, 1977).

Brady, John. *The Interviewer's Handbook: A Guerilla Guide* (Waukesha, Wisc: Kalmbach, 2004).

Clayman, Steven and John Heritage. *The News Interview: Journalists and Public Figures on the Air* (New York: Cambridge University Press, 2002).

Metzler, Ken. *Creative Interviewing: The Writer's Guide to Gathering Information by Asking Questions* (Boston: Allyn & Bacon, 1997).

Sedorking, Gail and Judy McGregor. *Interviewing: A guide for Journalists and Writers* (New South Wales, Australia: Allen and Unwin, 2002).

Skopec, Eric W. *Situational Interviewing* (New York: Harper & Row, 1986).

Stein, M.L. and Susan Paterno. *Talk Straight, Listen Carefully: The Art of Interviewing* (Ames: Iowa State University Press, 2001).

Stewart, Charles J., and William B. Cash, Jr. *Interviewing: Principles and Practices,* 12th ed. (Boston: McGraw-Hill, 2008).

6

Reporting What Others Say

Chapter Objectives

- To identify what spoken material is best quoted
- To explain the best use for different kinds of quotations
- To demonstrate how to punctuate quotations and use attribution correctly
- To explain how to write effective speech and interview stories
- To discuss how to present results of surveys and material from government documents
- To summarize ethical considerations regarding the use of quoted material

---

Weaving Interviews Into News Stories

When journalists write news stories, much of what they write is based on their interviews—talking to people to ask them what they think has happened or is happening. The rest of the story is typically based on checking records and documents, some of which, like people, provide information. As a journalist, you must find a way to take all the words you hear from people and find in documents and weave those words into the inverted pyramid story structure.

An essential problem in writing any news story is finding a way to present statements that people make and documents supply. First, you must make some decisions about the worth and usefulness of those statements: Are they valid? Valuable at all? Absolutely necessary to include in your story? Or of limited value just for their information? Or just for their use of language? Or for both?

Next, any information obtained from a personal interview or a document (that is, any information that isn't **common knowledge**) must be attributed, or identified as coming from someone or something. Common knowledge is generally defined as information readers could find in any number of general sources; it is indisputable and widely disseminated. For example, the height of Mount Everest would be common knowledge. The height of a piece of sculpture just purchased by an art gallery would not be, so you would need to identify the director of the art gallery or the artist as the source of information about that dimension. Similarly, the current population of the United States is common knowledge, but the number of students in your college's incoming freshman class is not. Thus, in a story about enrollment, you would have to attribute information about class size to a source such as your college or university's admissions director.

At the very least, you should always identify the source of the information when the information is not common knowledge and it clearly is not coming from your mind. You must indicate that you have the information because some person or a published text provided that information. As noted earlier, failure to give credit for someone else's ideas or work is **plagiarism**, the theft of another's intellectual property.

In addition, if you take any particular language from someone and use it verbatim, you must attribute it and set it off by quotation marks. Presenting someone else's words in this way is known as **direct quoting** or using **direct quotations**. Using direct quotations, with quotation marks, tells readers that you are reporting exactly word for word what your source said. Therefore, anything that appears within quotation marks must be precisely verbatim what the person said. It is not acceptable to eliminate words or tighten phrasing to make the quotation "read better."

This chapter provides guidelines for making judgments about sources. It discusses which material to use from sources, how to use it correctly, and how to apply guidelines about the use of quotations in specific situations, such as covering speeches and interviews.

What is Quotable?

Sometimes what someone has said is called **quotable**, meaning that the words said were so valuable or said so uniquely that they should be printed in the news story word for word. At other times, people say things that journalists need not necessarily quote directly but only attribute, that is, give the source of their information. You must use good judgment in determining which statements are quotable and which are not.

Generally, when a source says something badly or in a confusing way or in language using technical jargon, you should simply report the content of what was said in your own words. Attribute only the *information* as coming from someone or someplace else. In other words, merely identify the source.

If, on the other hand, a person has said something in a particularly effective way, or has voiced a strong statement of personal opinion, or has spoken about an extremely controversial situation, then you should probably quote the source's words verbatim. Direct quoting ensures that readers know that the strongly opinionated words or the colorful, unique words are not yours, but rather those of the person quoted.

Using Quotations

Direct quoting accomplishes a great deal. It gives readers the flavor of someone else's speech, lets them listen to more colorful language than the reporter's. Direct quoting lends the news story an air of immediacy: Readers sense they are hearing the words directly from the source's mouth. This feeling of immediacy enhances the story's credibility and encourages readers to respond directly to the speaker and his or her ideas.

Journalists typically use direct quotations in their news stories to let sources amplify their ideas. Such direct quotations allow interviewees to expand, offer their justifications or descriptions, elaborate their positions, give details about their experiences or plans. Direct quotations are also especially useful in allowing people in news stories to say what they think, hope, feel and believe—that is, to express their human emotions directly.

One thing that quoting someone word for word does *not* achieve is eliminating the possibility of a libel lawsuit. Anyone can say anything about anyone else in the privacy of his or her home or office, but the injurious statement becomes libelous when it is printed in a newspaper, even with quotation marks surrounding the quoted material. It is the wide dissemination of the injurious statement that makes it libelous (unless the statement is protected by privilege or fair comment), not the presence or absence of quotation marks. So, if you hear someone say something that might be libelous, don't use that person's words, or even his or her libelous ideas, in your story. Particularly, don't put the words in quotation marks thinking that because you have identified the language as coming verbatim from someone else, you no longer have to worry about a libel lawsuit.

Direct, Partial, and Indirect Quotations

If a direct quotation is a complete sentence, then that quotation is termed a **full, direct quote**, that is, a full and complete sentence quoted verbatim. If a quotation is only a word or a phrase, it is called a **partial direct quote**, typically shortened in conversation to **partial quote**, meaning it is a partial sentence, quoted verbatim.

Media writers use people's statements in other ways as well. You may use language fairly close to the language of the person you have interviewed: Most of the words are there, but you're not promising a verbatim transmission. In that case, you have written what is called an **indirect quote**. On the other hand, if the information from the source is there but not in similar language—that is, if it is summarized or **paraphrased**, restated primarily in the writer's own words—then the quotation is called a **summary statement quote**.

In print, indirect and summary statement quotations look alike: Neither uses quotation marks as punctuation. Thus, the distinction between indirect and summary statement quotations is perceptible only to you, the writer. To everyone else reading the news story, there is no distinction. Readers never hear the original statements; they don't know what the person you interviewed actually said, and thus don't know whether you summarized that information in your own words or quoted the individual's words fairly closely.

As a result, since it's not a widely understood term, reporters generally don't talk about summary statement quotes. They mention only the two kinds of quotations: direct and indirect. It doesn't hurt, however, to remember this distinction as you write, and to realize that even when you're summarizing ideas in your own words, you are quoting—that is, taking material from another person or a written document.

Attribution

For full, direct quotations, partial quotations and indirect quotations, as well as summary statement quotations, the identification of the source is a necessary ingredient in a story, even when the words are entirely your own. **Attribution** has to accompany any information that is not common knowledge. Typically, for a direct quote, we call that attribution the **speech tag**. It identifies ("tags") the speech with a speaker, and most commonly is a *he said* or *she said* type of phrase.

Wording of Attributions For information that comes from a person, the standard attribution simply is the doer of the action with the verb *to say*; in print, it is typically *said* (past tense):

> *"American women still work longer hours than men and are paid less for doing so,"* the ***president*** *of a leading women's rights group **said** today.*

Generally, the tense of the words of attribution varies according to the type of media. Print journalism prefers the past tense (*he* or *she said*). Broadcast favors the present tense (*he* or *she says*) because it makes the speaker seem to be talking immediately, at that moment, to the listener or viewer, and thus stresses the broadcast's timeliness. To create the same sense of immediacy, many print journalists use present-tense attribution in feature stories to boost the story's sense of liveliness and drama. Public relations writers use whichever verb tense is more appropriate for the medium for which they are preparing a news release—past tense for newspapers, magazines and newsletters, present tense for radio and television.

When you're writing news stories, it may seem boring to write over and over again the simple *he said* or *she said* speech tag. But such repetition, although bothersome to you, is not bothersome to readers. In fact, its very dullness and simplicity enable readers to focus on what they should focus on: the content of the material quoted rather than the attribution. The goal in news writing is to play down the speech tag. It has to be there but it shouldn't call attention to itself.

Writers can use other words of attribution instead of *said,* but only with care. For example, use *announced* only if the speaker did in fact make an announcement, *stated* only if the speaker made a formal statement, *argued* only if the speaker was arguing a point, *explained* only if the speaker was giving an explanation, *observed* only if the speaker was making an observation, and *declared* only if the speaker was making a declaration. Don't use body movements or facial expressions as speech tags. Rather than saying *he laughed,* say *he said with a laugh*; rather than saying *she grimaced,* say *she said, grimacing.*

In feature writing, as opposed to news writing, the speech tag can become more elaborate and more tinged with emotion. In feature articles, you might find a speech tag verb like *chortled* or a speech tag with a description phrase: *he said with a grin.* The point of such usage in features is to be amusing and to offer readers emotional depth. The point in news articles, however, is to be objective and to offer readers a neutral environment in which to encounter information.

If the information you're quoting in news articles comes from documents, use the standard *said* or also the words *according to*, as in the following examples:

According to the report of the Federal Aviation Administration, pilot error caused the airplane crash. (Note that the *according to* phrase is separated from the rest of the sentence by a comma.)

A Federal Aviation Administration report released today said pilot error caused the airplane crash.

According to is generally not used as a speech tag for people; it applies to texts that speak. Don't write: *According to John,* . . . The *according to* phrase and the speech tag are set off by a comma. Also, don't attribute direct quotations to buildings or groups of people. For example, it is incorrect to write *"War is likely," the Pentagon said,* or *"There will be a massive protest," the peace group declared.* Names of individuals should be attached to each of these direct quotes. To judge the veracity of the statements, your reader wants to know who the military representative is or who in the peace group predicted a protest.

There are, of course, exceptions to this rule. If Al-Qaida issues an anonymous threat by fax or e-mail of impending terrorist strikes, that organization would be quoted as though it were a speaker. You've noticed, too, that phrases like *the White House said* and *the governor's office declared* are used in wire service and broadcast copy. The terms are not precise, however, and should be avoided.

Placement of Attributions   In a news story, the speech tag usually goes at the end of a short direct quotation, especially if that quotation is a single brief sentence. With longer quotations, speech tags are generally buried in the middle of a sentence or unit of sentences, in part to make the quotation more readable. You should place your speech tag at the first convenient, natural break in the language. In a multi-sentence quotation, place the break at the end of the first sentence; in a single long sentence, place it at the end of a phrase or clause. Do not place the attribution in such a way that it breaks a quoted sentence awkwardly. It should not split subject and verb, different words of a title, a preposition and its object, and nouns and the adjectives that describe them.

Even if a quotation consists of several sentences, use only one speech tag until you interrupt the long quotation with some other unquoted material. Then put in a speech tag the next time you use a direct quotation.

The major reason for avoiding a speech tag at the beginning of a quotation is that this placement calls attention to the speech tag. Particularly if a string of quoted sentences comes paragraph after paragraph, the *he said* or *she said* at the beginning of each paragraph seems to leap visually to the readers' eyes. It suggests a rigid, formulaic pattern, with all sentences beginning the same way.

In certain circumstances, however, the speech tag should go before the quotation. For example, when two direct quotations follow one another and the speaker of each quoted sentence is different. In that case, the speech tag goes before the second set of directly quoted sentences. This placement signals to readers that a new speaker is uttering the words of the new quotation:

"This year, taxes will go down," the president said.

The speaker of the House of Representatives replied, "Not as much as I'd like."

Note that a new paragraph begins every time speakers change.

Another reason to put the speech tag first would be to emphasize the source, as in this indirect quote:

Police said the victim had been sexually assaulted.

These guidelines for placement of speech tags are widely observed. However, you may break the rules if doing so eliminates confusion. Clarity, as stated previously, is a major principle of good journalism.

Punctuation With Attributions

When you place the speech tag at the end of a direct quotation, end the quotation with a comma inside the quotation marks. Note the construction of the earlier example:

"This year, taxes will go down," the president said.

When you place a speech tag in the middle of directly quoted material, you must decide where, in a grammatical sense, the speech tag should occur. If it is in the middle of a single sentence, end the first part of the quotation and the speech tag with commas and do not capitalize the second part of the quotation:

"This year," the president said, "if I have my way, Congress will reduce taxes, giving credits for college tuition and deductions for capital gains."

If the speech tag is at the end of the first sentence and before a subsequent sentence, the speech tag ends with a period and the subsequent sentence begins with a capital letter:

"This year, taxes will go down," the president said. "It seems certain that Congress will pass a bill giving tax credits for college tuition payments and eliminating taxes on the money people make selling stocks."

A multi-sentence quotation is sometimes called a **long, running quote**. As long as the quote runs without interruption, you need only one speech tag:

"This year, taxes will go down," the president said. "I will ask Congress to pass a bill giving tax credits for college tuition payments and eliminating taxes on the money people make selling stocks. The gasoline tax will be reduced. You could even see a reduction in personal income tax for all taxpayers."

Even if the quoted sentences run on for several paragraphs, only one speech tag is required. Omit the ending quotation marks from all but the last quoted paragraph, and then place them at the end of the quote's final sentence:

> *"This year, taxes will go down," the president said. "I will ask Congress to pass a bill giving tax credits for college tuition payments and eliminating taxes on the money you make selling stocks.*
> *"The gasoline tax will be reduced. You could even see a reduction in personal income tax for all taxpayers.*
> *"You will not, however, see a reduction in the payroll tax."*

When the speech tag comes first, a comma follows it when a single sentence is quoted. If you are quoting more than one sentence, a colon should follow instead.

> *The vice president said, "Actually, I'm in favor of raising taxes for the rich."*

> *The vice president said: "Actually, I'm in favor of raising taxes for the rich. I don't believe tax breaks for the rich stimulate the economy. The rich only reinvest the money. We need to give tax cuts to the middle class, who will spend the money and boost the economy."*

Every change in speakers, and thus every change in direct quotations, requires you to begin a new paragraph.

With all direct quotations, commas and periods at the end belong inside the quotation marks. Don't double up on either mark of punctuation—for example, by ending a quoted sentence with periods both inside and outside the quotation marks. One period or comma is enough:

> Not: *"We are waiting eagerly", she said, "for our taxes to go down".*

> But: *"We are waiting eagerly," she said, "for our taxes to go down."*

Placement of a question mark depends on the meaning. If the quoted sentence asks a question, the question mark goes inside the quotation marks, as in the following example:

> *"What will Congress do," the president asked, "if I refuse to hold the Easter Egg Roll on the White House lawn?"*

If the quoted material is part of a larger question, the question mark goes outside:

> *Does the poet tell readers whether human beings are ever "truly, truly happy"?*

When additional quoted material occurs inside a quotation, use single quotation marks inside double quotation marks:

> *"The raven's immortal word 'Nevermore' in Poe's poem had a great effect on my love of poetry," she said.*

Variety in the Use of Quotations

In their news stories, journalists usually vary the summary of factual material with the use of direct and indirect quotations. Reporters want to avoid too much of any one type of writing. A story without any direct quotations lacks immediacy, credibility, color and emotion; a story with too many resembles a transcription, with the reporter functioning only as a recorder, incapable of selecting, summarizing and organizing material. A story with only indirect quotations or with too many one- or two-word partial quotations seems written by someone either not on the scene or not capable of effectively gathering entire sentences of spoken information.

Occasionally, a particularly well-spoken source may explain a special situation more clearly and colorfully—and with catchier, more expressive colloquial language—than a reporter could write. In such an unusual circumstance, the reporter may choose to quote that person extensively, to let readers hear the entire story directly from the source rather than from organized paraphrases and a mix of indirect and direct quotations. The story then becomes in essence one extremely long direct quotation.

Speech Stories

One of the most common quotation-filled stories that reporters write is the speech coverage story (as opposed to an advance story, which briefly announces an upcoming speech and tells the title of the speech, as well as the time, location and cost of the event). A similar quotation-filled assignment is covering a news conference at which a formal statement or statements are given.

When you're writing a speech coverage story, you are essentially operating as the eyes and ears of those who cannot attend the event themselves. You perform a service for those readers by attending an event in which they are interested, then giving them the highlights of that event, reporting to them the most significant statements and happenings.

Covering the Entire Event

Any reporter covering a speech or news conference should cover the *entire* event. Although your primary purpose is to report on what the speaker (or primary speaker) said, you must also follow your reportorial instincts. Take note of all the people involved, how many were in the audience (were a number of seats vacant during the candidate's campaign appearance?), the way the speaker (or main speaker) is dressed, the audience reaction to the speech, the name of the person or people who introduce the speaker (or speakers), the questions asked of the speaker following the speech, and anything unusual that happens during the event.

Watching the speaker react to hecklers or questioners can also prove important to a reporter. What the speaker says after the speech or during off-the-cuff remarks to a heckler (or nonverbal responses) may provide the most interesting material of the entire event. Don't fail to report what the speaker said simply because it wasn't in the advance speech copy you received, or what you expected to hear and were sent to cover.

At a news conference, similarly cover the entire event. Stand well forward and pay attention to all speakers, as well as to all questions put to the speakers from other reporters or members of the audience.

If the event seems to be fairly routine, the beginning of the coverage news story will emphasize the substance of the speech. Any additional material that seems worth including can go further down in the inverted pyramid. If, however, something out of the ordinary happens, put the unusual in your lead or high up in the story. (Of course, you still must provide comprehensive speech coverage of the event slightly lower in the story.)

Reporters frequently receive advance copies of speeches or statements to be made by public officials, heads of corporations, and organization representatives who are speaking, holding a news conference, or presenting testimony at a hearing. Public relations practitioners supply reporters with advance speech copies in the hope that the coverage will contain substantial and accurate quotations taken from the prepared text.

Handheld speech copy can be valuable to a reporter, but such assistance should be limited. Never rely entirely on the advance printed text of a speech. Instead, study that text so you understand the speaker's topic more clearly and know what to expect the speaker to say. Beware of what is called the **textual deviate**: Speakers often depart from what they intend to say. Those variations from the advance copy sometimes provide the most interesting news material of the speech event. An obvious example would be when the speaker scraps the prepared text and responds to a late-breaking news development. Or a speaker makes a major announcement, such as announcing his or her retirement, as a preamble to that speech or instead of delivering the prepared speech.

Challenges of Covering Speeches

The good news about speech reporting is that, for a speech, unlike an interview, you have little responsibility for the success of what is said. The speaker is going to say what he or she wants to say whether or not you show up, are prepared, or make encouraging or supporting responses. The speaker is probably already nervous, so your notepad or recorder or camera won't make any difference—unless you set off the flash in the speaker's face. In addition, it is likely that several other reporters will be around, so if you momentarily fumble in your note-taking, you can always ask another reporter to bring you up to speed on what just happened.

The bad news is that all those other reporters are around, as well as the audience listening to the speech and perhaps other less important speakers. If the quotations in your coverage story are inaccurate or you missed the general meaning of the speech, several people will be able to attest to your failure to cover the story properly. So be careful: Directly quote only what you definitely have fully and accurately in your notes or on tape.

Leads for Speech Stories

The speech coverage story or the news conference story is never told chronologically. Rather, as the writer, you decide which statement of the speaker was the most significant. Use that statement in your lead, usually quoting it **indirectly**, although partial quotes may be included:

> *American soldiers made a significant impact in bringing peace to Iraq and returning the country to stability, the Secretary of Defense told a group of Army veterans Tuesday night.*
> *Speaking in Washington to about 200 veterans on the White House lawn, Mel Moreguns praised soldiers for their "restraint and sense of humanity."*

The lead in the preceding example takes two paragraphs to completely tell where, when, and to whom the speech was given. Speech coverage stories frequently begin with two-sentence (or two-paragraph) leads. The first paragraph starts telling the most important statement the speaker made, where, when and to whom. The second elaborates on this information and completes the idea expressed in the first-sentence indirect quotation.

In general, and especially when covering speeches for newspapers in smaller communities, you don't lead with the name of the speaker. If the president or governor visits your town and says something newsworthy, it is appropriate to begin the first sentence with his or her name; the "who" *is* the news story. However, as in the earlier example of not leading a police story with the unfamiliar name of a suspect, do not begin the lead of a speech story with the unfamiliar name of the speaker. The person isn't important; what he or she said is. If that person was hit by a truck as he or she crossed the busy street in front of your college or university while walking to the auditorium to give the speech, someone could pick up the scattered papers and read the text in his or her stead after the ambulance drove away. The *who* is usually not as important as the *what*.

Box 6.1
Recipe for a Good Speech Story

Advance Speech

Speaker

Occasion (sponsor? purpose?)

Title of Speech

Time, date (day), place

Cost, if any (if not, the speech is said to be free and/or open to the public)

Biographical material about the speaker

Speech "Cover"

Striking statement or most noteworthy point

Speaker

Time, date, place (time may be less exact: *Tuesday night*)

Occasion

Size of audience

Audience reaction

Title of speech (optional)

Content of speech (using quotes, transitional lines)

Biographical material about the speaker

Other people who spoke (if appropriate)

Information from the Q&A session following speech (if one took place)

Using a Quotation as a Lead for a Speech Story

Although you can lead a speech story with a direct quotation, remember the perils of leading *any* story with a direct quotation: The quotation, as a self-contained unit, must make sense or the lead itself won't make sense. A lead that starts with a direct quotation such as *"Soldiers make great peacekeepers," the Secretary of Defense said* . . . may be arresting, but leaves readers puzzled as to the particular context in which soldiers are great peacekeepers (in barroom brawls? during civil unrest in an American city? In Mideast hot spots?).

Only rarely does a direct-quotation lead adequately capture what was said in a speech as well as an indirect quotation summary lead, because the direct quotation tends to be too specific, and to make sense only in context. Generally, the indirect quotation allows you to more clearly, yet briefly, report the entire significant sense of what the speaker said.

For an advance speech story, the lead paragraph should give the topic of the speech along with details about who is sponsoring the speech and when and where it will take place, as in this example:

> *The findings of a major report on the state of the local economy will be presented at a 7 p.m. dinner meeting of the Junior Chamber of Commerce tonight at the City Center Hotel.*

For a speech coverage story, the lead should use an indirect quote giving a key point of the speech:

> *It is only a matter of time until astronomers find other inhabited worlds in the universe, a Nobel Prize-winning astrophysicist told 400 high school students attending the Young Scientists National Conference in Roswell, N.M.*
>   *Dr. Ulysses F. Osborne, the event's keynote speaker . . .*

Structuring the Speech Story

The indirect quotation or summary quotation lead should incorporate the main theme of the speech and may end with the name of the speaker or an impersonal identifier (for example, *a noted food scientist said last night*).

The second paragraph should cover the essential background: the name of the speaker if not used in the first paragraph, and the rest of the what, when, where, why, and how (some of this information can also go in paragraph one). Tell your readers more of what the speaker said in a speech, to what group, when and where, and how it was received or delivered. This paragraph may also include any awards presented or additional information about the speaker's organization or issue. (If it would interrupt the narrative, some of this material can be left to later paragraphs.)

The paragraph after that begins with a direct quote that relates to the first paragraph. Ideally, this paragraph will contain a good, rich, substantive quote that logically continues into the next paragraph. If you have trouble fleshing out this paragraph, perhaps your lead does not really capture the main idea. Consider revising.

Box 6.2

Basic Format for a Speech Folo (Follow)

There is now enough food in the world to feed everyone, but poor use and distribution leaves millions malnourished or starving, a United Nations food scientist said last night.

Summary lead that capsulizes what the speaker had to say.

Dr. Virginia Bountiful, development director of the Food and Agriculture Organization and a writer in the field of nutrition, said the accelerated increases in world population must be checked if food problems are to be overcome.

Fully identifies the speaker and further summarizes what was said.

"At present, there is enough food grown on earth to insure each human being a healthful diet and, barring cataclysmic circumstances caused by global warming, this situation should continue to endure for some time to come," Bountiful said.

Begin this paragraph with a quote that relates back to the first paragraph. It ties the elements of the story together.

She noted world population is increasing at a rate of more than 100 million persons a year, and "it is rendered even more dangerous by the fact that it mostly takes place in the poorest areas of the globe.

"It is occurring in these areas which are experiencing the greatest nutritional difficulties."

While it's important to quote from the speaker, don't over quote. Often you can say as much or even more by paraphrasing or using partial quotes.

Bountiful also said grains were being used more and more to feed livestock instead of for direct consumption—a more efficient use.

"Wealthier nations have had spectacular increases in meat consumption, draining even more grains from use in poorer parts of the world," she said.

She noted that the use of corn to produce ethanol for motor fuel was driving up food costs for poorer nations.	You as the reporter may decide this is more important and re-work this for your lead.
"There will be disruptive social consequences on a global scale if this gets out of hand," she warned.	
Bountiful spoke at a panel on the world food crisis after receiving the Rice-Pilaff Award from (your school). The award, citing Bountiful for her work in nutrition, carried a $5,000 honorarium.	This gets remaining details out of the way. An editor could cut or make this the story's third paragraph.

For subsequent paragraphs, move on to other aspects of the speech. Follow what is called the **concept/quote format**. Set up a concept, then follow it with a direct quote; for example:

> *In addition, the award-winning journalist said, blogging has distorted the process of news gathering.* (Follow this concept with a quote in which the speaker makes this point.)

Continue this format through the balance of the story. Most speeches lend themselves to the development of three or four major themes. If you identify and logically tie them together, the story virtually writes itself.

Keep in mind, by the way, that this is a basic "can't-go-wrong-if-you-follow-the-formula" style of reporting speeches. As you become more experienced as a reporter, you will develop your own style of writing and approach to news. Just as there are other ways to write a story than by always using the inverted pyramid, so too, is the case for speech reporting. Master the format, develop your own shorthand, learn to take good notes, then become adept in analyzing what was said and you'll be on your way toward being a skilled reporter of this type of story.

Interview Stories

The difficult aspect of personal, one-to-one interviews and the stories that grow out of them is that you are responsible for the success of the "event," and thus for making your subject comfortable and talkative. Listen attentively and use positive body language to help keep the speaker loquacious. Follow up the subject's interesting statements with further probing questions or pursue unusual lines of questioning. If the interview lags or goes off on a tangent, ask more stimulating questions or those that return the subject to the original focus of the interview.

The good news about writing interview stories is that subjects seldom make recordings of the interview and few have the type of memory that allows them to recall precisely what they said to you, exact word for exact word. Therefore, with regard to capturing less important words (e.g., the articles *a, and,* and *the* or prepositions such as *around* noon rather than *about* noon), you aren't likely to get sued if you misquote. (However, some public relations practitioners advise their clients or the executives of their organizations to tape themselves when interviewed by news reporters, especially if the interview concerns a controversial topic.)

What interview subjects do remember is what they believe and think; therefore, it is especially important that you understand the *meaning* of what they were trying to convey in the interview, the *content* of what they said and the *context* in which they said it. Most people don't issue accusations of misquotation as long as you correctly represent their meaning, especially if any words left out or remembered incorrectly were minor and insignificant. They will complain if your quoting totally misrepresents their point of view on a particular subject.

Listening well to what someone says is as important as writing down individual words. Don't concentrate so much on taking verbatim notes that you stop listening to the speaker's meaning.

However, despite the tolerance of most interview subjects, accurate direct quoting is important in one-to-one interview stories. Quote directly only what you are certain you wrote correctly in your notes. If you are uncertain of the speaker's words, use an indirect quote, partial quote or a paraphrase of what was said, with appropriate attribution.

What If the Source Misstates?

Most journalists are fairly generous about grammatical slips of the tongue and nonsense phrases (*ah, um*) that occur during a spoken interview. The usual test of whether to keep the spoken "error" in your printed version of the quotation is whether what you heard represents a deviation from standard speech that occurred simply because the person was speaking rather than writing, or something more significant. If the person had written the statement instead of spoken it, would he or she have used the same language? Would he or she have written that *um* sound? If not, then you probably don't need to re-create that sound in your news story.

If, however, the subject's words reveal a flaw in credentials relevant to a particular job, then the public needs to see those words. If the person is a candidate for mayor and talks like

---

Box 6.3

"Fun" Interview

Beware of having too good a time in an interview!

As usual, when I was doing an interview for a lengthy feature profile, I used my tape recorder. I expected it to make a beeping sound when it came to the end of the tape. But I was having such a good time laughing at my subject's jokes and sharing a few stories of my own that I never heard the beep or noticed the tape recorder stop.

I compounded the error by nonchalantly popping the tape recorder in my pocket at the end of the interview. (I didn't want to look uncool to my new "friend.") I dug a deeper hole for myself by waiting a few days before I settled down to write the feature story—and came to a place where my tape abruptly halted. Frantically, I studied my notes, but after the few days' delay, the full direct quotations in my notes simply weren't reliable.

Fortunately, my subject never noticed that none of the direct quotes in my story came from the final 20 minutes of the interview. But I knew I had a hole there, and I also knew enough to keep my eyes and ears constantly checking that tape recorder in the future.

—*JER*

a gawky teenager (*so, like, ya' know*), then you must decide whether it is important that the public realizes that this political candidate has that particular speech pattern and creates that impression. Most reporters would likely say that the speech pattern should be included in the quote. Similarly, if the superintendent of schools commits numerous grammatical errors in speaking, most reporters would not clean up those errors in writing the quotation for print. Voters have a right to know the educational level of their school administrators.

If a person makes a misstatement of content during an interview, you might gently query whether he or she really meant what the words seem to have said. But if a member of Congress makes a crucial error in stating something he or she should know about, you might not raise the issue during the interview but rather simply report the error for the public to note and judge.

Writing Interview Stories

An interview story, like a speech story, generally leads with an indirect quotation, relating the most significant or interesting statement the subject made. For the interview story, however, you do not cover the entire event as you would in a speech story or press conference—in fact, just the opposite. Although some personality profile feature stories give elaborate descriptions of the interview setting, most news interview stories deemphasize the particulars of the interview itself. The interview situation is relatively unimportant; what matters is the information given in the subject's statements. Thus, in the interview story lead, the indirect quotation usually carries only a brief phrase, such as *in an interview today* or *said in a telephone interview*, rather than giving the precise time or location at which the interview was conducted.

Understand also that the reporter is relatively unimportant to the story. Readers don't much care about you; they care about what the subject said. Don't focus on your trials and tribulations obtaining the interview or arriving for it. Don't write:

> *After driving through the pouring rain, huffing and puffing up four flights of stairs and waiting interminably for the bell to be answered, I finally got to interview Greta Glamour, who said she loved her latest film, "Street of Desire."*

Keep yourself out of the story.

Also, the story should not focus on the questions you asked. Avoid the *when asked if* formula for presenting quoted material. That sentence treatment takes up column space with unnecessary words by needlessly repeating the question. Instead, simply state indirectly what was said in the response:

> Wrong: *When asked if he was going on vacation this summer, the president said he "wasn't sure."*
>
> Right: *The president said he was not sure whether he was taking a vacation this summer.*

Like speech stories, interview stories are generally told in inverted pyramid structure. To organize the story, consider the several issues that the subject discussed and arrange the topics from most important to least. Then similarly prioritize the quotations and what the subject said within that list of topics. Write effective transitions to verbally lead your readers from one topic and set of quotations to another.

You may want to work some biographical material into the story. This information usually appears soon after the initial indirect quotation. Use first those biographical details that will explain why the person was worth interviewing. Less important biographical material can be worked into the story toward the end, in the final paragraphs.

Sometimes, rather than biographical information, you might want to provide information that ties the interview to another news story—something like a natural disaster reported the previous day on the front page. Then your news-peg tie-in is a brief sentence or two recapping the highlights of the news event and this person's role in it, for those readers who missed the initial story.

Question and Answer Stories

Occasionally, the interview story is written in a question-and-answer (Q&A) format; that is, the story is presented chronologically, with first the reporter's "Q" and then the subject's "A"— the idea being that the reader "sits in" on the interview. The story definitely creates a feeling of immediacy: The reader is right there, experiencing every word the person being interviewed says. The story also creates a sense of honesty: The reader knows exactly how the questions were asked, in what order, and in what words; he or she also knows exactly how the questions were answered. For certain testy, controversial subjects and for emotionally charged situations, a Q&A story is especially suitable. It is also suitable when the reporter is suspected of having a conflict of interest or the publication is suspected of being biased.

There are two drawbacks, however, to using the Q&A story. The first is that it takes longer and demands more column space to convey the same information as an edited story. Summarizing the general meaning of what someone has said is usually shorter than relating every word he or she used to say it. The second drawback is that emphasis tends to fall on the reporter, detracting from the interviewee. Readers may resent having to wade through the reporter's questions to get to the real substance of the interview—that is, the subject's responses. They may quickly feel that the reporter has not sifted through the information and made judgments about what is most important and necessary to know. There may be a lingering sense that the reporter took the easy way out, shrugged off responsibility, and said to readers, "Here it is; you figure it out."

Then too, the "honesty" of Q&A stories is something of an illusion, because most have been edited in a limited fashion. The order of the questions may have been followed faithfully, but presumably some of the least effective questions and dullest answers have been deleted.

Survey Stories

The third most common news stories using extensive quotations are those about surveys, polls and other social science measurements. Survey stories may originate from a reporter covering a news conference in which results of a survey are announced or from the reporter reviewing published material announcing survey results. Either way, when you do a survey story, you will be quoting several people: those conducting the survey and those speaking through the survey by providing comments.

Covering surveys is tricky because, as noted previously, the science of measuring public opinion is imprecise. Any survey has statistical limitations or imperfections; therefore, it is important not to convey the sense to readers that the results are absolute truth. Rather, they are a limited version of the truth—a momentary snapshot of what a group of people learned about what another group of people think, believe, or prefer.

Be sure to attribute findings as coming from those who conducted the survey. Indicate who conducted the survey—that is, who paid for it, who studied its results and who actually administered it. These details permit readers to judge the survey's validity. In addition, tell readers the sample size, the type of poll or survey (for example, telephone, mail or in-person), and the circumstances under which it was administered (late at night, on a particular day, during a 10-day period). Indicate any relationship between pollster and the organization, product, service or opinion being studied. Explore whether there is any vested interest about which the readers should know. Again, this information helps readers judge the validity of the findings.

Usually, the story's lead gives the most significant finding—again, in an indirect quotation or a summary statement. Then, in subsequent paragraphs, material about the survey's administration is incorporated, as in the following example:

Almost seven out of 10 young Americans believe they will have fewer opportunities in the future to own their own homes, according to a survey released today by the American Association of Mortgage Lenders.

Most Americans believe a home to be "financially impossible" unless the government steps in to help, said survey researchers, who questioned 300 residents, aged 21 to 30, in five American cities.

Unlike interview stories, survey stories frequently include the questions asked of respondents, particularly if the wording of a question might influence the way it was answered. For example, readers might find the word choice of interest in this survey:

When asked whether they agreed that women are "unable to think logically," nine out of 10 survey respondents disagreed.

Surveys typically ask both closed- and open-ended questions, such as *do you prefer Coke, Pepsi, Dr. Pepper or another brand of cola* and *tell what quality makes you choose that soft drink over any other.* When reporting the results of this type of research, summarize the significant hard statistical information first: *More than half of 19-year-old American males prefer Pepsi.* Then give open-ended responses in subsequent paragraphs as partial or full direct quotations: *One survey respondent said he preferred Pepsi because of "that image thing."*

Stories From Official Documents

Government and corporate documents, as well as sponsored surveys, also can be sources of quoted or attributed material for reporters. The material in such sources is usually heavy on statistics and light on quotable statements. Even if there are summarizing statements you can use, study them carefully and connect them with the original numbers to see whether the conclusions presented are reasonable, relevant, and important to your readers.

A vast quantity of numbers provides a screen behind which to hide a specific unpleasant number. Your responsibility as a reporter is not to be fooled, to study all the numbers to see what they tell you.

If the numbers raise questions, talk to the people who gathered the information and quote what they say in your story. Also interview other experts, have them analyze and comment on the government information. Colleges and universities are great sources for such experts because professors are likely to be relatively unbiased in helping you and your readers understand the information in the government document.

When reporting from documents or surveys, translate the language of the results into sentences and paragraphs readers can understand. Eliminate technical jargon, present complex material clearly and concisely, and state numerical information in a form easily grasped. Round off complex numbers with phrases that are immediately understandable (don't write *74.83 percent* but write instead *three out of four*; not *975 out of 1,899* but *nearly half*).

Citing Quotations

Generally, newspapers and other print media do not cite textual sources of information the way scholarly articles or term papers cite them. Instead, minimal information is given—just enough so that the reader can find the original source in a good library or through a well conducted computer search. The reporter usually incorporates as much information as possible in the text of the news story itself, occasionally including the necessary publication material in parentheses. For example, the reporter might give the name of the author of quoted work as a source and relate the title of the particular work in a phrase:

> *George Block, noted author of numerous books on the needs of children, has this month published a new text on adolescent development,* Living With Your Teenager *(Houghton Mifflin), which argues that American parents are too soft on their children.* (The reader knows the author and his area of expertise, month of publication, title and publisher.)

The reporter also might incorporate the citation of a magazine in this way:

> Time *magazine noted last week (May 6) that the presidential candidates had raised more than $12 million in campaign contributions since the beginning of the year.*

Or the reporter might cite a news report this way, by including all pertinent information in the sentence wording:

> *The World Health Organization, in a report this May in its in-house publication* Staying Alive Today, *argued that scientific evidence indicates there is no need to inoculate for tuberculosis.*

Remember, too, that citing information so that readers can seek it out in the original demonstrates that you are willing to have someone double check your research. You know that if readers seek out the source or sources you used, they will find the information exactly as you have reported it.

Ethical Considerations

Whether you are writing about a speech, interview, poll, survey, or a government document, your primary responsibility is to make judgments about the considerable information that you heard or read. Decide what your readers most need and want to know, and speak to them as a guardian looking out for their welfare. Prioritize the information you heard or read and then present it in understandable language. Give readers an appropriate number of direct quotations so they have a clear sense of what the original speaker or document said.

Accurate and Fair Quotations

We previously discussed libel and other legal and ethical considerations in using quotations and in other media writing, as well as the ethical responsibility not to preconceive an interview—that is, not to write a story that reflects personal bias rather than what actually occurred. Two final ethical considerations regarding the use of quotations need to be mentioned here.

Be careful in assembling quoted material for writing interview, speech, survey, or government-document stories. Do not cut and paste quoted words in such a way that your cutting and pasting do not accurately reflect the sense of what the person or document stated or the context in which that sense was stated.

In terms of the general presentation of topics in your story, reorder the information gathered into an inverted pyramid structure; however, in terms of the individual sentences, do not reorder phrases or sentences so that words spoken appear incorrectly as having been said together or in a different order. Do not make two sentences appear to have been said consecutively if they were not, and don't cut a word from one directly quoted sentence and paste it into the middle of another. Anything that appears in quotation marks should be *exactly* as the speaker said it.

To create distance between direct quotations said at different moments, use your own language to include additional factual information or to summarize a statement. Provide clear transitions from one general topic to the next.

In addition to maintaining the general order of specific sentences, phrases and words, be faithful to the speaker's patterns of speech. Don't reorder or alter quotations so that a speaker doesn't sound like himself or herself.

Box 6.4

Misleading Reading

We're all familiar with misleading blurbs in print advertising for books or movies. A single phrase is lifted from a review—something like *fantastic reading*—when the actual full-direct quote was *This is fantastic reading for a sadistic bloodsucker hung up on violence and gore.* Such a borrowed phrase, called a **lift**, is false advertising: deliberately misleading readers in order to sell them something. Don't be guilty of this sort of misrepresentation. Use quotations so they reflect the tenor and order of the language as it was said.

Denials by Interview Subjects

If you have been faithful to the tenor and order of the language, and if you believe that your notes and memory are accurate, then stand by your story, even if the subject accuses you of misquotation or misrepresentation. In coverage of speeches, surveys and government documents, your accuracy can be quickly verified. The more difficult situation involves the personal, one-on-one interview. Occasionally, an interview subject makes a foolish or controversial statement. When you quote it, the subject is likely to deny that he or she ever said those words, say he or she was misquoted, or say the statement was taken out of context. Respond to the subject's complaints as politely, kindly and firmly as possible. Your considerate behavior will be instrumental in diffusing the subject's anger. But don't admit to a wrong you didn't commit and don't apologize for telling what you believe is the truth.

Sometimes subjects will argue after an interview but before publication that they didn't realize at the time how terrible what they said sounded. They may then ask you not to use a particular quotation in your story. In print journalism, the call is yours. (In broadcast, of course, the story has probably already aired.) If you haven't agreed before hearing something to its off-the-record status, you are not bound to comply with the subject's request—at least, most journalists believe this freedom to use what was said is ethically appropriate. If the quotation is important to your readers, you will probably go ahead and print it.

Be aware, however, that printing something the subject doesn't want printed can cause everyone from you to your publisher considerable aggravation, especially if the subject decides to accuse you of lying or misquotation. If you print a quotation against your subject's wishes, be sure that you're standing by the story because what was said is necessary to the story's meaning and the welfare of your readers. Don't assert your right to control the story and publish whatever *you* want to publish because you're playing "gotcha" journalism or because you believe that you have to win the power struggle.

In public relations, the call will likely not be yours alone. Public relations practitioners are writing to create good will within as well as outside of their organizations, so they rarely print something that they've been asked not to (and stories are routinely proofread for accuracy and appropriateness). In fact, a superior may simply instruct you to remove a quotation from the story. In public relations, unless you can make an argument that changes your superior's mind, you will follow instructions. That is part of what being on the organization's team means.

A Great Responsibility

The use of spoken and written sources requires your best intelligence, honesty, ethical judgment and news sense. Because you are the only one who knows what you selected from all that was said or was available in written form, your responsibility to readers is greatest when you gather information for them. No one, not even the severest editor, can look over your shoulder to know what you left behind on the bookshelf or computer screen, what you heard but did not quote, what you read but ignored. Nor can anyone easily determine the accuracy of the information you present or your faithfulness in recapturing its original sense. Most editorial corrections to the story before publication are made to the writing, not the reporting. Errors in the use of material are usually revealed only when sources complain or when someone writes a letter to the editor pointing out an inaccuracy or omission.

There have been ongoing cases of reporters found guilty of fabricating quotations and descriptions as well as stealing material from other reporters. These ethical lapses demonstrate how much a reporter can get away with unless, and sometimes even when, editors are keeping a watchful eye. It's surprising, too, how few sources may call to complain of inaccuracies or misquotations, especially if the newspaper involved seems powerful or impersonal.

The fallout from these incidents, which shake public confidence in all media, not just newspapers, is also a reminder of how much damage a reporter's lying can do to a news organization's credibility. The essence of journalism is the trust readers have that what they are reading, seeing, and hearing in your writing is the truth. If you want to have respect as a journalist and if you want your writing and reporting to survive, you must honor that trust. Too much of the welfare of the media profession rests on each reporter for you to risk lying about your reporting or what your sources said—even if that lie may not be readily discovered. When readers and editors are most putting their faith in you is when you need most to justify that faith.

Discussion Questions

The following are discussion questions drawn from Chapter 6:

1. What is attribution? When is it necessary to use in a news story?

2. Under what conditions should indirect and direct quotes be used?

3. What are the rules for placing speech tags in a news story?

4. What are the guidelines for using commas and other punctuation marks in conjunction with quotation marks?

5. What is the format for a speech story?

6. What is the general structure of an interview story?

7. What cautions should be observed in assembling and writing interview, speech, survey, and official document stories?

CHAPTER EXERCISES

Exercise 6.1—Speech Tags

 Review a newspaper and examine how speech tags are used. Can you find any examples of different styles for different types of stories? Are any of the stories confusing because of careless placement of speech tags? Bring to class different examples.

Exercise 6.2—Choosing Quotes

From the following interview statements, decide which material you would use in a direct or partial quote and which material you would rewrite in your own words.

> Senator Dudley Pompous, in an interview today: "Of course I'm going to vote for term limits. It's absolutely ridiculous that senators and representatives to Congress serve year after year after year. Some senators haven't had a new idea in their heads in 20 years. We need a breath of fresh air in Washington. Term limits will encourage integrity and responsibility. If we had term limits, senators and representatives would vote their consciences, not for any bill their campaign chairperson tells them to support for reelection. And this bill is only a start. Then the Congress should take up serious campaign reform."

Exercise 6.3—Sentence Punctuation

Punctuate the following sentences. The italicized words are direct quotations.

1. The mayoral candidate said that the incumbent was a *scoundrel of the lowest order.*

2. *I believe we can correct this situation* the bank manager said *Of course we will try.*

3. The attorney asked *Did you actually see her with the vial of poison in her hand.*

4. *After giving it much thought* the chairman said *I have decided to release my old tax documents.*

5. The defendant said she had promised to do *whatever it takes* to maintain custody of her child *I couldn't live without my little girl* she said *I'd die first.*

Exercise 6.4—Editing Quotes

Identify what is wrong in each of the following statements.

1. "I can't see any use for this project," sneered the mayor.

2. "There," he said, "is nothing to the rumor that I am leaving the company."

3. "This is foolish reasoning on your part. If you want to graduate on time you should plan ahead and count credits carefully. Every sloppy registration mistake adds to the costs of your education," Dr. Ralph Mentor said.

4. "Jane Austen was an outstanding British writer," said Herbert Howath. "Her novels should be on every college reading list," he added. "If you aren't familiar with Austen, you just don't know literature," he declared.

5. The captain of the team looked at his teammates and said that "It was a good thing the toughest game was at the end of the season."

Exercise 6.5—Writing History

Ask your instructor to read aloud a well-known speech, such as John F. Kennedy's inaugural address or Martin Luther King Jr.'s "I Have a Dream" speech. Write a speech coverage story, then compare your coverage with that in a newspaper the day the speech was given and/or with your classmates' coverage. (You can do the same exercise with a current speech, such as your governor's most recent state-of-the-state address.)

Exercise 6.6—Group Interview

Conduct an all-class interview with an official of your college or university. Then, working individually, write a story from the interview. Compare the different approaches you and classmates have taken.

Exercise 6.7—News Conference

As a class, arrange for a public relations class at your school to hold a mock news conference you can cover, or attend a news conference your college president is holding. Working individually, write a news story. Then discuss with others in the class your decisions about what was quotable.

Exercise 6.8—Superintendent of Schools

James K. Betzhaec, superintendent of the West Cornfield School District, made these remarks during the "superintendent's comments" portion of the agenda of the school board meeting yesterday evening. Cover them for the next morning's edition of your town's paper:

"Our district faces some very difficult and painful choices, because the state has cut education budget allocations so severely. As it stands right now, the costs have been passed down to the local level. These costs represent a six percent cut for all school districts, including our own. The money once raised by state taxes now must be raised by all school districts. We'll have to make some difficult choices.

"There are at least three reasons for the state's current budget problems: the instability of the stock market, the unwillingness of local voters to approve increased taxes for schools, and the increased pension costs of state employees. And we still don't know exactly what impact the weather will have for our school district on the increased use of fuel and higher utility costs. We really have our work cut out for us. Clearly we are in a dire situation, as are all school districts.

"We must, however, not neglect the important quality that has to be maintained in this district. Safety is our highest priority. We must support student achievement for all groups of students. We must maintain the district's physical plant and facilities.

"It's unfortunate that the news of the state cuts comes at a time when standards for performance are being raised and when the schools in West Cornfield have begun to make significant progress in meeting those performance requirements. Nonetheless, we will absolutely meet all state mandates and requirements.

"I seek your support for West Cornfield's schools and renewed commitment to using money efficiently and wisely in this school district as we tackle the problems that lie ahead.

"Just a reminder—the district will hold a budget workshop, our first, Monday at 7 in the evening at the Administrative Building, 2093 Salva Nostra Drive, West Cornfield." ∎

Exercise 6.9—*Covering a Major Speech*

Go to the Web site of your United States senator at www.senate.gov. Click onto the text of a major speech of his or hers. Assume that speech was given at your college or university last night, part of the "Issues for the 21st Century" series of lectures, and you were the reporter for your local paper. Write a speech coverage story, using the principles discussed in this chapter. After you have turned in your story, look at how your local newspaper or a Washington newspaper covered the story, if at all. Also, go to the senator's Web site and analyze how it reported the speech. ∎

Exercise 6.10—*Cassandra Naysayer*

Following the format outlined in this chapter, write a speech folo story of approximately eight paragraphs from the following background information and your notes from her text:

Background: Nationally known social critic Cassandra Naysayer, who has written a half dozen books critical of the quality of contemporary American culture, spoke last night in Memorial Auditorium for part of your college or university's "Issues for the 21st Century" series of lectures. Her speech to approximately 450 people was entitled "Turn That Thing Off!"

Your Notes From Her Text: I think television is an evil, and we'd be far better off if it had never been invented. Television is entertainment for the disabled and the homebound, a valuable distraction in institutions for the mentally ill. But for the rest of us, it's been a disaster.

TV is an effective communicator of major news events such as rocket launchings, weather disasters and national celebrations. Public television carries significant cultural events and tasteful entertainment, as do the commercial networks on rare occasions. Are these benefits worth the price? Probably not.

TV networks and stations are controlled by men and women oriented not to news, entertainment and education, but to advertising, accounting, and promotion. Thus, TV news is fragmented and superficial, turning the high drama of life into sound bites and "good" visuals that often feature death, deprivation or destruction. "Reality based" programs make us voyeurs of people's private lives or encourage us to share their foolish impulses. Most entertainment series are vulgar and degrading, relying on suggestive humor and racial or gender stereotypes that someone ought to have the good sense to avoid. TV has corrupted sports, turning it into a commercial madhouse where the goal is to win for the biggest bucks and future product endorsements. We could live without these shortcomings.

The worst curse of television is what it has done and is doing to our young. It's a disastrous influence. Let's start with the most shocking statistic: Between the ages of 6 and 18, the average child spends 15,000 to 16,000 hours in front of a TV set. The same child spends about 13,000 hours in school!

Television appears to be shortening the attention span of the young, eroding their linguistic power and ability to handle mathematical symbolism. It causes them to be increasingly impatient with deferred gratification.

TV is deepening the chasm between the poor and the privileged. Surveys found that the poorer the household, the more time the kids spent watching TV. The higher you go on the economic scale, the more attention is paid to reading and homework. In effect, the dilution of word-and-sentence literacy of the low-income TV watchers is training them for low-level jobs. TV, as a curriculum, molds the intelligence and character of youth far more than formal schooling.

I'm not sure, given the necessity of both parents working, that latchkey kids who watch TV aren't losers in another way. Look at the messages on video music channels—the sexually suggestive, antisocial portrayals children see. Skimpily clad female backup singers wiggle provocatively, reinforcing the message that the sole purpose of the female is to gratify the desires of the male. No wonder we have a teen pregnancy rate that is going through the roof!

Aside from the antisocial messages coming across on music video channels or the inane garbage kids soak up from sitcoms, what about commercials? In the first 20 years of an American child's life, he or she will see about one million TV commercials. The commercials instruct the child that all problems are quickly resolved with a pill to cure a cough or go to sleep, with a shiny sports car being driven in a way to make a professional racer blanch, with a flight to Jamaica to relieve weariness, or with a cold beer to provide instant camaraderie. In the world of commercials, problems are solved happily and decisively in a matter of minutes. In the world between commercials, problems are solved happily or violently in 25 or 50 minutes.

Is there any hope? Only for children whose parents will not let them turn on the TV set just to pass time. I advise all Americans: Turn that thing off!

■

Exercise 6.11—"A Chill Wind Is Blowing in This Nation . . ."

Excerpts of a speech given by actor Tim Robbins to the National Press Club in Washington, D.C., on April 15, 2003

Background: Actors Tim Robbins and Susan Sarandon had been invited to a celebration at the Baseball Hall of Fame in Cooperstown, New York, to mark the 15th anniversary of the baseball movie *Bull Durham*. The invitation was canceled after the actors spoke out against U.S. participation in the war against Iraq. Robbins was then invited to speak to the National Press Club.

Assume the speech was given at your college or university. (Portions of the original speech have been deleted in the interests of space and currency.) How would you write the coverage story for the speech? How would your local newspaper report the event? TV station? How would the local community react to the speech? Would that influence the way it was covered (or not covered)?

TIM ROBBINS: Thank you. And thanks for the invitation. I can't tell you how moved I have been at the overwhelming support I have received from newspapers throughout the country in these past few days. I am extremely grateful that there are those of you out there still with a fierce belief in constitutionally guaranteed rights. We need you, the press, now more than ever. This is a crucial moment for all of us.

For all of the ugliness and tragedy of 9/11, there was a brief period afterward where I held a great hope, in the midst of the tears and shocked faces of New Yorkers, in the midst of the lethal air we breathed as we worked at Ground Zero, in the midst of my children's terror at being so close to this crime against humanity, in the midst of all this, I held on to a glimmer of hope in the naive assumption that something good could come out of it.

I imagined our leaders seizing upon this moment of unity in America, this moment when no one wanted to talk about Democrat versus Republican, white versus black, or any of the other ridiculous divisions that dominate our public discourse. I imagined our leaders going on television telling the citizens that although we all want to be at Ground Zero, we can't, but there is work that is needed to be done all over America. Our help is needed at community centers to tutor children, to teach them to read. Our work is needed at old-age homes to visit the lonely and infirm; in gutted neighborhoods to rebuild housing and clean up parks and convert abandoned lots to baseball fields. I imagined leadership that would take this incredible energy, this generosity of spirit and create a new unity in America born out of the chaos and tragedy of 9/11, a new unity that would send a message to terrorists everywhere: If you attack us, we will become stronger, cleaner, better educated, and more unified. You will strengthen our commitment to justice and democracy by your inhumane attacks on us. Like a phoenix out of the fire, we will be reborn.

And then came the [president's] speech: You are either with us or against us. And the bombing began. And the old paradigm was restored as our leader encouraged us to show our patriotism by shopping and by volunteering to join groups that would turn in their neighbor for any suspicious behavior.

In the months since 9/11, we have seen our democracy compromised by fear and hatred. Basic inalienable rights, due process, the sanctity of the home have been quickly compromised in a climate of fear. A unified American public has grown bitterly divided, and a world population that had profound sympathy and support for us has grown contemptuous and distrustful, viewing us as we once viewed the Soviet Union, as a rogue state.

[Robbins noted that he and his wife had recently gone to Florida for a family reunion.] And the most frightening thing about the weekend was the amount of times we were thanked for speaking out against the war because that individual speaking thought it unsafe to do so in their own community, in their own life. Keep talking, they said; I haven't been able to open my mouth.

A relative tells me that a history teacher tells his 11-year-old son, my nephew, that Susan Sarandon is endangering the troops by her opposition to the war. Another teacher in a different school asks our niece if we are coming to the school play. They're not welcome here, said the molder of young minds.

Another relative tells me of a school board decision to cancel a civics event that was proposing to have a moment of silence for those who have died in the war because the students were including dead Iraqi civilians in their silent prayer.

A teacher in another nephew's school is fired for wearing a T-shirt with a peace sign on it. And a friend of the family tells of listening to the radio down South as the talk radio host calls for the murder of a prominent antiwar activist. Death threats have appeared on other prominent antiwar activists' doorsteps for their views. Relatives of ours have received threatening e-mails and phone calls.

Susan and I have been listed as traitors, as supporters of Saddam, and various other epithets by the Aussie gossip rags masquerading as newspapers, and by their fair and balanced electronic media cousins, 19th Century Fox. (Laughter.) The United Way canceled Susan's appearance at a conference on women's leadership. And both of us were told that both we and the First Amendment were not welcome at the Baseball Hall of Fame.

A famous middle-aged rock-and-roller called me last week to thank me for speaking out against the war, only to go on to tell me that he could not speak himself because he fears repercussions from Clear Channel. "They promote our concert appearances," he said. "They own most of the stations that play our music. I can't come out against this war."

[Robbins noted that veteran White House correspondent Helen Thomas found herself banished to the back of the briefing room and uncalled on after asking the president's press secretary whether our showing prisoners of war at Guantanamo Bay on television violated the Geneva Convention.]

A chill wind is blowing in this nation. A message is being sent through the White House and its allies in talk radio and Clear Channel and Cooperstown. If you oppose this administration, there can and will be ramifications. Every day, the air waves are filled with warnings, veiled and unveiled threats, spewed invective and hatred directed at any voice of dissent. And the public sits in mute opposition and fear.

I am sick of hearing about Hollywood being against this war. Hollywood's heavy hitters, the real power brokers and cover-of-the-magazine stars, have been largely silent on this issue. But Hollywood, the concept, has always been a popular target.

Today, prominent politicians who have decried violence in movies—the "Blame Hollywooders," if you will—recently voted to give our current president the power to unleash real violence in our current war. They want us to stop the fictional violence but are O.K. with the real kind.

And these same people that tolerate the real violence of war don't want to see the result of it on the nightly news. Unlike the rest of the world, our news coverage of this war remains sanitized, without a glimpse of the blood and gore inflicted upon our soldiers or the women and children in Iraq. Violence as a concept, an abstraction—it's very strange.

As we applaud the hard-edged realism of the opening battle scene of *Saving Private Ryan*, we cringe at the thought of seeing the same on the nightly news. We are told it would be pornographic. We want no part of reality in real life. We demand that war be painstakingly realized on the screen, but that war remain imagined and conceptualized in real life.

And in the midst of all this madness, where is the political opposition? Where have all the Democrats gone? Long time passing, long time ago. (Applause.) We need leaders, not pragmatists that cower before the spin zones of former entertainment journalists. We need leaders who can understand the Constitution, Congressmen who don't in a moment of fear abdicate their most important power, the right to declare war to the executive branch.

In this time when a citizenry applauds the liberation of a country as it lives in fear of its own freedom . . . when people all over the country fear reprisal if they use their right to free speech, it is time to get angry. It is time to get fierce. And it doesn't take much to shift the tide . . . A bully can be stopped, and so can a mob. It takes one person with the courage and a resolute voice.

The journalists in this country can battle back at those who would rewrite our Constitution in Patriot Act II, or *Patriot, The Sequel*, as we would call it in Hollywood. We are counting on you to star in that movie. Journalists can insist that they not be used as publicists by this administration. (Applause.) The next White House correspondent to be called on by [the president's press secretary] should defer their question to the back of the room, to the banished journalist du jour. (Applause.) And any instance of intimidation to free speech should be battled against. Any acquiescence or intimidation at this point will only lead to more intimidation. You have, whether you like it or not, an awesome responsibility and an awesome power: The fate of discourse, the health of this republic is in your hands, whether you write on the left or the right. This is your time, and the destiny you have chosen.

We lay the continuance of our democracy on your desks and count on your pens to be mightier. Millions are watching and waiting in mute frustration and hope—hoping for someone to defend the spirit and letter of our Constitution, and to defy the intimidation that is visited upon us daily in the name of national security and warped notions of patriotism.

Our ability to disagree and our inherent right to question our leaders and criticize their actions define who we are. To allow those rights to be taken away out of fear, to punish people for their beliefs, to limit access in the news media to differing opinions is to acknowledge our democracy's defeat. These are challenging times. There is a wave of hate that seeks to divide us—right and left, pro-war and antiwar . . . let us try to find our common ground as a nation. Let us celebrate this grand and glorious experiment that has survived for [more than] 227 years. To do so we must honor and fight vigilantly for the things that unite us—like freedom, the First Amendment and, yes, baseball. (Applause.)

(Posted on www.commondreams.org/views03/0416–01.htm.)

Suggestions for Further Reading

Anderson, Rob, and Robert Agnew, Eds. *Interviewing: Speaking, Listening, and Learning for Professional Life* (Cary, N.C.: Roxbury Publishing, 2007).

Botts, Jack. *The Language of News: A Journalist's Pocket Reference* (Ames: Iowa State University Press, 1993).

Bragg, Rick. *Somebody Told Me* (Tuscaloosa: University of Alabama Press, 2000).

Brooks, Brian S., James Pinson, and Jean Gaddy Wilson. *Working with Words*, 5th ed. (Cappon, New York: Bedford/St. Martins, 2003).

Cohn, Victor, Lewis Cope and Jay Winsten. *News & Numbers* (Ames: Iowa State University Press, 2001).

Knight, Robert M. *A Journalistic Approach to Good Writing: The Craft of Clarity* (Ames: Iowa State University Press, 2003).

Plimpton, George, Ed. *Writers at Work: The Paris Review Interviews* (New York: Penguin, 1992).

——. *Women Writers at Work: The Paris Review Interviews* (Random House, 1998).

——. *The Associated Press Guide to Punctuation* (Cambridge, Mass.: Perseus Publishing, 2003).

7

Obituaries, Rewrites, and Roundups

Chapter Objectives

- To present guidelines for constructing complete and accurate obituaries
- To introduce the principles of ethics and good taste in the writing of obituaries
- To give guidance about updating news stories for later and online editions, localizing information, and writing follow-up articles
- To explain the process of rewriting news releases for newspaper publication
- To describe balanced, interesting, and accurate roundups

Moving Beyond the Inverted Pyramind

Although most news stories in print journalism use the inverted pyramid structure, which requires the journalist to present information from the most important to the least important, a few other types of news stories call for a somewhat different organization. In those news stories, material needs to be considered differently even before writing begins. Three common types of stories that require a variation on the inverted pyramid approach to standard news writing are **obituaries**, **rewrites**, and **roundups**.

Obituaries

Newspapers recognize a person's death in several ways, publishing these kinds of stories:

- **Obituaries**: relatively brief news articles about the deaths of ordinary people, published on the obituary pages (*obituary* is often shortened to *obit*)

- **Death notices**: brief articles usually in small type, ordered by the family, typically through the funeral home, and paid for in the same way as classified advertising
- **Celebrity obituaries**: longer stories giving full biographies of famous people, such as those obits done by the *New York Times*
- **Obit editorials**: opinion articles passing judgment on the value and worth of the lives of prominent individuals, as seen in *The Economist* news magazine
- **News articles**: articles about the death of people, most commonly seen when that death is caused by a traffic accident, fire, airplane crash, or as a result of a crime.

Journalists consider obituaries to be the nuts-and-bolts stories of their professional writing. Many reporters are assigned to write obituaries as a first task on their job because those basic stories test a beginning journalist's accuracy and thoroughness. Writing obituaries can be a good way for reporters to practice the discipline of accurate reporting and writing. Also, of course, newspapers simply need many writers to produce the numerous obituaries that must be written daily. Extra help is constantly needed.

Public relations practitioners also may write obituaries for a company newspaper or newsletter and/or an external publication in order to recognize deaths of members of the organization or employees of the company. In addition, public relations writers sometimes provide the media with the obituaries of their eminent executives.

Both news organizations and public relations offices often keep on hand up-to-date biographical narratives or prewritten obituaries of prominent people. Then, if any of those people die unexpectedly, the organization has the necessary background for promptly writing his or her obituary.

To journalists, writing obituaries of people who are not prominent—average private citizens—may seem routine, even boring; however, to the family of the deceased, obituaries are anything but routine. They are the final published record of their loved one's life, the last document attesting to the worth of someone about whom they cared greatly. Family members and other readers remember with bitterness mistakes published in an obituary of their loved ones, and they remember them for a long time. Therefore, journalists must consider that well-written obituaries—although "routine"—can win admiration and gratitude for the news organization that does them well. When done poorly, obituaries often generate contempt and condemnation for the newspaper that publishes them.

The Obituary Formula

Standard news obituaries are unusual journalistic stories because they blend a formulaic non-inverted pyramid form of writing with the more traditional inverted pyramid sense of which information is more important and thus should come first. As a journalist, you will write obituaries to a pattern that orders the information—that is, you will write to a formula, a template other than the inverted pyramid—but you will still use some news judgment about which information should be more prominent in the story as well as within each paragraph or unit of paragraphs.

Box 7.1

A Typical Obituary Formula

A reading of obituaries in the *Boston Globe* suggests that the newspaper uses the following formula—a fairly typical one:

- lead (name, age, address by township, occupational title or identifying description, fact of death, when, where, sometimes why)

- information about where the deceased was born and reared

- education history

- employment history

- military service

- honors

- memberships

- hobbies

- survivors

- funeral arrangements

Each newspaper determines its own obituary writing formula. It establishes an order for a predetermined number of topics, including the deceased's occupational history, military service, education, place of marriage and birth, information about funeral and burial arrangements, memberships, honors, and names of surviving relatives. (If you are a public relations practitioner, one of your tasks may be creating such a formula for your newsletter or other organization publication.)

The purpose of creating this formula is to achieve fairness. One person's obituary should not be constructed entirely differently from another's. Newspapers have enough concerns about disappointing friends and family with inaccuracies in obituaries without worrying about causing ill will through the appearance of favoritism. Thus, all reporters at a given newspaper write obituaries about average citizens in a similar way.

Basic information for the obituary is supplied by the deceased's family members who complete forms at the funeral home, which then passes that information on to reporters. Reporters may supplement this information by telephoning the family directly, or perhaps talking with a family member or colleagues of the deceased.

Formulaic obituaries have what is called a **first-day version** of the formula or a **second-day** or **later version**. For the first-day obituary, one written on the day of death or shortly thereafter, the lead typically begins with the name of the deceased and the fact of death. For a story written at the end of the second day, or for an evening edition when there has already been a morning-edition obituary, or when news of the death has already been announced on the radio or TV, the lead begins with information on funeral arrangements. Thus, a typical second-day lead begins *Funeral services for [name] will be held* . . .

News Judgment in Writing Obituaries

Despite the existence of a writing formula, writing obituaries still demands news judgment. Although a formula ensures basic fairness, a reporter must continue to be aware of differences in people's lives and make judgments about what to include from all the information that fits each category of the formula. When the life of the deceased was varied or he or she was prominent, or involved in many interactions with the public, an obituary writer may have more information from which to select. Thus, obituaries for some people may be longer than those for people who were less active or who moved more frequently or who won fewer honors.

Sometimes families provide reporters with additional personal information or with anecdotes about the deceased that can be added to the article according to the reporter's judgment. Sometimes a reporter has time to seek more information by calling outside sources or checking local public records and histories, adding details, anecdotes and description to the obituary.

News judgment also comes into play in writing the lead of the obituary. The reporter must sift through all the information about the deceased and choose for the lead the one or two points of most interest to readers or of most significance in the deceased's life. The aim is to find something about every person that makes him or her unique.

The lead combines special information with an identifying description, or at least an occupational title, with the full formal name of the deceased, his or her address and age, the day (but not time) of death and, usually, the cause of death or circumstances surrounding it, for example, *died Wednesday after a brief illness*; or *suffered a fatal heart attack Sunday, two days after his wife of 51 years died.*

As a reporter, you may need to make many other decisions when writing an obituary, but most will be made according to established newspaper policy—always allowing for some exceptions. For example, writing the lead can involve at least three special decisions. First, would you include in the obituary a nickname, if there were one? If so, would you include it in the lead in place of the formal first name of the deceased, put it in parentheses after the formal name, or work it into a later paragraph in the obituary?

A second decision involves the deceased's address. Should you give the exact address or only the deceased's hometown, city section or suburb? Burglars may prey on empty houses of relatives attending funerals, so newspapers often omit from obituaries street addresses of both the deceased and the survivors—even though an enterprising thief could look up the addresses in the telephone directory.

Box 7.2
Some Obituary Leads

Here are some common ways of writing first-day obituary leads:

W. James Hassleblatt, 78, of East Lansing, former chairman of the English Department at Lansing Community College, died Tuesday in Mercy Hospital after a short illness.

Plumber, building contractor, and folk singer John B. Constance of the Town of Tinapple died Wednesday in Millard Fillmore Hospital. He was 64.

Nancy Whire, 94, a retired Latin teacher at St. Louis Academy, died Monday in her home following a long illness.

Box 7.3

Suicide Judgment Call

As a newspaper city editor, I approved copy for an obituary of a well-known, well-liked nurse whose death was reported on my shift. The nurse had committed suicide and it was the paper's policy to refrain from being judgmental. Thus, we attributed the death to suicide, and the reporter accurately reported that she had suffocated herself by tying a plastic bag over her head.

This was a fairly new policy for the newspaper, which had previously not mentioned the specific cause of death, and the paper went even further in this case by publishing unpleasant details about the circumstances. After the paper hit the streets, a number of readers made critical phone calls to the city desk, the editor, and the publisher.

In response, we revised our obituary policy to note when a death was suicide but to refrain from providing details. (Such details, however, might be used in news stories about prominent persons.)

—*RDS*

Finally, what about cause of death? Would you include it at all? Some readers and journalists believe the cause of a private citizen's death is a private matter and do not think it should be published at all. Or do you state the cause of death in a stock phrase (*died after a long illness* rather than *died of cancer*)? Do you publish the cause of death if it is a suicide, or only if the suicide occurred in a public place? Do you give the cause of death if it is AIDS? Do you give the cause of death only if the deceased is young? What information does the public need to know? For what reason?

Such decisions typically rest on a consideration for the general public's welfare. Does the public need to know that an elderly widower took an overdose of sleeping pills? Probably not. But perhaps it *does* need to know whether a teenager died after binge drinking so that citizens can consider whether such drinking is a habit in the community. Newspapers are aware that obituaries are terribly important to readers and they don't go out of their way to make judgments or cause offense. But in serious cases, their obligation to the greatest number of readers will override their consideration of the feelings of a single family or family member.

Other problems arise as you continue writing through your obituary formula. Do you mention criminal behavior if it occurred 50 years ago, when the deceased was young? Do you mention previous marriages and divorces? Do you list live-in companions among the relatives of the deceased? Do you treat children and stepchildren identically? Do you give names or only the number of grandchildren? Reporters and their newspapers generally try to make those decisions by establishing and following principles to be used equally for everyone.

Listing Family Survivors

For some of those decisions, such as whom to list as surviving relatives, the newspaper's policy may be simply to follow the family's wishes as stated on the form provided by the funeral home. Thus, the obituary lists surviving family members as they are identified and described by the family. Exceptions to the typical survivors' list are often made in cases in which the family wants them or where the deceased has few living relatives. For example, if a distant cousin has been the caretaker for the deceased, he or she will likely be listed as a survivor, even if distant cousins are generally not included in survivors' lists.

However, most newspapers would refuse to list a faithful dog as a survivor, no matter what the family wants. A detail about pets, however, might be worked into the story, as in a sentence ending . . . *who lived alone with her 11 cats.*

Listing many names of surviving relatives requires careful punctuation. Most newspapers create a formula for the order of survivors' names—for example, giving first the name of the husband or wife (not *widower* or *widow*), then parents (if surviving), children, brothers and sisters, grandchildren and great-grandchildren. Each category of relative is separated by a semicolon (used as a strong comma), while commas separate the elements within the category. A semicolon precedes the final *and*:

> *Surviving Mrs. Smith are her husband, Paul; her parents, Mr. and Mrs. James Jones of North Beuly, N.Y.; her sons, Robert of Siwell, N.H., and George of Lake Placid, N.Y.; her daughter, Mary Evans of Atlanta, Ga.; her sister, Linda McCrae of Longview, Texas; three grandchildren; and one great-grandchild.*

It could also be written: Mrs. Smith is survived by her husband, Paul; by her parents . . . etc.

Checking Accuracy and Completeness

Although most newspapers receive obituary information from funeral directors or mortuaries with which they are familiar, a reporter may receive a call from an unfamiliar funeral home.

Box 7.4

Language for Obituaries

- Don't replace the simple *died* with euphemisms such as *passed over, went to the great beyond, bought the farm,* or *cashed in his chips.*

- Most editors feel that death, when it comes, always takes the same amount of time; it is only the cause of death that is fast or slow. Therefore, don't use the phrase *sudden death* or say someone *died suddenly.* Often, the phrase you want is *died unexpectedly.*

- When giving place of birth, don't say someone was a *former native. Native* indicates place of birth. If someone was born in Warrensburg, Mo., and died in San Francisco, he or she is still a native of Warrensburg.

- A Roman Catholic Mass is *celebrated*; don't say *held.* Be sure to capitalize *Mass.*

- Don't omit the *the* before *Rev.,* as in *the Rev. Clarice Jones.* Check the *Associated Press Stylebook* for proper terminology for other members of the clergy.

- Remember *Stylebook* order for events: time, date, place. This includes obits. *Funeral services will be conducted at 3 p.m. Thursday at the First Evangelical Church.*

- Don't misspell *cemetery* as *cematary.*

If that happens to you, be sure to confirm the reported death with a return phone call, using a number from the telephone book or information. People have been known to play hoaxes on newspapers, calling in friends or enemies as "deceased" who are alive and well.

Also be careful of potentially libelous information received from funeral homes, neighbors or friends, especially in small communities. People may share private suspicions about others: *She had a daughter who ran off to Cleveland with a casino gambler,* someone may tell you. *Must have been pregnant, everyone figured . . .* Gossip is common, but it becomes libelous if you put it in the paper. Don't print information unless you can prove that it is true.

Before writing an obituary, check your newspaper library for clippings about the deceased. There could be significant information that the family has not mentioned.

If information in the paperwork from the mortuary doesn't make sense or is vague, call the family. You may not look forward to calling grieving relatives, but most people will be glad to talk to you if it means the obituary will be accurate and more complete. They will see the newspaper as caring about telling the correct story of the person they loved.

Double-check as many names and dates as you can against telephone books and other directories and sources of information. Relatives filling out forms at funeral homes are usually under great stress; they may make mistakes in spelling names and giving dates.

Rewrites

A second major category of stories requiring a different approach to writing involves stories that need to be rewritten rather than created as original stories. **Rewrites** fall into the following categories:

- Rewrites of news service stories
- Rewrites of stories in earlier editions for later editions of your paper, or for online editions of your paper (or of online versions for the next day's edition of your newspaper)
- Rewrites of information (doing a follow-up story) based on stories published elsewhere, particularly on blogs or non-newspaper online sites
- Rewrites of news releases sent to your newspaper by public relations practitioners or readers volunteering news stories about their organizations and clubs

At the very least, rewrites require that you first decide the news value of the original story. Is it still timely? Is it of value to your readers? Is the information in it reliable? Should you use all of it or only part? Is it worth a rewrite, or do you want to use it simply as information or a tip that provides a starting point for your own follow-up story, or for reporting and writing a different but related story?

Next, if you decide the story as written is basically worthwhile and reliable, you concentrate primarily on making cosmetic changes and updating information. If not, you need to do more work reporting, organizing and writing additional new material.

Rewriting News Service Stories

If the story to be rewritten is from a news service your paper subscribes to, consider ways to change it so your newspaper's version does not appear identical to the version picked up by broadcast outlets or other publications that might use it at the same time. You may want to slightly rearrange the story's sentences, using new words. Direct quotations may be cut or paraphrased. A quotation may be moved lower in the story or brought closer to the lead. You may want to write a snappier news lead or a feature lead. If appropriate, you could combine several related news service stories by summarizing them into a single more general article.

More substantial rewriting might be necessary to **localize** the story, finding ways to emphasize the local connection or add local human interest, perhaps by interviewing a local citizen on whom the news event has had a special impact. You may need to do some further reporting and interviewing to write a new lead that ties the story into your community or connects it to local citizens.

Recycling the Story for Later or Online

When a story is rewritten for a later edition or for an online version of your newspaper, you create what is called a **second-cycle story**, in which at the very least superficial changes are made so the story will sound fresh and different. You might simply rewrite the lead to emphasize the most recent developments. You could also add new information by making phone calls to obtain updates, for example, about injury or damage figures, newly released test results, public officials' reactions, or the pressing of criminal charges.

The original story must be reviewed, and outdated or now-irrelevant information edited out. Be sure that when you do a second-cycle story you reread the original article in its entirety, making necessary editorial changes to remove outdated information throughout. It is particularly important to be conscientious in second-cycle editing for online journalism, where speed is of the essence and mistakes can be made. Obviously, the need to add new developments to the story is paramount for a timely online publication.

Follow-Up Stories

Sometimes a more developed **follow-up** news story can answer questions raised in the original story. At times, the reporter may simply follow up with basic reporting, solidifying information that is printed as "rumor" on a blog, or news on a less-than-reliable online publication, and adding fresh new information along the way. At other times, an enterprising reporter does some deeper investigative reporting or considers a local angle or uses an unusual feature approach to writing a follow-up story.

When the reporter initiates a relatively new subject or direction to an original story, it is called an **enterprise** story. After a newspaper has published an article on a business going bankrupt, for example, an enterprising reporter, using computer-assisted reporting techniques, might decide to seek information about the number of bankruptcies in the city or county that year. He or she might decide to investigate whether a particular sector of the economy is weak nationally or weak in that particular region. The reporter might write about whether a business

---

Box 7.5

An Explanation that Didn't Explain

In her syndicated column (April 6, 2007), Ellen Goodman cites an incident that makes clear why reporters should particularly check the accuracy of information they read in blogs. Goodman describes an ABC Supreme Court reporter, Jan Crawford Greenburg, noticing that Supreme Court Justice Ruth Bader Ginsburg took an "unusually long time getting on her feet after a hearing." Blogging on "Legalities," Greenburg suggested that it might be time to consider writing about Justice Ginsburg's retirement. The rumor of retirement traveled across the Internet rapidly, according to Goodman, until a *New York Times* Supreme Court reporter, Linda Greenhouse, offered an alternative, more pedestrian explanation. Ginsburg was getting up slowly, Greenhouse wrote, because she couldn't find one of the shoes she'd kicked off under the table!

---

is in trouble for a cultural reason, perhaps because there's a trend developing against an image or product. A story about the impact on the community's social services or welfare rolls when a company goes under could provide another angle, as would a human interest feature on how the owner of the bankrupt company is handling the disappointment and stress.

A reader may e-mail or call in information after seeing the first edition of a news story, leading to a follow up. Check e-mail sources as you would any other source, making sure that you have the writer's correct identity—that the e-mail source is indeed a real person who can be given as a source—and that the shared information is accurate and verifiable or, if an opinion, can be quoted with attribution.

Police reporters may call the rewrite desk when they have the information but not the time to write a series of reports for the next edition of the newspaper. News writing under those conditions is tricky because there is a chance for error in taking down information on the phone or in not knowing the reliability of your source. Be sure to verify the spelling of all names and addresses and ask which information is safe to put in the story. Make sure you have all the facts; after you hang up, the police reporter may not be available again.

Rewriting News Releases

News releases sent by public relations practitioners and representatives of organizations and clubs also require cosmetic changes so that the articles don't appear in your newspaper exactly as they appear in other local newspapers and broadcast outlets. In fact, some newspapers have a policy that all news releases must be rewritten because those newspapers don't want to have the same wording in their stories as in other publications.

Beyond cosmetic changes, what you do in rewriting a news release depends to a great extent on who submitted it and your judgment of its news value. If the news release comes from a well-trained and professional public relations practitioner, one you know to be reliable and accurate, you may have relatively little additional work to do. A good public relations professional studies the styles of various publications in the market, then tailors each news release to fit those styles. If a reporter or newspaper page editor is pressed for time—especially on a small newspaper—and if the news release resembles something the newspaper's reporter would have written, it is likely to be printed in close to its original form.

Even with the best news releases, however, you would double-check the writing to make sure it conforms to Associated Press style or to the stylebook your newspaper uses. Also verify that the story's lead is the best lead it could have, in your judgment and sense of your readers' best interests.

The story may also need to be cut because public relations practitioners will likely send more information than you need or for which your paper has room. It's their job to try to gain the greatest number of column inches for their organization and it's your job to keep each story limited to the column inches its worth requires, in order that the paper has space to publish as many other different stories as possible.

More Extensive Rewriting

If you have received a news release from someone untrained in publicity or with no journalistic background, perhaps someone working on behalf of an organization or club, your job will likely be more extensive. To reduce work for some volunteer public relations workers, some newspapers supply standardized who-what-where-when-why-how forms with space for additional comments. In those cases, you would be essentially writing the story from those forms.

With a news release written by an amateur or from a form completed by a non-journalist, you always need to do serious double-checking. Accuracy is the main concern, followed by the need for the story to conform to journalistic news judgment and writing style, particularly the judgment and style of your newspaper.

In their zeal to write an article promoting their organization or cause, some untrained individuals include in the news release insignificant material that needs to be edited out of the story. Study the article to determine what is of genuine news value and then delete all the material that is not—for example, self-serving quotations glorifying the "new," "special" or "unique" qualities of a product; background on the company or organization irrelevant to the news event; **puffery** material about how happy or pleased everyone is; and invitations or pleas to the public to attend events or support projects or drives. (Note to future public relations practitioners: that statement is probably being kind—those types of releases often wind up in the recycling bin because editors and reporters don't want to waste their time rewriting and editing them.)

Responsibilities of the Journalist

Public relations practitioners serve as advocates for their organizations and are trying to provide your readers with news of what their organizations do. The best public relations practitioners know they can do that by writing like professional journalists and providing stories of true news value. The worst among them, however, present you with hyped or artificial news, hoping it will be used as is simply because you are in a hurry, too lazy to do additional reporting, or in need of last-minute material to fill space.

Journalists, on the other hand, are advocates for the general public: They determine whether to pass along information they receive from news releases if it truly helps their readers, but not if it merely helps a particular organization gain free advertising or publicity, or if the news doesn't help their readers as much as other items competing for space in the newspaper.

What's Missing?

Regardless of how much rewriting the news release requires (assuming you decide to use it), read the release with an eye for what might *not* be there. If the public relations practitioner or member of an organization is trying to tell readers the good news, he or she may be softening, downplaying, or not telling the bad news. Does the announcement of a new product, for example, mean that workers producing an old product will be laid off? As an advocate for the paper's readers, you need to consider all aspects of the story, those in the news release as well as those that are not. Public relations practitioners, of course, need to be prepared for the likelihood that a journalist may pursue the less positive aspects of the story.

Consider other stories that might spin off the original. They might not necessarily be bad news; they just might arise from a different approach—from a local angle, a concern for citizen reaction, a need for background explanation, a follow-up development. Although public relations practitioners are generally available for further questions and interviews, you may want to interview people not connected to the organization and follow other lines of investigation.

Remember not to take the news release at face value. Even if it comes from a public relations practitioner you have worked with often, regard highly, and trust, approach what the news release tells you with an open mind and a nose for news.

Roundups

Another kind of writing that requires a slightly different journalistic approach is the writing of **roundups**, a collection of brief articles. Some are rewrites (for example, a roundup collection of movie, book, or restaurant reviews distilled from longer reviews published throughout a given period) and some are new stories (such as brief descriptions of local politicians and union leaders involved in contract negotiations). Some roundups are page one news briefs about the day's events, which reduce into capsules longer versions of the articles on inside pages.

Roundups are also used for routine police, highway patrol, or sheriff's department news, for theft and vandalism and other petty crime reports, and for traffic citations or arrests.

Some small papers publish hospital admission roundups, although privacy laws make this practice increasingly rare. Others print a roundup of church or social activities, listing the names of those attending. (Don't misspell any of the names or leave anyone out. You'll never hear the end of it!)

For news briefs on page one, your primary consideration is brevity and impact. For those stories, you're actually doing intense lead writing, making sure that if the one or two sentences are all the reader will read, then he or she will understand the essence and impact of the news. Of course, the news brief is often the first two paragraphs of a news story running on an inside page, with the roundup run almost as a teaser on page one.

Box 7.6

It Happened to Me: How to Lose a "Friend"

The small-town paper on which I worked routinely did roundups of traffic incidents, including DWI stops. I thought this was a good idea because, in a small town, if people didn't know something already, they'd read about it in our paper. Maybe people would drive more safely.

I went through the list of weekend sheriff's stops and saw the name of a neighbor. He had been stopped for DWI shortly after midnight. I knew he was going to be unhappy, but I went ahead and wrote it up.

After all, if we stopped including the names of our friends and acquaintances who transgressed, we would lose our credibility (as well as any claim to fairness).

When my neighbor saw the news report, he was livid. "How could you do that?" he angrily demanded. "You *know* me, and you still put that in the paper! I'm never going to speak to you again, you %#@*!"

No real loss. As they say, it goes with the territory. — *WRW*

For roundup collections, another consideration is balance—creating evenness to the collection of stories. Usually, the most noticeable evenness is established by having an approximately equal length to each part (each story) of the whole (the roundup as a whole visual unit). All the separate sections of the roundup should be about the same number of words and occupy the same amount of space on the page.

Evenness also typically requires a similarity in tone, sentence structure and language. You wouldn't write, for example, a colorful, casual, feature-like round-up bio of one politician and then an absolutely straight, formal and news-like longer bio of another. In the interest of fairness, all parts of a roundup are usually similar in tone, sentence structure and language, unless the roundup consists of a series of opinion articles explicitly signed by different reviewers or columnists, when each element would therefore be expected to reveal individual differences in style.

Before you begin to write roundup articles, decide on the length and type of lead for each section of the story, as well as the general content and tone for all sections. Then apply your stylistic decisions across the board as you write the individual roundup components.

Misspelled or omitted names in a roundup can be a cause for complaints to the reporter and newspaper. Therefore, although individual items may seem brief and relatively unimportant, roundups are still worth the reporter's careful attention to accuracy and detail.

A Good Training Ground

Editors often assign obituaries, rewrites, and roundups to newly hired reporters. Those stories are considered safer for inexperienced reporters than major breaking news articles because the emphasis is on writing and editing rather than on reporting. The newcomer, under an editor's close supervision, can follow a fairly predictable pattern of action in each situation. For obituaries, he or she conforms to the formula; for rewrites, corrects writing faults and non-journalistic style; and for roundups, weighs and balances the evenness of words, phrases, sentences, and the tone of each element of the whole.

Yet, "safer" does not mean insignificant. Those stories can be as much of interest to readers as any inverted pyramid news story—perhaps of more interest to the busy, scanning reader. For reporters, the discipline of writing those stories is important to professional development and to their winning approval of the editorial staff. Shaping meaning and form to fit an alternative structure—disciplining your writing beyond the inverted pyramid—is valuable training. It helps writers become wordsmiths in control of form and content—masters of language and communication.

Discussion Questions

The following are discussion questions drawn from Chapter 7:

1. Why are obituaries important, even though they may seem to be routine?

2. Which elements are included in an obituary?

3. When does news judgment come into play in writing obituaries?

4. What questions need to be asked before beginning the rewrite of a news-service or online story or a news release?

5. Give some examples of cosmetic changes that can be made in rewrites.

6. What are second-cycle and follow-up stories? Enterprise stories?

7. What are the differing roles of the public relations professional and the journalist in preparing news for publication?

8. What are the hazards of working with news releases supplied by people with no journalistic background?

9. What writing and editing cautions should you exercise in preparing roundup articles?

CHAPTER EXERCISES

Exercise 7.1—Writing an Obituary

Assume that the order of an obituary for your newspaper is the following:

- Lead: name, age, address, day of death, circumstances of death, occupation or identifying characteristic

- Paragraph 2: life chronology, including birth and early childhood information; schooling; military, employment or professional history

- Paragraph 3: honors, memberships and hobbies

- Paragraph 4: survivors

- Paragraph 5: funeral and burial arrangements

Write an obituary using this information:

- Deceased: James Richard "Happy" Hapalong

- Day of death: today

- Cause of death: heart attack

- Circumstances: in Mercy Hospital

History:

Hapalong was born in Roanoke, Va., on May 10, 1934, then moved with his family when he was eight years old to Columbus, Ohio. He was valedictorian of his 1952 Abraham Lincoln High School class and worked in his father's hardware store, earning enough money to attend Ohio University, where he studied medicine.

After high school, Hapalong joined the Army and served in Korea for three years, rising to the rank of captain. He left the Army in 1955, having served as a radar technology instructor.

Hapalong returned to Ohio and was graduated from Ohio State University in 1960 with a degree in secondary science and math education. He worked as a high school math teacher in the Columbus, Ohio, City School District for 20 years. He earned a master's degree from Ohio State in secondary education administration in 1979, then became the first principal of the new Dwight D. Eisenhower High School in Bexley, Ohio, in 1980. He served as principal until 1986, when he retired. In that same year he won the award of "Outstanding High School Principal in the Midwest" from the American Association of High School Principals.

Hapalong lived on 22 Hill Street in Columbus. Hapalong was married twice. In 1955, he married Jean A. Johnson, a native of Fort Lauderdale, Fla.; they have a daughter, Katherine Fitzhugh of St. Albans, Fla. The first Mrs. Hapalong has died. The couple was divorced in 1965.

Hapalong was married again in 1969, to Josephine W. Wickham, daughter of John Wickham, mayor of Columbus, Ohio, in the 1960s. Their wedding was a huge society event; their son, H. Robert Hapalong, serves now on the City Council of Akron, Ohio, and resides in that city. Another son, Joseph Allen, is, like his father, a math teacher for the Columbus City School District and resides in Columbus. Joseph has a daughter, Julie.

Hapalong's wife survives him. During his retirement, the couple worked together for Best Buy Real Estate Corp.

Hapalong will be buried Saturday in Hillcrest Cemetery, Bexley. A Memorial Mass will be offered at 10 a.m. Saturday in Nativity of Our Lord Catholic Church, South Amherst Street and Thorn Avenue, Bexley. Calling hours will be at the John Roth Funeral Home, Friday from 7 to 9 in the evening.

Hapalong was a member of the Nativity of Our Lord Church, the Greater Columbus Rod and Gun Club, and the Columbus Youth Bureau. An avid tennis player, he was a member of the Hickory Hills Swim and Tennis Club, and served as club president for 10 years. The family has requested that donations be given to the American Heart Association. ∎

Exercise 7.2—Series of Rewrites

Practice rewriting. First, write the lead for a story for your morning newspaper based on the following information:

Two seniors at South High School were involved in an accident when their car skidded into a tree along a deserted road. The accident occurred at 2 a.m. today. Both students, John Raake and Fred Hohe, were admitted to General Hospital. You do not know the extent of their injuries, but paramedics indicated they are not life-threatening.

Now, write an update for the early-afternoon edition based on the following new information:

You have just learned that the police are charging both students with underage drinking and the driver (Raake) with driving under the influence of alcohol. Additionally, the passenger (Hohe) is being charged with possession of a controlled substance for a small bag of cocaine that was found in his possession. Both sustained only minor injuries in the accident.

Finally, write an update for the later-afternoon edition from these new facts:

Both students are starting players on the school's conference-winning football team. The principal, James Hardnose, has issued a statement that both students are immediately suspended from practicing and playing football with the school team because of the charges involving illegal use of alcohol and other drugs. The principal cites a school policy, signed by both the players and their parents or guardians.

You have a statement from the coach, Ara Byczyk, who said it will now be difficult to win this weekend's game against North High School, South High's biggest rival. ∎

Exercise 7.3—Rewrite of a News Release

Assume you are rewriting the following news release from a local business for your local newspaper. Eliminate or rewrite what you think is necessary to transform the news release into a usable article:

The Happy Pup Corp. is pleased to announce that its president, Aaron Spanielson, has appointed Doretta Dachshund-Beagle as the new director of customer relations.

Spanielson founded the Happy Pup Corp. in 1991. It is now the third-largest pet food manufacturer in the state and the only one using a patented process that guarantees the highest protein content. Dog owners throughout the state have put their trust, and their pets, in the hands of Happy Pup.

Ms. Dachshund-Beagle will be directing a staff of 15 dedicated workers in the customer relations department. Her important job there will be to deal directly and personally with dog breeders, pet stores and dog owners to answer any questions you might have about Happy Pup products. We at Happy Pup are confident she will do a splendid job with this new assignment.

Spanielson first hired Ms. Dachshund-Beagle about 10 years ago to be his personal secretary, so he has seen her work up close for all this time. He says he is convinced that she is the best person for the job, which is a new position in the Happy Pup Corp. He has the highest confidence in her ability to deal with customers from this position.

Exercise 7.4—Writing the Roundup

Try one of the following four roundup writing assignments:

1. Gather a collection of six movie reviews from newspapers or magazines. Rewrite them into a what-to-see-this-weekend roundup for the Friday night edition of your local newspaper.

2. Write a roundup guide for a fall edition of your student newspaper telling freshmen places to eat or hang out near campus.

3. Do a roundup presentation of information about students who are candidates in campus government elections.

4. Do a brief roundup of this week's crime report on campus, available from the police blotter of your campus security force.

Exercise 7.5—More Than Meets the Eye?

After the story of the promotion of Doretta Dachshund-Beagle (Exercise 7.3) appeared in the paper, you get calls from two employees of Happy Pup, one of them a junior executive of the firm. They independently say that her promotion came after Aaron Spanielson broke off their intimate relationship, which had gone on for years. Dachshund-Beagle threatened to file a multimillion dollar sexual harassment suit, your sources say, unless she received the promotion, a hefty salary increase and lucrative stock options. What do you do? And, if you are Happy

Pup's director of public relations, what do you do if the reporter calls and makes an inquiry? And what happens if you tell Spanielson about the call and he says, "Oh, no! How'd they find out?" (Note: "Quickly update your resume" is not an option, given today's job market.) ■

Suggestions for Further Reading

Harrower, Tim. *Inside Reporting* (Boston: McGraw Hill, 2006).

Lauterer, Jock. *Community Journalism,* 3rd ed. (Chapel Hill: University of North Carolina Press, 2006).

Levi, Ragner. *Medical Journalism: Exposing Fact, Fiction, Fraud* (Ames: Iowa State University Press, 2001).

Morgan, Arlene Notoro, Keith Woods and Alice Irene Pifer. *The Authentic Voice: The Best Reporting on Race and Ethnicity* (New York: Columbia University Press, 2006).

Miraldi, Robert. *Muckraking and Objectivity: Journalism's Colliding Traditions*, Vol. 18 (New York: Greenwood, 1997).

Schulte, Henry H. and Michael Dufresne. *Getting the Story: An Advanced Reporting Guide to Beats, Records, and Sources* (Boston: Allyn and Bacon, 1994).

——. *A Field Guide for Science Writers: The Official Guide of the National Association of Science Writers*, 2nd ed. (New York: Oxford University Press, 2005).

8

Research in Communication

Chapter Objectives

- To explain the role of research in the writing process
- To describe the research process and criteria for effective research
- To illustrate a variety of reliable news sources
- To introduce the concept of computer-assisted reporting
- To provide a sample of useful Internet Web sites for research
- To provide a primer in math for journalists
- To explain principles of survey research, including sample selection, the writing of effective questions, and the use and misuse of statistics
- To raise the issue of plagiarism and the ethical problems it presents

Check It Out

A classic adage in the newspaper business advises, "If your mother says she loves you, check it out." It's not cynicism; rather, the expression points to the need to verify even the most certain-seeming information. "Check it out" is good advice for anyone in the business of communication, whether print, broadcast, or public relations.

Everyone has biases and occasional hidden agendas, and reporters need to be sensitive to this reality. People sometimes use reporters to achieve their own ends, and it's not unheard of in the news business for sources to engage in outright lying. But if a misrepresentation is published in the paper or aired on the evening news, it is perceived as fact because audiences seldom pay attention to the subsequent correction. While excessive caution may result in lost audiences in today's competitive media environment, and ultimately, advertising revenue, checking it out is always the safe and preferred practice.

Research and Analysis

The term **research** is not confined to white-coated technicians in a laboratory. Those involved in the communication professions engage in research every day. Coupled with research is **analysis**—using critical thinking when obtaining measurable facts or data and asking "What does it all mean?" when confronted with information of any type. Research and analysis allow hunches to be compared to reality, combining into a thought process of forming and answering questions to eliminate as much uncertainty and bias as possible.

Newswriters like to say that they engage in objective reporting, which is impossible, of course, as the individual differences theory would predict. We all have biases based on our unique background experiences that color the way we interpret information or events. Good research, however, tends to minimize the subjectivity everyone feels about an issue.

Ultimately, research is simply the process of gathering information and it advances to a higher level when it becomes systematic. Research propositions flow from what is termed **reasoned judgment**: whether there is cause to believe that a relationship exists among events, variables or conditions. Opinion has a role in this process, because research often begins with opinions and beliefs, as well as interest or curiosity. Thus, research and analysis are not mechanisms to frustrate intuition or imagination. Rather, they are the means of systematic inquiry about a topic to understand why things are the way they are and to allow change when change is deemed necessary.

A news reporter who covers a series of automobile accidents at a particular intersection, for instance, may begin to suspect something is unsafe about the location. That suspicion needs to be tested, possibly by investigating the reasons that drivers give for the mishaps, such as weather conditions, time of day, or light levels. Only when the supposition is supported by facts can a relationship between that intersection and the frequency of automobile accidents be claimed.

Box 8.1

It Happened to Me: Oops! Got It Wrong!

The journalist cannot afford to take things at face value; perceptions may at times be wrong. I once covered an auto–train collision. Although the train engineer's statement wasn't yet available, the position of the car seemed to leave no doubt about what had happened. Even highway patrol officers at the scene came to the same, seemingly logical conclusion as I did. My interpretation went on the 11 o'clock news.

The next day I found out what actually happened. What appeared to have been a northbound car hit by the train had actually been heading *south*. It did no good to say to one of the law officers, "But you came to the same conclusion." A minor matter, perhaps. My station had correctly reported the vital information about who was involved and the extent of their injuries. Nonetheless, every mistake chips away at the credibility of a newspaper, radio or TV station, or public relations representative.

—WRW

The Research Process

Formal research begins with a **concept**, an idea or question about something, and evolves into a **hypothesis**, a precise statement of relationships that can be tested by manipulating measurable **variables**. The resulting conclusions, when evaluated, lead to the formulation of a **theory**, a set of related propositions that explains why events occur as they do.

In the case of the suspect intersection, the reporter's concept is that something is wrong because accidents occur more frequently at that intersection than at others. A simple hypothesis is a suggested explanation, stated in terms of measurable variables such as accident data for other intersections, time of day, weather conditions, and levels of driver impairment. Based on the research results, the reporter may either develop a theory or reject the hypothesis and consider a new one.

Criteria for Useful Research

Computer scientists have an expression: GIGO, for "Garbage in, garbage out." The same principle applies in research. The research design and data quality must meet certain standards to assure that results are meaningful.

Research should have **validity**, meaning that it is relevant and accurately explains objective reality. Sometimes research generates results that show a strong association between two variables, but the results are inaccurate because the researcher failed to identify the actual underlying cause. For example, a study might test for a link between students' grades and the hours they spend watching television. Research that tests only those variables might find that the two are linked; however, if the true source of poor grades is a lack of parental involvement, the results are not valid.

Research should also have **reliability**, meaning that it permits **replication**—repeating the study generates the same results. If one study shows that the more hours spent playing video games, the lower are students' grades, a second study should find the same relationship. When a researcher's study is repeated with the same results, reporters can have more confidence in accepting the study's conclusions.

Finally, research should have **generalizability**, also called **external validity**, meaning that the results not only accurately reflect the facts about the sample studied, they also describe a wider population. In the example of frequent traffic accidents at the intersection, testing the reason will be less generalizable if the research is conducted only on a holiday weekend. The results may then reflect conditions only on holidays or on that particular holiday and may not apply to the work week.

The criteria of validity, reliability, and generalizability depend on how well the research is designed and on the quality of the data gathered. The research should use a representative sample of the population and attempt to include all relevant variables. Data quality is at times a greater problem than might be expected. The accuracy of some governmental statistical records can be questionable: keypunch entries may not have been checked, data read into a computer by optical scanning devices may contain errors because of alignment or formatting problems, or other information may be missing.

News Sources

News reporters and public relations practitioners do not operate in an informational vacuum. Those who work in the public media must be acutely aware of the world around them, especially as it applies to their media specialties. A print journalist, for instance, must be knowledgeable about a variety of topics and familiar with many others. Beginning general-assignment broadcast reporters face many of the same challenges; they do not specialize until they reach the major market or network level or begin work for a market-specific cable channel. Public relations practitioners, especially those who will work for a variety of clients, need a broad range of general knowledge. Those working within an organization should know virtually everything possible about it. A continually updated knowledge of people and events shaping the community, the nation and the world is essential for anyone working in the mass media.

Cultivating Primary Sources

On a daily basis, media professionals deal with what are known as **primary sources**—the participants in an event or the people directly involved. These include police, victims, perpetrators, prosecutors, attorneys, politicians, community activists, business leaders, and others who are thrust into the news spotlight for various reasons. Interviews with sources are the most commonly used information-gathering tools.

Although interviews can be conducted on the telephone, by mail or online, in-person interviews are the most effective because the reporter can "read" body language and assess the veracity of what is being said. Reporters should also make an effort at **multicultural sourcing**, the process of seeking sources for stories from various ethnic and racial groupings whenever possible. Differing points of view are based on cultural demographics and, in fairness, those viewpoints should be represented in news columns and broadcasts.

As noted in the earlier news chapters, reporters are often assigned specialized responsibilities known as **beats**, such as police, courts or city or county government, and are expected to develop news sources and to be aware of events transpiring on their beats.

Cultivating sources is especially important in covering criminal and civil courts because attorneys, prosecutors, clerks, and bailiffs often provide information beyond the official record or facts that might otherwise be overlooked. Reporters often have better success interviewing people in administrative positions who can still speak authoritatively; for example, the deputy court clerk, the executive assistant to the county executive, the administrative assistant to the school superintendent. They often have more information, facts and figures, because they work with the budget numbers, case files, or documents related to an issue. They can arrange an interview with their supervisor if you need quotes or policy statements. Treat secretaries well, by the way: They are effective gatekeepers who can either be a facilitator or a barrier in access to sources.

Public relations or public information specialists are often extremely valuable to beat reporters. Because a reporter cannot know everyone or everything about an assignment, public relations representatives provide a useful link between an organization and the media. Although both may have an agenda, a professional relationship is mutually beneficial.

Box 8.2

Supporting Our Troops

One of the neglected beats that needs to be further developed in the post 9/11 environment is that of covering the armed forces. The increased deployments of National Guard and Reserve units make the local military an important news story.

Understanding and reporting about what local Guard or Reserve personnel do and what they need is part of the traditional "watchdog" function of the media. The slogan "Support Our Troops" means doing more than merely shooting a colorful video news piece of departing or returning units, or running a back page photo spread with flags and men and women in combat fatigues. There have been too many instances of units being deployed without adequate equipment, training or protective gear. The news reporter has a role to play in looking out for the welfare of those who are potentially going to be sent in harm's way. It also means looking out for the welfare of returning service personnel. If they're not getting the care or support to make the transition back into civilian life, it needs to be made known so that something can be done.

The best way to effectively cover local military is to know its key personnel. Every unit has a designated public affairs officer who is tasked to be an effective liaison between the military and civilian community. Learn what that unit does. Go out on training exercises with them, if possible, and become qualified to report the story if your local unit gets called up.

Don't take the easy way out in covering things like call up departures, especially around end-of-the-year holidays. Yes, there are going to be some weeping wives and tearful children, but the story is the mobilization and what the unit will be doing. Our volunteer military is composed of professionals who understand their obligation and responsibility. Coverage should reflect that reality.

Write any story about the armed services simply and directly. Acronyms and jargon routinely used by service members will be incomprehensible to a civilian population that has had no experience with the armed services. The military beat reporter has to understand that language and culture and be able to translate it for the average reader, listener or viewer.

In some respects, it becomes the job of the reporter to serve as a bridge between the community and the Guard or Reserve units, or a nearby military base, if such is the case. With an all-volunteer force, it is inevitable that there is going to be a division between them and the civilian world. At times the reporter's role becomes that of a mediator to smooth over differences and tell the military's story, just as it is expected that the stories of other important community groups will also be told.

That doesn't mean a reporter should be a cheerleader or turn a blind eye to problems that exist or something negative. The military should be no more exempt from scrutiny than any other segment of society. But because local Guard and Reserve units have become vital components of our national defense structure, they deserve the same level of coverage given to other important segments of the community.

—WRW

Using Reference Materials

To provide depth in an article, reporters also rely on **secondary sources**—traditionally printed material, although information is increasingly available online or in compact-disc read-only memory (CD-ROM) format. Preplanning is important when you are beginning to research. Clearly identifying what information is needed and its likely location can prevent hours of frustrating searching. A good reference librarian can help you wade through the ever-increasing volume of available data. In addition to the secondary sources described in this section, standard sources such as local and regional telephone books, city directories, almanacs, yearbooks, fact books, encyclopedias and bibliographical directories such as the *Who's Who* publications can be valuable.

News Magazines   News magazines are a useful reference source, as are the magazines and newsletters published for people working on a reporter's beat. A story in a law enforcement or urban government magazine can lead to ideas for feature stories, especially if the story concerns a pilot program being tried in the coverage area. Many people do not realize that what they are doing is newsworthy; it is up to the beat reporter to tell the story. Because a reporter spends a lot of time waiting to interview news sources, reading professional publications can provide potential story ideas.

Meeting Agendas and Minutes   Media writers should also read agendas of meetings that they will cover and then read the minutes afterward; there may be discrepancies. The maps, charts or statistical data attached to agendas as supporting documentation provide valuable background material in preparing stories. If your community has a Web site listing upcoming meeting agendas, you can write advance stories to alert the public of important issues.

Budgets   Reporters covering public entities should obtain copies of budgets, budget summaries or digests. Before a new budget is presented, it's important to review the current one. This process allows reporters to familiarize themselves with how the budget is organized and to ask questions needed to interpret the new budget when preparing a story on deadline.

Court Transcripts   Court reporters should read transcripts of grand jury proceedings when indictments are returned, as well as study lower-court preliminary hearing transcripts to become thoroughly familiar with important court cases.

Academic Directories   An underused resource is the talent available at local colleges and universities. Most institutions of higher education publish a directory that lists the areas of expertise of faculty members who are generally available to media outlets. In addition, the *Directory of American Scholars* and *Who's Who in American Colleges and Universities* publish lists of resource people in various fields.

Indexes and Abstracts   Other good resources are the indexes of the *New York Times* and the *Washington Post*, *News Bank Index*, and *Canada News Index*. The *Reader's Guide to Periodical Literature* has long been a good source for articles published in various magazines, and specialized magazine indexes are available in the arts, humanities, sciences and social sciences. Abstracts supplement indexes with brief summaries of papers, articles and other published materials.

Government Reports   Local, regional, state and federal governmental agencies publish a wealth of data valuable for general background information, as well as for writing specific news articles. At the federal level, Census Bureau reports provide authoritative snapshots about communities and regions, as does the *Statistical Abstract of the United States*, an annual U.S.

Department of Commerce report that contains information on various aspects of American society. If you are covering a story with an overseas news peg, consult the U.S. Department of State's area reports about specific countries, or the Central Intelligence Agency's (CIA) *World Factbook*. Publications, reports and news releases are distributed by a number of governmental agencies, some of which provide telephone or online assistance.

Other Published Reference Materials   Written records, newsletters or annual reports of city or county agencies, school districts, major businesses and charitable organizations provide good background material. *The Encyclopedia of Associations* is an excellent source of information about organizations, their services and the informational materials provided. Other good sources include the *Clearinghouse Directory*, *Information Industry Directory*, and *Instant Information*.

Because online or database charges can be expensive, fixed databases are increasingly stored on CD-ROMs. This technology combines print, visual and sound information on prerecorded digital CDs designed to store and replay data on a computer. CD-ROMs offer economical access to unchanging information such as census data, budgetary information or economic statistics. Examples include Educational Resources Information Center of the U.S. Department of Education (ERIC); the Federal Data Base Finder; InfoTrac; Business Index; Medline; and encyclopedias, dictionaries, and other specialized information sources. Using keyword searches that can be converted into topical bibliographies, the *Guide to Reference Sources* contains thousands of entries to reference CD-ROMs and online databases, laser disks and other titles. Commercial publishers are developing CD-ROMs to accompany textbooks, as well as hypertext databases on CD-ROMs that contain as much as a year's worth of scholarly journals.

Box 8.3

Using a Newspaper as a Reference Resource

Don't overlook the morning newspapers as good sources of information. As a television reporter, I relied on newspaper reports for background of stories on my beat. In covering city and county legislative sessions, for instance, the paper often had an in-depth advance of the upcoming meeting, issues and personalities. Of course, I still had to comb through the often 10- to 12-page agenda for other stories, especially those that would lend themselves to visual treatment. After my meeting report was written, I would keep in my file a copy of my script, a clip of the newspaper follow-up story and my meeting notes. Because there was always the chance that one of the minor issues we did not cover could erupt into news three weeks or three months later, the newspaper story was a valuable resource because of its greater depth than my TV version.

Newspapers often provided leads for advance stories. Because newspapers tend to dominate their markets, many public relations professionals and those working for community organizations sent news releases only to the paper, forgetting about the broadcast media. Advance stories were often routed to the assignment editor for inclusion in the monthly assignments book—although the assignment editor read the same newspapers and often clipped the same leads as I did.

—WRW

If you are covering a beat, get your name on the mailing lists of organizations that distribute news releases and information about it, and join e-mail lists related to the topic. Finally, a most thorough and timely reference source is local and regional newspapers; reading them should be a daily ritual, even on your days off.

Computer-Assisted Reporting

Until recently, investigative reporting required sifting through masses of information, often coming up empty-handed because the reporter did not know exactly what to look for. For years, federal, state and local governments have maintained public records from aviation to zoning, but until the early 1980s, most were inaccessible to journalists. When the computer revolution hit newsrooms, it became possible to transfer data from bulky government-controlled mainframe computers to reporters' personal computers. This technology led to what is probably the biggest change in news reporting methods since the invention of the typewriter and the telephone: computer-assisted reporting (CAR). At most newspapers, the morgue—once a collection of musty envelopes filled with clips—has been computerized with background stories filed according to keywords.

Computer-assisted reporting involves the use of a storage and retrieval system to access, organize and analyze large columns of data from various electronic database sources. It has become an essential part of daily beat reporting, and all the recent Pulitzer Prizes for investigative reporting have been awarded to newspapers using CAR techniques. In addition to the traditional attributes of a good journalist, to be successful today in communicating via the mass media, you need the computer skills to understand how to access electronic resources and build databases and spreadsheets.

The primary advantage of database reporting is the convenience of being able to gather vast amounts of information without leaving the newsroom. Increasingly, print and broadcast reporters use online sources for daily assignments by examining what has already been written about a subject or by generating names of experts as interview sources.

Governments are placing more public records in full-text electronic storage, which means that all words in the database have been indexed and are searchable, with the actual text of selected records displayed on the user's screen. With a few keystrokes, reporters can access databases through keywords or menus to generate on-screen data that would have taken months to research otherwise. Because databases show local, national or international trends, cross-indexing eliminates wading through extraneous data and allows reporters to fit together seemingly unrelated pieces of information. However, professionals caution not to overload CAR stories with data, and they also recommend that personal interviews be included to provide perspective and interest.

Commercial Databases

The following are several commercial database systems for newsroom use. All are continually undergoing expansion and improvement, and provide an amazing amount of data, information and resources.

- Lexis/Nexis (www.lexisnexis.com), commonly available in college and university libraries, provides research service information to legal, corporate, risk management, government, law enforcement, accounting and academic markets. It publishes legal, tax, and regulatory information via online, hardcopy print and CD-ROM formats. Its Web site offers comprehensive company, country, financial, demographic, market research, and industry reports from more than five billion searchable documents, utilizing more than 32,000 legal, news and business sources. It provides access to thousands of worldwide newspapers, magazines, trade journals, industry newsletters, tax and accounting information, financial data, public records, legislative records, and data on companies and their executives. Its academic and library Web services are tailored to meet the needs of researchers and students.

- Dialog (www.dialog.com), which bills itself as the world's first online information retrieval system, offers (according to its Web site) depth and breadth of content coupled with the ability to search with precision and speed from a collection of more than 900 databases that deliver more than 17 million document pages per month. The service includes "articles and reports from thousands of real-time news feeds, newspapers, broadcast transcripts and trade publications" designed to meet specific needs of clients.

- Factiva (www.factiva.com) from Dow Jones combines the *Wall Street Journal*, the *Financial Times*, Associated Press and the content of Dow Jones and Reuters Newswires, and offers multilingual content of nearly 10,000 sources from 152 countries in 22 languages. The service provides content from newspapers around the world and from more than 370 continuously-updated newswires, as well as television and radio transcripts and key magazines.

- ProQuest online information service (www.proquest.com) offers more than 100 products and services for research and learning to schools, colleges and universities, and libraries, accessed at the rate of more than 2.5 million page views per day. Users have access to more than 4,000 newspapers and periodicals, more than a million dissertations, as well as a wide range of other content.

- Ingenta (www.ingenta.com) is a library-based service that offers access to more than 14 million articles in approximately 27,000 academic and professional publications, including 5,400 full-text online journals. According to its Web site, Ingenta has agreements with more than 250 publishers that grant subscribers access to the online full text of thousands of publications free of charge. Non-subscriber researchers may purchase individual articles on a pay-per-view basis.

- PR Newswire (www.prnewswire.com) is a leading source of corporate news for media, business, and financial communities and private investors. With offices in 11 countries, it sends news to outlets in 135 countries in 40 languages. Its Internet, satellite and fax network provides targeted or mass distribution of news releases, video, audio and photos to consumers. More than 70,000 journalists access the content of PR Newswire and more than 22,000 media outlets receive content. PR Newswire for Journalists provides individualized news and advisories.

- ProfNet (www2.profnet.com), a subsidiary of PR Newswire, is a collaborative network of 14,000 public information officers representing thousands of organizations in

North America and Europe. Linked by the Internet to provide journalists with convenient access to 20,000 expert sources, queries may be sent anywhere in the world. ProfNet 3.0, their Web site declares, permits communicators to not only filter and fine-tune interactions with reporters, but with "non-journalist professionals, including authors, bloggers, meeting planners, government officials, academic and corporate researchers, publishers and analysts."

- Time Life Photo Collection (www.timelifepictures.com) has millions of pictures from decades of photojournalism. Registered users may browse the collection, obtain information about the photos and purchase licenses. Getty Images (www. gettyimages.com) allows one to search, purchase and download photography, illustration, film and editorial images. Business users can create, manage, share and distribute marketing materials, using a centralized library to store materials and application tools.

The Internet

The **Internet** is a virtual world of information, communication, entertainment and commerce, with text, pictures and sound. Originally set up in the late 1960s to permit defense scientists and academics to exchange information, the Net grew rapidly during the 1980s as software was developed to make access easier. Now, more than 75 percent of the U.S. population regularly accesses the Internet or online services. Companies have created private "intranets" for internal-organization communication and "extranets" with business links to customers, service providers and suppliers. American research universities and the government are building Internet II, which is dedicated to academic traffic without commercial users, as the Internet was less than 20 years ago.

Users access the Internet through commercial online services or by **Internet service providers** (ISPs) that provide basic Internet access with easy-to-use software, technical support and unlimited access at an increasingly-lower monthly cost.

The World Wide Web

An offshoot of the Internet that has seen an explosion in growth and use is the **World Wide Web (WWW)**, with millions of sites for information, entertainment and interactivity. Web sites feature home pages with hyperlinks of underlined or highlighted text; clicking on the image draws you deeper into information at the site. Web-based browsers have transformed the Web and Internet from an exotic toy into an essential communications tool.

A Valuable Resource

One advantage of the Web for a public relations writer is the ability to interact with people looking for information about an organization. Although some hits to a Web site are from "surfers"—users who are merely browsing—a high proportion come from people seeking specific information. Web sites and e-mail provide public relations practitioners with access to those individuals. The Web also allows the easy transfer of multimedia applications viewable by anyone with the required software so that sound, photographs or increasingly-sophisticated video can be incorporated in publications and presentations.

The Internet is a valuable journalistic research and public information resource, providing access to Web sites that offer constantly updated sources and background material. Updated Web sites are usually more reliable and useful than dated ones; the sites of governmental agencies, educational institutions and national organizations are generally the most credible. There is no problem with going to a Web site that has a bias, however. The Doctors Without Borders site, for example, has a link to the 10 most underreported humanitarian crises during the past year, its effort to bring those stories to the attention of journalists. There's nothing wrong with using its information if you are aware of the bias and you verify statistical information with another source (such as the U.S. Department of State, the United Nations High Commissioner for Refugees, or other human rights organizations). Likewise, the Web site of Greenpeace or other environmental organizations have their particular perspectives. Cross-check the data with United Nations statistics, the U.S. Environmental Protection Agency (EPA), or industry sources. If you're doing a story on gun control, check the Web sites of gun-control advocates and the National Rifle Association. Your story might not only be the significance of the data, but also who's manipulating the numbers and for what purpose.

CAR reporters recommend that when you download or copy Web information, copy the Web address and paste it into your document. Web sites are frequently discontinued; without the URL, it becomes difficult to attribute a source. A few words of caution are appropriate, too: So many Web sites are available that there are bound to be some ringers. For the most part, the Internet is not juried as is traditionally published material, and something is not fact just because it's on the Internet. Hate groups and conspiracy buffs have found the Internet an effective way to chat with kindred spirits and distribute their distorted versions of truth. More than one person or organization can share an e-mail address, and e-mail addresses and home pages can be faked. (Even the CIA and U.S. Department of Justice have had problems with hackers breaking into their Web pages and changing content.) Journalists using Internet information should pass along doubts as well as facts to their readers and must apply their news judgment even more critically to Internet sources.

The Internet as an Information Source

Search Engines

Finding data, statistics, and information of all kinds has become progressively easier in the recent past with the development of more sophisticated search engines that wend their way through the more than three billion documents stored on various WWW servers around the world. **Search engines** are simply Web sites that help find information on the Internet. Each compiles a database from robot programs that travel the Web looking for sites based on criteria spelled out by search engine programmers, who rank them in order of importance. The more specific you can be when searching, the better. Generally, if you combine words or phrases that likely appear in a document or Web site, you will be more successful. Most search engines provide search tips on their main page or make suggestions about how to refine a search if the initial results are too broad. Usually, the first two or three pages of search results will be the most helpful. Read the descriptors and addresses to effectively select the appropriate Web site to visit.

The question of which search engine to use is often a matter of preference, familiarity and comfort, as well as what you are looking for. There are two basic types of search engines: **individual**, which scan their own Web databases, and **meta**, which search databases of multiple individual search engines simultaneously.

Google.com, the leading search engine, ranks sites by popularity. It is particularly good at tracking down distinctive words or phrases. **Yahoo.com** provides access to communications tools, forums, shopping and search services, personalized content and branded programming. Microsoft's **MSN.com** provides news and entertainment in addition to basic search capabilities.

There have been consolidations among the search engines in the past several years. Other popular crawler-based search engines, designed to follow hyperlinks throughout a Web site, include the following:

- **Ask.com**, which uses a system of "subject-specific popularity" to select pages considered expert on the topic of a search and ranks a site based on the number of same-subject pages referencing the topic being searched.
- **AlltheWeb.com** includes billions of Web pages, millions of PDF and Microsoft Word files, and supports searches in 36 languages. News Search indexes hundreds of stories from around the world every minute, and image, audio and video searches include hundreds of millions of multimedia files.
- **AltaVista.com** provides integrated search results, including multilingual and translation support, with access to Web pages, multimedia files, and up-to-the-minute news. Topical searches place information into highly segmented indexes, helping users to refine their searches and quickly access the most pertinent information.

Meta search engines search clusters of search engines. Among them are:

- **Metacrawler.com**, which simultaneously searches a combined pool of the Internet's top search engines for the best results, instead of obtaining results from only one search engine. It also provides users the option to search for images, audio, video, news, yellow pages and white pages.
- **IxQuick.com** prioritizes results by relevance of keywords, deletes duplications and searches in 17 languages, including Chinese, Japanese and Korean. Other features include an international phone directory to find people and businesses and an international price comparison, with more that 5,000 merchants, to find the lowest prices worldwide.
- **Copernic.com** queries more than 90 search engines grouped into categories, combines their results, removes duplicates and keeps only the very best of the information. It also saves searches for later use. Users can click on a previous search to instantly see, modify or update the results.
- **SurfWax.com** delivers results from a broad range of sources, including the visible and invisible Web, news feeds and intranets. Users can construct their own meta-search tools to meet information needs. Features include LookAhead, which helps

users find, summarize and use information. The site has a blog search feature, News Accumulator provides a choice of 50,000 news topics from 4,200 news sources, WikiWax allows searches of Wikipedia, and ShopEasier is a tool for shopping the Web.

One caution about meta-search engines is that they only come up with about 10 percent of search results from the search engines they visit. However, with potentially thousands of relevant Web sites, perhaps the top 10 percent is a fairly adequate return.

Directories

Internet directories are human-selected Web sites grouped into categories and subcategories by editors and experts. To search, one goes from a general concept into more specific subtopics until the desired information is reached. Useful directories include the following:

- **About.com** features nearly 600 expert "guides" on hundreds of topics, listed alphabetically. There is a link with journalism-related articles at http://journalism.about. com/.
- **Refdesk.com** bills itself as "the single best source for facts on the Net," with the stated goal of indexing quality Internet sites and assisting visitors in navigating them. More than 20,000 links include national and international newspapers on the Web, almanacs, maps, and directories of people and places.
- **AcademicInfo.net**, an online subject directory of educational resources for high school and college students, has detailed academic subject links, especially for country studies, a reference desk with directories and search engines, and background links for news and analysis of important world events.
- **SearchEngines.net** has specialized, foreign language and "pick of the best" search engines and directories to incorporate into personal Web sites.
- **Infomine.ucr.edu**, a virtual library of more than 110,000 Internet resources for university faculty, students, and research staff compiled by university librarians, contains useful Internet resources such as databases, electronic journals, electronic books, bulletin boards, mailing lists, online library card catalogs, articles and many other types of information.
- **Librarians' Index to the Internet**, www.lii.org, with its motto, "Websites You Can Trust," is an efficient, searchable annotated subject directory of Internet resources selected by librarians for their usefulness to public library users.

Online News

Major newspapers, magazines and broadcast outlets have established Internet sites as a means of distributing specialized publications. The easiest way to find a Web publication, of course, is to run the name through your favorite browser. For a wider base of publications, there are several good directories:

- **NewsDirectory** (www.newsdirectory.com), with more than 14,000 free worldwide links to English-language newspapers, magazines, television stations, colleges, visitor bureaus and governmental agencies.
- **ABYZ Newslinks** (www.abyznewslinks.com) has links to hundreds of online news sources from around the world. Although primarily composed of newspapers, it also includes broadcast stations, Internet services, magazines and press agencies.
- **World News Connection** (http://wnc.dialog.com) is a valuable research tool for those needing to monitor non-U.S. media sources provided by the Open Source Center, a governmental agency. It monitors and collects news and information from thousands of non-U.S. media sources, providing daily news from foreign countries.
- **Google News** (www.google.com/news) presents news and information from approximately 4,500 news sources worldwide, automatically arranged to present the most relevant items first. Headlines, stories and photographs are updated continuously throughout the day from thousands of sources worldwide, allowing users to compare how different news organizations report the same story. The Google news service is compiled solely by computer algorithms, without human editors. Although the sources of the news vary in perspective and editorial approach, inclusion is without regard to political viewpoint or ideology, guided by the editorial judgment of online news organizations to determine which stories are most prominent and deserving of inclusion.

Major online U.S. newspapers include the **New York Times** (www.nytimes.com), the **Washington Post** (www.washingtonpost.com); the **Chicago Tribune** (www.chicagotribune.com), the **Los Angeles Times** (www.latimes.com), and the **Wall Street Journal** (www.wsj.com). Even smaller-market newspapers have gone on the Internet, providing a useful source of "local" news, especially in cases of disaster. Various magazines are just a mouse click away through your favorite browser. Radio and television stations are broadcasting on the Web. Access to news is global, thanks to the technology. Popular international Web sites include Britain's **Guardian** newspaper (www.guardian.co.uk) and the **British Broadcasting Corporation** (news.bbc.co.uk).

Government Databases

Thousands of federal government databases have been placed on the Internet including the following:

- **USA.gov**, the U.S. government's official web portal (www.usa.gov), "a rich treasure of online information, services, and resources," provides official information and services from the federal government. The site contains a listing of government departments and commissions, state government agencies, local government offices and services, and Native American tribal listings.
- The **White House** Web site (www.whitehouse.gov) has press releases and the text of presidential speeches and briefings, with links to cabinet and executive branch officials. Position papers reflecting the administration's views on issues such as the

economy, defense, education, immigration and national security, among other topics, are part of the site.

- The **Library of Congress** (www.loc.gov) provides library catalogs with print, multimedia and online resources, historic maps, photos and documents with audio and video, and a "global gateway" of multilingual resources on world culture. A section known as "Thomas" (as in Jefferson) provides federal legislative information, including bills and resolutions, Congressional activity and committee information.

- The **House of Representatives** home page (www.house.gov) provides information about members and committees, listing members according to state, and allows the finding of a bill, amendment or debate. There are links to legislative branch agencies, including the Congressional budget office, the cabinet, Supreme Court, and state and local government. The **Senate** Web site, with similar information, is www.senate.gov. Most **State** sites are found at www.state.xx.us, with the two-letter state ZIP abbreviation substituted for "xx."

- The **Supreme Court** Web site (www.supremecourtus.gov) has biographies of current justices and features an historical overview of the court and its traditions. It archives court decisions and provides a calendar of cases and scheduled arguments.

- **DefenseLINK** (www.defenselink.mil), the official Web site for the U.S. Defense Department and the starting point for finding information about defense policy, organizations, functions and operations, provides access to department news releases, photographs, contract awards and briefing transcripts.

- The **Central Intelligence Agency** (www.cia.gov) publishes a World Factbook, a detailed almanac that includes information about every country and territory in the world, and a directory of all world leaders and members of national cabinets.

- The **Census Bureau** (www.census.gov) releases reports, including an up-to-the-second U.S. and world population projection. Data on income, economic indicators, trade and labor statistics are among those provided, and a link to **FedStats** (www.fedstats.gov) makes statistics available from more than 100 agencies.

- The **Centers for Disease Control** (www.cdc.gov) provides health tips and authoritative information about diseases, traveler's health and physical fitness. A related site from the National Institutes of Health, http://health.nih.gov/, provides information about disease and health issues, with links to specific disease-related Web sites.

- The **Securities and Exchange Commission** (www.sec.gov) has made available every document required to be filed by publicly traded companies, with information on contracts, EPA settlements, lawsuits and marketing campaigns. The site carries regulatory actions, investor information, news releases, speeches and testimony, and litigation summaries.

Sites for Journalists

Several Web sites are of value to journalists—too many to list, given the introductory scope of this text. Student journalists should visit and bookmark the following sites and others relating to interests that develop. Tips that help study skills, improve writing, and develop attitudes necessary for success in this highly competitive profession are all available at these sites:

- **A Journalist's Guide to the Internet** (www.reporter.umd.edu), by Christopher Callahan of the University of Maryland School of Journalism, is a one-stop resource of topics including sources, directories, records, politics and government, Freedom of Information, Net strategies, listservs and news groups, and new developments.
- **Newslink** (www.newslink.org/spec.html) has 8,000 free media links and provides access to 3,600 online U.S. and Canadian newspapers. Resources include news services; links to journalism organizations with e-mail forums; a segment on new media newsletters with reports, marketing research, and other lists of news sites; search tools; and a "Starting Points for Journalists" section with resources for broadcasters, photojournalists, and print reporters.
- The **Poynter Institute** (www.poynter.org) offers workshops and seminars to professionals and educators in reporting, writing, and editing, and has a variety of

---

Box 8.4

NGOs for Journalists

There are human rights Web sites of **Non-Governmental Organizations (NGOs)** of interest to journalists that provide story leads (and show how well off reporters are in the United States). During the past two decades, a number of journalistic watchdog groups have arisen to look out for the welfare of reporters around the world and to oppose restrictions on print, broadcast and, increasingly, Internet reporting.

One of the best known sites is the **Committee to Protect Journalists** (www.cpj.org), which promotes press freedom worldwide by defending the right of journalists to report the news without fear of reprisal, publicly revealing abuses against the press in 120 countries and acting on behalf of imprisoned and threatened journalists. CPJ also publishes a number of reports, including its annual "Attacks on the Press," which details the number of journalists killed, attacked or imprisoned each year. Other reports include "World's Worst Places to Be a Journalist" and "Enemies of the Press," an annual indictment of 10 world leaders who make conditions for journalists in their countries particularly bad.

Reporters Without Borders (www.rsf.org) also vigorously condemns any attack on press freedom worldwide by keeping the media and public opinion informed through news releases and public-awareness

campaigns. The organization is working to improve the safety of journalists worldwide, particularly in war zones, and assists in the rebuilding of media groups. To ensure that murderers and torturers of journalists are brought to trial, RSF's Damocles Network provides victims with legal services and represents them before the competent national and international courts.

Article 19 (www.article19.org), named after Article 19 of the Universal Declaration of Human Rights that says the free flow of information is a fundamental right, works worldwide to combat censorship by promoting freedom of expression and access to official information. It monitors, researches, publishes, lobbies, campaigns, and litigates on behalf of freedom of expression wherever it is threatened, and it develops standards to advance media freedom, assists individuals to speak out, and campaigns for the free flow of information.

Other NGOs concerned with information rights issues are **Amnesty International** (www.amnesty.org) and **Human Rights Watch** (www.hrw.org), which make their concerns about repression of expression part of their regional and annual reports. Although not an NGO, the **U.S. Department of State** (www.state.gov) every March issues its annual "Country Reports on Human Rights Practices," which exposes repression of freedom of expression and of the press.

articles about the craft of journalism. Its "Hot News/Hot Research" link lists Web resources for current news topics.

- **Freedom of Information** resources include those of the Society of Professional Journalists (http://spj.org/foia/index.htm) and the University of Missouri Freedom of Information Center (http://foi.missouri.edu/).

- The **Resource Center of Investigative Reporters and Editors** (www.ire.org/resources/center) contains a rich reserve of handouts and guides that can be used as a research starting point, along with 12,000 investigative stories indexed by subject, source and year.

- **Investigative Reporters and Editors (IRE)** and the **National Institute for Computer Assisted Reporting (NICAR)** have a Web project (www.reporter.org) that is home for several different professional journalism organizations and mailing lists, including IRE and NICAR, the **National Association of Black Journalists** (www.nabj.org), the **Asian American Journalists Association** (www.aaja.org), and the **National Association of Hispanic Journalists** (www.nahj.org).

- **Public Agenda Online** (www.publicagenda.org) is a free online service for journalists and researchers that provides concise nonpartisan overviews of social policy issues, key facts and trends, polling data, and links to related issues-oriented Web sites. The **Pew Research Center for the People and the Press** (www.people-press.org) reports survey results on attitudes about press performance, politics and public policy issues.

- The **Foundation for American Communications** (www.facsnet.org) provides background and sources to help reporters cover stories about major issues, leads to highly selective annotated links to Internet resources, and lists of names, telephone numbers and e-mail addresses for sources who can answer questions.

- The **National Press Club** (http://npc.press.org/sources) lists news and journalism resources for research and information by category, organization, and keyword.

- **YearbookNews** (www.yearbooknews.com) is an interactive guide to thousands of the country's leading experts and sources. A link, **Daybook**, provides journalists with a daily or weekly e-mail distribution list of news releases, a particularly valuable venue for public relations professionals. If a company has a news release or is planning an event that should be announced to the national news media, the information can be supplied to DaybookNews.

- Several other useful public relations resources include those of **prnewswire.com**, **prweb.com**, **uwire.com**, and **businesswire.com**. Increasing numbers of public relations practitioners and educators are participating in Public Relations Forum (www.prforum.com), a lively international discussion of practical aspects of the profession. It has breaking public relations and marketing news and has added an accreditation conference for those taking the Public Relations Society of America's accreditation exam.

- The Web site of the **Radio–Television News Directors Association** (www.rtnda.org), an information resource to assist member broadcast journalists, includes a "Reporter's Toolbox" with links to experts, associations, companies and government agencies to help broadcast reporters research, develop, and write stories.

- The **American Press Institute** (www.americanpressinstitute.org/pages/toolbox/) provides a similar service with sources and story ideas on current news topics.
- **JournalistExpress** (www.journalistexpress.com/) is another rich resource, with numerous links to wire services, magazines, newspapers, broadcast outlets, directories, archives and other references.
- **Journalism Reviews**, which critically examine a broad range of journalistic issues— a "must-read" for professional development—include the **Columbia Journalism Review** (www.cjr.org), **American Journalism Review** (www.ajr.org) and, focusing on online journalism issues, **Online Journalism Review** (www.ojr.org).

Mailing List Discussion Groups

Another computer research tool on the Internet is a **mailing list** news group to which one can subscribe. Computer users register with a server run by a moderator who, generally in the form of e-mail, sends to individual subscribers all the information sent to everyone else on the list. News professionals have found them to be good places to find facts or locate knowledgeable people for interviews, although some are also venues for mindless chatter and pointless debate. They differ from **news groups**, which are electronic bulletin boards where people with similar interests can discuss and debate specific topics and issues. Among the most recommended of the mailing lists are the following:

- **SPJ-L**, of the Society of Professional Journalists, covers a broad range of issues in print, broadcast, and online journalism.
- **SPJ-ETHICS** and **JOURNETHICS** focus on ethical issues and journalists.
- **CARR-L** is for discussion among journalists, educators, librarians and researchers about issues related to the use of computers in journalism.
- **IRE-L** is a news story discussion list of Investigative Reporters and Editors.
- **NICAR-L**, sponsored by the National Institute for Computer Assisted Reporting, discusses online searching and data analysis.
- **CORR-X** is a discussion group for foreign correspondents.
- **COPYEDITING-L** is for copyeditors.
- **ShopTalk** is a newsletter about TV news from Syracuse University.
- **STUPAP** is a discussion group for online campus newspapers.

Two comprehensive search tools for finding mailing lists on the Web are www.reference.com with more than 100,000 indexed mailing lists, searchable by keyword, and www.liszt.com. Major search engines and directories also have lists of news groups: Google (http://groups.google.com) has thousands filed alphabetically.

Math and Media Writers

The mantra of "check it out" not only applies to facts but to figures too. Reporters and public relations writers frequently do stories containing numbers: vote tallies, percentages, census data, budget growth, crowd estimates, etc. The problem is that creative people drawn to the professions of journalism, public relations, advertising and other communication-based disciplines are often stronger in writing than in math. However, interpreting numbers and statistics is a required skill for media writers.

As reliance on polls, percentages and surveys has increased, the potential for their abuse has also risen. Numbers can be misleading and statistics are at times misused by those providing information to journalists. Therefore, every set of numbers needs to be examined to ensure that what is being purported is indeed true. The data should then be put into a context members

---

Box 8.5
Looking for a Job on the Internet

Job seekers will find the Internet valuable for career information guidance and resources. Here are some Web sites to get you started:

- **Newslink.org/joblink**, "the fastest way to a journalistic job," according to the Web site, bills itself as "the world's largest, best-read active listing of journalistic jobs, online or in print." Quick Search gives job seekers access to the most frequently searched categories of job ads, and its Detailed Search lets job hunters look at ads matching exact criteria. Standard ads submitted online by job seekers are posted free.

- **SPJ.org**, the Web site of the Society of Professional Journalists, offers to member subscribers a job bank, a listing of internships and fellowships, and career advice.

- **Rtnda.org/jobs**, a free job-search service of the Radio–TV News Directors Association, lists broadcasting jobs and provides other resources, including statistics on salaries, and information about working in electronic journalism.

- **TVjobs.com** displays a wide range of broadcast positions in North America. Subscribers have access to hundreds of jobs listed each month.

- **Editorandpublisher.com**, with a basic and a premium subscription service to the newspaper magazine, enters resumés into a database of more than 5,000 that can be accessed by employers.

- **PRSSA.org/JobCenter**, a career resource of the Public Relations Student Society of America, allows members to search for jobs and internships, post resumés, view the resumés of others, and use other PRSSA career resources.

- **PRSA.org/JobCenter** is a service of the Public Relations Society of America, with browsing and posting of jobs and resumés, and has a database, PR Power, for freelancers.

- **Monster.com** is the most comprehensive employment database on the Web, with more than 800,000 worldwide job postings, searchable by region, industry or titles. Job hunters are able to complete applications and interviews, have jobs e-mailed, and access thousands of pages of career information and advice.

- **CareerTalk.com** provides tips and counseling for job seekers.

- **CareerBuilder.com** allows visitors to search for jobs by category, post resumés and connect with hundreds of employers.

- **JobWeb.com**, sponsored by the National Association of Colleges and Employers, links 1,600 colleges and universities with employer organizations. The site provides tips on resumés and interviews, hosts an Online Career Fair, and has a virtual library with career and job search information.

of the audience can understand. This section provides an overview of some of the more common types of mathematical calculations that find their way into news reports and public relations pieces.

Misleading Averages

Averages are often of limited value. For instance, an average daytime temperature of 37.5 degrees in the weather statistics could mean a range in temperature between 37 and 38 or between 15 and 60 degrees. The number is relatively meaningless. Likewise, in a labor dispute, both sides may use the same figures and come up with different conclusions. Management says the average salary is $40,000, the union says it is $25,000. It all depends on whose salary is used to determine the average. Do the numbers range from the CEO's salary to skilled laborers on the assembly line or do they start with skilled laborers and go down to the part-time stock clerk barely making minimum wage?

When we casually talk about "average," the word can have three different meanings. Journalists, public relations writers and other careful wordsmiths need to be clear about the intention. Let's set up a scenario and then look at the three kinds of averages. In a company with a boss and seven employees, the boss earns $100,000 a year. The vice president earns $60,000, and two project managers each earn $39,000. Four staff specialists earn $25,000 each, and a trainee earns $15,000.

The **mean** is the sum of all the elements, divided by the number of elements. So it's the sum of all the salaries, divided by the number of employees. $100,000 plus $60,000 plus $39,000 plus $39,000 plus $25,000 plus $25,000 plus $25,000 plus $25,000 plus $15,000. That's $353,000 divided by eight. So the mean is $39,222. The mean is the kind of average we most often think of when we use the term "average." Sometimes the mean is a useful calculation; other times, it doesn't really tell us much. In this scenario, for example, the mean would be helpful to the accountant, but it doesn't reveal a lot about the workforce compensation. The mean average is a salary higher than 78 percent of the employees; only two individuals make more than the mean. So how average is the mean?

Suppose this were a city agency instead of a private company. Same salaries, but now perhaps the average would be useful information for taxpayers. But be careful about averages. You could add another staff specialist, decrease the average salary (mean), and still end up spending more money for salaries.

Another at-times misleading number is the often-reported **median**, the midpoint or center of a distribution where the number of units above the median is equal to those below. Line up all the salaries, and find the one in the middle. That's the median. So we line up the salaries: $100,000, $60,000, $39,000, $39,000, $25,000, $25,000, $25,000, $25,000, $15,000. No need to add anything; just look for the middle number, item No. 5, $25,000. In this scenario, the median gives even less useful information than mean. More light is shed on this scenario by using the mean average—$39,222—along with an explanation that two employees earn more than this average and six earn less.

Context is important. How accurate, for instance, are reported median income figures when there's a wide disparity between households with incomes in the hundreds of thousands of dollars and those with a sizeable percentage below the poverty line? Or measures of the educational level in a community where there is a college or university compared to one where there is not? While averages of any type become more reliable as the sample size increases, a small sample with extremes at either end can skew results and render them virtually meaningless.

Mode is a less commonly used type of average. It refers to the most frequently-occurring in a set of numbers. In the salary scenario, the mode is $25,000, but it's not a very useful concept. But take the example of an intercultural communication class on your campus with 25 students; 15 are of white/European descent, four of Hispanic origin, three African-American, two Asian-American, and one Native American. What is average? There is no way to calculate a mean, and the median doesn't make much sense because there is no logical way to line up the elements in the set. But using the mode—the most frequently occurring element—you can say that the typical or average student taking this course is white.

In conclusion, when presented with averages of any type, news reporters or public relations professionals should ask how they were calculated. If possible, check the **standard deviation**— that is, how dispersed the data points are from the arithmetic mean. The more closely data clusters around the mean, the more reliable is the average. At least look at the maximum and minimum values: If the values are widely dispersed (or the standard deviation is large), the data are probably suspect. Apply the rule of common sense: Are the numbers logical? If not, do some checking because if the numbers don't add up, there goes your credibility.

Currency converter

You are writing a travel story about the cost of things in various countries. Two things to keep in mind. One, money has different values in different countries. Two, the same item may have a different cost in different countries.

About the first, be aware that the American dollar may be the standard reference point for your readers, but you'll need to calculate the exchange rate if you want to make comparisons with another country. Go to an up-to-date currency exchange calculator—easy to find with an Internet search engine—and you'll find two numbers. One is what a dollar is worth in the basic unit of currency in another country; the other is what the other country's unit of currency is worth in dollars. Take the euro. Let's say that one dollar is worth 0.68, which also means that one euro is worth $1.47. Thus an American traveling in Europe who spends €50 on a meal is spending the equivalent of about $73. A European visitor who spends $50 on a meal in America is spending the equivalent of €34.

The other thing to remember about currency is that not everything has the same value in different locations. In the U.S., a decent burger may cost $9 in Cleveland but $25 in Manhattan. Go international, and differences in value can be even more extreme.

Another way to calculate relative cost is to compare it to the amount of time a person has to work to earn the money needed to buy something. UBS, a Swiss bank, calculated in its 2006 Prices and Earning report that a Big Mac would require 20 minutes of work in Taipei, 13 minutes in New York City, and 10 minutes in Tokyo (where a burger costs most, but where average wages are higher than in most other cities). A Big Mac requires 97 minutes of work in Bogota, Colombia, where wages are very low. The worldwide average (mean) is 37 minutes of working to afford a local Big Mac.

Box 8.6

Hardship Living

Percentages are often misleading. When I had returned for the summer from a teaching assignment in Egypt, American newspapers reported that the Egyptian government had sharply increased the tariff (tax on imported goods) and had raised the price of Stella, the refreshing local beer, by 100 percent. Friends commiserated about this manifest example of hardship living until I explained that a 100 percent increase meant that the price of a 22-ounce bottle of beer would be raised from its U.S. equivalent of 60 cents to $1.20—still a bargain by any standard!

Not too long ago, in the verbal jousting over trade policies with Japan, the U.S. government threatened a 100 percent tariff that would have raised the cost of luxury Japanese automobiles from $45,000 to about $90,000. Now *that* would have been significant!—*WRW*

Cost-of-living is also a finicky number. As noted above, prices can vary dramatically from one place to another, but so can salaries. It's a wise college graduate who, when comparing salary offerings for entry-level jobs, also factors in the local cost of living. That $20,000 a year job offer in Pittsburgh, Houston or Louisville would require a matching offer of $36,000 in San Francisco and $44,000 in Manhattan to make an even playing field. Here again, Internet search engines can identify good cost-of-living calculators.

Percentage

When numbers are integral to what you are writing, try to put them in context. Readers often find that percentages are more meaningful than raw numbers, because they put the numbers into the perspective they need. For example, if you learn that the student population in your department increased by 50 since last year, what have you really learned? Okay, the enrollment is increasing, but how significant is the increase? You won't know until you compare the growth to the base. The enrollment may have increased from 60 to 110, or from 900 to 950. One is huge; the other is just a blip.

First, some basics. Convert percentages to decimal numbers by moving the decimal point two places to the left (45 percent is the same as .45). And vice versa, .37 is the same as 37 percent.

Compute percentages by dividing the portion by the whole. Example: 200 divided by 50 is 25 percent (the whole is 200, the portion is 50). Think it through differently: 50 into 200 is 25 percent.

Sometimes the portion is larger than the whole. For example, what percentage of 200 (whole) is 300 (portion)? Same process, 200 divided by 300. The percentage change is 150 percent.

Percentage Change

A related issue is percentage change. We often want to know how the percentage has increased or decreased. Let's say your department offers 50 sections of communication courses this semester; 45 sections were offered last semester; 60 sections are planned for next semester.

The current 50 is 111 percent of last semester, an 11 percent increase. The planned 60 sections is 120 percent of the current ($60 \div 50$); it could just as easily be written as a 20 percent increase. It's also 133 percent or a 33 percent increase over the previous semester ($60 \div 45$).

Be careful in the words you use to indicate percentage change. An outcome that is twice as big may be 200 percent of the original, but it is not a 200 percent increase. If the 20 students applied for a journalism scholarship last year and 40 applied this year, this year's number is 200 percent of last years' application total ($40 \div 20$ %). But it's only a 100 percent increase, a doubling. If 50 applied, it would be 250 percent of last year ($50 \div 20$ %), a 150 percent increase.

Now let's say that the number of individual faculty members in the department (both part-time and full-time) is 25 this semester, compared with 22 last semester. Next semester some additional full-time hires will replace several part-timers, and the department will still have only 25 individual instructors. The number of full-time faculty this semester represents a 13 percent increase over last. Next semester will be a zero percent increase over this semester.

Let's consider the number of students in a particular class. Last year the department had an average of 19 students in each writing class. A new policy this semester limits the number of students in such classes to 15. What's the percentage change? Calculate the new divided by the old ($15 \div 19$ %). That's 79 percent this semester of what the average enrollment was last semester, an obvious decrease. How much? Calculate 19×21%.

Sometimes you know the present value and want to calculate backwards the percentage change from a previous time. Let's says you are writing an article for the student newspaper about recent changes in dorm costs. A basic two-person dorm room at your university costs $5,000; you are told that's a seven percent increase over last year (or 107 percent of the previous year). What was the dorm fee last semester? Divide the current value by the percentage change. Calculate $5000 \div 107$%. Last year's tuition was $4,673.

Remember that a 100 percent increase is a doubling, a 200 percent increase is a tripling, and so on. Note also that a 50 percent decrease cuts something in half; a 100 percent decrease results in zero.

Correlation, Cause, and Common Sense

Be particularly careful in making comparisons between two sets of numbers. In particular, don't confuse correlation with cause. Snow and cold temperatures correlate with the number of people who go skiing, but the number of skiers doesn't cause the snow. Correlation, but not cause.

Does using a cell phone in the car cause higher traffic accidents? Perhaps, but it also might be that high-risk drivers likely to be in traffic accidents use cell phones while driving more than other motorists? Or perhaps it's that some drivers, the ones likely to be in accidents, are simply not paying attention to their driving. Take away their cell phones, and maybe they'll find something else to distract them from the boring traffic. So is it cause or correlation?

Urban legend holds that red cars are more likely to get speeding tickets and be involved in accidents. Is it the paint job that causes the ticket or accident, or rather the likelihood that more risk-taking drivers prefer the color red?

Number Analogies

Often the best way to make sense of big numbers is to translate them into something that allows the reader to grasp them. Writers often provide an analogy to create such perspective. Take the situation of space distances. Earth is 235,000 miles from the moon, 93 million miles from the sun. Big numbers. Vast distances that are difficult to comprehend. So an analogy can help make sense of the numbers.

Traveling 55 miles an hour and not stopping, it would take 21 or 22 days to drive across the U.S. and 19 days to circumnavigate the earth (if only there were an equatorial bridge). It would take six months to drive to the moon, and 54 years to get to Venus, our closest neighbor planet. Two centuries to get to the sun. That's what 93 million miles is like.

Here's another such analogy: If the sun were the size of a quarter, earth would be a tiny speck (smaller than a grain of salt), and it would be 10 feet away. The distance to Pluto (the newly defined "dwarf planet") is that of a football field, 350 feet away. And the next nearest star would also be the size of a quarter—500 miles away.

Per Capita

A per capita number allows you to generalize a total cost over a population, which is more meaningful than raw numbers. Consider this scenario: You are preparing material for your university admissions office about the 545 students each year who receive scholarships. Impressive, but what does it really tell you? You know that the university has about 11,500 students, so you can calculate that the per capita rate of scholarships is about one in 21. That's much more meaningful to potential readers of your report.

If you are doing a story about travel safety, you may look at data from 2006, the latest year available at this writing. California had 4,236 highway deaths; Wyoming had 195. Does that mean that California roads are more dangerous than Wyoming's? You have no way of knowing anything about road dangers from this data, only the number of deaths, which could be caused by any number of factors. But look at the per capita rate of highway deaths. California had 36.4 million residents that year; Wyoming had only 515,000. Now you find that California's high death rate of 11.6 per capita (the number of deaths for each 100,000 of the population) was much lower than Wyoming's 37.9 per capita. You still have no insight into the cause of the deaths, so you can't conclude that Wyoming roads are more dangerous than California. But you do have a much more realistic picture because the raw numbers are in perspective.

Miscellaneous Math for Journalists

Journalists sometimes are called up to perform other mathematical calculations. Suppose you are covering a protest demonstration in front of City Hall. Other than counting legs and dividing by two, how do you estimate crowd size? You know from your research that in a loosely-packed crowd, each person takes up about 10 square feet. You know that in your town, a block is approximately 100 yards long. The staging area for the rally is a park that is a block long and roughly half a block wide, and the crowd is loosely packed. To estimate the crowd size, convert the space into square footage (300 ft × 150 ft = 45,000 sq ft), then divide that by the space taken by each person (10 sq ft). The estimate is 4,500 people at the rally. Another useful mathematical tool is the **ratio**, which describes how many times as large one number is to another. Your academic department has 16 faculty and 400 students, so it has a ratio of 25 to 1, that's 25 students for every one faculty member.

Probability

Sometimes we want to write about the likelihood that something will happen. The weather station reports that there's a 70 percent chance of rain today, so you'd better take the umbrella. That's presuming you are listening to a station that isn't wrong 50 percent of the time.

But be careful with confusing probability with quantity. Let's say you are working on a story about hospital deaths in your county. At County General, 112 patients died last year during heart surgery. At City Medical, 64 patients died during similar surgery. You might write, "It is more dangerous to have heart surgery at County General than at City Medical." But you shouldn't write that, because it may not be the truth.

Check the records for the raw numbers. You may find that County General performed 1,700 heart operations last year, nearly five a day. City Medial performed 500 such operations. Now let's compare figures. At County General, 6.6 percent of patients died during surgery; at City Medical, 12.8. So perhaps you should write, "At City Medical, it is nearly twice as likely that a patient will die during heart surgery." Both statements are accurate numerically, but the latter puts the numbers in perspective and gives a truer understanding of the facts.

Surveys and Formal Statistics

Journalists and public relations writers often deal with formal research, such as surveys. Because their credibility is on the line, professional researchers are careful to measure the accuracy of their findings before this information is released to the media and public. Reporters, though, must still be on the lookout for occasional abuses, misrepresentations and methodological blunders in data presented for their use.

Not-So-Random Sampling

A **sample** is a subset of the population being studied. But **random sampling** is not merely standing in the mall and asking any shoppers who will talk to you what they think about the proposed tax increase. That's a mix between a volunteer sample and a convenience sample and neither is trustworthy. Random sampling is much more scientific. It is random precisely because every person in the population (each shopper) has an equal chance of being asked to participate in the survey—the inner-city resident as well as the suburbanite, the senior citizen as well as the teen, the bargain-basement shopper as well as the patron of upscale boutiques.

One of the most widely abused reporting methods is the person-on-the-street interview in which reporters stop people who look as though they may be willing to talk and ask them questions about which they may know nothing. Put 10 of those interviews together, however—especially if virtually everyone takes the same position—and "public opinion" has miraculously been measured. So much the better if that opinion matches the reporter's bias. The reporter takes those interviews back to the paper or broadcast station and creates a "Voice of the People" story for the next edition or newscast. If nothing else, the reporter doesn't want to admit to wasting several hours of company time doing something of no value.

Another category of useless efforts, it seems, is telephone polls conducted by local TV stations. The station invites audience members to call a 900 number at 95 cents a minute and vote their bias, one way or another. The results may be entertaining, but they're not worth anything as information. This type of poll surveys a non-representative, self-selected sample: Only those who feel strongly about an issue will bother to call.

Surveys and Questionnaires

Questionnaires are often used to provide a gauge of public thinking about an issue. When properly designed, they can be valuable tools to measure public opinion; when not, they can be less than worthless. How many times have you looked at the rating form to evaluate the food in a restaurant? *My meal was (a) Splendid, (b) Wonderful, (c) Just like Mom makes, (d) Satisfactory, (e) Needed more salt.* That's an example of an invalid survey question, designed to elicit compliments, not constructive criticism.

Problems With Survey Methodology

Many surveys are flawed. How many times have you seen a national poll in a magazine or on television with only two choices or two positions? Answer "yes" or "no," "favorable" or "unfavorable"; no middle ground. Those types of questions, often about issues for which there is a third or even fourth legitimate position, tend to distort findings.

Some survey questions skew the results by quoting unpopular people to prod respondents into giving alternative positions: *Most people jailed on drug charges say that possession should be decriminalized. Do you agree or disagree?* Of course, respondents aren't going to agree, even though some public officials are saying the same thing. If the question were, *The local police chief says drug possession should be decriminalized. Do you agree or disagree?*, the results might be reversed.

Another flaw in survey methodology is asking people questions about which they know nothing. This method yields a high "don't know" or "no opinion" response with a low "yes" or "no" rate, which can then be used however the questioner desires. Good survey questions should have opposing alternatives that accurately measure a range of responses of whether people are for or against a position, if they agree or disagree about an issue.

Reporters sometimes receive news releases about surveys that match the public position on an issue taken by the sending organization. Often, those surveys come from groups that take one side or the other on controversial public questions, such as health care, gun control, abortion, or environmental concerns. The biggest offenders seem to be polling organizations for political campaigns. Questions can be misstated or phrased in such a way as to deceive the respondent, reader or viewer; for example:

> *The president has ordered additional U.S. troops sent abroad as peacekeepers. Do you favor such a policy that wastes taxpayers' money and puts our military personnel at risk?*

Obviously, no one wants to say he or she favors wasting tax money and putting troops at risk.

Not all sponsored surveys are flawed, but anyone who works in the communication media should be careful about how survey information is gathered, used and disseminated. Journalists should first evaluate the organization that sends the report. What bias does the sender have? Who will gain from dissemination of the survey results? Journalists should also examine questions that form the basis of the survey. Were they understandable and free of bias? Did they measure what the sponsoring organization said would be measured? Do the findings make sense? If so, journalists may pass on the results to readers, viewers or listeners.

Characteristics of Good Surveys

Good survey research questions should meet the general criteria for research methodology, discussed earlier in this chapter. The questionnaire must have internal validity, meaning that the questions measure what the researcher says they're going to measure: how people respond actually measures their beliefs or feelings. The questionnaire should be reliable, meaning that if it is used several times, the results should be the same. Finally, those results should be generalizable to the overall population.

Ideally, a survey should contain **closed-ended questions**, meaning that respondents give a "yes" or "no" answer or rate their agreement using a scale (generally numbered 1 to 5 or 1 to 7, with 1 being "strongly agree" or "strongly disagree" and 5 or 7 being the opposite). **Open-ended questions**, which ask respondents to answer in their own words, can be helpful in research intended to disclose feelings.

Conducting Survey Research

Media writers, especially those in public relations, may need to conduct survey research to measure opinion about an issue or determine how segments of a community are dealing with conditions unique to them. Planning is essential: Unless the research effort has focus or direction, the value of its findings will be questionable.

Sample Selection   Often the most vexing methodological issue in survey research is determining an adequate **sample size**. Whether individuals, households, or businesses are being surveyed, the objective is to use as few units as possible while still maintaining precision. Although no set sample size is available for every research project, using a rule of thumb of a sample of 100 for each category being examined is generally adequate. Most surveys yield meaningful results if the sample is between 100 and 500 cases; samples or sub-samples of fewer than 100 could be non-representative, with a high error level. Many researchers question whether the extra cost justifies going beyond 500 because a sample size of more than 1,000 is seldom needed.

Sample size is generally dictated by the time and money available, as well as the objectives of the study. A preliminary investigation or pretest can make do with a smaller sample than one in which major changes or a significant expenditure will be the outcome. The more precision needed, the larger the sample should be. If the sample is too small, the results are subject to

Box 8.7

Conducting a Survey

A carefully selected group of 250 students may be the survey sample for a study of all 15,000 university students. It is important for writers to indicate how the sample was selected. Let's say your study is about the candidate whom students are likely to vote for in upcoming campus elections. One candidate is the football quarterback, out for the season with an arm injury. The other is president of the math club. If we take the 250-student sample from among people waiting to enter the football stadium for the big game, we might get far different answers than if we used a systematic random sample of every sixtieth name on a list of full-time registered students. So the writer must know the integrity of the sample.

Reports about surveys usually include information about the accuracy of the study. The **margin of error** is a percentage, often written as a plus/minus number, that indicates the likelihood that the result is true. Usually the margin of error is reported along with the **confidence level**, which indicates the amount of certainty the researcher has in the result.

In the campus-election scenario, let's say the margin of error is ±6.15 at a 95 percent confidence level, which is the same as ±5 with a confidence level of 90 percent. This means that the researcher is 95 percent confident that the results are accurate to within 6.15 percent, or 90 percent confident that they are accurate to five percent. Note that higher certainty comes with a potentially greater discrepancy among the findings. Professional surveys usually report margin of error at the 95 percent confidence level.

---

error, which makes the conclusions suspect. Above a certain point, however, it is not worthwhile to increase the sample. Part of the consideration in sample size is the expected response. If replies to questions are expected to be similar and nearly unanimous, a smaller sample will suffice. Where it is likely that respondents will split 50–50, that sample must be larger.

The main determinant of the quality of a sample is the degree to which it represents the population from which it is drawn. Not even the most carefully drawn sample will be perfectly representative of the population because there will always be some degree of sampling error. To increase precision, some researchers engage in **stratification**, the grouping of members of a population into homogeneous groups. This grouping usually reduces the variation in population and permits a smaller sample size.

You may need to conduct what is called a **non-probability sample**, such as when surveying business leaders or directors of social-service agencies. Also called **purposive sampling**, it involves using your own judgment about who should be included. Purposive sampling is generally considered less reliable than probability sampling, in which everyone is a potential respondent. How that overall sample is winnowed down, whether by the use of a table of random numbers or by a systematic way of selecting every twentieth name, is decided by the person conducting the research.

Construction of the Questionnaire

Equally important is the construction of the questionnaire or testing mechanism to be used. When drafting questions, try to work from an outline of objectives or modify questions from another questionnaire that sought similar data. Careless wording can have devastating results in a survey: Writers should use simple words and grammatical structures and avoid ambiguous wordings, loaded adjectives, qualifying statements and overlapping alternatives.

Survey questions should be clear, brief and relevant. Avoid the following pitfalls:

- items that oversimplify the issue and provide no middle ground and/or no alternative

  Do you support higher graduation requirements or lower graduation requirements?
  (What if I support maintaining the current graduation requirements?)

- double-barreled items that ask two questions but allow for only one answer

  Is Niagara Falls a friendly and quiet town?
  (What if I think the town is very friendly and very noisy?)

- biased items that ask unbalanced and misleading questions

  Would you rather read an interesting book or just watch some television?
  (This question can lead to results that might be misinterpreted as more people preferring to read a book than watch TV.)

- leading questions that suggest a "proper" response

  Like most residents of Youngsville, do you read a newspaper every day?
  (Am I prepared to say, "No, I'm not like most of my neighbors"?)

Box 8.8

Guidelines for Writing Survey Response Categories

- Keep in mind that open-ended responses are difficult to codify and compare.

- Avoid yes–no categories. Instead, use response categories that gauge intensity of feelings:

  Likert scale: *Strongly agree, agree, neither agree or disagree, disagree, strongly disagree*

  Rating scale: *Disagree 1–2–3–4–5 Agree*

- List possible response categories in a balanced progression, with equal numbers of positive and negative responses:

  Negative example: *Media history class is (a) useful, (b) easy, (c) pleasant, (d) required,* *(e) a waste of time.* This is neither balanced (four positive, one neutral, one negative) nor progressive (each item refers to a different aspect rather than a range of similar ones).

  Positive example: *The college's new dorm policy is (a) reasonably permissive, (b) somewhat permissive, (c) neither permissive nor restrictive, (d) somewhat restrictive, (e) unreasonably restrictive.* These choices are balanced (two positive, two negative, one neutral) and they measure equally across a permissive-to-restrictive continuum.

- questions asking for too much detailed information that respondents are unlikely to have

  In the past 30 days, how many hours of TV has your family watched?
  (How can I calculate that? Better to ask about the last week or a typical weekday.)

- double-bind questions that "get you" no matter how you respond

  Do you still have a drinking problem?
  (If I have never had a drinking problem, would I respond, "No, I don't still have a problem," thus implying I used to?)

- embarrassing or intrusive questions that respondents are likely to find too personal

  Have you ever abused any illegal drugs?
  (Will anyone really confess drug use to a stranger? And will anyone really admit that this drug use, if in fact there was any, amounted to abuse?)

- questions calling for information beyond the capabilities of the average respondent

  Do you think the United States should promote fission or fusion as the approach for generating power?
  (How am I, a non-scientist, expected to understand the difference? And of what value are the resulting data when I simply guess and provide irrelevant information?)

Avoiding Plagiarism

Plagiarism is the offense of presenting somebody else's words as your own. Academically, it is cheating; journalistically, it is fraud. Whether intentional or the result of negligence, plagiarism is a serious breach of professionalism. It is a specific violation of the code of ethics of organizations such as the Society of Professional Journalists and the Public Relations Society of America. It's also a career-breaker. Journalists who are discovered plagiarizing are summarily fired, as several recent highly publicized cases have shown.

Writing coach Roy Peter Clark, of the Poynter Institute, calls plagiarism the "unoriginal sin." His institute colleague, Christopher Scanlan, sees it as a matter of honor. "If you plagiarize, you dishonor yourself because you are dishonoring another writer."[1] We would add that it also dishonors your readers, perhaps the gravest offense of all.

In addition to being an unoriginal sin, plagiarism also unfortunately is a common one. Every year, it seems, some otherwise respected newspaper or magazine writers are accused of plagiarism. Meanwhile, colleges and universities are strengthening both their warnings about and penalties for plagiarism, which is apparently becoming more prevalent on campuses.

Sometimes the boundaries of plagiarism are fuzzy. The writer's role is to share information. Specifically, the job of a reporter or public relations writer is to tell readers what newsmakers are thinking and saying. In the academic world, meanwhile, ideas are meant to circulate freely, with new knowledge consciously building on the past. Nevertheless, in both fields, the credibility of the writer is enhanced by the honest indication of the source of information. Indeed, readers are more likely to feel that a writer has done a thorough job when a variety of sources are cited in a piece of writing, whether a news article or a term paper.

Plagiarism Defined

Those who commonly review writing—teachers and editors, for example—observe that plagiarism can fall into several categories. Copying word for word from another source without using quotation marks is plagiarism. Copying from another source almost verbatim while changing only a few words is plagiarism. Presenting somebody else's original ideas without noting the source is plagiarism.

Plagiarism is about co-opting somebody else's work as your own, and it has nothing to do with permission. Copying from a friend's academic paper or from a colleague's news report without attribution—even with that person's permission—is plagiarism, as is turning in a term paper purchased from somebody else. Sometimes students are accused of plagiarism when they more rightly should be charged with sloppy attribution. Perhaps the intent was not to steal somebody else's work and pass it off as their own; rather, the writer was merely inept at quoting, paraphrasing and summarizing.

Unfortunately for the student, intent is seldom the issue. Plagiarism is in the product; an "I didn't mean to cheat" argument is not likely to hold up against the weight of evidence that, regardless of motive, the information was plagiarized.

Let's define a few related terms: A **direct quote** provides the original wording of a phrase, sentence or longer passage. Obviously, this verbatim information needs to be used with quotation marks and attribution to the original source. A **paraphrase** includes all or most of the original source's information with nothing added, but it is presented in your words, often in an effort to simplify complicated information. A paraphrase also must be attributed to the source. A **summation** provides a short overview or synopsis of information from another source, presented in your words as the author of the report or paper. Because such a summation highlights somebody else's ideas, the source must be cited.

Public relations writers have more flexibility about direct quotes and paraphrases than reporters. Part of a public relations writer's job may be to develop a quote that would be attributed to a boss, colleague or client. This is not plagiarism because it is an original quote. It is like the situation of a speechwriter or adviser. The only offense related to plagiarism is if the quotation were not original (either to the writer or to the person within the organization to whom it would be attributed) but rather was lifted without attribution from some other source.

Steps to Avoid Plagiarism

Ethicists debate the reasons why some writers plagiarize the work of others, and editors and teachers grapple with what to do about it. Our intention is to presume that you do not want to plagiarize, so we present some guidelines for avoiding the problem.

Note-Taking   Avoiding plagiarism begins with careful note-taking. Approach your research first with a clear idea of the information that you want to obtain. Follow that with a practical list of potential sources, whether they are people or documents likely to have the information you are seeking.

During your research, whether you are interviewing somebody or working with already published information, make sure that your notes accurately indicate when you are quoting verbatim. Reporters and other researchers often underline direct quotes to distinguish them from paraphrased information, or they may use a color-coded system, such as writing direct quotes in red ink or pencil or using a highlighter.

Always include in your notes the full information about the source. For an academic report, that means full bibliographic information about the original written document. In journalistic research, it means noting not only the person being interviewed, but also the time and place of the interview, so the newswriter will have a clear paper trail if one should be needed to answer accusations of misquoting or libel.

Avoid quoting more than necessary. Usually, paraphrased information is more useful to writers and shows more of the writer's insight. Verbatim quotes should be reserved for particularly important information or for strong and memorable phrases.

Writing Time Give yourself enough time to review the appropriate sources, digest the information, and put it down on paper. A well-written article or paper is one in which the author clearly understands the relationship among the various items of information and has taken time to organize them in a way that is clear, logical, and insightful. Even when you are writing on deadline, you must take the time to avoid plagiarism.

Attributing Sources Make sure that your readers know when you present information from a source other than yourself. In an academic paper, attribution generally follows the quoted, paraphrased, or summarized information. Any information after the attribution citation is presumed to be the original thoughts and writings of the author. It is not necessary to document when writing from your own experience or presenting the results of your own research. Nor do you need to document your own observations, insight and conclusions, or to attribute basic facts and easily verifiable information. A good test for determining what is common knowledge is to observe whether you find the same information in several different sources. If so, it does not require attribution. If in doubt, write a citation.

It is necessary to attribute judgment or speculation, especially if particularly unique wording is involved. For example, when the FBI was asked about an Oliver Stone film that promoted the theory that a TWA airliner was shot down by a missile—after the FBI ruled out that possibility following a lengthy investigation—a named FBI spokesman told Associated Press: "The real facts are glossed over by the likes of Mr. Stone and others who spend their life bottom-feeding in those small dark crevices of doubt and hypocrisy." That's a great quote with some powerful language that could add a lot to a news article or a report. There's no way to present it without attribution to the FBI source.

Penalties for Plagiarism

Most news-gathering organizations have specific policies against plagiarism. Newspaper and magazine reporters have been demoted or fired because of sustained charges that they plagiarized. Some have had their bylines banned. Reporters and reviewers with TV and radio organizations have been sanctioned, from being reassigned to entry-level duties to being fired. Book authors, too, have been embroiled in plagiarism controversies.

In academia, students have been expelled or have lost scholarships for plagiarism. Most colleges and universities have written guidelines outlining the range of penalties for plagiarism. The penalties generally can be invoked at the sole discretion of the instructor, ranging from failing the specific writing project to automatic failure for the entire course. Some schools reserve the right to dismiss an offending student from college.

Remember, too, that it often takes a professor less time to track down where a suspicious paper came from on the Internet than it did for the writer to locate and download the document. Many schools are investing in computer software to help spot plagiarized papers and some colleges and universities are considering legal pressure against companies and Web sites that sell term papers to students.

Avoid problems: Don't pass off work as being your own when it isn't.

Research and the Challenge of Communication

Today's media writers must possess a broader knowledge base than ever before, due in part to the proliferation of data and information. Yesterday's reporters and public relations writers were generally reactive—they covered meetings and reported what people said, they went to crime scenes, they interviewed politicians, listened to speeches, and uncovered the occasional good feature. Now the emphasis is shifting. News sources, public relations professionals and journalists are becoming more proactive. Instead of passively letting news happen, reporters dig, investigate, and ask questions more than ever before. Inquiry, research, and analysis are therefore vital in the communication process for the print or broadcast journalist and the public relations practitioner. If you plan to work in this field, you need to develop the critical thinking mindset that will make it possible for you to succeed.

Discussion Questions

The following are class discussion questions drawn from Chapter 8:

1. Why do we need research in media writing, and how important is research to the journalist or public relations professional?

2. Why is "objective" reporting impossible? Or is it?

3. Differentiate between primary and secondary sources. Why are they important in beat reporting?

4. What is CAR? What has been its impact on journalism? Has this impact been good or bad?

5. What are some of the cautions media writers should use in analyzing the results of polls and surveys?

6. What are some of the ways to avoid inadvertent plagiarism?

CHAPTER EXERCISES

Exercise 8.1—Freewriting

Freewrite for five minutes on the following topic: "How important is research to a journalist or public relations writer?" Then share your views with others in class. ∎

Exercise 8.2—Exploring Databases

Ask your college or university research librarian if the library provides student access to Lexis/Nexis or another full-text news archival service, or inquire if the library provides student access to an abstract news archival service.

Using one of those services, spend an hour exploring the information database. Look up a news event of interest to you and see how it was reported by different publications. Look up a business or nonprofit organization of interest to you and see how many news articles have been published about it. ∎

Exercise 8.3—Web Sites

Spend an hour exploring some of the Web sites noted in this chapter. Also check out the Web sites of your college and another college or university. How are they structured? Are they user-friendly to navigate? What generalizations can you make about the writing? ∎

Exercise 8.4—Government Information

With a consumer's eye, spend an hour exploring some of the Web sites of federal government agencies mentioned in this chapter. Then look at what material is available in your state Web site. What do you conclude? ∎

Exercise 8.5—Test Your Math Skills

Test your skills with these writing scenarios in which math plays a significant part in your reporting and writing. (Answers appear after Exercise 8.7, but no peeking!)

1. You are working on a report about a power outage in a city neighborhood. The neighborhood includes 40,000 residents in a city of about 150,000. What is the percentage without power?

2. If the power went out at 3:16 a.m. and was not restored until 2:49 p.m., how long was the power out?

3. You are preparing a report on the college budget. Tuition was $19,500 last year. It will be $21,300 next year. What is the percentage of change?

4. You currently work in St. Louis. You are offered a job in Chicago, where the cost of living is 25 percent higher. You currently earn $35,000 a year. What must the salary offer be for an even switch to Chicago?

5. You also are offered a job in Little Rock, where the cost of living is 6 percent lower than in St. Louis. You won't move unless you can realize a 20 percent increase in your salary. What must the offer be to meet that requirement?

6. Your instructor gives the following grades in a media writing class: 5 A's, 8 B's, 4 C's, 2 D's. What is the median grade?

7. What is the mode?

8. With the grades above, an A is worth 95%, B 85%, C 75%, D 65%. What is the mean average score (rounded to the nearest whole point)?

9. The journalism program has 88 majors, including 9 scholarship recipients. The public relations program has 125 majors with 14 scholarship recipients. What is the per capita rate of scholarship holders for the journalism program?

10 What is the per capita rate of scholarship holders for the journalism program (to the nearest decimal)?

11. Based on the information above, does journalism or public relations attract better students (to the nearest decimal)?

12. The campus bookstore sold 150 media writing textbooks last semester and 125 this semester. What is the percentage of this semester compared with last (round to nearest whole number)?

13. What is the percentage of increase or decrease (round to nearest whole number)?

14. The bookstore sold 200 mass communication books last semester and 25% fewer this semester. How many books were sold this semester?

15. The bookstore sold 21 introduction to journalism books last semester. This semester sales were at a 100% increase. How many books were sold this semester?

16. Using an online margin-of-error calculator, indicate the margin of error at a 95% confidence level for a sample of 300 out of a population of 15,000.

17. Here are exchange rates for several currencies: Argentine peso = $0.322, dollar = 3.1 peso. British pound = $1.95, dollar = £0.510. Kuwaiti dinar = $3.45, dollar = 0.289 dinars. South Korean, won = $.001, dollar = 938.9 won. How much would a watch purchased for $150 in America cost in each of the foreign currencies?

18. How much would an American visiting these countries spend on a piece of jewelry costing 180 pesos, 45 pounds, 15 dinars, 10,000 wons?

19. Last year, three students in your department participated in internships at a national television network. This year no students did such an internship. What is the percentage change from last year to this year?

20. 178 students took an entrance exam to your department; 35 failed. What percentage passed (round to the nearest whole number)?

Exercise 8.6—Survey Reports

In a newspaper, magazine or online, find an article that reports the findings of a survey. Determine how many of the following elements the article reports:

- sponsor of the survey
- researcher who conducted the survey
- sampling techniques used in the survey
- methodology for administering the survey
- number of respondents
- specific wording of key questions
- specific wording of response categories for key questions
- margin of error or degree of reliability

Exercise 8.7—Penalties of Plagiarism

Do a Web search to locate an incident of plagiarism by a journalist or book author. What was plagiarized and what was the penalty for the writer? How was he or she viewed by peers, critics and the public after the incident came to light? Report your findings as part of a group discussion in class.

Answers to Exercise 8.5—Test Your Math Skills

1. 27 percent without power

2. 11 hours and 33 minutes without power

3. 9.2 percent increase in tuition

4. Current salary equivalent to $43,750 in Chicago

5. 25 percent increase in current salary ($43,750) equivalent to $41,125 in Little Rock

6. B (median grade)

7. B (mode)

8. 83 (mean average)

9. 10.3 per capita for journalism

10. 11.2 per capita for public relations

11. Data does not indicate which program attracts "better students"

12. 83%

13. 17% decrease

14. 150 books this semester

15. 63 books were sold this semester

16. Margin of error is ±5.6

17. 465 pesos; 76.5 pounds; 42.25 dinars; 140,835 wons

18. $57.60 (peso); $87.75 (pound); $51.57 (dinar); $10 (won)

19. 100% decrease

20. 80% passed

Suggestions for Further Reading

Investigative Reporting

Aucoin, James. *The Evolution of American Investigative Journalism* (Columbia: University of Missouri Press, 2007).

Cohen, Sarah. *Numbers in the Newsroom: Using Math and Statistics in News* (Columbia, Mo.: Investigative Reporters and Editors (IRE), 2001).

DeBurgh, Hugo. *Investigative Journalism: Content and Practice* (New York: Routledge, 2000).

Gaines, William. *Investigative Reporting for Print and Broadcast* (Belmont, Calif.: Wadsworth, 1998).

Hinton, Derek. *Criminal Records Manual: The Complete Guide to the Legal Use of Criminal Records* (Tempe, Ariz.: Facts on Demand Press, 2004).

Houston, Brant, Len Bruzzese and Steve Weinberg. *Investigative Reporter's Handbook* 4th ed. (New York: St. Martin's Press, 2004).

King, Dennis. *Get the Facts on Anyone*, 3rd ed. (Lawrenceville, N.J.: Arco, 1999).

Mann, Thomas. *The Oxford Guide to Library Research*, 3rd ed. (New York: Oxford University Press, 2005).

Meyer, Philip. *Precision Journalism: A Reporter's Introduction to Social Science Methods,* 4th ed. (Lanham, Md.: Rowman & Littlefield, 2002).

Rose, Louis J. *How to Investigate Your Friends and Enemies,* 3rd ed. (St. Louis: Albion Press, 2004).

Computer-Assisted Reporting

Callahan, Christopher. *A Journalist's Guide to the Internet: The Net as a Reporting Tool*, 2nd ed. (Boston: Allyn & Bacon, 2002).

Ciotta, Rose. "Baby You *Should* Drive This CAR," *American Journalism Review,* March 1996, pp. 35–39.

Houston, Brant. *Computer-Assisted Reporting: A Practical Guide*, 3rd ed. (New York: St. Martin's, 2004).

LaFleur, Jennifer, and Andy Lehren. *Mapping for Stories: A Computer Assisted Reporting Guide* (Columbia, Mo.: Investigative Reporters and Editors (IRE), 2005).

Paul, Nora. *Computer Assisted Research: A Guide to Tapping Online Information*, 4th ed. (St. Petersburg: Poynter Institute/Bonus Books, 1999).

Reavy, Matthew M. *Introduction to Computer-Assisted Reporting: A Journalist's Guide* (Mountain View, Calif.: Mayfield, 2001).

Salwin, Michael, Bruce Garrison, and Paul Driscoll. *Online News and the Public* (Mahwah, N.J.: Lawrence Erlbaum, 2005).

Sankey, Michael L., and James R. Flowers Jr. *Public Records Online,* 6th ed. (Tempe, Ariz.: Facts on Demand Press, 2006).

Schlein, Alan. *Find It Online,* 4th ed. (Tempe, Ariz.: Facts on Demand Press, 2007).

Uplink, newsletter of the National Institute for Computer Assisted Reporting.

Internet and Web Resources

Maxwell, Bruce. *How to Access the Federal Government on the Internet* 4th ed. (Washington, D.C.: *Congressional Quarterly,* 1998).

Callahan, Christopher. "A Journalist's Guide to the Internet" at http://reporter.umd.edu.

"USUS Internet Guide for Journalists and Reporters," www.usus.org.

Polls, Surveys, Statistics and Research

Mauro, John. *Statistical Deception at Work* (Hillsdale, N.J.: Lawrence Erlbaum Associates, 1992).

Poindexter, Paula, and Maxwell E. McCombs. *Research in Mass Communication: A Practical Guide* (Boston: Bedford/St. Martin's, 2000).

Wickham, Kathleen W. *Math Tools for Journalists*, 2nd ed. (Oak Park, Ill.: Marion Street Press, 2003).

Wilhoit, G. Cleveland, and David H. Weaver. *The Newsroom Guide to Polls and Surveys* (Bloomington: Indiana University Press, 1990).

Note

1. Christopher Scanlan, "Tips for Avoiding Plagiarism," *The Writer*, January 2001, vol. 114, no. 1, p. 8.

9

Feature Writing

Alternative Story Formats

Particularly in today's competitive media atmosphere, newspapers and their online versions are eager to publish not only stories that readers choose to read for information but also those that readers elect to read for pleasure—articles that offer readers a variety of writing styles, structures and subjects. These alternative stories, called **features**, are frequently found in "Lifestyle" or "Today" sections of the newspaper, as well as in special Sunday sections such as "Travel," "Home" or "Health." They can also appear on front and inside pages of news sections.

Most of the more creative journalistic writing styles and structures are associated with these feature stories, ones that tell "softer," less timely news. Feature stories are typically seen as entertaining, optional stories that don't *have* to be written or read but that nonetheless offer readers an enjoyable reading experience. Beyond lighthearted entertainment, features can offer readers serious optional background information or give them a closer look at current events or trends. Features can present a different perspective on a news happening or on a prominent person. In such instances, the "enjoyment" of the reading experience would come from learning something new or from having one's eyes opened to a new interpretation of reality.

When, as a reporter, you face an especially dramatic, emotional or humorous situation, consider your writing options and think about writing a feature. Indeed, to be a first-rate reporter, you need to be always on the look-out for unusual stories that can be told in an alternative format—stories that might be suitably written, for example, as human interest features or exciting narratives.

In most instances, first consult with your editor before writing something that strays too far from the inverted-pyramid. A quick editorial conference can save you from wasting time on a more creative effort only to end up rewriting the material in the news format that your editor still wants. However, don't forget that even if you do write the straight news story, a feature article can be a good second-day follow-up to the inverted pyramid story.

Characteristics of Features

Features have been defined as nonfiction stories written using the writing techniques of fiction. Feature writing techniques, then, may already be familiar to you. You have likely noticed them in your reading of short stories and novels, even poems and plays.

The most important distinction between fiction and journalistic writing (nonfiction) is that fiction originates in the imagination; that is, it is a written text created from material that exists only in the mind of the author. Features, on the other hand, are texts created from reality, from information reported from real-life situations. The content of a feature story is never imagined or created, although it may be treated imaginatively and creatively. Features must tell the truth and provide accurate information.

Generally, features are not written under strict deadline pressure; in fact, they are sometimes defined as "alternative" because they are *non-deadline* journalistic stories that do not need to be published on a given day. Thus, features can be as long or short as suits the story content. If adequate space is not available to publish a feature on a particular day, the feature can be held until the next day or week, when adequate space for it is available. It doesn't need to be cut from the bottom. It is a feature's freedom from the "cutability" requirement of a news story that creates the ability to write it in other than the inverted-pyramid style.

Nevertheless, feature stories, like news stories, must be clearly written and economically constructed. Every word in the feature article must be important—must *need* to be there—because the feature story takes away column inches from a potential news story or another feature article, or fills space that could be used for advertising.

The alternative, fiction-like writing styles associated with features can sometimes be integrated into a more timely "hard" news story. Using these styles and structures in limited ways (perhaps just writing a feature lead) is called giving the story **feature treatment**. When an entire news story is written throughout with the stylistic devices of a feature story, but it has an inverted-pyramid structure and contains hard news information, that story would be called a **news feature**.

If a regular feature story accompanies a news story, that feature is generally called the news story's **sidebar**. For example, a human-interest sidebar that tells the hard-luck story of a local person affected by the death of a child might be published next to the story about the

---

Box 9.1

Comparing Features and News

Features are *unlike* news stories in that they:

- are not done rigidly for a particular day's deadline

- are more casual, conversational, and cleverly written

- do not structure information in an inverted pyramid

- have leads that may or may not be one paragraph

- offer readers entertainment or the enjoyment of learning something new or experiencing something in a new way

Features are *like* news stories in that they:

- must be accurate in every detail

- must be based on real events and people, not composite characters or reordered or imagined happenings

- must be written economically and clearly

---

plane crash in which the child died. Today's concept of a sidebar is that it accompanies a hard news story but need not be literally *beside* it; the sidebar for a front-page story may be on an inside page of the paper.

Generally, a traditional full-fledged feature story does not cover a news event. If the feature story was suggested by a news event or is related to it, the feature writer ties it to that event. A "news-peg" paragraph reminds readers of which recent event or news story the feature article relates.

Readers usually can enjoy features long after a news event is past. A news story about a traffic accident is more or less finished after it is published, but a dramatic feature story on the heroism of a driver who rescued his passengers from a burning car with only moments to spare will be interesting five years after the event. Features are timeless rather than timely.

Feature Treatment

When is it appropriate to give a straight news story feature treatment? A variety of news situations might call for such treatment.

A common reason for feature treatment is to freshen up a story that has been around for a while. The story might need alternative treatment because the information in it has already appeared in an earlier edition of the newspaper and has been picked up and repeated by the broadcast media. If the story is to be recycled, it will benefit from fresh language and a snappier feature lead.

Another reason is to liven up a story that is otherwise fairly dull. The topic, for example, might be a change in insurance regulations or the statistical results of a set of person-on-the-street interviews. Such information must be reported, but the story needs spicing up to make it palatable to the average reader.

On the other hand, perhaps a news story reports a lighthearted event, such as the appearance of the Easter Bunny at a charity fund drive or the arrival of hundreds of volunteers to participate in a folk dance at the county fair. Hard news treatment, with its bare-bones, semiformal tone, might not harmonize with the character of the event or accurately relay the tenor of what happened. Feature treatment is appropriate.

In the same vein, perhaps a news story is dramatic and exciting, such as an armed robbery's being foiled by a courageous bank teller or a drowning teenager being rescued by his friends. To relate the story's information in an absolutely straightforward way might lessen the story's emotional impact and human interest appeal. More compelling feature-like writing would be appropriate and consistent with the content of the article.

Box 9.2

Public Relations Uses of Feature Stories

Like other journalistic formats, feature stories offer particular benefits to public relations writers. Feature stories can be packaged as releases for newspapers and magazines, paralleling the style of a reporter-generated feature. They also can be used internally in organizational print media such as newsletters and in-house magazines. Additionally, features offer a wealth of possibilities for organizational Web sites. Here are some ways public relations writers use features.

Features about people may include biographical narratives or personal profiles about people associated with an organization, such as the profile of a school principal nearing retirement, a newly appointed corporate executive, or a long-time volunteer at a nonprofit organization. Features might also be based on interviews with employees having a particular expertise or interest.

Features about organizations include histories of companies or nonprofits, as well as profiles of the organization and its role within the community, industry or profession. For example, the NGO Doctors Without Borders uses its Web site to provide information about its history and its health programs throughout the world.

Features about issues allow public relations writers to focus on topics of importance to their organizations and clients. Examples of such features are a how-to article disseminated by a psychiatric counseling center with suggestions on reducing emotional stress during the holiday season, a Web-site service article by a law firm on how to save money while preparing a will, or tax tips from a CPA around tax-filing time. Public relations writers also use background features to provide perspective on an issue of current interest, such as a university engineering department outlining the pros and cons of wind energy or a teachers' organization reviewing options for state-wide education restructuring and reform.

Don't ignore **visual elements** in features. If a feature lends itself to an accompanying photo, shoot one or have one produced. Digital technology makes picture-taking easy, and a photo along with a feature story will increase the possibility of its use, especially in weekly or suburban newspapers. If your organization has a video unit, send stock footage along with a fact sheet or news release and let the television station create its own feature. Or, call an assignment editor about a feature that you have planned with visual components and encourage them to send a camera crew and reporter. Print and broadcast media have voracious appetites that constantly need to be fed. If you can generate a newsworthy feature, your company, organization or candidate gets some free space or air time. That's the best kind.

Feature Leads

By far, the most common way to give a story feature treatment is by writing a feature lead to begin the article. A feature lead omits some, if not all, of the usual facts about who, what, where, when, why and how. The writer adds the missing details after the lead.

Feature leads are not limited to the single-sentence, single-paragraph hard news lead format. Rather, feature leads are more like opening sections of stories. They may consist of a single short sentence or phrase, or they may be two paragraphs, three paragraphs—even a dozen paragraphs. The feature lead sets the direction and tone of the story and is finished when the introductory unit is complete—for example, when the description is ended, the anecdote related or the riddle answered.

What today we call a summary news lead, in fact, grew out of the common use of what was originally thought of as a brief feature lead—one used to succinctly and directly summarize somewhat startling information. Such a summary feature lead would be something like *Rebecca Wainwright spent her entire Fourth of July eating watermelons,* or *Max Morton has no house, no car, no job and no family.* These leads are considered good because they quickly summarize for readers information that on its own merit is exciting or intriguing enough to grab their attention and hook them into reading the story.

In general, most feature leads are conversational, using contractions such as *won't* or *can't.* They also can be written in sentence fragments, such as the phrases people use in talking to one another (rather than in the complete sentences used in formal news writing).

Feature leads often use the direct-address pronoun *you* (or *you* understood—that is, the word *you* is implied). Feature leads ask readers questions *(Are you happy with the size of the daisies in your garden?),* give readers advice *(For a successful holiday party, consider these new low-fat recipes),* or tell readers anecdotes or little stories *(Winston Churchill was known for his quick wit and furious temper. One day when his military aide was slow to respond to a request, Churchill . . .).*

It is not unheard of for a reporter, in a feature lead, to refer to himself or herself in order to draw readers into the story by personalizing it *(I remember my high school prom, class of '97).* In a context where it will not sound condescending, a feature writer can also write a lead using casual language such as slang or dialect *(So, y'all, head on down to the fab festivities . . .).*

Silly words *(zippity de do da)* or onomatopoeic words (words that sound like what they mean: *crash! bang!),* and alliterative phrases (many words beginning with the same sound) are also common in feature leads. Feature writers, then, are expected to write leads that are clever, that entertain readers with creative language and draw people into reading the story.

Sometimes feature leads attract readers by astonishing them with amazing facts or statistics; sometimes they arouse readers' interest by springing surprises on them or by ending with an unexpected piece of information or a twist in the turn of events (an **ironic lead**). Feature writers may also attract readers to a story by so intensely describing a location that readers can imagine being there (a **descriptive** or **color lead**). Sometimes feature leads tease readers with an intriguing statement that makes little apparent sense but tells them just enough to awaken their curiosity (a **teaser lead**).

In fact, feature writers have a great deal of latitude in writing their leads—they can pretty much write anything. As long as the lead attracts readers to a story, it is considered well written.

Box 9.3
Writing Interesting Feature Leads

Here are some interesting feature leads. Note the length of the leads, the unusual language, and the way readers, after finishing the lead, would want to keep reading to find out more.

CLERMONT—"Eeuuuuuwwww!"

Tabitha Ramirez gripped the sides of an oak barrel and lowered her feet into the cold, sweet-smelling slush.

The message on her 4-year-old face was something between "Get-me-outta-here, NOW!" and "Let-me-AT-it."

The whistle blew, the music began and Tabitha started stomping grapes at Lakeridge Winery and Vineyard.

(*Phil Long, Miami Herald*)

This was Doris Duke's dilemma. She was worth $1.2 billion, but had no relatives or friends she particularly cared to enrich so massively when she died. Instead, she decided with immodesty befitting one of the world's richest women that her estate would go toward "the improvement of humanity," as her will said. Her money would allow dancers to dance, artists to paint, doctors to cure diseases, animals to escape the cruelty of people.

It was a wonderful vision. But it overlooked what turned out to be the first effect of Miss Duke's largesse: It allowed lawyers to eat.

(*Matthew Purdy, New York Times*)

TORONTO—Astronomers took a long, long look into the future and foresaw a cold, black, dying universe without planets, stars, galaxies or life as we know it.

Fortunately, they said, that day won't come for an unimaginably long time. To designate the number of years before the last scrap of matter disappears, you would have to write 1 followed by 100 zeros (a googol). That is:

10,000,000,000,000,000,000,000,000,000, 000,000,000,000,000,000,000,000,000,000, 000,000,000,000,000,000,000,000,000,000, 000,000,000, 000—or many times more than the total of atoms in the universe.

(*Robert S. Boyd, Knight Ridder*)

If you decide to give an inverted pyramid news story feature treatment by writing a feature lead, you too can have this latitude about what you write. Almost anything goes—but be sure your lead is consistent with the purpose and content of the story. If it is not, the difference between lead and story can be unpleasantly jarring. You wouldn't, for example, write a zany teaser like *What goes bang and thump?* as a lead for a story on the number of accidental deaths caused by guns.

Types of Feature Stories

Narratives

As described previously, a chronological narrative is occasionally integrated into sports, accident and other inverted pyramid news stories. A narrative structure can also be the basis of a feature.

A **narrative** by definition relates events chronologically, although its "once upon a time" story-telling can be modified and rearranged to allow for flashbacks or foreshadowing. Frequently, a narrative is used to create suspense; readers keep reading to find out what happens, to see if the subject of the story survives some ordeal or gets out of some danger. Writers of narratives deliberately withhold the story's conclusion, keeping readers in suspense; therefore, such narratives are sometimes called **suspended-interest stories**. Any time you modify a straight news story, presenting some of its information in a story-telling manner that keeps readers guessing about what happens next, you are adding narrative structure and using a feature writing technique.

Narrative feature stories can help readers understand the moments before or after a tragedy, whether that tragedy is public or personal. Narrative features can also chronologically relate what happens in the day in the life of someone, whether a public servant, such as a highway patrol officer or firefighter, or a private individual, such as an orderly at a nursing home or a janitor in a college dormitory. Narrative features can recount steps in a process of recovery or breakdown. They can re-create the events of a bygone time, pacing the reader through a nostalgic journey.

Narratives With Inverted Pyramid Stories

Narratives can be combined with inverted pyramid stories in various ways. An **hourglass story**, as described by Roy Peter Clark of the Poynter Institute for Media Studies, consists of two large sections connected by a slim paragraph. The first section of the story summarizes in a few paragraphs the highlights of the reporting, using standard inverted pyramid style. Then comes the **turn**, a slim paragraph that says something like *it all began when . . .* Finally, the second major section of the article retells the story chronologically with greater detail and many quotations, giving readers a clearer and more satisfying version of what happened.

Narrative passages also can be alternated with inverted pyramid sections of news stories, particularly in longer stories, so that storytelling can break up the duller, more solid factual reporting.

Narratives can also **frame** news stories; that is, they can serve as the beginning and ending units of inverted pyramid articles. Typically, the framed story (sometimes called a **focus story** or a *Wall Street Journal* **story** after the newspaper that popularized its use) leads with several paragraphs telling the story of one person affected by a news event:

> *Bob Jones walked home slowly with his layoff notice in his hand . . .*

Then a brief paragraph relates the fact that the single individual's story is only a part of a more significant set of events:

> *But Jones is only one of several hundred auto workers laid off this week.*

The major full-length section of the story presents information (for example, about the layoffs) in an inverted pyramid structure. The last few paragraphs complete the single person's narrative story begun in the lead:

Jones says he's not discouraged. He said he'll be at the employment agency first thing tomorrow morning.

Personal Narratives

Other stories, called **personal narratives**, entail individuals relating to readers what happened to them, using the first-person pronoun *I*. Personal narratives are, to some extent, integrated in some way into straight news stories whenever the reporter uses a long extended direct quotation from a person who was interviewed.

Personal narratives in news features might consist of a reporter telling his or her own experience covering an event. For example, the reporter might give an hour-by-hour description of witnessing the execution of a criminal or seeing hurricane winds do their damage. Narratives are frequently written by war correspondents during battles or military invasions, giving people back home a special way to learn—through the eyes and ears of the reporter writing personally what is happening far away.

Occasions that call for personal narratives sometimes include instances of **participatory journalism**, in which a reporter deliberately participates in an action (usually incognito) to discover first hand what such an experience is like. The participatory experience may represent serious investigative reporting, such as a reporter testing airport security by trying to take prohibited items through inspection. Or the experience may represent relatively lighthearted, casual reporting, giving readers a human-interest insight into roles people play (being a mall Santa Claus for an afternoon, for example).

Color Stories

Another alternative writing style that can be used for stand-alone features or news features, or can be integrated into inverted pyramid news stories is **color** writing—that is, using a writing style heavy with descriptive language. Color feature stories, as full-fledged features or news features, focus on place, giving readers a strong sense of what it's like to be at a particular location, whether a courtroom, a concert or a Caribbean island.

Color feature stories are relatively unstructured. The article begins with a description of a special meaningful place and ends whenever the writer wants. Writers typically use the present tense in the article rather than the traditional past tense.

Color features may be unified, not by an inverted pyramid structure, but rather by a repetition of verbal elements, such as words, sounds, metaphors or details about people or places. The unifying element is consistently repeated throughout the article, creating a rhythmic structure that enlarges meaning with each repetition.

Color stories also may be held together by a skeletal narrative, for example, a color description held together by the order of events at something as newsworthy as a Super Bowl or an Olympic skating competition, or something as familiar as bingo night at the local fire hall. The story is then a narrative–color combination, with a heavy dose of description and a light dose of narrative.

Color stories also can be chaotic—as chaotic as the reality they represent—with story information arranged in a kaleidoscope of images. The chaos represents the confusion the reporter might have actually perceived, for example, at an anti-abortion rally or a rock concert.

Color features and color news features make extensive use of sensory language. Sensory writing, as the name suggests, addresses the senses—describing what readers would see, hear, smell, feel and taste if they were on the scene. These stories are known also for their richness of observed physical detail. Writers of color stories are masters of observation and careful, precise descriptive writing. Nothing of relevance is lost to them; they have an eye for the factual reality that conveys an emotional meaning:

The five-foot office desk is a deep brown mahogany. (Its owner is rich and powerful.)

Writers of color stories also go for language that is loaded with connotative meaning; *blue eyes* become *sapphire eyes*. Such language calls forth more emotional responses from readers than the neutral descriptive language of news articles.

Color stories often use poetic imagery. Similes (comparisons using *like* or *as)* and metaphors (comparisons not using *like* or *as)* describe the unknown in terms of the known, helping readers understand the nature of the unfamiliar through what is familiar, as in the following:

The flowers, cranberry-red, bloomed in profusion.

Personification (ascribing to inanimate objects human characteristics or behavior) is used to help inanimate objects come alive:

A large portrait of Gen. Wilkes glared down from the far wall.

Observed physical detail, of course, can be used effectively in straight inverted pyramid news stories, as can colorful sensory description. A limited dose of color can improve many news stories, particularly those about events with an interesting location and atmosphere. When similes, metaphors and personification give color treatment to an inverted pyramid news story, they add to the fullness of its coverage:

At the convention, balloons danced in the air while the candidate gave an acceptance speech the length of a commencement address.

Human Interest Stories

A third type of feature article, the **human interest story**, also can influence the style of a straight inverted pyramid news article. Some professionals argue that all journalistic stories are human interest stories, because all stories appeal in some way to the shared human values of readers. Few writers would contest that argument; however, at least in the traditional sense, a human interest story is understood as one that *particularly* emphasizes human values and has sympathetic people as story subjects. A human interest article especially considers what it means to experience the defeats and victories, joys and sorrows of the human condition.

In terms of story structure, human interest features generally take the form of lengthy interview articles. They use extensive long direct quotations so readers feel they are hearing

---

Box 9.4

It Happened to Me: Happy New Year?

As a TV reporter, I was called out early one New Year's morning to cover a spectacular predawn house fire. Fortunately, the family—husband, wife, and six children—escaped without injury. I photographed the husband and wife watching firefighters battle to save their newly built home—the family had lived there only three weeks—but I could not locate the family's six children, although fire officials said everyone was safe.

Later that morning, I went back to the ruined house. I felt somewhat awkward when I realized the man standing in front of me was the homeowner, inspecting the damage. I introduced myself and asked whether he minded if I walked through the house. "Not at all," the man replied. "I'll go with you."

I had strapped on the portable sound camera, so as we moved through the ruined rooms, our feet crunching in the debris and ashes, I commented, "Rough way to start a new year, isn't it?"

"No," the man replied, "not at all." He felt that way, he said, because most important of all, they were all alive and safe. They had insurance and, although they had lost some things of value, most possessions would be replaced.

What was most gratifying, the man said, was the fact that neighbors they didn't even know took in the children, one here, two there, and gave them a place to sleep, dressed them in clothes belonging to their own children, and fed them breakfast the next morning. How fortunate, he said, to live among these generous people.

His words made for a powerful interview story and a great New Year's Day human interest feature on an otherwise uneventful holiday. —*WRW*

---

the story's subject and/or the people around the subject share feelings directly and immediately, talking to readers one-on-one. Speech tags are more elaborate, substituting other words for *said* and including descriptions of human actions or facial expressions accompanying the spoken word:

> *"Why did he do this to me?" she cried, shaking her fist at her husband's framed picture on the table.*

Human interest stories are often about an individual's experience with a run of hard luck or a sudden reversal of fortune. They tell about people who are dealing with loss: of health, of money, of a loved one, of life itself. Some human interest features are positive and inspirational; others are negative and full of a sense of futility and despair.

Human interest features tend to be relatively short, concentrating on creating in readers a single emotional response; too long a story can break the reader's mood. These articles use everyday straightforward language, suitable for expressing the concerns of most human beings.

Straight inverted pyramid news stories can be given strong human interest treatment when they permit interview subjects to talk extensively about their experiences or when the articles present certain aspects of the story from a human interest perspective. Such articles, for example, would consider the outlook of the players rather than the star of the game. They would describe individual human beings rather than the collective members of a large group.

Profiles

In contrast to human-interest, color and narrative writing, which can be used for features, news features and feature treatment of news stories, other kinds of articles are generally defined as features only. Probably the most familiar is the **personality profile**, which looks for the key to the subject's character and psyche. A brief personality profile may be called a **personality sketch**, or a **thumbnail**, when it is briefer still. A personality profile differs from a news interview story, which seeks to discover information that the interview subject holds, in that a profile article studies personality and attempts to present to readers the complex and unique psychology of a human individual.

Profiles usually take the form of lengthy one-to-one interview articles. They also typically include background biographical information and a lot of description of the subject and his or her environment or "natural habitat."

Most profiles are written about celebrities. Feature writers also sometimes write profiles of unusual and eccentric characters or of people who have memorable or inspiring personal histories. Places and organizations, too, can be "profiled," in the sense of the feature story's examining their essential character or nature, just as in profile stories of people.

Brights

Brights are brief humorous feature stories intended to brighten the reader's day. (They are called **kickers** in broadcast writing.) Many brights, like jokes, include only the most necessary relevant details—those that "build" economically to a punch line that ends the article with an unexpected twist.

Some brights relate extraordinary things that happen to ordinary people, telling about coincidences and actions entirely unplanned and unexpected. Their humor comes from a sort of "isn't life crazy?" message. In other brights, the writer offers personal reflections and observations, or playfully considers obscure but amusing facts or pieces of trivia. Playful brights might examine, for example, strange phobias or silly habits, or investigate the origins of certain words or clichés.

Backgrounders, Reaction, and Analysis Stories

Backgrounders are lengthy, serious features that typically explain the how and why behind a news event or trend (which is the "foreground," so to speak). Backgrounders explain the historical context of a controversy or conflict, helping readers understand why people or institutions are behaving as they are.

Certain background articles, called **reaction stories**, use the premise of the news event to give readers information about how other people—particularly people with education and experience—are interpreting reality. Learning about how others view the news—for example, reading about a how a general judges the progress of a war or how a doctor views a new health-related science discovery—provides readers with a better understanding and evaluation of what is happening around them. **Person-on-the-street** reaction pieces can add local interest to a national or international event, but they have less value as educational pieces.

Backgrounders can also take apart the elements of a current event, organization, or business to analyze it, helping readers see how the parts work together to make an effective or ineffective whole. Such an **analysis story** dissects reality to examine it. A typical formula involves analyzing the past, present and future of the situation, organization, or event. For example, the story might describe the current situation of a disease, such as diabetes, that affects the general public, then give a history of how the disease was discovered and has been treated, then ask experts and scientists what the future will be like: Will the disease be conquered, when and how?

Some backgrounders explain scientific phenomena to readers, helping them understand, for example, new surgical techniques or increased computer capabilities. Other backgrounders dispassionately present two sides of a conflict or controversy, enabling readers to learn the pros and cons of each side's point of view.

Many backgrounders deal with topics on readers' minds, but some are the result of the enterprise of reporters and editors who deliberately bring to readers' attention in-depth information about topics that the editors believe readers should understand. Examples include new capabilities of genetic alteration, the threat involved in the destruction of the rain forests, or the relevance of the discovery of a new galaxy.

Backgrounders are similar to news stories in that they are written in an objective and fairly formal style. Unlike news stories, however, they have a clear explanatory, "teacherly" intent. And, unlike editorials and personal columns, they teach but do not preach. They make no attempt to persuade the reader to any point of view; rather, the reader is educated so he or she can make judgments independently.

To teach, backgrounders must define terms clearly and provide numerous examples and illustrations. They must make statistics and numbers relevant and put them in a context that readers will understand. They must explain complex technical and scientific ideas in direct simple language that makes such ideas understandable but not simplistic.

The content of backgrounders imposes further demands on the writer. Because backgrounders are usually quite long, they need a consistent focus and steadily paced material. Because they are complicated, they require clear transitions that keep ideas following logically one after another.

Anniversary Stories

Another type of feature story that many reporters are called on to write, an **anniversary story**, not only marks anniversaries but also the regular occurrences of holidays or seasonal changes. Such stories are written routinely and their routine nature makes them difficult: How do you say something about this Veterans Day that hasn't been said already about the last 20 Veterans Days? Such feature-writing occasions can severely test a reporter's ability to come up with a fresh story or a fresh way of writing a familiar story. Anniversary stories are often rotated among reporters to ensure a different perspective each time.

Anniversary stories, along with **holiday** and **seasonal stories**, are usually brief and written with a common, simple touch, as befits an article marking an occasion that many readers share and value. They are frequently done as extended interviews, with the reporter (and reader) listening, for example, to the recollections of someone who lived through D-Day or the fall of

---

Box 9.5

It Happened to Me: Circus

"The circus is in town. Go do a feature," my editor growled. I didn't bother to tell him that I was six years old the last time I went to the circus and I got sick on the peanuts and scared that the high-wire artist was going to fall and started crying and never went back. My editor said, "Do a feature," so that's how I was going to spend the next few hours.

But what to do? Editors often don't give more direction than that. It's up to the ingenuity of the individual reporter to come up with a story. It was a beautiful, sun-splashed early summer day, with temperatures in the low 80s. I walked over to the Civic Auditorium, where the circus was going to be, and was attracted by the sound of grunting and stomping. The noise came from a half-dozen elephants in the parking lot, chained together by their feet, who seemed to be enjoying being hosed down by a circus attendant to keep them cool. He told me that keeping the animals healthy was a constant problem and if they became overheated and dehydrated, death could follow in short order. I noted that down, as well as a picture idea for one of our photogs.

Inside, it was controlled chaos, with roustabouts shouting as banners were being strung and various props were put into place. I was particularly intrigued by the high-wire setup. The trapeze artist was standing next to the riggers, meticulously supervising every aspect of the setup, testing wires for tautness, directing how cables should be tightened or loosened a quarter turn so that they were exactly right. He told me this became a routine ritual after he once nearly fell because the settings weren't correct. After the wires were rigged, he added, one of the other high-wire artists would stay nearby to ensure that someone didn't bump into the rigging or otherwise change the settings. After all, he said, he did work without a safety net.

I walked back and looked at the lions and tigers in their cages (they looked unhappy, I later wrote) and talked with one of the clowns and a couple of other performers, gathering material for a story that was gradually starting to come together in my mind. I also talked with the circus publicist and made sure that I had times and ticket charges correct. No sense in writing a good feature about the circus if the information isn't accurate and people miss the show.

—WRW

Saigon, or hearing the reflections of someone who has helped feed the homeless every Thanksgiving. Some holiday stories offer helps and tips; still others try to consider a given holiday through a fresh perspective, by viewing it through the eyes of someone outside the culture or by comparing the present holiday to one from another time.

The key to the success of the holiday, anniversary or seasonal story is the writer's creativity in offering something fresh, either in style or content.

How-Tos

A feature especially helpful to readers is a **how-to**, which—as the name suggests—is a story explaining to readers how to do something or how to do it better. How-to stories are almost formulaic. They usually begin with a lead that directly addresses the reader's need:

If you're having trouble sleeping, a good mattress may give you the sweet dreams you crave.

Then the story progresses to either a step-by-step set of directions (go to the mattress store, buy a mattress, bring it home) or a point-by-point discussion of relevant considerations (box springs, padding material, cover quality, stitching strength). The story ends when the set of directions or the advice is complete.

The expert of a how-to can be yourself, the reporter, or it can be someone you interview— that is, one or more authorities. However, be sure to include in the story the credentials of whoever is the expert (including your own if you are the expert), so that the article's advice has credibility.

The sentences and vocabulary in the how-to must be particularly clear and its directions or discussion easy to follow. The story must not simply rehash folk wisdom the reader already knows. To serve readers, a how-to must be truly helpful and offer new or advanced advice.

Labeled Feature Stories

Many other features have "labels" or "names"—not because they represent distinct types of writing but simply because the topic they concern is done so frequently that it becomes

---

Box 9.6

It Happened to Me: More Than Friends

One of the police officers in a neighboring community loved to ride his motorcycle after work, his way to unwind after a stressful day. One evening at dusk, he rode through what had been open land, only to run into a chain stretched across the road. He died instantly.

His funeral, as for any law enforcement officer, brought respectful delegations of police, sheriff's deputies, and highway patrol from a 50-mile radius. Police funerals are colorful, full of pomp and splendor. That alone made for a good TV news story.

But I was surprised to see one of his fellow officers standing quietly on crutches. What was amazing to me was that he had been severely wounded more than three years before, shot in the abdomen and partially paralyzed by a gunman whose attempt at holding up a supermarket had been foiled. I had covered the story and dutifully reported several days later that doctors said he probably would never walk again because of spinal injuries. Now, here he was on crutches!

I had had an ongoing interest in the man's story, and our station had done at least one feature on a fundraiser to pay for making his house handicap-accessible. One of the other officers told me the story. The injured officer had gone into a deep depression and his best friend, the motorcyclist, was determined to snap him out of it. The injured officer was undergoing painful physical therapy and every day his friend was there, encouraging him to do the exercises.

The months went on and the officer's condition improved. Not good, not pain-free, but he could get out of a wheelchair and eventually could shuffle along with a walker. His goal became to walk unassisted, and both worked hard at achieving that objective. "This is the first day he's walked on his own," the policeman told me.

I didn't talk with the officer; I didn't want to intrude on his grief, or his privacy. What I did was shoot some telephoto shots, mostly from behind and the side, interspersing video of him with that of the funeral procession. Coupled with the news story of the funeral, it made for a powerful human-interest sidebar feature.

—WRW

recognizable. The **dying-child** and **last-wish** story "names" refer somewhat cynically to human interest articles about people dealing with death. The **where are they now** and **native sons and daughters** stories are profiles—in the first instance, of people who have retired or moved on; in the second, of hometown people who have become celebrities. A **behind-the-scenes** story presents a scene through the eyes of the reporter or another witness who is behind the public facade during an event or at an institution. A **race against the clock** story is a narrative about accomplishing a crucial objective in a limited amount of time.

Consider the Possibilities

The list of story names could continue because journalists like to concoct labels almost as much as they like to concoct stories. However, what's important to know is simply that there are many alternatives to the inverted pyramid. In feature writing, the possibilities are limited only by your reporting and writing abilities. Develop an eye and ear for features just as you do for news. Look around you. Let your curiosity run rampant. Start thinking. If something interests you, chances are it will interest your readers too.

Read and study the varieties of feature stories you find in print and online newspapers, magazines, newsletters and journals. Through them, you may get ideas for stylistic techniques and structures that you want to integrate into your own particular toolbox of writing skills for print journalism. You may also see how alternative approaches to reporting and writing can enhance the news you report.

Discussion Questions

The following are class discussion questions drawn from Chapter 9:

1. What is the purpose of feature stories?

2. What are some of the characteristics of features?

3. How is a feature lead constructed compared to a traditional lead for a news story?

4. How is *narrative treatment* used in a news story?

5. What elements are present in *color* stories? *Human interest* stories?

6. What is it about the *personality profile* that distinguishes it from other forms of journalistic writing?

7. Why are *backgrounders* important and how are they written?

8. What traits do you need to develop to become a good feature writer?

CHAPTER EXERCISES

Exercise 9.1—Spin-Off Ideas

Discuss in class some possible feature stories that could be generated by the publication of the following news story:

> A man who stole a box of diapers and a bag of groceries from a car in a discount store parking lot was sentenced Tuesday to 25 years to life under California's "three strikes" law.
>
> Superior Court Judge John D. Simons sentenced David C. Frazier, 30, for the robbery, following his two previous convictions for petty theft and attempted robbery. Under the new "three strikes" law passed in 1994 to punish repeat offenders, Frazier's sentence is automatic. He will not be eligible for parole for 20 years.
>
> Frazier, out of work and father of a newborn baby girl, said he took the diapers and food because he and his wife were desperate. "I know it's wrong to steal," he said, "but I never thought I would be spending the rest of my life in jail for it."

Exercise 9.2—Giving a News Story a Feature Lead

Find a news article in your local newspaper that is about a slightly silly or offbeat event. Write a feature lead for the story.

Exercise 9.3—Gathering Impressions

Sit in a crowded public place like a zoo, ski resort or public library. Write down in your notebook the conversations you overhear, the sights you see, the sounds you hear, the colors and textures of physical objects around you.

Discuss in class which of the observed details you should include in a description of the place. How could you give people a sense of what it was like to be there? What overriding impression would you convey in a descriptive lead or color story?

Exercise 9.4—How-To Story

Consider a topic about which you know a lot. Write down everything you would want to tell someone who was just learning about that subject. Then organize the information. Does it work better topically or chronologically? Write a how-to story with yourself as expert.

Or, think of a topic about which you would like to know more, such as what equipment to buy for mountain climbing or for water or winter sports. Who would you interview to get information for a how-to story? What are the strengths and weaknesses of these various potential sources as credible teachers? Would you prefer to interview just one of them at length or talk to as many people as possible? Why?

Exercise 9.5—Professor Profile

Write a profile of one of your teachers for your college or university's student newspaper or public affairs newsletter. Interview your source for at least 45 minutes. Be sure that you observe his or her natural surroundings. What clues to character can you find in your professor's office?

Consider your subject's appearance carefully. Be sure you note details—like the color of hair and eyes—details so specific that, after reading your story, readers could identify this person from, say, five other people in a group. Look for physical characteristics or mannerisms that reveal character: laugh lines, tapping feet, hands flying around while he or she talks. Which details would you include?

How will you find out biographical information about this professor? Does your college public relations office give out vitae (resumés) of staff? Are vitae on file in department offices or the campus library? Has the professor written any books? Are they listed in *Books in Print?* If you Google him/her, what will you find?

How much negative and how much positive material will be in your portrait? Which is the best representation of reality, as you experienced the interview? After you've written a full profile, distill what you've written into a six-paragraph sketch.

Exercise 9.6—Crime Feature

Take the following crime story information and give the story an interesting feature twist:

There was a holdup at the nearby Short Stop convenience store at Grant Street and Forest Avenue today.

Police say a man walked into the market, pulled out his wallet, and asked for change for a $20 bill. When the clerk opened the register, the man drew a handgun and demanded money. He then sped off with about $300 in stolen cash.

He forgot something: his wallet.

When police arrived at the scene, they looked inside the wallet and found three traffic citations. After matching the address to a partial license plate number spotted by the store clerk, officers arrested the man, Jessie Dillinger, 1512 Gunn Ave., at his home.

He was charged with armed robbery and is being held in [your] local jail. Dillinger told police he held up the store in order to have money to pay the traffic tickets.

Exercise 9.7—*The Four Seasons*

Write a 400-word feature on some aspect of the beginning of the new season to be used on the first day of spring, summer, winter, or fall. Incorporate interviews as well as your own impressions. When you are finished, put the different features onto a class e-mail distribution list or Web site. Read and discuss them in terms of writing, organization, originality and interest.

Suggestions for Further Reading

Aamidor, Abraham. *Real Feature Writing* (Hillsdale, N.J.: Lawrence Erlbaum, 1999).

Bloom, Stephen G. *Inside the Writer's Mind: Writing Narrative Journalism* (Ames: Iowa State University Press, 2002).

Blundell, William E. *The Art and Craft of Feature Writing: Based on the* Wall Street Journal (New York: New American Library, 1988).

Chance, Jean and William McKeen, Eds. *Literary Journalism: A Reader* (Belmont, Calif.: Wadsworth, 2000).

Franklin, Jon. *Writing for Story: Craft Secrets of Dramatic Non-fiction* (New York: Atheneum, 1994).

Friedlander, Edward Jay and John Lee. *Feature Writing for Newspapers and Magazines: The Pursuit of Excellence*, 6th ed. (Boston: Allyn and Bacon, 2008).

Jackson, Dennis and John Sweeney, Eds. *The Journalist's Craft: A Guide to Writing Better Stories* (New York: Allsworth Press, 2002).

Klement, Alice M., and Carolyn B. Matalene. *Telling Stories, Taking Risks: Journalism Writing at the Century's Edge* (New York: Wadsworth, 1997).

Garlock, David, Ed. *Pulitzer Prize Feature Stories: America's Best Writing, 1979–2003*, 2nd ed. (Blackwell Publishing Professional, 2003).

Garrison, Bruce. *Professional Feature Writing*, 4th ed. (Mahwah, N.J.: Lawrence Erlbaum, 2004).

Harpee, Timothy, Ed. *The ASJA Guide to Freelance Writing* (New York: St. Martin's, 2003).

Lewis, Anthony, Ed. *Written into History: Pulitzer Prize Reporting of the Twentieth Century from the New York Times* (New York: *New York Times* Books, 2001).

New York Times. Portraits 9/11/01 (New York: *New York Times* Books/Henry Holt and Co., 2002).

Ramsey, Janet E. *Feature and Magazine Article Writing* (New York: McGraw-Hill College, 1998).

Sims, Norman and Mark Kramer, Eds. *Literary Journalism in the Twentieth Century* (New York: Oxford University Press, 1990).

Weingarten, Marc. *The Gang That Wouldn't Write Straight: Wolfe, Thompson, Didion, and the New Journalism Revolution* (New York: Crown, 2005).

Witt, Leonard. *The Complete Book of Feature Writing* (Cincinnati: Writer's Digest Books, 1991).

Wolfe, Tom. *The New Journalism* (New York: Macmillan, 1998).

10

Writing Broadcast Copy

Chapter Objectives

- To compare the difference between writing for print and broadcast
- To explain various types of leads used in broadcast copywriting
- To demonstrate effective word choices that make copy clear and lively
- To introduce formats appropriate for radio and TV copy
- To show the importance of freshening broadcast copy
- To explain news judgment in assembling stories for a newscast

---

News is Often Unexpected

It was shortly before 5 p.m. on a Friday, often a quiet news day. Most pieces of the 6 o'clock news had fallen into place, and the mood in the newsroom was low-key, relaxed. Several members of the staff were already debating whether to hold a post-newscast critique at the usual watering hole or try a new place up the street. Suddenly, a tremendous explosion downtown rattled our windows, even though we were more than two miles away. A boiler had exploded in a department store, sending glass and debris rocketing into the city's main intersection; five people were killed and more than 100 were injured.

The news team sprang into action and reporters switched into "automatic," deciding instinctively what to use, preparing riveting copy to go along with powerful visuals. The program producer, with production's technical director, tied together the various field reports, visuals, background "wild sound" and graphics to produce a comprehensive report that lasted well into the evening.

It was great television, but it wouldn't have been half as good had it not been well reported and well written. Writing is the essential ingredient in radio and TV news broadcasting. No matter how dramatic the sounds or visuals, it is the writing quality—interesting leads and crisp copy—that attracts and holds listening and viewing audiences.

Writing copy for radio and television news and for organizational broadcast media used in public relations is both more difficult than it seems and easier than it looks. To become a good broadcast writer, you must write on a regular basis and listen analytically to broadcast reports. When you do, you will realize there are essential basics to writing good broadcast copy.

First, radio and TV stories are designed to be spoken over the air. Because radio–TV copy is written for the ear, not the eye, it has many limitations, one being that the listener or viewer does not have an opportunity to return to something that was missed or seemed unclear. Instead, the listener or viewer must absorb information as it is presented or miss the story. Some people do other things while their radio or TV is on, so broadcast copy must be written to catch their attention when the TV or radio is used as background sound.

To grab attention, broadcast copy must be simpler than print and convey the essence of the story in a limited amount of time. Simple direct style enables greater understanding. A basic principle in broadcast writing is that scripts must be written conversationally, as though the writer were talking to a friend. Also write with your announcer in mind so that he or she does not stumble over phrases or mispronounce words. The goal is clarity so that listeners understand what is being communicated.

Time is often the determining factor in how a story will be written. Although newspapers have a finite amount of space, when a major story breaks, pages can be added or ads can be pulled to provide more column inches. Not so in broadcasting: The clock is a tyrant because there is just so much time in a 30-minute TV newscast or a five-minute radio news summary. In addition, today's audiences live in an increasingly fast-paced world. Broadcast news copywriters must take into account that not only is the audience rushed, but listeners and viewers also have shorter attention spans, perhaps because they have become accustomed to the speed and brevity of TV advertising.

Except for popular "magazine format" programs such as *60 Minutes* or tabloid news shows, the average listener or viewer will not spend time with a long detailed news report. Instead, audiences want essentials. A broadcast writer sometimes must tell in 30 seconds a story that a newspaper writer may relate in eight to 10 column inches.

Condensing Copy

Copy must be pared to accommodate a precise and limited number of minutes and seconds. This means there is no latitude for wasted words. While some redundancy is sometimes necessary to aid comprehension, copy is lean and spare for the most part.

The inverted pyramid format for setting priorities applies equally well in broadcast copywriting. What should go first? What's the most important? How to get into the story and bring along the listener or viewer? Those are questions the radio or TV newswriter instinctively asks. Details are often cut. Ages are usually left out unless they are germane to the story. Precise addresses are often eliminated. Quotes are generally too lengthy for a routine story, unless

Box 10.1

What to Cut?

It's all well and good to say that copy should be lean and spare, with useless words and phrases eliminated. But how does that translate into practical advice?

First of all, get rid of wasted words. This writer's personal favorite is *"that,"* as in "The mayor said *that* he didn't know how the city was going to avoid layoffs." *That* doesn't add a thing.

Ages are another. There's no reason to say, "The *24-year-old* driver was booked for D-W-I." Age doesn't matter. Now, if an 84-year-old driver loses control of a vehicle and causes an accident, age probably needs to be mentioned because it introduces an unusual element into the story. If the age of one participant is used, fairness implies that the ages of others are mentioned. But if there are several persons of similar ages, reporting ages complicates the script and takes away from other detail.

Directions usually can be cut, as in "The speeding *westbound* auto . . ." If something happened "today" you don't need to say so in your copy. "The fire, which broke out at 4:30 a.m. today . . ." can be pared to *"The predawn fire . . ."*

Eliminate unneeded words. "The accident occurred at the corner of Grant Street and Forest Avenue" can be cut to *"The accident occurred at Grant and Forest."* Five words gone with no sacrifice of clarity—but five words here, two or three there, and suddenly there's another line to add more detail.

Occupational titles can be tightened up. "Scientists at the University of Oregon" can be *"University of Oregon scientists."* Two words gone. "The Secretary of Defense, Mel Moreguns, said . . ." becomes *"Defense Secretary Mel Moreguns said . . ."* Another two words. Some can't be changed. The Secretary of State is the Secretary of State, not State Secretary. But where titles can be abbreviated, do so. Try this one: "The Commissioner of Finance of the County of Erie." Four words can be chopped. See how easy it is?

In sports, is it necessary to refer to "the hard-throwing left-hander"? That seems to be one of those clichés like "the fleet-footed running back." Now, a sportswriter may *want* to use those phrases because sports writing is more informal than news copy, but question whether it's desirable. Always look for ways to cut words and simplify phrasing.

---

they can be used as a final punch line to add impact. Less important detail, which might flesh out a print story, generally has to be sacrificed.

The reason is simple: In a half-hour television newscast, the actual time for news is about 12 minutes. First, the newscast is only 28 minutes and 30 seconds long, not the full 30 minutes. Subtract at least eight minutes for commercials, another minute and a half for various verbal bridges between stories and getting in and out of the newscast, four minutes for sports, and about three for weather. There's not much time left. If there's 12 minutes for news and each story runs 30 seconds, it means there is a maximum of 24 items that can run in a newscast. But some pieces may run a minute and a half, or sports or weather may need more time. The latitude in radio news is even smaller. Subtract a couple of minutes for commercials within a five-minute news-on-the-hour format and there's little time for more than expanded headlines. Audio cuts have to be trimmed to just the essentials. Tight writing is a must.

Stories are often assigned a specific length. If a reporter goes over that allocated time, it means another story must be cut or dropped from the newscast, and the other reporter won't be too happy about it. Or someone else will cut the story to length; the risk being that essential details may be inadvertently dropped. Learn to write to length.

Composing "Good-Sounding" Copy

Like any good copy, print stories included, broadcast copy should "read" well. In the case of radio–TV writing, this quality is not just desirable but also essential. "Write as you speak," many experts advise. Write conversationally and explain complex events in understandable language. Know your audience and have a purpose in writing. Aim your news reports at the listeners or viewers who did not have the opportunity to attend the city council or school board meeting or sit in on budget hearings or observe a sensational criminal court arraignment or trial. You are their eyes and ears, so write clearly and concisely in a way that makes them listen and ensures that they'll understand what happened.

Good broadcast copy should have rhythm and cadence, an ordered flow of sounds that makes it interesting. You can develop those qualities by reading the copy as you write, shaping and editing phrases so they blend together well. Good broadcast writing, as in print journalism, almost always involves rewriting. For radio, you are painting a word picture; for television, you are creating a fusion of words and visuals.

Informality and Clarity

Broadcast news copy, by its nature, is more informal than newspaper copy, but not so informal that it loses respect or credibility. Various writing formulas have been developed over the years to quantify how long broadcast sentences should be. One of the most effective may be the "**Rule of 20**," in which each syllable in a sentence counts as one unit. A count of 20 units, the rule says, is the maximum a broadcast sentence may run and still be easily understood. (The previous sentence, for instance, has a count of 31; read it aloud and see how cumbersome it becomes toward the end.)

Not every sentence should be the same length. (That sentence has a count of 10; note the difference in ease of understanding.) Variation in sentence length gives copy rhythm and a pleasing flow. Some sentences will come close to a 20 count, others may run only eight to 10.

As a general rule, keep sentences brief, energetic and simple, with only one thought or idea to each sentence. Broadcast writing permits an occasional sentence fragment (lacking either subject, verb or complete thought), but be sure you know the difference between a complete sentence and a sentence fragment and can justify the fragment's use. Beginning writers run into trouble when they use sentence fragments without realizing they're doing so.

Readability

Don't ignore the ability of the person who will be reading the copy on air. Some announcers have trouble with words or phrases, so the copywriter should be aware of any unique problems. Remember, broadcast copy is written to "read" well for the announcer, as well as the audience.

Be careful about using hard-to-pronounce words and try to avoid too many words ending in *s* or *th* because they generate hissing sounds over the air. Also, watch out for words ending in *ing*: they are hard to pronounce and tend to disrupt the rhythm of sentences. Alliterative phrases—words in sequence that begin with the same sound—can create a similar problem, especially if the announcer stumbles over them.

Box 10.2
An Anchor's Secret

A good broadcast writer should take an interest in the story being covered and convey that interest and the story's importance to listeners and viewers. My first news director, Jess Marlow, who went on to a successful career for KNBC-TV and became the top-rated news anchor in the Los Angeles market for years, was always interesting to listen to, even when he read the most routine of stories. His secret, he explained, was to treat each piece of copy he was reading as the most important one in the newscast and to carry that feeling throughout the news program from beginning to end. —*WRW*

Writing the Lead

A print story can have a long complicated lead, especially if it takes the form of a single-paragraph news brief or summary. Where some newspaper leads are as short as 15 words, most range from 30 to 35 words, and some run more than 40 words. Try that length in a broadcast lead, though, and your audience is lost. The newspaper story packs as many facts as possible into its lead paragraph. Broadcast leads, on the other hand, must have enough substance to attract the listener's interest, but not so much information that confusion results.

Don't lead with a question; your listeners will expect a commercial. Instead, your lead should answer the implicit question, *Have you heard about . . .?* The reporter generally determines the most important fact in a story, then leads with that piece of information. If you're in doubt about how to lead a story, the same advice holds as previously discussed. Think about how you would tell the information to a friend over a cup of coffee: "*Hey, did you hear . . .?*" What follows is the lead. Don't "crowd" a lead with too much information, however, and avoid long complex introductory phrases. Putting too much information into a print lead makes it difficult to understand; doing so in a broadcast lead encourages the audience to tune out.

Types of Broadcast Leads

Because of the constraints posed by time and the need for simplicity, broadcast leads do not have the variety found in print leads. Three of the most common broadcast leads are the **single-act lead**, the **umbrella** or **comprehensive lead**, and the **chronological narrative lead**.

Single-Act Leads   Probably the most common of broadcast news leads, the single-act lead relates who did what or what happened. It begins by telling who did something, what happened, or when it occurred: the president makes a speech, a tornado devastates a farming community, a predawn fire sweeps through an apartment complex.

Those are the easy leads to write because the facts are obvious and the story often tells itself. Many stories may be written in the form of a circle with three sections: the latest (timeliness, again), what happened (the body of the story, with most of the facts), and the end (a related aspect of the first section). Write a strong lead, then follow with details to fill in an explanation of how or why. The challenge in this type of story is to hold back information from the lead, saving some facts for later to keep your audience interested and to prevent the opening sentence from becoming too complex.

An offshoot of this type of lead is to put events into perspective, as in this example:

The biggest blizzard in 10 years struck the city overnight.

Just make sure that it *is* the biggest or else you have created a credibility problem for your station.

Umbrella or Comprehensive Leads   Reports about city council and school board meetings or related crime stories often use an umbrella or comprehensive lead, which ties together related events or incidents: the city council or school board takes several important actions, a series of automobile fatalities occur, the evening is particularly violent and crime-filled. In each case, a lead wrapping up several events draws listeners and viewers into the news report.

Box 10.3

Bloody Sunday

One of the late-night weekend newscasts I produced opened with a crime summary of a day with two homicides within hours of each other, a violent and bloody fight downtown, and a terrible two-car auto crash with multiple fatalities.

My lead: "It's been a bloody Sunday in the South Bay." From there, we presented video of the two murder scenes; a narrative of the fight, with descriptions of the participants and their conditions; and video of the traffic accident.

Perhaps it would have been better to have scattered those stories to maintain viewer interest throughout the newscast—we debated that in a staff meeting the next day—but a comprehensive lead set the stage for what was to follow.

—*WRW*

This type of story organization also lends itself to a reaction lead later in the day, focusing on what a participant or one of those affected feels or plans to do. Is the president of the teachers' union threatening a strike after the school board changed working conditions? Are police beefing up patrols to prevent a recurrence of last night's violence? Those are questions your audience will be asking and it is your responsibility as a newswriter to answer them.

Chronological Narrative Leads   A more difficult lead is the chronological narrative lead, which describes events stretched over time. It often begins by telling the first thing that happened, then carries the story to the ending. Some news events lend themselves to this treatment.

Others tell the latest happening in a series of events, then go back to the beginning and carry the story to the end. Some stories begin more effectively with a summary lead, then move to a transition line that carries the listener into the narrative.

Box 10.4

Death in the Early Hours

On one occasion, I covered a story where a mentally disturbed woman threw herself to her death from a freeway overpass at four in the morning. Police reports, filed chronologically, showed a clear pattern: her walking away from the county hospital mental health facility at 1:30 a.m., being committed at 10:30 p.m. the night before, and accounts of irrational behavior earlier in the evening and in the afternoon of the previous day.

Linked together in narrative format and tied together with video, the sequence of events made for a powerful human interest story. —*WRW*

Soft Leads

Radio–TV copy often uses what is referred to as a **soft lead** or **soft intro** into news, a gradual easing into the story. Other terms include a **warm-up lead** and a **tune-in lead**. Whatever they're called, these leads are designed to catch listeners' attention and prepare them for what comes next:

> Traditional lead: *Hurricane Kristy, bearing down on the big island of Hawaii, is expected to cause torrential rain accompanied by gale-force winds as it moves along the western edge of the Hawaiian Islands chain tonight and tomorrow.*

> Soft lead: *The Hawaiian Islands are bracing for high winds and heavy rains. Hurricane Kristy is bearing down . . .*

The information remains the same but the way the soft lead presents it is less formal, more conversational—the way one person would relate facts to another.

Unless the story concerns a prominent person, broadcast leads do not begin with who but instead use an "impersonal who" treatment. For example, *Howard Heavyfoot is in jail tonight after leading police on a 110-mile-an-hour chase earlier today* would not make it as a broadcast story. No one knows Heavyfoot, and the fact that an unknown person is in jail is not news. What would work would be *A high-speed chase lands a local man in jail. Howard Heavyfoot is behind bars tonight after leading* . . . Woven into the soft lead is deliberate repetition to prepare the listener for what is to come.

This story is a good example of the circle format discussed earlier. "The latest" is that Heavyfoot is in jail after leading police on a high-speed chase. "What happened" means the writer goes back to the beginning: *Pursuit began when Heavyfoot's car was clocked at more than 80 miles per hour.* The body of the story is told with as much detail needed for comprehension. The end is exactly that: *Heavyfoot will be arraigned in court tomorrow morning on a number of traffic violations.*

Let's say, by the way, that Heavyfoot is charged with unsafe operation of a motor vehicle, speeding, driving with an expired driver's license, resisting arrest, having a broken tail light, and a couple of other charges that haven't yet been determined. While that information can go in the newspaper story, there's no time to list all of them in broadcasting, and listeners and viewers are not really interested. Thus, heed an important concept: When deciding how much detail needs to be included in a story, always consider whether anything important will be lost if some facts are left out. Delete from one story to be able to add to another.

In many respects, the soft broadcast lead functions the way a newspaper headline does: Its goal is to catch listeners' attention to orient and prepare them for what is to follow. Because TV and radio listeners are at times not paying attention, it is necessary to provide some key words to interest them in tuning into the report. A soft lead doesn't work for every story; in fact, too many in a newscast wastes words and takes time that would have been available for other stories. Some reporters refuse to use any soft leads. However, because the broadcast writer's challenge is to compose copy that catches and holds the interest of listeners and viewers, remember that the soft lead is an effective device to create a change of pace within a newscast.

Names and Numbers

Warm-up leads often work best in the use of names and numbers. Unless a person is well known, do not lead a story with a name. Rather, use an identifying title. If a person is well known, omit the first name and use the title and last name, such as in references to the president of the United States. If a person is not well known, use the title and the name, as in *British Prime Minister Penelope John-Bull* and *Secretary of State Harold Globehopper*. Remember that titles can be condensed. As discussed earlier, broadcast copy can refer to *Mel Moreguns, Secretary of Defense,* as *Defense Secretary Mel Moreguns.* Lengthier titles can be shortened or paraphrased or portions of the titles may be eliminated.

Another way of dealing with names is to begin with a warm-up lead and use the name in the next sentence:

> *A local lawyer has been suspended by the state bar association. Louis Litigious was stripped of his right to practice law for two years . . .*

If the name is not well known but is necessary, use an identifier before the name:

> *Last night's winner of the 21-million dollar lottery, Marian Nouveau-Riche, says . . .*

Middle initials are generally dropped unless they are essential to the name or are a necessary part of the identification in a crime story.

Don't begin broadcast copy with numbers, figures, or facts crucial to the story. If a writer begins with *Five people were killed in a fiery auto–truck collision early this morning,* the fact that five people died will have to be repeated in the story.

Box 10.5
Leading With Numbers

Beginning with a number is a rather easy mistake to make. I once wrote a lead about a multiple-fatality accident, starting with the number of people who died, but didn't repeat the fatality total. When I returned to the newsroom, the phone rang for the next 10 minutes. Everyone asked, "How many were killed?"

Don't begin with numbers, figures or facts crucial to the story! If you must, make sure you repeat the information later in the story. —*WRW*

Clarity in Broadcast Copy

Like all good writing, broadcast writing must be clear. However, clarity is especially challenging for radio–TV writers because written reports must be clear for two "audiences": those who read the reports over the air and those who listen to or watch the reports. Therefore, clarity includes a writing style that will be easy for even casual listeners to understand, as well as techniques for making pronunciation obvious.

Pronunciation

The person reading a story must know how to pronounce difficult or unknown names or terms. To convey this information, use a pronunciation guide with simplified phonetic spelling of hard-to-pronounce names, places, and technical terms. "**Pronouncers**," as these are known, follow the word and are enclosed in double parentheses to prevent any confusion for the announcer reading the copy. Each syllable is written separately, connected by a hyphen, with all caps for accented syllables:

The incident occurred in Versailles ((ver-SALES)) Missouri.

The plane made an emergency landing in Cairo ((KAY-roh)) Illinois.

A great white shark ate five surfers off the coast of La Jolla ((La HOY-ah)) California.

Generally, the wire services run a pronunciation guide during the overnight feed. Save the guide and keep it where others can refer to it.

Learn local pronunciations, especially if you are new in an area. For instance, the Arkansas River is the "ARK-an-saw" when it flows through Colorado and Arkansas, but it's the "ar-KAN-zes" when it winds its way through Kansas. Nothing leads to a greater loss of credibility than a broadcast reporter who cannot pronounce a local name or who mispronounces a word because the newswriter did not include a pronunciation guide. If you're a public relations writer, you will enhance your reputation among broadcast journalists if you help them avoid the embarrassment of mispronouncing what you've written.

Consider, too, whether names of unfamiliar places need to be used. It may be just as effective to use general geographic locations or refer to distances from the nearest large city, especially to describe non-U.S. news events.

Box 10.6

Writing Pronouncers

To write pronouncers, create phonetic spellings using the following guides:

Consonants	**Vowels**
S for soft C (*city*)	AY (*hate*)
K for hard C (*canal*)	IH (*fit*)
Z for hard S (*disease*)	A (*bat*)
G for hard G (*grape*)	AH (*cot*)
J for soft G (*gentle*)	AW (*draw*)
SH for soft CH (*machine*)	AI (*hair*)
CH for hard CH or TCH (*channel*)	EE (retreat)
	EH (*bed*)
	EYE (*file*)
	OH (*wrote*)
	U (*foot*)
	UH (*putt*)

An acceptable alternative to using a phonetic guide is to use a common rhyme with a word:

James Rwytt ((sounds like write))

The key to writing effective pronouncers is to use simple basic spellings so that mispronouncing the word is virtually impossible.

Strong Words

As in writing for print journalism, use strong, declarative subject-verb-object sentences with action verbs. Active, vital verbs give copy action, impact, color and interest. One writing suggestion is to use positive verb forms for stronger sentences; focus on what people decided to do rather than not do, even if they decided to take no action.

Also, remember what was discussed earlier: Use the active voice, starting the sentence with the person or thing that did the action:

Active: *A lone gunman held up the liquor store.*

Passive: *The liquor store was held up by a loan gunman.*

The second example, in the passive voice, makes sentences limp and lifeless. Limp and lifeless copy does not make it in broadcasting!

Try to avoid the past tense. In broadcasting, things are happening "now," not last week. Broadcast writing differs from print writing in that verb tenses can be mixed because radio–TV copy often describes events that are taking place now, have taken place or will take place. To keep copy lively, writers often use the present perfect:

Firefighters have freed the driver who was pinned in the wreckage. He has been flown by Mercy Flight to a downtown hospital.

The key is to write a sentence that makes sense.

Pronouns and Phrasing

Be specific in referring to people and things. Use personal pronouns such as *he, she, it, his, him,* and *our* or *this, those, these,* and *their* sparingly and near to whatever noun they refer. Repeating the original phrase is better than using a reference that could be misunderstood. Never use the word *latter* or *former* to refer to individuals. Generally, to say a newscaster has just been told something, the accepted pronoun is *we*:

We have just been informed that . . .

Use of the pronoun *I* is limited to editorials and commentary.

Phrases at times in the wrong place wind up, which makes sentences (such as this deliberately confusing example) difficult to understand. It's an easy trap to fall into:

The firefighters will be decorated for heroism during today's football game.

The enraged bull injured the farmer with an ax.

Or the classic,

Throw Mama from the train a kiss.

To arrange phrases properly, follow the guidelines in Chapter 3. They apply equally well to broadcast copy.

Simplicity and Economy

Radio–TV copy strives to be economical. The tighter the copy, the more information can be transmitted during the five-minute radio *News on the Hour* or the approximately 16 minutes of time available in a 30-minute telecast. Writers should avoid long descriptive clauses or participial phrases at the beginnings of sentences. They're difficult to follow and bog down the flow of writing. Banish modifying phrases and clauses, and don't write long or confusing copy between the sentence's subject and verb. People don't speak in rambling sentences with dependent clauses and misplaced modifiers. Don't write that way!

Because copy blocks are so short, repeated uses of words can be annoying. A writer should look for other words: a fire can also be a *blaze* even an *inferno* if it's really huge (although never a tongue-twisting *conflagration*).

However, it may be necessary to repeat words. If it is, do so and don't reach for an inappropriate word just to give a sentence variety. One of the best rules passed around in the tradition of broadcast news writing is: If it is necessary to say "banana" five times, say "banana" five times, not "banana" four times and "an elongated yellow fruit."

How often should *said* be said? Words like *explained, declared, pointed out, noted* and *replied* are alternative verbs. But be careful about using *insisted, claimed, implied, alleged* and *alluded to.* As was noted in the print section, these are opinion verbs that may misrepresent the motives of the speaker.

In covering a speech, instead of reporting that the speaker *said* something, for variety write that the speaker *told* a group something. In broadcast copywriting, *says* is often used as a substitute for *said,* especially when the news is fresh. For several hours following the mayor's news conference, for example, it is appropriate to use a present-tense verb, as in *The mayor says he'll veto the city council's spending plan.* By late in the news day, however, the *says* should be changed to *said.*

Be careful about using colorful nuances. Is the bank really *in difficulty?* Just because co-workers say someone was *acting suspiciously* or *appeared agitated,* is it necessarily true? Or are you distorting events by using such phrasing? In addition, as discussed in Chapter 3, avoid clichés.

Simplicity in writing means avoiding the use of big formal words. Also, try not to use jargon, foreign words or technical expressions that your audience won't understand. If it's necessary to use them, make sure they are simplified or explained. If others use difficult words, simplify them. If they are necessary, then carry them inside quotation marks so that the announcer can change inflection for emphasis.

Transitions

Word bridges help to take your listener and viewer from one story to another, especially in radio copy. Transitional phrases include *Locally, In other business news, Meanwhile, in the state capital,* or *In a related development.* Transitions can be used to link similar stories, especially if there is an extreme contrast between the two events. For instance, a failed rescue effort by firefighters at this morning's two-fatality fire can be coupled with a story about a firefighter assisting in the birth of a baby whose mother didn't quite make it to the hospital.

Don't force transitions, however. A pause and an obvious change of locale is enough of a cue for audiences to realize that one story has been concluded and the announcer is beginning another.

Contractions and Abbreviations

Because broadcast writing is conversational, radio–TV copy uses contractions more than print. Contractions sprinkled throughout the copy give the newscast an informal flavor. Some stories may be too formal or serious for the lighter touch, however, so newswriters must use good judgment. Don't use contractions that are difficult to say or might be misunderstood on the air *(mightn't* is a particularly bad one) and don't use contractions in a quote if the speaker didn't.

The best rule for abbreviations is to keep them simple and spell out words or names if the audience or announcer may be in doubt. Common abbreviations that are easily recognized, such as *Mr., Mrs.,* or *Ms.,* can be used in copy, as well as *St.* (for "Saint") in cities, as in *The St. Louis Cardinals won.* Obviously, however, the football team would not be the New Orleans "Sts."

Words like *Street, Avenue, Boulevard, Drive, Road, Parkway* and other street designations should be spelled out in broadcast copy. Local option should rule on whether nearby Interstate 90 is spelled out or referred to as "I-90"; what will your audience understand?

Names of well-known groups and government agencies readily known by their initials may be abbreviated. To clarify pronunciation, hyphenate commonly used acronyms that are pronounced by saying the letters, such as *F-B-I, C-I-A* and *U-N.* Acronyms that are pronounced as words should not be hyphenated: *NATO* and *AIDS,* for example.

To clarify an acronym that might be unfamiliar, follow the acronym with an explanation:

OPEC—the oil-producing cartel—says it will decrease production to raise prices.

Overly Informal Language

Be sparing in your use of slang or colloquialisms. While they may have a place in a print or broadcast feature story, they are rarely used in hard news. If a prominent person uses a slang term, make it clear that this term is a quote, as in the following example:

The mayor said that no matter how the spending plan was "gussied up," it is still a new tax.

When the announcer reaches the word in quotation marks, inflection will be changed to provide an audible quotation mark around the phrase that will be understood by listeners. New terms, especially those related to changing lifestyles, should be explained to listeners who might not be part of or familiar with the culture.

Just because phrasing makes its way into the language doesn't mean that it should be used on a newscast. Newswriters ought not to succumb to what might be called "creeping conversationalism." Police officers should never be referred to as "cops"; the California city is San Francisco, not "Frisco", and, to be bi-coastally correct, it's Philadelphia, not "Philly."

Needless to say, never use dialects of nationalities, sections of the country, race or ethnic background. Most listeners and viewers, not just members of the group being portrayed, will consider the use of a dialect insulting and offensive.

Avoid obscenities. The 1934 Communications Act still has provisions prohibiting profanity and obscenity on the air, even though these rules are increasingly ignored in "shock radio" formats and reality-based TV programming. News is different, however. Profanity, off-color phrasing or suggestive language in a news broadcast will offend some in the audience. Even "gutter language" that is neither obscene nor profane should be avoided. If obscenities lace an audio or videotape, the news producer ought to consider whether it should be used. If the piece adds to the comprehension of the story, the debate then becomes whether to bleep out portions of the objectionable language. The principal consideration for using such language is that it aids understanding of the news event, not that it will garner additional listeners or viewers.

Punctuation

As in the previous discussion of abbreviations, punctuation for broadcast at times differs from punctuation for print. The period, comma, dash, and hyphen are the most frequently used forms of punctuation. Semicolons should be eliminated from broadcast writing. While they are understandable in print, semicolons tend to create overlong sentences for broadcasting. Use a period in place of the semicolon, then start a new sentence.

The period is the most important punctuation mark in broadcast writing. Periods mark the end of a sentence, the end of a thought. By their nature, they elicit a pause. The comma calls for a shorter pause than a period. The dash, typed as a double hyphen, indicates a pause or parenthetical material, as in *The president—back home after a 10-day European trip—says Congress* . . . The dash can be overused, so writers should be cautious. Likewise, use colons sparingly.

The hyphen is used to separate letters in an abbreviation or to link words that should be read together. Use hyphens for clarity in words that might be difficult to pronounce without them, generally words that begin with *non, anti, co*, or *semi*. Thus, make it *non*-smoking, *anti*-war, *co*-worker, and *semi*-literate.[1] Consider whether other words, such as *well-being*, might require hyphens if there is a possibility for confusion.

Use a comma only at places where the announcer should pause. In print, the city is *Washington, D.C.*; in broadcast copy, it's *Washington D-C.* With the comma, the announcer will read, "Washington (pause) D-C."

Some writers suggest the use of periods between words for pauses. Be careful; in print writing, the use of three periods typed together—an ellipsis—indicates that something is missing. Using periods for inflection or emphasis may be confusing to the announcer, so make sure your purpose is clear.

Quotations

Use quotations sparingly because the listener or viewer cannot see them. Likewise, it's inadvisable to use a quotation lead because it is not immediately clear who has made the statement. In fact, the audience might even perceive the newscaster to be giving his or her opinion about events:

> *"Last night's city council meeting was a disgusting spectacle." With those words, Mayor Sprawl said* . . .

When using quotations, broadcast copywriters should avoid long quotes. Instead, paraphrase the material into shorter indirect quotes. Paraphrasing not only eliminates unnecessary words, it also often aids clarity.

If a longer quotation is necessary, break it in the middle with words naming the source. For instance, a longer sound interview with the mayor might be summarized as follows:

> *Mayor Sprawl says he will veto the pay raise the city council voted for itself last night, denouncing the hike as "an unjustifiable raid on the public treasury." The mayor added he*

would support a recall drive of council members voting for the raise. "I'll sign a petition myself," he said.

Writers and announcers should avoid using the words *quote* and *unquote* in their copy, although these words can occasionally be used for effect. Typically, announcers signal a quotation with a voice inflection:

The mayor said the city council's action was "absolutely outrageous," and he vowed to "fight them tooth and nail" over the issue.

To use the same wording without quotation marks would seem to imply that the comments were the newscaster's opinion.

Making Attributions   Don't bother to attribute obvious information or uncontested facts, but when a statement might be controversial or if the reporter cannot verify information from the source, begin with an attribution to enhance credibility: *Police say they have evidence linking the suspect to the murders* rather than *There is evidence linking the suspect to the murders, according to police.* Don't complicate writing by inserting the attribution as a dependent clause in the sentence: *There is evidence, police say, linking the suspect to the murders.*

Although use of identifying attribution enhances a news report's credibility, be careful who you quote. Sometimes sources have their own agenda, and some topics—forecasts of racial unrest or violence, hurricane or tornado danger, flood or earthquake predictions— must be handled carefully. Don't unquestioningly accept the word of sources, no matter how reliable. Instead, cross-check information whenever possible. Also, be careful in using anonymous attributions such as *usually reliable sources said* or *sources told Eyewitness News.* Such expressions don't add anything and they raise suspicion that the reporter may be using the phrase as a ruse to add his or her own opinion. If a story seems speculative, it's a good idea not to go with it unless it can be confirmed by two sources, one of whom can be named.

Avoiding Ethical and Legal Problems   Don't write a sensationalized lead, followed by the name of the source:

Flying saucers have been landing in the hills around the city for the past three years. That, at least, is the opinion of Professor Ulysses F. Osborne, who says he's done extensive research on extraterrestrial visitors.

Your audience will hear only the first words and may react accordingly (see Welles, Orson, 1938 "War of the Worlds" broadcast).

Just as in print writing, banish the words *allegedly* and *alleged* from your broadcast vocabulary. They do not provide a defense in a libel action and, in a crime story, they unnecessarily cast doubt on the victim, especially in rape and other abuse stories where there has already been enough trauma. Don't write *the alleged victim*.

If there is doubt, quote a source, as in *Police say burglars apparently entered the building through a ventilator shaft*. Consider whether names have to be used at all. A witness at an air crash, unless there is audio- or videotape of that person's account of the incident, can be left nameless:

One witness said the plane rolled over before it nosedived into the field.

Numbers and Statistics

Make statistics, figures and numbers understandable. Don't use detailed statistics unless necessary because most listeners and viewers either won't understand, remember or care. For the same reason, don't use lists of numbers.

Round off numbers whenever possible. A city budget deficit of $24,719,440 can be expressed as *24-point-seven million dollars*. Another way to simplify numbers is to use approximations such as *some, nearly, almost* or *more than* (never *over*, which indicates position rather than amount), unless the story requires the exact number to be used. Thus, the amount of the city budget deficit can also be expressed as *nearly 25-million dollars*.

Note the broadcast writing style for reporting dollar amounts. Omit the dollar sign and simplify the numbers. This prevents an awkward pause while the announcer figures out on the air how to say $24.7 million, which is the Associated Press style in print writing.

Also, for ease in readability, hyphenate numbers in street addresses:

The incident took place at 2–14 High Street.

If ages are used—and increasingly they are not unless they play some part in the story—hyphenate it before the noun, as in *the 21-year-old driver*. Write out decimal equivalents and fractions, as follows:

The stock market was up three-tenths of a point.

Three-fourths of those surveyed agreed.

Set off telephone numbers with hyphens:

Call 1–800 5–5–5 1–2–1–2.

Be careful how numbers sound on the air. Professionals advise using the phrase *one million* instead of *a million* because the *a* may be heard as *eight*. Likewise, to avoid confusion for the announcer, spell out the numbers 1 and 11 in copy as *one* and *eleven*.

Make numbers relevant to listeners. It is all right to say *The gas company has been given approval to raise rates by 12-million dollars,* but it is more meaningful to listeners and viewers if you write *Gas company customers will pay three dollars a month more, due to a just-approved rate hike.* (If the wire service report doesn't have this information, call the gas company public relations representative and ask what the numbers mean.)

Make numbers understandable as well. For example, tell listeners that an aircraft carrier flight deck more than 900 feet long is the length of three football fields; then they will more easily understand.

Making Newscasts Interesting

The news producer has the challenging job of assembling what are essentially information blips into a comprehensive pattern for the listener or viewer, who may be only half paying attention. Thus, it is important to freshen news copy. If a radio station takes the same story used when listeners were stuck in 8 a.m. traffic and reads it during the 5 p.m. going-home commute, the message is that nothing important has happened. Listeners will change stations for something fresh and immediate. Even TV copy should be rewritten; at least rewrite the lead in a video piece used on both the early and late-night newscasts. Ideally, an entirely new piece should be written and edited.

You can freshen copy by inserting new information: Why did the fire start? Why did the accident occur? If there's nothing new, then report that fact:

Fire officials say they still have no cause for the early-morning blaze that took three lives.

This type of lead subtly tells listeners and viewers that your news operation is staying on top of stories so that when a cause is known, listeners will hear it first from your station.

Try to develop a new angle. If a tax hike was approved at last night's school board meeting, find out the reactions of teachers, parents and taxpayers' groups, and use that information as your updated lead. Likewise, if someone was appointed or elected last night, freshen the story by finding out what the person intends to do in office. The appointment or election is fine for the drive-time news program or the local TV news cut-in to the network morning show, but by noon, there ought to be something new.

Again, avoid using the word *today* because stories are expected to have taken place today unless otherwise noted. Instead, use *this morning, late this afternoon, a predawn fire, an evening rush-hour fatality,* or *a daring daylight robbery.* If something happened last night or last week, there's no avoiding the fact. Say it once and be done with the time factor.

As in print journalism, localizing stories is important. If the Pentagon releases the names of five military personnel who died in a helicopter crash over the weekend and one is from your regional listening area, report the local story angle. Some news broadcasts tend to localize too much, however. If a wanted international terrorist is arrested somewhere, don't have the local newscaster point out that the fugitive once changed planes at the nearby airport. Be careful not to over-localize!

News Judgment in Broadcast News

Working journalists often find many stories to be routine. After a while, the same things seem to happen again and again; only the names change. You can't let your writing become routine,

---

Box 10.7

Tips for Writing Broadcast Copy

---

1. Remember, broadcast copy is written for the ear, not for the eye. Simple writing style increases understanding. (If people don't understand what you've written, you've wasted your time and theirs.)

2. Broadcast copy is conversational. Radio–TV scripts should "read" well. Write as you speak.

3. Give your copy rhythm and cadence, an ordered flow of sounds that makes writing interesting to listen to. Vary sentence length.

4. Avoid hard-to-pronounce words, and write copy that considers the ability of the announcer who will read it.

5. Don't crowd broadcast leads with too much detail. Use enough information to attract listeners' attention, but not so much that it confuses them.

6. Remember that the soft or warm-up lead, which attracts the listener's attention and prepares him or her for what comes next, is an effective writing device.

7. Do not lead broadcast stories with unfamiliar numbers or names. Simplify names and titles, and remember that in broadcasting, titles *always* come before names, and both *always* come before a quote. Round off numbers to facilitate understanding.

8. Simplify pronunciation of difficult or unknown names or places by using a pronouncer (a guide with an understandable phonetic spelling of hard-to-say names, places, and technical terms).

9. Use strong declarative subject-verb-object sentences with action verbs. Write using the present tense and active, not passive, voice.

10. Remember that broadcast copywriting is governed by the clock. Prepare tightly written copy that makes every word count.

11. Keep abbreviations simple. Spell out words or names where the audience or announcer may be in doubt.

12. Good writing involves rewriting. Polish, freshen, and update copy.

---

however. Each story should be composed with an interesting blend of writing techniques. Lead with what is most important, tell as many of the details as possible, and provide the significance of the news story—tell why, not only who and what. And try to do it in a unique way every time; writing stories the same way day after day can cause newscasts to become stale and uninteresting. When that happens, people switch radio stations and change TV channels.

News Bulletins

One of the most troublesome responsibilities a radio or TV program producer has is dealing with bulletins. A news flash comes through on the wire service or someone calls on the telephone with a breaking news tip. What do you do? Because your station wants to be first with the news, one of the worst conversations to have is trying to tell your news director or station manager why you sat on something for 20 minutes while the competition had it. On the other hand, an even worse conversation is answering how you could possibly run something like that and why it wasn't checked out because you should have known it wasn't true.

Bulletins are tricky because at times they are rescinded by the wire services—not often, but often enough to be worrisome. Bulletins are serious: War has been declared, a political leader has been assassinated, a plane has crashed, a natural disaster has occurred. If you're the program producer, call the news director or station manager to clear a decision to break into programming with a bulletin.

For the broadcast writer, the challenge is to get as much information out as quickly as possible. This is difficult because initial details are sketchy. To cover yourself, give as much attribution as possible. If a plane has apparently crashed, cite the Federal Aviation Administration or air traffic controllers at the airport as sources. Make it clear in your copy that details are incomplete, but that listeners or viewers should stay tuned for updates as they are received. If it's a local story, tell your audience that a news team is en route. Generally, the first line of the bulletin is repeated at the end for those just tuning in.

Wire copy is received in broadcast newsrooms around the country so, unless that copy is rewritten, everyone's newscast will sound the same. An initial use of wire copy as written is fine; CNN does it all the time on late-breaking stories. However, after the initial story has broken, rewrite it. Rewrite wire copy. Rewrite the 10 a.m. news before the noon broadcast. Rewrite, freshen and update before the 6 o'clock news. Good writing and reporting always involves rewriting.

Content of the Newscast

Some news producers suggest building a newscast of "peaks and valleys" of information. Audiences cannot be hammered with one bad story after another throughout most of the newscast, nor can they be bombarded with a series of fact-filled pieces, important as they may be. Instead, news programs should have an ebb and flow, with some hard news stories mixed with lighter feature material. These "valleys" present an ideal opportunity for public relations professionals to suggest story ideas or provide copy or video. Editors want to ensure that a variety of stories is offered, just as it is important for reporters to seek out and cover a mix of stories.

Finally, avoid editorializing in newscast copy. Gabriel Heatter, a radio newscaster of the 1940s, used to begin his broadcasts with "There's good news tonight" or "There's bad news tonight." Although most people might agree whether the events are good or bad, newswriters should let their audience decide without being prompted. Increasingly, network and cable news correspondents seem to be closing reports with an opinionated summary, at times not necessarily consistent with the facts. This practice crosses the invisible line between objectivity and subjectivity. It's not the newscaster's place to try to convince an audience about something; just write and report the news. Leave the interpretations to the listeners or to commentators.

Print or Broadcast: Which is "Better"?

Any comparison as to which writing form is "better" than the other misses the point. It's not the form that's important, but rather how it is used. English is one of the most expressive languages ever developed. Print and broadcast writing forms demand a mastery of the mechanics, nuances and shadings of the language to effectively transmit information.

Print writing, for instance, allows greater development of stories. Sit down with a copy of *The Economist* and read from its "Science and Technology" section about the latest discoveries about quasars and pulsars from the far side of the universe or about ethical considerations involved in cloning of humans. Even with good visuals, broadcasting could not approach that level of depth. Radio, television, and—increasingly—the Internet blend immediacy, visuals, and sound to involve listeners and viewers in the event.

Discussion Questions

The following are class discussion questions drawn from Chapter 10:

1. Radio–TV copy is written for the ear, not the eye. What are some of the rules for writing good broadcast copy?

2. Differentiate between a *single-act lead*, the *umbrella* or *comprehensive lead*, and the *chronological narrative lead*. When and why should each be used?

3. What is a *soft lead* and why is it used in broadcast news copy?

4. What are the guidelines for using names and numbers in broadcast copy?

5. What are some of the ways to add strength and clarity to broadcast copywriting?

6. How does punctuation used in radio–TV writing differ from that used in print?

7. The use of quotes and attribution differs from print in what way?

8. Why is it important to rewrite and freshen news copy?

9. Why do news producers build "peaks and valleys" of information into newscasts? What opportunities does this format present for the public relations practitioner?

10. "Don't editorialize." Why?

CHAPTER EXERCISES

Exercise 10.1—Condensing Copy

 Clip a crime, fire or accident story from your local paper and pare it down to a maximum of eight full-page width lines. Don't write a solid block of copy. There should be two or three paragraphs, each indented one tab space. How much information did you leave out? Why? What information should have been included but was not because of a lack of lines? What does this say about the drawbacks of broadcast copy compared to print?

Exercise 10.2—Comparing Newscasts

 Watch a local and a network newscast on the same day. What similarities do you see between them in terms of types of news stories used and the way they are presented? Differences? Write a comparative critique of 250 words. Discuss your observations in class.

Exercise 10.3—Three Leads

 Write single-act, umbrella, and narrative leads to go with the set of facts in Exercise 4.4, which describes a trustees meeting.

Exercise 10.4—Writing Warm-Up Leads

 Using the same set of facts as in Exercises 4.2 and 4.3, write warm-up leads for a broadcast version of the stories. Summarize the differences between the two versions.

Exercise 10.5—Creating a Pronunciation Guide

 Compile a list of 10 place names that look as though they would be difficult to pronounce or appear to have unusual pronunciations. Look up the names in a gazetteer or dictionary and develop a pronunciation guide for each.

Exercise 10.6—Updating a News Story

You are a reporter for your local radio station. Write a 30-second news story for your morning drive-time report, based on the following information:

> There was a holdup early this morning at the Short Stop convenience store near campus. (You provide the street location). Police said two white males in their early 20s, wearing sweat suits with the logo of your college or university on them and nylon pantyhose over their heads, took $250 at gunpoint from the attendant, Jason Roberts. The two fled on foot. The robbery occurred just before 2 a.m. (The store is open 24 hours a day.) Police are looking for the robbers.

Now update the first news report with a 30-second story that would air on your noon newscast using the following information:

> Police are continuing their investigation of the Short Stop holdup. The chief of detectives says several people saw two persons matching the description of the robbers fleeing the convenience store. One witness said she saw them run onto campus, then disappear behind the administration building.

Finally, incorporate those new details into a 40-second story for the afternoon drive-time newscast:

> There has been a break in this morning's holdup at the Short Stop convenience store. Police late this afternoon arrested two suspects. They are identified as Elbert Coinseizer, 21, and Frederick Lawless, 22. Both are criminal justice majors at your college or university. They are being charged with armed robbery and will be arraigned in court tomorrow morning.

In each update, pick up additional background material from the previously provided information to finish the story.

■

Suggestions for Further Reading

Broadcast Writing

Hewitt, John. *Air Words: Writing for Broadcast News*, 3rd ed. (New York: McGraw-Hill, 2001).

Hilliard, Robert C. *Writing for Television, Radio and Web Media*, 9th ed. (Belmont Calif.: Wadsworth, 2008).

Kalbfeld, Brad. *Associated Press Broadcast News Handbook* (New York: McGraw Hill, 2000).

Kant, Garth. *How to Write Television News* (New York: McGraw-Hill, 2005).

Meeske, Milan D. *Copywriting for the Electronic Media: A Practical Guide*, 5th ed. (Belmont, Calif.: Wadsworth, 2006).

Orlick, Peter B. *Broadcast/Cable Copywriting*, 7th ed. (Boston: Allyn & Bacon, 2004).

Papper, Robert A. *Broadcast News Writing Stylebook*, 3rd ed. (Boston: Allyn & Bacon, 2006).

Raiteri, Charles. *Writing for Broadcast News: A Storytelling Approach to Crafting TV and Radio News Reports* (Lanham, Md.: Rowman & Littlefield, 2005).

Tuggle, Charles, Forrest Carr and Suzanne Huffman. *Broadcast News Handbook: Writing, Reporting and Producing in a Converging Media World* (New York: McGraw Hill, 2006).

Note

1.   The tip comes from Sharyl Attkisson and Don R. Vaughn, *Writing Right for Broadcast and Internet News* (Boston: Allyn & Bacon, 2003), pp. 26, 256, who call it their "non-anti-co-semi" rule.

11

Reporting for Radio and TV

Chapter Objectives

- To describe the ways in which a news staff works together to produce a daily newscast
- To explain the difference between the various types of script formats and production techniques used in broadcasting
- To differentiate the role of radio compared to TV in today's news-gathering environment
- To describe the essentials of video logic and composition for a TV news report
- To present guidelines for reporters' behavior in covering disasters, hard news, and features
- To compare sports and weather reporting with other newswriting forms
- To review principles for preparing and using public affairs programming, editorials, and commentary

Inside the Newsroom

Those who go into broadcast news have to enjoy the challenge of working to tight deadlines in an environment of what is at times controlled chaos. Step into a TV newsroom right before the newscast, especially in a small-to medium-market station where everyone seems to have the workload of 1.2 persons. Reporters are putting finishing touches on late-breaking copy, the producer is yelling at someone because several scripts are not in hand, a tape editor is cursing one of the balky machines and the fact that no others are available, and the sports editor is rehearsing copy in a corner. Police and fire monitors continue to blare and telephones ring.

In the studio, engineers are checking cameras, the floor crew is rearranging lights not put back in place following the taping of a commercial for tomorrow night's late movie, and one of the advertising sales reps is ushering a prospective client into the viewing booth behind the technical director to watch the news program.

Minutes before airtime, the anchor, co-anchor, sportscaster, and weathercaster come on the set. The jingling computerized *Eyewitness News at Six* theme fills the control room, and as the computer readout clock turns 6:00, the anchor begins the telecast. If all goes as planned, the show runs smoothly. Cameras and microphones work, videotapes run without incident, sports actually gets an additional 30 seconds and, much to the satisfaction of the advertising rep and the prospective client, the commercials run without a glitch. When it's over, everyone gets ready to do it again for the late news.

TV Newsroom Organization and Responsibilities

Day in and day out, TV stations around the country follow similar routines, made possible by a formal organizational structure. News departments are generally headed by a **news director**, who is responsible for overseeing the operation of the news department in terms of personnel, budget and policy. The news director hires and fires, battles with other department heads for fiscal resources, and determines what the station will cover and how. The news director does not operate in a vacuum, however. He or she reports to a **program director** or **station manager**, who in turn reports to a higher level manager. Management sets policy for sales, programming and news, and department heads in those areas are responsible for seeing that policy is carried out.

The smaller the station, the more likely it is that each person will have several jobs. For instance, the news director is often the lead **anchor**, the station's primary on-air news talent, or—if not given air responsibilities—might even be the program director or station manager. On occasion, the news director will double as **assignment editor**, responsible for sending reporters and videographers to cover stories and coordinating the work of **stringers**, who are freelance correspondents, generally in distant locations, that supply reports the station would not otherwise have.

The assignment editor usually starts the day by scanning local and regional newspapers to ensure awareness of upcoming events or make sure the station has not been scooped by the competition. News tips come via wire-service advisories or are faxed to the newsroom by those seeking coverage. Beat reporters are also responsible for knowing about upcoming events. If the mayor is going to present an award at 10 a.m. to a police officer who rescued someone from a burning building, the police beat reporter not only will have told the assignment editor about the scheduled event but will probably also have pushed for video coverage. Public relations professionals are also frequent and useful sources of ideas for assignment editors.

Reporters at small- to medium-market TV stations are likely to be **general assignment reporters** with multiple responsibilities. Those covering the police department might also cover the sheriff's office and state police or highway patrol. Court reporters cover various levels of jurisdictions, often combining courtroom visits with trips to the court clerk's office or the district or prosecuting attorney's office. That same reporter may end the day covering the city council, county legislative body, or school board. In between, these reporters will be expected to generate interviews, create news feature **packages**, and be available to cover breaking news events. Good reporters, like assignment editors, read local newspapers and listen to the news radio station on the way into the newsroom or the first stop on their beats.

Other people affect the news department's operation, as follows:

- The **chief photographer** is responsible for maintaining portable video equipment and training videographers.
- The **editorial writer** prepares station editorial positions in consultation with management.
- The **technical director** is the engineer responsible for taking the news program that has been prepared and directing its delivery over the air.

Putting the Pieces Together: The Producer

The news program **producer** combines the efforts of everyone in the newsroom into the station's various newscasts. He or she confers with the assignment editor to assess the importance of various news stories. Often, local stories are paired with regional or national news events to give a logical continuity within the newscast. For instance, a national product recall may be localized to see how merchants are going to handle returns or how an auto dealer plans to make mandated repairs. The producer schedules where every story will go in the newscast. He or she may at times have to alert sales or management to a potential problem, especially in smaller markets, where there is greater potential for advertiser pressure.

Box 11.1

Leave the Driving to Us

Transportation carriers are understandably reluctant to air commercials if there is adverse news about their mode of conveyance. For instance, airline companies often ask that their ads be dropped from the newscast when an air crash occurs, even if it involves a competing carrier.

One station I worked for had a daily segment sponsored by a national bus line. There was never any pressure not to air the story of a bus accident. Instead, sales had standing orders to pull the company's commercials. Although such a story understandably had news value if fatalities were involved, the producer would probably question whether to run any less serious story involving a bus accident, especially if it was far from our viewing area. After all, because we served a small market, commercial backlogs were few and the time occasionally went unsold because we could not insert another advertisement on short notice. The bottom line was that the station needed all the revenue it could get, and that need had the potential to influence news judgment.

—*WRW*

Most stations have a standard format for the newscast. Commercials divide sections of the newscast, fixed time blocks are set for sports and weather, and time is allotted for program introductions and conclusions ("**intros**" and "**outros**") and transition lines ("**tosses**") between air talent or into commercials.

In smaller market stations, where news is scarce or few reporters are available to cover stories, the producer rarely has too much material. On slow days, in fact, stations may run stories that otherwise would not ordinarily make the news. The alternative would be visually dull wire service copy read by the anchor.

In larger markets, more reporters are trying to put material on the air. (Being productive is one way to increase salary when a contract comes up for renewal and to showcase one's talent if the competition or a consultant for a larger market station is watching.) The producer often has to argue and cajole to convince people to cut story length or to agree to hold a feature for a day or two. Time for sports and weather, much to the chagrin of sportscasters and weathercasters, is often cut to make room for news reports that must run that day.

Working Relationships

Interpersonal relationships are important in the successful operation of any broadcast station. The business is known for attracting big egos and working with those people can be a challenge. Remember, though, that radio or TV broadcasting is a team effort. At times, everyone seeks or must do favors.

A good general rule is not to unnecessarily make anyone angry with you because you never know when things will come back to bite you. The engineering and floor crew, for instance, is vital for the night-after-night success of the evening news. Any member of the news team who treats studio personnel shabbily might find that microphones don't open or camera shots are less than flattering.

The word gets around in the professional community, by the way, that someone is difficult to work with. A reputation for being troublesome, no matter how talented an individual may be, is often the "kiss of death" for advancement or even for having the opportunity to compete for plum assignments. A proverb warns not to muddy the water because you might have to drink from it some day. That wisdom also applies to broadcasting!

Writing for TV News

TV news reports, designed around sounds and visuals, are uniquely able to let listeners and viewers "go" to an event through aural or visual stimulation, which enables TV to involve its audience emotionally. Audience expectations must be considered even more than they are in print because viewers have so many choices of media channels.

Consider the person for whom copy is being prepared. Although most stations have a standard length for copy, announcers or anchors do not always read to those speeds. In writing a TV script in which visuals are tightly cued, for instance, the newsreader should time each sentence—or even phrases within sentences—so that video can be precisely edited.

The days of ripping copy off the wire-service machines are over in most news operations. Wire-service copy is now available on individual computers and broadcast reporters can access the same online sources available to print journalists. Larger-market TV stations use computer systems to produce their news. The computer gathers and sorts the newswire copy, and enables the writer to put it on half the screen while rewriting for the local market on the other half. After the story is filed into the newscast, the producer can edit and sort scripts into program segments, rearranging stories as needed. The computer automatically times each story and the total newscast as it is assembled. The computer also feeds the TelePrompTers in the studio during the newscast, and some computers automatically insert graphic material listed on each script.

TV Scripts

Scripts are headed by a **slug line**, which is the name for a story—*fatal auto ax*, for instance—and often contain the name of the writer and the date. Scripts also contain technical information such as the length of audio cartridges or videotape reports, the length of sound segments, and in and out cues. The TV technical director also marks up the scripts before the newscast to indicate which cameras and microphones will be used.

There are several varieties of TV scripts. The most basic, the **reader**, is a non-video script and consists of copy read without any supporting visuals. Some studio scripts are read with a graphic over the anchor's left shoulder or with full-screen still shots to illustrate a story. Stories shot in the field without any sound bites and read by the anchor in the studio are called **voicers** or **voice-overs** (**V-O**). TV stations differ as to the order in which V-O scripts are written. Some write the script first, then edit the video; others, to preclude the writer's calling for nonexistent shots, edit the tape first and then write a script to the length of the edited scenes.

Reporters also put together interview stories that are **SOT**, or sound on tape. Here, a reporter writes an introduction that the anchor reads and then the interview rolls. Because many are visually uninteresting, SOTs have been derided over the years as "talking heads."

The most complex piece is called a **standupper**, in which the reporter in the field—often standing in front of the camera—produces a self-contained video package. Scripted, it begins with copy read in the studio introducing the news event and the reporter. The video begins with the reporter, then typically goes to **B-roll**, a leftover term from film days for video that replaces the picture of the on-the-scene reporter with video of what the reporter is talking about. The piece can either end in B-roll or can come back to the reporter, who concludes the report and tosses the newscast back to the anchor in the studio.

In terms of script format, TV uses a vertically split page, with technical cues on the left and announcer copy on the right. To ensure that the anchor does not inadvertently read the visual cues, the left side of the page is often written in capital and lowercase letters; the right side is in all caps. However, be sure to follow station style: Some stations use all capital letters in their copy to enhance eye contact with the camera; other stations ask for copy in caps and lowercase because that is how people are used to reading. Whether you use all caps or caps and lowercase, copy corrections should be few and should be clearly marked. Any scene changes or changes from V-O to sound video should begin on a new line in the copy.

Writing Style

Remember that broadcast writing is both simple and conversational. As discussed in the previous chapter, write as you speak because in radio and TV, you're *telling* a story. Copywriters need to consistently follow the style of their news organization; to not do so could be confusing for the news producer or the announcer. Often, a script or video piece is prepared immediately before or even during the newscast, and it is essential that copy and instructions are clear because the technical director has not had the opportunity for a preview. In this case, the producer and technical director ideally should talk about the late arrival, where it goes in the show, who will read it, and any technical adjustments it requires. Only then will the piece flow smoothly into the newscast. The technical director often is taping automobile, supermarket and other commercials or promos just before the newscast; that package of news scripts is just one more chore to be done before day's end.

The same rules of clarity apply when going live to a scene or taking a late-breaking network cut-in. Networks or satellite services give exact times for starts and finishes of inserts, with in and out cues, timed to the split second. It is essential that scripted instructions are clear.

Sound Bites

When a **sound bite** is incorporated within a story, not only does it provide factual information but background sounds also say a lot about the scene. Sound bites also permit an assessment of the speaker: radio listeners can detect hesitation or evasiveness, and TV viewers can not only listen to what the speaker says but also interpret body language.

Scripts are written with sound bites in mind because the nature of the sound bite and the time available for it dictate how the story will be shaped. Copy should move into the sound bite, leading the listener or viewer logically to what is going to be heard. Because audience attention spans are short, sound bites are too. Most TV sound bites don't run more than 15 to 20 seconds, and radio actualities often run far less. Time is short, so the sound bite needs to be complete, with an introduction that is written understandably avoiding the need to run the reporter's question at the beginning of the audio- or videotape. Short sound bites may lack perspective; therefore, it is important for the reporter to bring in background and update the audience about what's happened before.

The sound bite needs to be clear and understandable, free of interfering background noise and devoid of professional jargon. Law enforcement officers, social workers, engineers, computer buffs, along with military personnel, often speak their own unique language. Sound bites should enhance, amplify, describe and explain. Reporters, editors, and producers look for interesting interview segments and choose those that explain—the how and why questions encapsulating the nub of the story. In a broadcast news interview, it's necessary to get the idea across quickly by asking open-ended—not yes-or-no—questions. Sound bites should be chosen not only for factual information, but also for colorful language or for opinion and reasoned speculation.

Sound often adds drama to a radio or TV story. Fire, accident and rescue scenes all carry background **natural** or **"wild" sound**, which heightens listener or viewer interest in the piece. Be careful not to overuse background sound, however, and don't exploit a tragic situation.

Lead-Ins

Although there is often a lot of interaction between station personnel, the reporter who writes the script or prepares the on-the-scene report—either live or as a self-contained package—is the essential building block of the newscast. An important element of a radio or TV story produced in the field is what is known as the **lead-in**. A report from a network correspondent on the other side of the world or one by a local reporter live from downtown isn't just dropped into the newscast. Instead, the announcer must introduce the event and the field reporter. The lead-in gives a short version of the story and sets up listeners or viewers for the reporter's expanded telling, as in this example:

> *The annual Computer Expo opened at the convention center today. Organizers say it's bigger and better than ever. With a report, here's Fred Hacker.*

Note that this example works equally well for radio. Hacker can expand on what's going on and incorporate various interviews into his piece. If Hacker is really industrious, he can compile several short features to be sprinkled throughout the day's newscasts so that repeat listeners don't hear the same report. In the case of TV, the visuals drive the thrust of the story. Hacker will look for something that is visually interesting, working in details such as the hours and days that the exhibit is open.

This scenario, by the way, provides an ideal opportunity for the public relations professional working for one of the exhibitors. Come up with something visual, watch for those digital recorders or cameras, and your company nets some free publicity.

Lead-ins perform several functions. They identify the next voice to be heard, whether that of the correspondent, a public official or an eyewitness to something that occurred. Lead-ins also provide an opportunity to update news reports, even after the correspondent has left the scene. Presumably, the report has been filed to permit updating so that new information can be inserted at either the head or the end of the report.

Teasers

Broadcast newscasts, especially those on TV, not only must reach out and grab the audience, but also must keep viewers once they've got them. One strategy to accomplish this is to write what are called **teasers**, brief one-liners during the newscast or a series of short statements before the newscast that preview what's coming without giving away any solid information. In the newscast, one-liners are written to precede commercial blocks and designed to keep the viewer's finger off the remote control:

> *A local family deals with a double tragedy tonight. That, and more of tonight's news, right after this.*

Or, another example:

> *Will this good weather continue? Find out when we come back.*

Program teasers are often run a half-hour before the early-evening or late-night newscasts:

> *There's been a break in today's downtown bank robbery. And find out why Neartown residents are unhappy with their school board. Highlights of tonight's game. And get those umbrellas ready. All that and more, coming up on Action News at Eleven.*

Teasers don't say much, but that's the point: that's why they're called teasers. There are hazards to using them, however. If you tease a story before every break but don't air it until the last minute of your newscast, you risk alienating viewers. Research has shown this to be a strong source of dislike among audiences; do it enough and they'll switch to your competition.

How teasers should be written has generated some debate among the writers of this text. Teasers used to be small blips of information. Instead of saying, *And find out the latest in the ongoing hostage drama in the Middle East*, the reporter would say, *That hostage standoff continues in the Middle East. We'll have details at eleven.* Some of the teasers that are used today almost turn news anchors into sideshow barkers, diminishing their credibility with viewers. Ideally, a teaser should provide a little news along with an invitation to tune in to hear details.

Radio News Coverage

Radio used to enjoy the news-gathering advantages of today's TV. With this lightweight and portable medium, radio reporters had the advantage of being on the scene and on the air at a moment's notice with a breaking news event. Now, TV increasingly dominates breaking news. Even during the workday, TVs are available and audiences would prefer to see rather than merely listen.

Given the deregulatory trend being followed by the FCC for the past two decades, radio stations are no longer being held to the news and public affairs standards they were in the past. With more than 11,000 AM and FM stations on the air and satellite radio part of the mix, the FCC reasons that the marketplace should determine which programming services are provided. Increasingly, it seems, even in this post-9/11 world, people would rather listen to programs other than traditional "news" over radio.

These factors pose a particular challenge to the radio newswriter. Record numbers of stations have been downplaying or eliminating their news departments, relying on satellite feeds from network or other sources for news and information. Often this "information" takes the form of "infotainment," with a fixation on stars and celebrities. For stations doing local news, traffic updates and weather are considered most important by listeners. As might be expected, station format is an important determinant of news depth and content, with the greatest effort made by an all-news station or one with most of its broadcast day devoted to news.

Radio Reporters

The object of radio news is still to get information out as quickly as possible and to get it right. The technology of radio is dramatically different from that of the past, however. Reel-to-reel tape recorders, if they're still on hand, are convenient holders for coffee cups or decorative plants. Carts, cassettes and editing audio tape by cutting it with a razor blade are things of the past. Now, everything is digital in most stations, stored in a computer. Radio stations stream their programming on their Web sites, and many even stream video of their DJs or air personalities while they are doing their shows. Some radio reporters even take a digital camera with them on stories and shoot pictures for the station's Web page.

Radio reporters, unlike TV reporters, tend to work alone because most stations have a small staff. Although this solitude gives the radio journalist significant freedom and latitude in selecting stories to cover, he or she faces constant deadline pressure. Some small-market radio news staffers never get out of the studio. Instead, they use the telephone to record interviews, edit audio feeds from a network or other source, and announce the newscast.

Radio Scripts

Because radio news is non-visual, it requires speed, brevity, and simplicity—and it must be interesting. To add interest and give listeners a sense of being where news is being made, radio relies on field-produced, telephone, or studio sound bites known as **actualities**. Increasingly, digitized tape inserts are stored in computers. Radio field reporters are their own engineers, responsible for microphone placement and proper recording levels. The announcer, reading from copy on a computer screen, can double as his or her own technician during a live newscast, playing sound inserts with a keystroke or mouse click.

Cues in the radio script include an identifying name of the person speaking, the running time of the actuality, and an **out cue**—the ending words spoken. Hearing them, the announcer continues to read the program script. Many stations put **in cues**—the first words on the actuality—into the script so that the producer knows whether the correct piece is being played. Because confusion can result if an announcer moves onto another item immediately after an actuality, stories often have a **tag line**, a concluding sentence that ties the piece together before the announcer continues.

One of the most common types of radio copy is the **voicer**, a field report without an actuality. This is generally preceded by a studio lead-in and is used for updates on ongoing stories or reports about events:

Local firefighters are mopping up this morning's two-alarm fire on the waterfront. Peggy Pyro has an update.

Pyro's report about the fire, generally no more than 30 or 40 seconds, then airs. In this scenario, the piece would begin with a summary of where things are at this time, then offer background about the story:

The fire began early this morning when . . .

Finally, it projects from the present into the future:

It will take some time before things return to normal . . .

Voicers can either be done live or be digitally recorded and be sent to the newsroom through the Internet. If they're prerecorded, the studio announcer will often use a tag line for additional late-breaking details.

Some radio pieces are written as **wraparounds**, self-contained stories that are taped by the reporter and include an actuality. The script depends on the audio track available, and the words composed must lead into what is going to be heard without duplicating what the subject says on the actuality. Let's go back to Peggy Pyro's piece on the fire:

> *The fire began early this morning when oil-soaked rags burst into flames after a lantern was kicked over by a cow. Battalion Chief Augustus Nero said the blaze spelled trouble for his firefighters:*
>
> *"This fire was very smoky, very hot, and we had trouble keeping it from spreading to other buildings."*

Pyro then continues with another bridge to an actuality:

> *Nero said three of the firefighters were hospitalized.*

The chief's voice then continues:

> *"One of our guys dislocated a shoulder when part of a wall collapsed on him, and two others suffered from smoke inhalation. This was a tough one to fight!"*

Note that the sound cuts are brief, to maintain listener attention, and would probably be enhanced by the background sounds of the firefighters at work. Such pieces carry a standard station out cue:

> *Peggy Pyro, reporting from the waterfront for Comprehensive News.*

If the story is used hours after filing, a new lead-in (called a **new top**) may be written to freshen copy:

> *That two-alarm fire on the waterfront is finally out, and area traffic is slowly returning to normal. With an update, here's reporter Peggy Pyro.*

Since her last report, Pyro has been gathering facts and has written a new intro:

> *Fire investigators are already combing the ruins of the waterfront warehouse that went up in flames early this morning.*

Some elements of the earlier story will air in this piece. The battalion chief is with the arson squad, but his sound bite about how difficult it was to fight the fire will probably be in the updated piece. And if one of those firefighters who suffered smoke inhalation is still at the scene, that's another sound possibility.

As with TV, elements within radio newscasts must flow together. Radio producers need to pay attention to story order and types of news reports—the audience cannot be hammered with a series of "bad news" reports. Instead, audio contrasts are important: mixing serious stories with less dramatic ones, and often ending the newscast on a lighter note.

Radio News Releases

Public relations professionals have been successful in providing radio stations, especially smaller ones with limited staffs, with **radio news releases**. Prepared in the same way as the traditional radio news wraparound report, the radio news release gives organizations the opportunity to get their message out to the public. It's an enhanced print release with a message that not only includes the facts but also the voices of those in the organization making news. Some stations only use clips from lawmakers, and only if the piece is timely and they can't be reached by the station. Increasingly, sound clips are sent via MP3 in an e-mail.

Copy Preparation

Radio scripts generally run across the page but, like TV scripts, they must follow station format to accommodate production cues. (A public relations writer planning to send materials to a particular station on a regular basis should ask the news director for a copy of a model script and find out in what form the piece should be submitted.) Clearly mark in and out cues, the time, and the text of each actuality. When a public relations writer prepares a script, he or she is the reporter, editor and announcer, providing a finished news segment that can be dropped into a newscast without editing. Some stations, of course, have their announcers read the lead-in copy, then use the actuality unedited. In any case, a radio news release is a good vehicle to help both the station and your organization.

A Picture is Worth a Thousand Words

Radio has elements of drama and immediacy, but most people now prefer television because of its visual components. TV can literally be anywhere—recall the live battlefield scenes shown during the Iraq war or CNN's immediate coverage of the aftermath of terrorist strikes anywhere in the world.

TV images, especially in times of disaster or breaking news, are particularly powerful. Picture in your mind scenes from the events of September 11, 2001, or natural disasters such as California earthquakes or wildfires in residential neighborhoods, hurricanes in Florida, and tornadoes and floods in the Midwest. In each case, the sheer captivating drama of the visuals in the event dictated its presentation. "Television is a *visual* medium." An obvious statement, one might think, even a simplistic one. But the visual elements dominate television, and at times even determine whether the story will make the newscast or be buried in the announcer's non-visual "fill" copy at the end of the program.

Although this textbook focuses on writing, it is difficult to separate the writing process from the reporting and production aspects of the profession, especially in TV. For this reason, this section offers not only a primer in broadcast writing, but also in reporting and production techniques.

It is important for the reporter and photographer to conceptualize the video package before shooting begins. Good visuals don't just happen. The reporter and photographer must agree on a theme for the story so that each can cooperatively contribute to the final product. Conceptualizing is particularly important in smaller markets, where students are likely to get their first job, because the reporter is often the photographer as well as the scriptwriter and tape editor.

Planning is helpful to arrange setup shots that take advantage of visual elements. Here's where the public relations contact has to take the initiative, whenever possible, and think about which visuals the reporter and photographer might want. It's frustrating for a public relations practitioner trying to get airtime for his or her organization to hear a TV reporter say, "Gee, I sure wish we had pictures of—oh, well, it's too late now."

Sometimes arrangements cannot be worked out in advance; breaking stories do not lend themselves to planning. If the news crew rolls up just as a dozen barrels of paint thinner have exploded in the burning warehouse, everyone goes to work and gets as much of the naturally dramatic footage as possible. Writing the story comes later. Even then, those on the way to the scene of a breaking story should be giving some thought to how it will be covered. Thinking ahead helps the reporter or photographer effectively cover a breaking story, as well as a controlled feature.

Perhaps this is a good place to mention another aspect of preparation. Although TV is a visual medium, and visuals increasingly dictate what makes the air, you need to understand the story in order to write well and produce a good report. Often, a reporter must absorb significant background information before being able to do a field piece on a complex issue or interview participants about a controversial matter. If you don't know something, find out or ask others who are more knowledgeable. Public relations and public information specialists are there to furnish information to those in the communication field. Although reporters cannot be expected to know everything, not doing background homework is inexcusable.

Video Logic

Video pieces, especially voice-overs, in which the anchor reads over a video segment, follow a logic all their own in order to draw viewers into the story. A good piece begins with an **establishing shot**, which takes the viewer to the scene of the action and uses either a **wide shot** (WS) to show what the overall scene looks like or a **close-up** (CU) of a street sign or other identifying label to tell viewers where they are.

A CU establishing shot is generally followed by a WS. Once the viewer has an overall picture, the next scene is an **intermediate shot** (also called a **medium shot**, or **MS**) that draws the viewer further into the story. That shot can be followed by a series of CUs that illustrate details of the story. Editors often end the piece with an MS to take the viewer away from the central action, visually preparing them for the next event.

This format applies equally well in the standupper, the video report filed by the correspondent at the scene. The object is to let the audience see the whole picture without any extraneous details, then to move into the story—first midway, then close-up.

Whether the writer is working for the station's news department or is a public relations professional preparing scripts for corporate, educational or internal video productions, the challenge is to fuse words with pictures without being obvious about it. Words should explain, supplement, and mesh with the pictures and be cued as closely as possible to the video on the screen. Writers should use words that complement the picture, timing their copy to match what will appear on the screen.

Box 11.2

Video Terms for Broadcast Scripts

As with many other professions, video production has its own specialized jargon. Here are some basic video terms you should know:

ES or Est Shot: Establishing shot	Opening scene of a program, commercial spot, or news story; often an LS, it is also called a "cover shot"
ECU: Extreme close-up (also TCU, tight close-up)	Tight shot of someone's face or other scene details; an ECU of a street intersection sign is often used as an establishing shot
CU: Close-up	Head and upper shoulders shot of person; for dialogue or when registering emotion
CS: Close shot	Longer than a CU, a shot of a person to the mid-chest level; used most often for "talking-head" interviews (also called a head-and-shoulders shot)
MS: Medium shot	Shot of person to mid-thigh; provides for some background detail and limited movement of the individual within the shot
FS: Full shot	A head-to-feet shot
WS, LS: Wide shot, long shot	Any shot longer than a full shot

Camera Movement

Panning	Horizontal scanning of a scene, or following a moving subject with a stationary camera
Tilt	Vertical scanning of a scene
Traveling	Horizontal or vertical movement of the camera relative to the subject; horizontal camera movement is also referred to as "trucking"
Zoom	Movement of a scene between the range of ECU and WS, accomplished optically by changing the focal length of the lens, without a change in camera position

It's not correct to use the phrase *here we see* to describe action. Instead, copy has to be written so the announcer reads what the writer wants to call attention to as the image appears on the screen.

Novice writers may be tempted to blunt powerful pictures with wasted words. Sometimes, however, the best thing that can be "said" is silence, especially when the background on the video track carries some powerful natural sound, such as the wail of an ambulance siren or the sound of police message traffic coming from squad cars. When questioning whether silence is appropriate, err on the side of underwriting copy.

Because the viewer doesn't know anything about the story, the tape editor has to avoid **visual dissonance**—putting in visual images that confuse the viewer about what is being shown. This production error is common: a two-shot with both people unidentified or the anchor reading copy that doesn't match what is seen on the screen. In either case, the viewer's reaction is the same: confusion, leading to frustration. If viewers can't follow your video piece, they'll change channels. The basic goal of writers should be to lead the viewer through the piece with an understandable blending of copy and video.

Shooting Video

Smaller TV stations—and some of the bigger ones too, given recent staff cutbacks—ask the reporter to become what is being called a "**backpack journalist**" and to shoot his or her own video to go with the story rather than sending a videographer along. Thus, reporters need to know some video composition basics.

First, don't move the camera around. Let the subject move; don't pan, except to follow action. Once that action has started, let it go to its logical conclusion. If, for instance, emergency crews are loading a stretcher into an ambulance, follow the entire action: stretcher slides in, doors are slammed shut, and the ambulance takes off, siren wailing. You may not use the whole sequence on the air, but it's good to have in case it's needed, rather than the action ending abruptly.

They're not used as much as they once were, but get in the habit of shooting **cutaways**—scenes that can be used to avoid visual dissonance or to provide a bridge between scenes to collapse time. For example, in the ambulance sequence, the edited scene would be of the emergency crew beginning to put the stretcher into the ambulance, followed by a brief (2- to 3-second) cutaway shot of a rotating flashing light atop a police car, concluded by the ambulance driving away. Cutaways are also found in sound bites to provide a bridge between audio segments: the interviewer nods as the voice of the subject continues on the sound track.

Increasingly, **jump cuts** are permissible in TV, an example of which occurs in football reporting: The ball is snapped, the play runs to its completion, and the next scene shows the teams lined up ready for the next play to begin. In years past, photographers were instructed to get 2- to 3-second cutaway shots of the crowd reacting to the play that could be edited in to avoid visual dissonance.

Cutaways are no longer used to join different segments of interviews because their use was deemed misleading. Instead, sections of interviews are joined together directly. The jump cuts that result—whether from the camera being at a different width of shot, the subject moving, or a dissolve from one question into another—are accepted by viewers who understand that the tape has been edited.

Reverse questions are used to provide visual variety in an interview. After an interview has concluded, the camera is moved 180 degrees to an over-the-shoulder shot behind the subject, and the interviewer, shown on camera, repeats his or her questions. The questions should be worded exactly as they were originally asked, however; to do otherwise is a serious ethical lapse.

Whenever possible, the video should always complement the audio and not call attention to itself. Don't focus on the air or in the middle of a zoom; set your focus before you begin your shot. If that's not possible in an action situation, stay with a wider shot so that the camera lens won't go out of focus. Avoid **false reverses**—scenes that become confusing because the direction of the action is changed. For instance, when shooting a parade, don't work from one side of the street and then move to the other; where the action had been moving from left to right on the screen, now it's from right to left. Viewers will accept this if it's a live production using multiple cameras, but not on a one-camera shoot.

News stories should be shot logically with a beginning, middle and end. Stories will be written that way so the video should be shot that way as well. The best establishing shot should be chosen and visuals should flow together, just as if a member of the audience had come upon the scene and was walking in to inspect what was happening. Scenes should be edited to provide variety of length. A video piece in which every shot lasts five seconds will be visually uninteresting.

Although most video stories begin with about five seconds of copy read in the studio in order to roll tape or get ready to go live, sometimes dramatic footage will begin a story or even a newscast (a "**cold open**"). A producer needs to be careful in those cases because visual dissonance may result if the piece goes too long without any identification of what's happening.

Because TV is a visual medium, the reporter or videographer must be imaginative. Whenever possible, shots should include people engaged in action rather than static, empty shots. Don't shoot everything from eye level; it's amazing how many photographers never kneel down, lie down or climb up on something to frame an interesting or unusual video shot. Television's new HDTV format, with a different aspect ratio than analog TV screens (the relationship of length to width of the screen image), means that horizontal scenes are preferable to vertical composition.

Remember to eliminate background visual clutter in situations where the pictures are under the photographer's control. Don't have a telephone pole growing out of a person's head, stay away from harsh contrasting backgrounds that will drive the control room contrast balance crazy, and be aware of distracting clutter. If a shot doesn't look right in the camera's viewfinder, it's not going to look any better on the home screen. Because videographers at times don't pay attention to coffee cups or soft-drink cans on desktops, it's up to the public relations professional to check for and eliminate visual distractions.

An intern or novice videographer can learn from the techniques used by others on the news staff. Watch local and national news telecasts and study those techniques. If something looks good but you don't know how to do it, just ask; most working professionals don't mind sharing their secrets.

When Dramatic News Develops

One aspect of the news business is that dramatic events occur suddenly, without warning or the possibility of planning for them. A plane falls out of the sky, a fuel tank explodes, a tornado strikes, a sniper with hostages is shooting at police, a routine arrest sparks a riot. The response by news organizations is by nature reactive and spontaneous.

Box 11.3

We Interrupt This Lunch for a Bank Robbery

One of the TV stations for which I worked was more like an extended family than a traditional newsroom. Several of the spouses decided it would be nice to come in on a slow news day and everyone go to lunch. We picked a time and, as I recall, I had just turned on the ignition to head for the restaurant when the police radio blared into life. An attempted bank robbery had just occurred; ambulances and the coroner were en route. Needless to say, there went lunch!

Police had been tipped that the bank was going to be held up. Officers and FBI agents were waiting, and when the four bandits opened their topcoats and pulled out sawed-off shotguns, lawmen opened fire after the robbers refused to drop their weapons. The four were killed. It made for quite a story, and because we were there minutes after the shooting died down, we had some great visuals that the competition missed.

The newsroom spouses had a nice lunch, by the way.

—*WRW*

The first rule for reporters and photographers covering dangerous breaking events is to not become part of the story. Don't do something reckless that is going to get you hurt. This advice may seem obvious but, in the heat of the action, when you are on deadline and events are breaking around you, a natural reaction is to cover the story without thinking about personal safety. Watch out for downed power lines in the aftermath of a hurricane or tornado. Stay upwind from fires at chemical or insecticide production plants. Be careful around structurally weakened walls or roofs at a fire scene or after an earthquake.

At the same time, get the news. You may have to go into a burning building behind firefighters because that's where the dramatic footage will be. You may have to duck down behind police lines because if you raise your head, the sniper will fire at you.

Protect yourself and others on your crew in riot or unstable situations. If you feel you are in danger, get to police lines or leave the scene. Field reporters, by the way, have an obligation to watch out for their camera operators, who are more vulnerable because they are carrying heavy equipment and have limited visual range.

Stay out of the way: Don't impede police officers, firefighters or rescue personnel. Remember that you are at the scene because emergency response teams permit you to be. You have no "right" to be there, any more than do members of your audience. Yes, it's good public relations for emergency workers, but many also think that reporters and news crews are more of a nuisance than they're worth.

Confusion at the scene often makes reporting difficult. Reporters should talk to police and fire officials about what's happening, but they should be aware that officials may over- or under-estimate the number of dead and injured or the amount of damage. Be observant about who shows up at the scene. If the mayor comes to inspect fire damage at a shopping mall, it's reasonable to expect that he or she will have something to say for your newscast—at least ask. If the police chief comes to a scene of urban unrest or to a hostage standoff, ask if the chief will talk to you after getting an update on the situation.

Don't be too harsh on military personnel, by the way, if they are less than forthcoming after an air crash in a civilian neighborhood or a similar tragedy. The military has set procedures, and an investigative board will be empanelled to weigh the evidence about what went wrong and what needs to be done to prevent similar accidents in the future. If the public affairs officer speculates about what occurred, he or she could be putting at risk the careers of officers or enlisted personnel. Thus, expect that the military representative will tell you the what, when and where, but the who will have to wait until the next of kin are notified; finding out the how and why will take longer.

At an accident or disaster scene, talk to victims or their relatives. Don't ask an obviously distraught person "How do you feel?" but remember that people who have been through or witnessed a traumatic event often want to talk about it. Be sensitive to the privacy and dignity of victims. Take care while framing pictures; there's nothing lost in waiting for a rescue worker to toss a blanket over someone whose clothing is missing or disheveled. If someone who is injured objects to being photographed, stop—or at least back off to where the camera's not intrusive.

With today's instantaneous technology, live reports can be telecast from across town or halfway around the world. The advent of the 24/7 news cycle puts tremendous pressure on TV newsrooms because news has to be constantly updated and freshened. Producers are constantly telling reporters that they need to get some new visuals on the air. Electronic News Gathering (ENG) means there can be news any time, anywhere, as it's happening. This also means that the field reporter doesn't have time to think about the story. If the tempestuous city council meeting scheduled for 5 o'clock got underway 20 minutes late, the reporter still has to have a story for the early evening live cut-in at 6:03, whether or not anything has happened.

Although the reporter functions in a competitive environment, accuracy is of the utmost importance. Don't run with something sensational unless you've had the opportunity to check it out. Don't air speculation and rumor. Remember that careful reporting can be a public service: Getting verified facts to the public squelches rumors, warns people away from dangerous areas, provides information about help or services, keeps panic from spreading and helps put the event in perspective.

Major breaking news stories, of course, completely restructure the broadcast day. There are occasions when a local newscast is scrapped to stay with network coverage. Often, the network advisory does not come until shortly before news time, after a production crew has put together a local newscast that will never air (which you don't find out until 10 minutes before airtime!).

Reporting Hard News and Features

Broadcast reporters, like their print counterparts, cover hard and soft (feature) news stories. Hard news stories involve city and county government, politics, economics and the visually stimulating events that TV cameras pick up best: fires, accidents, and crime. Hard news tells the who, what, when, where, why, and how. Features are an important staple of broadcast news, although they're found more in TV than radio. Broadcast features involve people, animals, events, anniversaries, products, scientific breakthroughs, and anything interesting. The broadcast reporter, as is the case with print, has to be able to recognize, "Hey, that would make a good feature."

Reporting news, in many respects, is easier than doing features. Come up with the who, what, when, where, why, and how and you've got your story. With features, however, there's an additional layer. They can be amusing, warm, funny, unusual, odd (but non-embarrassing), compelling, informative, and—yes—emotional or opinionated. Features mean looking beyond the basics into the significance of events or examining the problems generated by what is happening.

A print feature can be riveting if it is well written and interesting if there are well-shot visuals to go along with a story. Not so in radio or TV; long audio cuts are deadly. Even on a program like NPR's *Fresh Air,* one really has to be interested in the topic to listen to the full interview. Talking heads on TV are visually dull and, in this time of multitasking, viewers will be doing other things and not paying attention.

CBS reporter Charles Kuralt, who did a series called *On the Road* for about 20 years, had one of the best jobs in TV news. He would find the odd, unusual and interesting features in small-town America: the moose-calling contest in Minnesota; the fence-painting contest in Hannibal, Mo., to commemorate the story of Tom Sawyer; and the mule ride down the Grand Canyon as the "Grand Canyon Suite" was laid over as an audio track. Kuralt went wherever he thought there was a feature; you're in for a treat if you have the opportunity to see a reprise of some of his work.

One defining aspect of broadcast features is that whereas they can be brief stories, they also may be extended reports or even magazine-type features such as those seen on *Dateline NBC* or *20/20.* For the most part, features go into greater depth than regular news stories and they're often enterprise pieces—the reporter must come up with a feature. The job of a reporter is to explain the significance of events, and features allow the participants to tell their stories and get their point across.

Features, either stand-alone stories or sidebars related to hard news, permit a reporter to put a personal stamp on the day's newscast. Like traditional news stories, they are built around radio actualities or TV sound bites with well-written narrative bridges. Reporters have greater subjective latitude in soft news stories about a group, organization, individual, or event. As discussed earlier in the text, there is nothing wrong with providing sympathetic or understanding treatment in constructing a feature. After all, if the journalists' ethic says that it is fair to do a hard-hitting exposé about fiscal mismanagement by a local charity, it's certainly acceptable to do a positive feature about a community organization with dedicated volunteers who are making life better for a number of people.

Generating features is one of the obligations of beat reporters, and they do so by talking with people and being observant. Many people, even some in public relations, don't always recognize the feature potential of everyday occurrences. A reporter should get in the habit of thinking about unique ways to cover a story. Ask what the listener or viewer would like to know.

Box 11.4

Two Examples of Features

I once did a piece on two little boys who had hemophilia, part of a piece we did on National Hemophilia Month. The public relations person who set this up did an exemplary job. The two boys were photogenic, full of life and fun, and their mother and father were devoted to them and each other. I shot video of the boys tossing a football back and forth. Each was wearing a protective helmet, protective elbow and knee pads, and other protective gear. While we watched them having fun, the parents also talked about what happened when there was uncontrolled bleeding and occasions when they wondered if one or the other was going to make it through the night.

At the end, we had a piece that not only explained an unfamiliar disease, but also one that gave hope to parents of other children with other maladies and provided understanding for those who had no experience with life-threatening illness. I didn't need to say, "What wonderful people." That came through in my piece as they told their story.

I always liked doing holiday features: Memorial Day, Fourth of July, Labor Day. There was always something going on. After my second cup of coffee and third donut, it was time to get out of the newsroom. "I'm gonna go do a feature," I would tell the assignment editor. He would nod, and I would vanish for a couple of hours. I would shoot people having picnics. They would always smile and wave at the camera. If there's water around, there are people on boats, and someone always says, "Hey, you want to go out on the water for a while?" Boats look even better when you're in one. I used to cover setting up for the fireworks display in the football stadium. The man in charge had a thick accent, but he patiently explained how he tied the various charges together so that they, not him, would light up and explode at the proper time.

If it sounds as though feature work is the best part of reporting, it often is. I remember many of the really interesting people who had some fascinating stories to tell. In many respects, that's what it comes down to: We're storytellers and feature work lets us do exactly that.

—WRW

Public relations professionals should look for good visual elements in a story involving the organization they represent. TV means visuals and if you can put together a way to visually illustrate an upcoming event, you may get the cameras there. Features are entertaining and audiences like them. They're a good way to end a newscast on an upbeat note (such features are known as "**kickers**"), but they also contribute to the change of pace necessary in any newscast to keep audiences paying attention.

Holidays make for good features, and broadcast reporters are often asked to do various features on health months—March of Dimes in January, Heart Association in February, and so on. These are occasions when the public relations professional can be helpful in setting up interviews and arranging to provide necessary background.

Sometimes advertisers want (favorable) stories. Although there is supposed to be an invisible line between news and advertising, those lines are sometimes blurred, especially in smaller markets. If you believe journalistic ethics are being compromised, tell the advertising department "no," and continue to report news based on journalistic criteria.

Even thornier are situations when advertisers threaten to pull their spots if a story they don't want to see reported is aired. If such a threat is made, let the advertising rep know that

---

Box 11.5
Supermarket Robberies and Advertising Sales

Sometimes you just happen to be in the right place at the right time. I was five minutes away when a supermarket holdup occurred. When I got there, the first pair of police cars was screeching to a halt. I went inside and started shooting video.

One of the cashiers was showing police how the gunman had ordered her to open the cash drawer and stuff money into a bag from under the counter. Then she turned to point out the door to show his escape route. It made for some good visuals. Suddenly, I heard a voice bellow from behind me, "What are you doing here?!" It was the store manager, and he was obviously unhappy that I was there.

I identified myself and started to explain that the holdup (about $10,000 was taken) was newsworthy. He said he couldn't care less (or words to that effect), ordered me out of the store, and threatened to have me arrested if I didn't go. I tried to talk him out of it, to no avail, so I kept shooting video as I backed slowly toward the front door. This made him even madder.

"We do a lot of advertising on your station," he shouted. "If you run this story, we're gonna pull all our ads and never advertise with you again." Although I didn't think the threat was real, I called the account representative when I got back to the station and warned him that the manager might call.

A half hour later, I got a call from the advertising rep. He thanked me for alerting him to the possibility of the store manager's call. The manager, still angry, did indeed call and threatened to pull advertising. The rep said, "I just told him, 'They're news and we're advertising. We don't tell them what news stories to run and they don't tell us what ads to carry.'"

—WRW

---

an irate client may be calling. The professionally responsible reps will take care of the problem and you'll never hear about it again.

A Plea for Ethics

There have been scandals over the years of reporters making up stories or lifting material from other publications, and broadcasting has not been immune to these problems. The field of communication, however, is a high calling. If you enter this profession, you will take on the responsibility of providing the audience with their view of the world. Your contribution should not only be as error-free as you can make it, but it also must be honest.

Don't Stage News Events

This doesn't mean that a messy desk shouldn't be cleared before the camera starts rolling, or that you can't reposition people to a better background, or move objects such as a flag into the picture. There's no ethical problem either in asking someone to demonstrate something for the camera—a rockhound polishing gemstones at a crafts fair, for instance. Reporters rely on events staged by others. The mayor and the police chief didn't just happen to be on hand to answer questions, hoping that journalists will show up in the mayor's office at 10 a.m. for a news conference.

Box 11.6

Egregious Staging

Here's an example of egregious staging: A photographer at a station where I worked was sent to the medical examiner's lab to get video of the body of a stabbing victim being brought in from the nearby state prison. He was late and the autopsy had already begun. The photographer convinced several of his deputy coroner friends to put a sheet over another body on a gurney, wheel it into the ambulance, shut the ambulance door, then open it again, and wheel the body back inside while the photographer had the camera rolling. He would have gotten away with it except that he bragged about what he had done when he got back to the station. The irate news director came close to firing him on the spot! — *WRW*

Don't Ask Someone to Do Something That Otherwise Wouldn't Have Happened

If you're at the scene where a noisy, surly crowd is gathered and police are concerned that violence may break out, don't get a group of people together to shout and wave signs, chant slogans or otherwise act up for the camera. Don't ask the rioter to wait a moment before throwing the brick through the window so that you can adjust focus. Don't show someone smoking, snorting, or shooting up just to have visuals for a feature on the latest drug statistics. When an organizer calls to tell you about an upcoming demonstration and you ask what time, if he or she asks what time you would like it to be, tell them you're not interested.

Don't Put Anything on the Air That Can't Stand Scrutiny

If the mechanics of news-gathering for a story are questionable, they will diminish the credibility of that piece as well as the work of everyone else. In any form of media writing, it is difficult to achieve fairness and balance because everyone brings his or her own perceptions to an interpretation of a news event. News sources can generate constant friction when the reporter does not report the news the way the source sees it. All you can do is try to maintain your ethical standards without unnecessarily upsetting anyone, which can be a challenge.

Sports Reporting

There was once a television comedy routine where the inept sports anchor said, "*And now today's baseball scores: Five, two, three, two, nine, seven . . .*" Sports reporting has come a long way from the time when the local sportscaster just reported the scores. Today's sports reporter almost needs to have minored in business to keep up with the contract squabbles of today's athletes! Way back when, sports reporters never had to cover drug or alcohol abuse and rehab by athletes, charges of recruitment violations, player tirades against fans or coaches, or domestic violence by athletes. Perhaps these problems existed years ago but just weren't discussed.

Today's sports reporting is different because the sports journalist has to know so much more. Consider how far treatment of athletic injuries has come and how often injuries are in the news. If a quarterback breaks an ankle, pulls a hamstring, or sustains cartilage damage in a knee, the sports reporter has to be able to explain to listeners or viewers the injury's impact on the team. A sports journalist also has to know all sports—men's and women's—not just football, basketball and baseball.

In many respects, good sports reporting and writing is merely good reporting and writing that focuses on sports. Just as a court beat reporter needs to know the legal system and the city hall reporter needs to know government, sports reporters need to know the details and nuances of the games they're covering.

In small- and medium-market TV stations, the sports department is often one person who is responsible for reporting, writing, and delivering the sportscast on the air. In radio, play-by-play announcing differs from sports reporting in that play-by-play describes game action instead of the behind-the-scenes coverage. Small-market play-by-play is a good place for beginners. Throughout much of America, Friday night means high school football, and the game is often one of the most listened to of local broadcasts.

Broadcast sports copy has to be lively, brisk, and easy to comprehend, especially in radio. Announcers or sportscasters can only give a rundown of scores; there isn't much time to dwell on details. But within those parameters, sports writing should try to convey as much of the excitement of the contest as possible, using a variety of adjectives to describe the action.

Good sports reporters develop contacts, just as other reporters do. When it comes to getting interviews and telling the story comprehensively, it pays for a reporter to get to know coaches, players, and trainers.

One of the biggest pressures on a broadcast sports director is to be a cheerleader for the team. For years, sports publicity offices for the colleges and the pros churned out reams of favorable copy for local teams. Reporters often traveled with the athletes on team buses or chartered aircraft. Acculturation, defined in Chapter 1 as identification with a news source, is equally strong in a sports environment and maybe more so, especially for fans.

Suppose you say on the air that the local team put in a dismal performance. You'll have to listen to angry callers accusing you of disloyalty or being mean to such a nice bunch of kids: Don't you know this will hurt their feelings, distract them, and hurt their chances of winning the next game? Whose side are you on, anyway? Or, if you break the story that a star player abused drugs or beat up his girlfriend, you might have to get an unlisted phone number. Some people take sports seriously!

At the risk of a cliché, audience reactions to negative stories go with the territory. Failure to report the news is bad journalism; to gloss over the obvious is to be dishonest with the audience.

Weather Reporting

Weather is news, too, even if the hurricane doesn't strike, the tornado doesn't materialize, or the snowstorm buries some other city. Remember the first part of Mark Twain's axiom: "Everybody talks about the weather." Is it important? If it weren't, would there be a Weather Channel?

As with other forms of specialized reporting, weathercasters need to know their subject. It's probably not necessary to have a meteorology degree, but if you don't know a high from

---

Box 11.7

Weatherspeak Quiz

Although everyone talks about the weather, not everyone uses terms correctly. What's your definition of the following commonly used weather terms? (Answers appear at the end of this chapter.)

- Blizzard
- Freeze
- Frost

- Gale
- Hurricane
- Ice Storm
- Sleet
- Storm Warning
- Storm Watch
- Tornado

---

a low or a cumulus from a cirrus, you'd better find out before you do your first weather segment on the 6 o'clock news.

The weather news reporter must convey technical information in terms that are accurate and understandable to listeners and viewers. Broadcast weather should be more than mere forecasts; listeners want to know why things are happening. Your weathercast must tell not only if it's going to be hot or cold, sunny or rainy, but also whether it's safe to travel, if airports will be open or delayed, whether schools are open or closed, and exactly when that storm front will hit. To answer those questions, most TV weather reporters must master a complex, specialized computer system that generates maps and displays for the weather segment.

The wire services periodically send out updated weather reports and forecasts. In addition, weather reporters should develop contacts at the nearest branch of the National Weather Service which are often located at even small airports around the country. During storm seasons, keep in touch with state police or the highway patrol, sheriff's offices and the division of highways. Build contacts with those responsible for snow removal and find out when they're most available to talk with you. Let them know your broadcast deadlines so that you can effectively communicate information the city or county needs to convey.

When stories involve extreme weather conditions, talk with people who experienced them. What did the tornado sound like as it came rushing down on the cluster of mobile homes? How do people feel as they are shoveling out after the season's first major snowstorm? How do folks cope? Are there any unusual stories or sidebars that will lend themselves to radio or TV coverage? These are questions the good weather reporter asks.

Many of the usual rules for copy apply. Make it bright, interesting, informative, and understandable. If winter storms are going to come howling across the Plains or Great Lakes behind a low front coming out of Canada, then say so. Explain wind chill factors or heat indexes in simple terms. Use visuals—maps, graphics and video—to illustrate what the weather has been like and what's ahead for the listener or viewer.

Remember, too, that not all weather news has to be bad. Look for the beauty after the first snowfall: kids build snowmen, dogs romp through the snow, ice skates and sleds come out, ski resorts go into operation. These are good visual stories that provide an up side to the news. Likewise, a sunny spring day, a warm summer evening or the beauty of an Indian summer are weather stories that can be pleasant to watch.

Video News Releases

Although **video news releases** (**VNRs**) have been around for years, they became popular—and somewhat controversial—during the 1980s. The VNR, like a radio news release, is a packaged public relations message designed for television. The format is that of the voicer, where the studio anchor reads copy to video prepared by the organization or to the TV news package, a self-contained news piece that includes one or more interviews.

VNRs had been used for years by members of Congress, who have their own production studio. (Have you noticed that every representative has the same office with a wonderful view of the Capitol dome?) Disney, McDonald's and Gatorade have all been successful in running well-crafted VNRs on newscasts around the country. Colleges and universities provide them, as does the military, and many nonprofit organizations have also found them useful.

What makes VNRs controversial is that some are so well done that it is difficult to tell them from regular news pieces. At times, the message is so embedded in the report that the audience never consciously notices. Some in the news profession argue that VNRs undermine the integrity of the newscast and mislead viewers. On the other hand, their use is increasing because understaffed TV stations rely on VNRs for helpful and accurate video pieces.

Public relations professionals can increase the chance of their VNR being used if the news value is apparent, if the story has a local angle, and if the pieces are easy to edit. Background sound should be kept on a separate channel so that the station can easily edit in its own announcer, for instance. It helps to include a written advisory indicating the news value of the VNR and the unique aspects of the visuals.

Some stations instead use B-roll—unedited videotape footage provided by an organization—and write and edit the story themselves. Not only does this save the public relations

---

Box 11.8
Getting Our Message out via VNR

As a Navy public affairs officer, I once coordinated media coverage for a change-of-command ceremony aboard the *USS Kansas City*, homeported in San Francisco. Because shipboard change-of-command ceremonies are routine in the Bay Area, media response was underwhelming. But I had an idea. I shot film of the ceremonies, got some general shots of the ship and the San Francisco skyline in the background, then had a processing lab make multiple prints of my film.

I prepared a shot list, stuffed it with a copy of the film and the change-of-command program into an envelope and addressed it to each of the news directors of the three network stations in Kansas City, Mo. I also included a stamped comments card, asking that it be returned if the film was used. Two out of the three stations said they did. I had done a VNR before I had ever heard the term, and the Navy got some positive publicity in heartland America.

—*WRW*

professional work, it may also mean that your message stands a better chance of airing on more than one station in a multiple-station market—each news organization has the opportunity to put its own unique stamp on the piece. Again, a script and a shot list should be included.

Public Affairs Programming

Since the FCC has been deregulating broadcasting, public affairs programming appears to be on the decline. TV is primarily entertainment, radio is a good advertising medium, and station managers looking at the bottom line don't want to take time to air **documentaries** or **public service programming**. It seems, especially in radio, that some good public affairs programs are wasted on the 7 a.m. Sunday morning time slot when there's virtually no audience.

TV is not much better. Most stations have followed the lead of the networks and have abandoned the traditional hour-long documentary. Nowadays, that format is mostly found on cable channels such as Discovery, A&E, and the History Channel. Although mini-documentaries ("**mini-docs**") are aired on local stations, many mix news with entertainment as a way to enhance ratings rather than an opportunity to inform listeners or viewers. Community service programs air at odd hours, either when no one watches or when infomercials won't sell.

If the opportunity arises, broadcast news reporters should be prepared to produce either documentary features or the more common mini-docs that stretch over several nights or a week as part of the newscast. Documentaries generally fall into two categories: an objective informative news report, or a subjective one that takes a position or makes a statement about an issue. These longer productions contain many of the elements of daily package reports but require much more research. If you work on documentaries or mini-docs, you will find them to be time-consuming and you'll have more footage and information than you can possibly use. They should be factual, however: no docu-dramas, no re-enactors. Just the news.

Box 11.9
Lumber Mill Closings Open Story Opportunities

While working at a small-market station in Oregon, I coordinated production of a half-hour program explaining why plywood-producing lumber mills were shutting down, unable to meet competition from Japanese mills. I had to spend days becoming familiar with how plywood was made, determining the costs involved, and sorting out differing stories from management and labor. Only then could I rough out the flow of the documentary and conceptualize where interviews would be dropped in.

One of the problems was that the story was changing rapidly, so several of the interviews we had shot, even as recently as a week before, had become outdated and had to be redone. We literally had to discard some sequences and redo them, although they had taken hours to produce. The interview segments were longer, more leisurely; we often were doing our background research as we talked with people on camera.

After the interviews we were going to use were done, bridges were written between sound bites, words were smoothed and polished, and standup pieces were written at the end of the project to make sure everything was tied together into a cohesive unit. When it was over, we had a report in which the station could take pride. —*WRW*

Editorials and Commentary

Another endangered species in broadcasting seems to be editorials or commentary. Because it's difficult to achieve fairness and balance, many stations avoid taking stands except on the blandest issues. This is unfortunate because radio and TV broadcasters have the potential to sway public opinion just as powerfully as the giants of print journalism during the 19th century.

The FCC, reacting to abuses by some radio station owners in the 1930s, slapped a decade-long ban on broadcast editorials in the early 1940s. "The radio broadcaster must not be an advocate," the FCC cautioned in its Mayflower decision (after the corporate name of the radio station in the ruling). The FCC later amended this ruling with its Fairness Doctrine, which said broadcasters had an obligation to seek out matters of public importance and controversy and to cover them fairly.

Faced with an activist FCC expecting broadcasters to take their public service obligation seriously, stations during the 1950s and early 1960s ran editorials and provided commentary on a variety of public issues. However, as the country became more polarized during the 1960s and 1970s, and as those with contrasting views sought increasingly expensive air time for rebuttal, the open marketplace of ideas began to seem like too much trouble. When the FCC finally abandoned the Fairness Doctrine in the mid-1980s, many stations had already dropped editorials and commentary.

If you are in a position to write station editorials, be aware that they require research. If you are going to advocate a position on a public issue, you must understand all sides of the question. If you take a position one way or another, be prepared to hear the phone ring off the hook.

Box 11.10

Controversial Commentary

At one station where I worked, the anchor did 90-second commentaries twice a week. They were sandwiched between commercial segments and, to further distinguish them from the newscast, he moved to a different set and the technical director superimposed the word *Commentary* at the base of the screen. We still got telephone calls demanding to know why the anchor was slanting the news or imposing his opinion on viewers. It did no good to protest, "But this is clearly labeled as commentary."—*WRW*

Some Final Thoughts About TV News

A pervasive tabloid formula on many of the nation's local TV stations is what has been called *Eyewitless News*, the action news program that is "On Your Side at Noon, Six, and Eleven." Blow-dried anchors, familiar to everyone in the community, have been turned into celebrities, with their pictures on billboards and buses everywhere.

Prior to 1970, news was something local stations provided to keep the FCC at bay, serving the public interest, convenience and necessity to keep their broadcast licenses. Now, local news is big business, and it has been for more than 30 years since the news consultants first came to station management and explained that there was big money waiting to be made. Sets were redesigned, news was redefined and increased attention was paid to the bottom line. Local TV news often concentrates on the superficial, using tabloid storytelling devices to relate personality, crime, health and consumer news, especially during ratings sweeps.

By its nature, TV has always been a simplifying medium. With television, we see snippets —only a piece of the whole—like going into a dark room and pointing a flashlight at objects. While print lends itself to critical analysis and thinking, TV generates feelings and impressions. Television relies on artificially predictable genres, whether in a sitcom, a dramatic production or news. The medium places a premium on physical appearance, demeanor, eloquence and clarity for the viewer to continue to pay attention and sit through the commercials.

Because they're not visual, important stories such as invisible social trends, economic development, global warming, Islamic fundamentalism and terrorism are not adequately reported on TV. Or they're reported in superficial (and often stereotypical) fragments in response to some development that can be made visually interesting. TV relies on symbolism, conflict, spectacle, color, sound, excitement and appearance to convey its message. That's always been a given. When tabloid elements replace substantive news, however, viewers who depend on television for most of their information are being shortchanged.

Why "If It Bleeds, It Leads" Isn't Good Journalism

There's been an axiom in the TV news business for years: "If it bleeds, it leads." Translation: A fatal automobile accident or a shootout between drug dealers on the city's mean streets will draw audiences. Yes, but . . . One has to question whether TV stations are meeting their social responsibility to viewers by showing this type of coverage night after night. The format may pull ratings numbers, but it's like feeding the audience junk food—in this case, there are no intellectual nutrients.

If you go into broadcast news the pressure will be intense on you to buy into this sensationalist formula. After all, stations around the country are making a lot of money catering to the lowest common denominator of the audience with easy-to-do stories, infotainment and a fixation on sports and celebrities. There's no sign they're going to stop now.

That doesn't mean that if there's a major fire, automobile accident or homicide to not lead with it. As a news producer, this author did so time and again. If traffic was tied up on a major roadway for an hour and a half during rush hour, viewers want to know why. If firefighters battled a stubborn blaze that sent up a plume of smoke visible throughout the city, the audience wants to know what it was. However, the interest of viewers is not being served if the newscast leads with a routine fatal automobile accident that is being used solely because the station paid a freelancer for the video.

Try to do what you can do to reverse the shallowness. As a reporter, look for stories of substance and figure out how to give them visual elements in order to make them interesting so that they're used on the newscast. If you become a producer, drop the exciting visuals in between the "boring" stories that nobody wants to pay attention to: what the school board did last night, how the zoning commission ruled on a controversial land use proposal, what the city council or mayor is up to. These stories are much more important than a visually enticing fire, accident or murder.

Remember, too, your function as a watchdog on behalf of your viewers. There are forces in every community that want people to be distracted by the visual "eye candy" that is currently the staple of many newscasts. Budget stories and zoning decisions are noted for the fine print that often benefits special interests or individuals. It's all right to chase ambulances or fire trucks; that's exciting—but even more exciting is to report about something that will make a difference in the quality of life in a community.

Look at what the competition is doing. Watch the competing news channels to see how and what they're covering and think about how you could do it better. Have your car radio set on the all-news station or at least listen to local news on the hour if any station in your region offers that service. Look at the Web sites of your competition and those of national flagship stations for ideas. If you can determine how to tell the story better, your listeners and viewers are going to be well served and they'll stay tuned to your station.

Remember that all news doesn't need to be bad. One of the criticisms of reporters is, "Can't you ever cover any good news?" It's a valid point.

Instead of spending time on the early morning single-car fatal accident, do a feature on the neighborhood group that turned a vacant lot eyesore into an urban showplace garden. Or one on an individual who is doing something special for people or the community. Good, upbeat features abound. No, they're not lead items, but often they are good ending pieces for the newscast or leads into sports or weather. Think about what you do and why you do it. Don't go along with mediocrity just because that's the way the station began defining the news two corporate owners ago.

Box 11.11

Turning Bad News into a Good Story

I once covered a story in which a tugboat had slammed into a bridge in the Sacramento delta, sending a span into the water. It made for some good visuals: I walked out onto the bridge, past the sheriff's deputies when they weren't looking, and I stood balanced on the edge of the damaged span, shooting into the water with the jagged shard of the bridge framing my shot. The trouble was, everyone else had the same visuals.

"How are the people on the other side going to get to work now?" I asked myself. A man with a motor-boat was picking up some easy money taking camera crews out to film the bridge from the water up. I asked him. He told me a couple of his friends were already getting their boats ready and an informal ferry system would be set up beginning the next morning. He hadn't told anyone else (because no one had thought to ask the same question) and I kept my mouth shut.

Instead, I was back at the crack of dawn, the only TV reporter there, riding across on one of the first boats and doing interviews with people who found they had 10 or 15 extra minutes to enjoy the sunrise and the water and, "Oh, look, there's a flock of egrets, look how graceful!"

My producer gave me two and a half minutes for the story (fortunately, it was a slow news day!). —*WRW*

Box 11.12
Weatherspeak Answers

The following are definitions for common weather terms from the *Associated Press Stylebook:*

- **Blizzard.** Wind speeds of 35 mph or more, considerable falling and/or blowing snow, and visibility near zero. A severe blizzard has wind speeds of 45 mph or more, a great density of falling or blowing snow, zero visibility and a temperature of 10 degrees or lower.

- **Freeze.** Describes conditions when the temperature at or near the surface is expected to be below 32 degrees during the growing season. A freeze may or may not be accompanied by frost.

- **Frost.** The formation of thin ice crystals, which might develop under conditions similar to dew except for the minimum temperatures involved.

- **Gale.** Sustained winds of from 39 to 54 mph.

- **Hurricane.** A tropical cyclone with a minimum sustained surface wind of 74 mph or more. Hurricanes are classified by category from 1 to 5, based on wind velocity, the level of coastal storm surge and damage.

- **Ice Storm.** The freezing of drizzle or rain on objects as it strikes them.

- **Sleet.** Solid grains of ice formed by the freezing of raindrops or the re-freezing of snowflakes. Sleet is already frozen before it hits the ground.

- **Storm Warning.** Severe weather conditions are almost certain to occur.

- **Storm Watch.** Severe weather conditions are possible.

- **Tornado.** The most destructive of weather phenomena, a violent rotating column of air in the form of a funnel cloud, usually accompanied by a loud roaring noise.

Discussion Questions

The following are class discussion questions drawn from Chapter 11:

1. What are some of the jobs in a typical TV newsroom? Which position would you like to fill and why?

2. What are some of the script formats? Which is most effective in reporting the news?

3. How do sound bites influence how scripts will be written? What are the characteristics of a good sound bite?

4. What is a *lead-in* and how is it used?

5. Is radio merely television without the pictures? How do you write good radio copy and present an interesting newscast?

6. What is basic video logic in covering a fire, accident, or similar breaking action story?

7. How do you avoid visual dissonance in TV?

8. What are some of the rules to follow in covering dangerous breaking events?

9. How do you deal with advertisers who want you to do stories or who threaten to pull advertising if you run stories they don't want aired?

10. How does sports and weather reporting differ from traditional news reporting? Or does it?

11. What are *video news releases* and why are they controversial?

12. What is the role of public affairs broadcasting, editorials and commentary in today's deregulated broadcast environment?

CHAPTER EXERCISES

Exercise 11.1—Sound Bites

Read the text of the speech by social critic Cassandra Naysayer in Chapter 6, Exercise 6.10. Highlight the sections you would use for a radio and a TV newscast. Explain your choices.

Exercise 11.2—Writing a Mini-Newscast

The following information comes from this morning's wire services and from input from your beat reporters. Write a five minute radio newscast. Follow your instructor's guidelines as far as an introduction to your newscast and an outro. For our purposes, figure that 16 lines of full-line copy equals one minute of airtime. Prioritize stories in terms of their importance.

1. For the past week, dead sea lions have been washing up on Oregon beaches. Scientists at the University of Oregon today said the animals contain the highest concentrations of dioxin ever recorded in sea life. The scientists think the animals died of something else, however.

2. There is a threat of a massive crude oil spill along the length of England's southern coast. The oil is spewing from a wrecked oil tanker, the 42,777-ton *Toxico Queen*. The tanker ran aground on an English Channel mud bank early this morning and now has flames roaring from its ruptured oil tank. The ship ran aground at about 5 a.m. and the fires have been burning for the past three hours. The ship was en route from Saudi Arabia and was due in Hamburg, Germany. The ship is owned by Toxico Oil Corp.

3. FBI agents arrested three men in Phoenix, Arizona, this morning. They were charged with a bank robbery that occurred in [your city] the ninth of last month. The men were charged with taking $31,000 from the Community Center Mall branch of the First National Bank. In the holdup of the bank, the two men, wearing ski masks and carrying sawed-off shotguns, forced bank employees and customers to lie on the floor while they took money from cash drawers. A driver waited in a car outside during the robbery. The three men who were arrested did not put up a struggle at six this morning when agents entered their plush hotel room in the Expensive Suites Hotel.

4. The Chamber of Commerce will hold a dinner meeting tonight. They will meet at the City Center Hotel at 7 p.m. Members will hear two reports: one on the progress of the organization's membership drive, which is now underway, and an analysis of a major study of the local economy conducted by the State Development Committee.

5. The Friendly Finance Company, 311 W. Main Street, was burglarized sometime last night. The manager, Harold Gold, reported the loss to city police this morning. Investigators found evidence that burglars entered the office through a ventilating shaft in the roof, cut a hole in the ceiling, and then broke into the safe. The reported loss: $800 in bills, $225 in coin, and $8,350 in checks. The loss was estimated by Gold.

6. A local man, apparently frustrated with his personal computer, pulled out a gun and shot it late last night. Police evacuated the man's townhouse complex in your city's north side after other residents heard the shots, then contacted the irate PC owner by telephone and persuaded him to come out. The computer, located in the man's home office, had four bullet holes in its hard drive and one in its monitor. "We don't know if it wouldn't boot up or what," said one police officer at the scene. No decision has been made as to whether any charges will be filed.

7. Choose two running sound bites from the Cassandra Naysayer speech (Exercise 6.10), and write an intro and a bridge between the two segments.

8. Don't forget a brief sports and weather summary.

Exercise 11.3—Video Pieces

Analyze video pieces used in a local TV newscast and compare them to those used by a network news organization. Do they follow the video logic described in this chapter? What similarities do you notice between the two? Is the network necessarily better? Discuss in class. ∎

Exercise 11.4—Sportscast Analysis

Test the proposition that not everything in sports reporting is a play-by-play recount, but that it involves a lot of real news reporting. Log the content of three TV sports segments within regular half-hour news programs. Tally how many stories deal with game reports, game previews, team or player news, and any other categories you identify. If possible, also watch a sports news telecast on one of the sports cable channels. What differences do you see in terms of content and subjectivity? ∎

Suggestions for Further Reading

History, Biography and Recollections

Arledge, Roone. *Roone: A Memoir* (New York: Harper Collins, 2003).

Blair, Gwenda. *Almost Golden: Jessica Savitch and the Selling of Television News* (New York: Simon & Schuster, 1988).

Bliss, Edward Jr., Ed. *In Search of Light: The Broadcasts of Edward R. Murrow, 1938–1961* (New York: Knopf, 1967).

Cloud, Stanley, and Lynne Olson. *The Murrow Boys: Pioneers on the Front Lines of Broadcast Journalism* (Boston: Houghton Mifflin, 1996).

Hewitt, Don. *Tell Me a Story: Fifty Years and 60 Minutes in Television* (New York: Public Affairs, 2001).

Schieffer, Bob. *This Just In: What I Couldn't Tell You on TV* (New York: Putnam, 2003).

Wallace, Mike, and Gary Paul Gates. *Close Encounters* (New York: Berkley, 1985).

Broadcast News Production

Cappe, Yvonne. *Broadcast Basics: A Beginner's Guide to Television News Reporting and Production* (Oak Park, Ill.: Marion Street Press, 2006).

Compesi, Ronald J. *Video Field Production and Editing*, 7th ed. (Boston: Allyn & Bacon, 2006).

Dobbs, Greg. *Better Broadcast Writing, Better Broadcast News* (Boston: Allyn & Bacon, 2005).

Freedman, Wayne. *It Takes More Than Good Looks to Succeed at TV News Reporting* (Los Angeles: Bonus Books, 2003).

Hausman, Carl, Philip Benoit, Frank Messere, and Lewis B. O'Donnell. *Announcing: Broadcast Communicating Today*, 5th ed. (Belmont, Calif.: Wadsworth, 2003).

Hyde, Stuart. *Television and Radio Announcing*, 10th ed. (Boston: Houghton Mifflin, 2004).

Keller, Teresa. *Television News: A Handbook for Writing, Reporting, Shooting and Editing*, 2nd ed. (Scottsdale, Ariz.: Holcomb Hathaway, 2005).

Shook, Frederick. *Television Field Production and Reporting*, 4th ed. (Boston: Allyn & Bacon, 2004).

White, Ted. *Broadcast News Writing, Reporting and Producing* (Burlington, Mass.: Focal Press, 2004).

Yoakam, Richard, Charles Cremer and Phillip O. Keirstead. *ENG: Television News and the New Technologies*, 3rd ed. (New York: McGraw Hill, 1995).

12

Public Relations Writing: Organizational Media

Chapter Objectives

Upon completion of this chapter, the student should be able to:

- Explain the role of persuasive writing and the scope of public relations
- Explain the relationship among publics, markets, and audiences
- Introduce effective speech-writing concepts
- Present techniques for preparing fliers and brochures
- Write effective articles for newsletters
- Write effective material for Web sites
- Write effective material for advocacy purposes

Persuasion in Communication

Print, broadcast and online journalism are rooted in a news-telling approach. Each uses technologies—different and changing though they may be—to accomplish a similar purpose: the presentation of information, set before an audience in a dispassionate and objective manner by an unbiased reporter. The approach reflects society's appreciation of impartial information and its expectation that this can be found in journalistic media.

Long before the advent of today's news media, however, writers engaged in another type of writing: persuasive communication. Throughout history, writers have intended not only to inform, but also to encourage acceptance of ideas and to inspire certain actions.

Even journalistic writers have been driven to support causes. Many American newspapers began as vehicles for particular political or social ideas. Some still carry remnants of this history in their titles, such as the *Rochester* (N.Y.) *Democrat and Chronicle*, the *Republican Journal* of Belfast, Maine; the *Springfield* (Mass.) *Republican*, and the *Tallahassee* (Fla.) *Democrat*.

In addition to partisan affiliation, some media also are associated with advocating various social causes. This is not a new phenomenon. Many of the earliest American newspapers were proponents of the separatist movement against Britain and others later championed the abolitionist cause. Today, alternative media encourage political, environmental, religious, feminist and racial ideologies, and other expressions of social activism.

Various perspectives about persuasion exist today, but for our purposes let's agree on the following understanding: ***Persuasion*** *is a process of communication that intends to influence others using ethical means that enhance society*. This definition has several important facets:

- **Communication**: To achieve their desired ends, persuasive writers focus on communication rather than on power, pressure, economics or other means of promoting their causes. Persuasion becomes an ongoing series of messages and responses, part of the cycle of interaction between writer and audience (or, in a broader context, between an organization and its various publics).
- **Influence**: Persuasive writers use information with the intention of influencing people in some way or enhancing an organization's relationship with them.
- **Ethics**: Attempts at persuasion should be based on socially acceptable professional standards. If communication becomes misleading or manipulative—whether by intention or negligence—it moves beyond the boundaries of persuasion into what often is called **propaganda**. If some people distrust persuasion as a concept, it is probably because they have seen subversive propaganda techniques used to manipulate unknowing or gullible publics.
- **Social role**: In a democratic society, everyone enjoys the right of free speech. Everyone may espouse a point of view, use legal means to share it in the marketplace of ideas, and thus attempt to influence others to adopt that point of view. Organizations often exercise this right to attempt to persuade. Likewise, people who receive an organization's messages have the freedom *not* to be persuaded.

What is Public Relations?

Public relations is a complement to journalism. It is a system of delivering newsworthy information to readers, listeners, and viewers. Going beyond the journalistic role, public relations also is a strategic process that involves research, planning, decision making, and problem solving. Its main function is to help an organization create a mutually beneficial relationship with its publics, using techniques that include many communication tools, including those associated with journalism and advertising.

An organization engaging in public relations first identifies the issues it faces and the publics that are important to resolving the issue. Next, the organization considers what it should do and say to enhance its relationships with key publics. Then it frames and presents its messages through communication tactics that require the same skills of clarity, precision and integrity that are needed for print and broadcast journalism.

Persuasive communication has been at the heart of much social and political development. It is a foundational element of democracy that played a major role in the American Revolution as well as the movements for abolition, women's suffrage and civil rights. Today, public relations is arriving in sub-Saharan Africa, Eastern Europe and other areas of emerging democracies where increasing accountability is expected of government, commercial and cultural leaders.

More than merely an ancient art, public relations also is becoming a contemporary science. This is nowhere more true than in the political arena. Recent political campaigns have become sophisticated strategic experiments with in-depth research, nuanced crafting of messages, careful and costly implementation, and ongoing evaluation. Unfortunately, they have all too often failed to demonstrate the proper role of ethics and integrity that public relations professionals expect.

The profession of public relations provides a base for much persuasive communication today. It is a growing field that offers many options for competent writers.

Public Relations Activities

Evidence of public relations abounds throughout the written history of civilization, suggesting that it is a natural and essential part of the fabric of society. Societies separated by miles and centuries display the elements of today's public relations practice: information, persuasion, reconciliation and cooperation. People sometimes fail to comprehend the breadth of public relations, seeing only some of its activities. Two aspects of public relations—publicity and promotion—often are mistaken for the whole. Here is a more comprehensive look at the range of public relations activities:

- **Media relations** attempts to develop a mutually beneficial relationship between an organization and the news media. This relationship involves pursuit of the news media as an outlet for organizational messages intended for various publics, as well as response to media inquiries about the organization and related issues.
- **Publicity**, or press agentry, is somewhat related to media relations, but its focus is more simply on soliciting positive coverage for an organization or individual.
- **Corporate communications** often is an umbrella term that manufacturing and service-based companies use to describe the full range of their public relations activities.
- **Internal relations** tries to develop mutually beneficial relationships within the organization. It is sometimes identified with more specific subcategories, such as **employee relations, volunteer relations, member relations, union relations**, and so on.
- **Events management** focuses on the development and implementation of activities in which the organization can take its message to its publics.
- **Financial relations** attempts to develop mutually beneficial relationships between the organization and these publics that provide its financial base. For businesses, this effort focuses on investors and financial analysts, and it frequently overlaps with financial media relations. **Investor relations** is an important subset. For nonprofit organizations, the focus is on the relationship with donors, foundations and corporate or governmental benefactors, often involving the specialized activities of **development** and **fund raising**.

- **Consumer relations** or **customer relations** tries to develop mutually beneficial relationships between an organization and its customers, clients, and patrons—the people who use the product or service provided by the organization.
- **Community relations** seeks to develop mutually beneficial relationships between an organization and its neighborhood or civic community.
- **Public affairs** focuses on the development of mutually beneficial relationships between an organization and governmental groups or those involved in public policy issues. **Lobbying** is a specialized part of public affairs. When the military or a government agency uses the term **public affairs**, however, it generally refers to the full range of public relations activities.
- **Issues management** is part of the research function of public relations that monitors the news media and the social-political climate. The purpose is to provide an early-warning system that identifies potentially troublesome issues in time for the organization to proactively deal with them.
- **Crisis communication** or **emergency public relations** involves an organization's readiness to communicate in situations involving physical disaster, accident or injury; financial problems; moral, social or legal offenses; ineffectiveness of a product or service; victimization or exploitation; and rumors about any of these.

As you can see, the discipline of public relations embraces a range of activities aimed at developing and enhancing mutually beneficial relationships with many groups of people who can affect or are affected by the organization and, therefore, are important to an organization's mission.

The public relations practitioner serves a vital function within an organization. This person manages the tools of communication, identifies and analyzes problems, interprets the organization's publics to the organization and the organization to its publics, and counsels on social responsibility. The public relations practitioner also monitors the process of producing messages—from research through development to dissemination. Through it all, the public relations practitioner is a writer—one whose writing should be clear, concise, focused and, most of all, effective.

Integrated Communication

Public relations is linked with marketing and advertising. Here are the important distinctions:

Marketing is a management function that identifies needs and desires of potential customers and offers products or services to satisfy customer demands. Marketing involves what are commonly identified as the four P's: product development, placement, pricing and promotion. Marketing activities parallel public relations within most organizations.

Whereas marketing and public relations are both management functions, **advertising** is a communication tool that can be used by either. Advertising generally involves the paid placement of an organization's promotional or sales messages in the media, though occasionally a media outlet waives the cost of advertising time or space for a nonprofit organization's public service message. Advertising is most commonly associated with marketing, which regularly uses it to promote products and services. But advertising can be used for public relations purposes, such as when an organization engages in advocacy or image advertising, when a political candidate campaigns, or when a nonprofit organization issues fundraising appeals.

The disciplines of marketing and public relations, and their associated tools such as advertising and publicity, come together in the concept of **integrated communication** (also called **integrated marketing communication** or **marketing public relations**). An emerging field, integrated communication seeks to combine both the functions and the various communication tools of each of these disciplines. As companies downsize and consolidate functions, integrated communication is becoming not only a good idea but also an effective practice. Thus, the public affairs office of a college might handle advertising, promotional publications, media relations, newsletters and special events, internal communications and public affairs.

Publics, Markets, and Audiences

As with all writing assignments, effective public relations writing begins with knowing for whom you are writing. The public relations writer, therefore, begins by identifying the organization's **publics**, which are groups of people connected in some way with the organization. You need to distinguish publics from other groups that are of interest to the organization. Publics sometimes are confused with audiences and markets, but there are some key differences.

- **Publics.** To a public relations practitioner, there is no such thing as the "general public." It's impossible because the very concept of public is specific and limited. Members of each public share a common bond of interest or concern related to an organization. Publics are, for example, patients of a doctor with AIDS, volunteers at a soup kitchen, homeowners whose side streets are congested by college students, and repeat patrons of a vegetarian restaurant. The public may be supportive of the organization (frequent customers) or nonsupportive (striking employees or picketing ex-members). Think about four basic types of publics: customers, producers, enablers and limiters. **Customers** are the people who use the organization's product or service (the doctor's patients, the university's students, the band's fans). **Producers** are the people who provide the product or service, such as employees, volunteers, suppliers and donors. Other publics are **enablers** who in some way make it possible for the organization to operate and communicate, such as professional colleagues, formal or informal regulators, and the media. On the other hand, **limiters** threaten or restrict the organization's performance, such as competitors, pressure groups and watchdog organizations.
- **Markets.** An organization's **markets** (also called **market segments**) are a specific type of public. They are groups of people whose defining characteristic is that they are potential buyers, customers, patrons, patients, clients or otherwise spenders who are sought out by a business. To distinguish publics and markets, think of them in terms of your personal relationships. Publics are like your family. You don't get to choose your relatives, nor they you. You exist in a relationship often not of your own making, which includes your friendly Cousin Chris, overbearing Uncle Fred and eccentric Aunt Bertie. Markets are more like friends. You can add or delete them at

will, usually based on your interest in having them around and their ability to please you. Sometimes, but not necessarily, publics and markets coincide, just as family members may also be friends.

- **Audiences.** An **audience** consists of the people counted among the readers, listeners or viewers of a particular medium. Beyond their reliance on that medium, members of an audience do not necessarily have anything in common. Audiences generally are passive; they do not seek the organization's message. Instead, they put themselves in a situation in which the organization can present its message to them despite their potential lack of interest.

Developing a Planning Sheet

After identifying the organization's publics, writers set about the task of communicating with them. Good writing progresses logically. It emerges from the mind of the writer, based on careful and clear consideration of the purpose for writing and the strategy for achieving it. Good writing evolves from a plan.

To help accomplish these objectives, public relations writers use a **planning sheet**, which forces the writer to think carefully about what he or she is writing, for whom, why and with what objective or outcome.

A planning sheet outlines what you must think about to make your message more effective. It forces you to consider who will read your work, what they want and need to know, what you want to accomplish with the writing, and other important decisions in the writing process. Journalists preparing a news story, editorial writers working on a persuasive piece, copywriters drafting a new advertising campaign, students writing term papers—all have found the planning sheet to be a useful tool for strategic thinking and effective writing. Keep this thought in mind: The planning sheet is meant to guide you toward an effective piece of writing.

Box 12.1

It Happened to Me: Asking the Right Question

A clear understanding of the public relations situation is crucial. Once, when I was serving as consultant to an organization concerned with alcoholism and substance abuse, I almost wasted a lot of time working on the wrong problem.

Most of the organization's work was with individuals affiliated with the police, courts, probation system, schools, and counseling agencies. The agency director wanted some materials vigorously presenting the agency's position, because "people don't like us, so we have to work harder."

From my initial research, I learned the director's assessment of the situation was wrong. People didn't dislike her agency. Rather, they hardly knew it existed and weren't sure what it did. Instead of dealing with hostility, we were dealing with obscurity—a much easier problem to handle. Had I jumped right in with the writing project as the director defined it, the response probably would have been, "Who are these people? And why are they so defensive?"

—*RDS*

A good planning sheet would address each of the following points:

- Define the public relations situation.
- Identify and analyze key publics, with attention to their wants, interests and needs.
- Note the benefit or advantage to each public.
- Note the appropriate tone for the piece of writing.
- Define the public relations objectives, such as levels of awareness, degree of acceptance, and hoped-for action from the publics.
- Indicate how the writing will be evaluated to determine its effectiveness toward achieving the objectives.

Choosing Communication Vehicles

This and subsequent chapters discuss various levels of communication tactics: personal communication, internal organizational media, news media, and advertising media. This chapter deals with ways to communicate on behalf of your organization through personal channels of communication and through organizational media. **Personal channels** include speeches and interviews. **Organizational media** include occasional publications such as fliers and brochures, periodic publications such as newsletters, and new opportunities on the Internet. What binds all these communication vehicles together is that through their effective use, the organization can control its message and communicate directly with its publics.

This is a major distinction with the following chapter, which deals with the **news media**, through which public relations practitioners present their messages through news releases, interviews and news conferences. Media gatekeepers decide if, when and how the organization's message is presented.

The subsequent chapter focuses on **advertising**, through which public relations practitioners, marketing experts and others engaged in integrated communication use paid promotional media to present their messages. Using advertising media, organizations control their own messages, but they pay a high price to deliver them to their audiences.

In selecting channels for communicating, public relations practitioners have a wide range of choices. They consider everything from high-tech possibilities involving computers and fiber optics to no-tech/low-tech tactics such as fliers and bulletin boards. Although we often use the term *media* to refer to all the various choices, some of the possibilities are unmediated communication channels such as small-group and one-on-one encounters.

Each communication vehicle has both advantages and disadvantages, and none is meant to be used exclusively, which is the concept behind integrated communication. Not every tactic will be appropriate for every organization in every situation. For example, a nonprofit organization with a lot of newsworthy activity can generate interest from the news media, whereas a company with a substantial budget but not much news might buy advertising.

Effective organizational writers assess all of the communication opportunities and select a mix of tactics to enhance the relationship between an organization and its key publics, which in turn translates into positive feelings, increased sales, or whatever else the objectives may be.

Speechwriting

Communication theorists and public relations practitioners agree on a crucial point: Face-to-face communication is the most persuasive of all the many communication tactics. Communication that is personal potentially has more persuasive impact with a smaller audience reach. Thus, organizational media such as a direct-mail brochure may cost-effectively reach great numbers of people; magazines and television may carry an organization's message to an even larger audience. But their effectiveness in persuasive communication pales beside the greater individual influence of direct, face-to-face communication, which should therefore be the first choice of public relations practitioners.

Not every speaker is a good communicator, however. As anyone who has ever sat through a boring lecture, talk or sermon knows, there is a big difference between talking at and communicating with an audience. Other than the problem of nervousness, anyone who can talk presumably can speak before a large group. But good public speaking takes a lot more than simply talking at people, more even than enunciation and other fine points of delivery. Truly effective communication is more a matter of content than form. Good public speaking requires a carefully honed message addressing the interests of the audience and engaging members of the audience in an internal dialogue with the speaker.

The Speechwriting Process

Public relations practitioners often must prepare speeches, either to deliver personally or to serve as scripts for others. Usually, the most effective way to deliver a speech is to work from an outline and notes rather than from a completed script. Occasionally, however, you must develop a full-blown script, such as when preparing a speech for someone who has not learned how to speak from notes or who will be delivering the speech in a formal setting such as a

---

Box 12.2

It Happened to Me: How *Not* to Write a Speech

Learn from my bad experience. As a Navy journalist working in the public affairs office of an aircraft carrier, I was assigned to write a speech for an admiral to deliver to a group of visiting dignitaries. The information came third-hand. I got directives from the public affairs officer, who had heard from the executive officer, who presumably had met with the admiral. The directions were a classic example of communication degradation or **entropy**—the loss of information as a message is transferred from one person to another. Because military protocol did not facilitate a face-to-face discussion between the admiral/speaker and the non-officer/speechwriter, the message was watered down by the time it got to me.

In the end, I was frustrated because I knew the speech text was not a good one. It didn't match the admiral's personal speaking style, and the message itself was mushy because I hadn't clearly understood what the admiral wanted to say. The admiral was displeased because he had to rewrite it. And the officers in the middle were embarrassed and annoyed.

There's a lesson to be learned: Establish a knowing relationship between the speechwriter and the speech giver. — *RDS*

congressional testimony or a keynote address to stockholders. Either way, the following steps provide a useful route toward preparing effective speeches.

1. **Learn About the Speaker.** Before writing anything, take some time to get to know the person who will be delivering the speech. If that's you, this step is a breeze. But if you will be writing a speech or preparing speech notes for someone else, take the time to learn about the speaker. Let's say you are drafting a speech for your company president to deliver before an important legislative committee in the state capital. For your president to do a good job, she will need a solid speech carefully tailored to her particular speaking style. Can she tell a joke well? Use an inspiring quotation? Share a personal story? Arouse an audience to passion? If she can, then you might want to include a joke, quotation, story or exhortation in the speech. However, if she hasn't learned how to tell a personal story without sounding wooden, it is better to avoid one. If her style of delivery would flatten even the most zealous appeal, by all means give her something else to say. How can you find out about the speaker's delivery style? Listen to a speech given by your speaker. Meet with the speaker and record the conversation, so you can later review how the speaker uses language. Ask about her comfort and competence in various presentation styles.

2. **Know What Needs to Be Said.** A good speechwriter needs to know what should be said. What is the topic? Why is the speech being given? What are the objectives of the speaker and the organization? What are the potential benefits to the organization if the speech is successful? What are the potential disadvantages if the speech is not very effective?

3. **Know the Audience.** An effective speechwriter also understands the audience. Knowing your audience includes knowing its relationship with your organization and the importance of both the audience and the organization to each other. Also, try to understand the context in which the audience finds itself. For example, there is a significant difference between an audience assembled primarily to hear the speech and one gathered for a celebration in which the speech is peripheral to the festivities. Audience expectations are likely to differ according to the type of speech, such as whether it is a keynote with a rousing thought or innovative concept, or a closing reflection with a thoughtful summary.

4. **Sketch out a Plan.** Having researched the speaker, the organization and the audience, sketch out a rough plan for the speech by using the planning-sheet techniques. Note the particular wants, interests and needs of the audience. Identify the general benefits or advantages that might be suggested. Give thought to appropriate tone for the presentation. Consider the educational level of the audience so you will be in a better position to write appropriately for your listeners. Consider how you will assess the effectiveness of the speech once it has been presented.

5. **Research the Topic.** Now that you have some kind of plan, dig into the topic of the speech. Review organizational documents, including previous speeches on this topic. If necessary, research the topic more formally, either by interviewing experts or obtaining information from libraries or online sources. Make sure you include up-to-date information.

6. **Outline the Speech.** The time you spend outlining your speech will be well spent. By outlining, you are focusing on the logical presentation of your information. Do this before molding the information into careful phrasing.

7. **Draft the Speech.** With your planning and research complete, turn your attention to the content of the speech as you draft the notes or text. It might be helpful to provide yourself with the conventional outline for a speech: introduction, proposition, subordinate points and supporting information, and conclusion.

The **introduction** is like the lead of a feature story. It gains the audience's attention and interest, setting the tone for what is to come. It creates rapport between the speaker and the audience and often establishes the speaker's credibility on the issue. The **proposition** is the main idea you wish to leave with your audience. Consider the three general types of propositions:

- **Factual propositions** serve awareness objectives by asserting the existence of something and providing information about it (such as the background of your political candidate).
- **Value propositions** address acceptance objectives by arguing the worthiness or virtue of something (the merits of your candidate).
- **Policy propositions** assist action objectives by advocating a particular course of action (signing a petition in favor of your candidate).

Support your propositions with logical arguments. **Subordinate points** and **supporting information** make the case that has been stated by the proposition.

Box 12.3

How to . . . Avoid Common Errors in Logic

To provide strong support for your propositions, avoid these common errors in logic:

- **Over-generalized arguments** make unwarranted presumptions based on limited information. Such arguments fail to persuade listeners or readers.

- **Unwarranted conclusions** occur when the writer begins with the conclusion and then goes searching for data to back it up.

- **Building on false facts** fails to make a credible case because opponents can easily point out the incorrect or uncertain data.

- **Arguing in a circle** is an attempt to prove a proposition by restating it. It may mean something in algebra to assert that if *a* equals *b*, then

b equals *a*. But in writing, a "proof" that relies on itself is no proof at all.

- **Criticizing the person rather than the issue** demeans the writer or speaker and insults (and alienates) intelligent audiences when they realize they are being manipulated by irrelevant arguments.

- **Appealing to tradition** works only when everyone in the audience unconditionally accepts the substance and source of that tradition.

- **Appealing to authority** weakens the speaker's claim if not everyone in the audience accepts the credibility of the authority. In the end, each argument must stand on its own merit, apart from the star quality of its supporters.

Box 12.4

How to . . . Write Effective Speeches

For both delivery notes and finished texts, speech-writers have learned the hallmarks of effective speechwriting. Consider the following guidelines:

Stick to the Topic. Some speeches wander from Boston to Albuquerque and back again. Bad move. Wandering first confuses and then bores the audience. Rather, identify a theme and stick to it. Keep the information simple and provide the audience with a few facts surrounding the theme.

Write for the Ear. Remember that people hear differently than they read. In reading, they can deal with lengthy titles, specific numbers and other types of detailed information. In listening, they generally cannot absorb such detail, so effective speechwriters provide more general information. Like broadcast reporters, speechwriters will write a *budget of more than three million dollars* rather than a *budget of $3,097,548*. When preparing speech texts or notes, use simple words and personal pronouns, active voice and simple sentences. Avoid unwanted rhyme or alliteration.

Get off to a Good Start. First impressions are crucial because audiences make quick judgments about whether they will allow the speaker to engage their attention. Speechwriters have found a variety of formats for developing that positive instant relationship—a compelling question, a shocking statement, an engaging anecdote, an appropriate quotation, a humorous observation, or simply a summary of the speaker's proposition.

Use a Variety of Structural Elements. No single structural element is required of speeches; they lend themselves to many different styles. Consider the various writing features that can be used in speeches —analogies, anecdotes, enumeration, examples, hypothetical situations, repetition, rhetorical questions, statistics and suspense. Effective speechwriters try a variety of writing elements, keeping those that seem appropriate for a particular speech and discarding those that may be less effective.

Use Quotations Sparingly. The testimony of experts and people in authority can be persuasive features in speeches, but use it carefully. Avoid it unless it is truly central to your key message, and then only if the experts are people the audience would recognize and respect. Remember that not every thought in a speech must be original to the speaker and not every idea must be documented.

Allude to Relevant Events. Public speakers often address the same topic on several different occasions, updating their presentation each time. An effective way to update is to include allusions to current events, activities, or incidents that will be familiar to the audience. During the research phase, the speech-writer should try to identify current local issues or activities related to the speech topic.

Avoid Clichés and Stereotypes. Language that is trite or simplistic diminishes a speech. As a writer, strive for fresh ways to express ideas. Then the speech will not be predictable but rather will energize an audience through its original phrasing.

Engage the Audience. Most people remember little of what they hear, but the retention rate increases when hearing is supplemented visually. Retention increases further when speakers interact with audiences, and even more when both are involved in discussion and sharing. It may not be possible to transform a formal speech into an interactive seminar, but speechwriters often try to build in rhetorical questions, pauses for self-reflection and other techniques for engaging the audience.

The **conclusion** leaves the audience with a carefully chosen thought. The writer may wish to summarize the information or dramatically reinforce the proposition. The conclusion may feature a challenge or a call to action, or it may leave the audience with an inspiring thought or perhaps a point for self-reflection.

Structurally, the conclusion often parallels the introduction. For example, both may present a rhetorical question. In the introduction, the question focuses the audience's attention on the issue and invites them into a mental dialogue with the speaker. The conclusion repeats the same rhetorical question in the hope that the audience will mull it over following the speech.

A common structure for speeches is found in this adage: "Tell 'em what you're gonna tell 'em; tell 'em; then tell 'em what you told 'em."

8. **Test the Speech Out Loud.** Read the text out loud or speak aloud from the notes you are preparing. Notice if you get tongue-tied or run out of breath. Observe whether the cadence is awkward or out of rhythm. If necessary, rewrite the text to eliminate those problems. Be present when the person who will deliver the speech practices. Be prepared to either coach the speaker toward a smoother presentation or revise the speech to accommodate the speaker's style.

9. **Prepare a Clean Script.** The last step in speechwriting is to prepare a clean transcript for the speaker to use. For guidelines on preparing scripts, review the information about broadcast writing in Chapter 10. Speechwriting follows similar patterns: Copy is written to be *heard* by an audience. Be conversational. Avoid complex sentence structure and the use of multi-syllable words. Both styles of writing use written numbers, phonetic guides for proper pronunciation and other devices to aid the person reading the written information. The text of the speech or notes should be typed large enough for the speaker to see without squinting. Keywords that require emphasis should be underlined. It is a good idea to mark sections of the speech that the speaker can eliminate if there is not enough time to deliver the entire speech as planned.

Writing Fliers and Brochures

By some accounts, fliers and brochures were the first written materials for public communication. Archeologists in Mesopotamia (modern-day Iraq) discovered 38,000-year-old stone tablets, the equivalent of today's fliers, that the Babylonians used in a public education campaign to increase agricultural efficiency. Fliers figured significantly in the successful public communication at the time of the Reformation in Western Europe, during the American Revolution, and subsequent national campaigns to end slavery and gain women's rights. In wartime, pilots have dropped fliers over civilian populations to persuade them not to oppose the invading armies.

Fliers and brochures continue to serve public relations today. Most businesses and organizations have brochures providing information about their products or services and about their various programs. Many businesses and organizations also have brochures outlining their history, mission, vision and values, as well as their accomplishments. Most organizations prepare a variety of brochures for strategic publics: new employees, retirees, customers, sales agents, stockholders, donors and so on. Additionally, virtually every organization uses fliers to provide information about activities and events.

The terms **flier** and **brochure** are often confused, in part because they have many features in common and because the terms are sometimes used interchangeably. Both are controlled media that allow the organization to determine not only the message content, but also the presentation of that message: timing, duration, repetition and dissemination. Both are stand-alone pieces published once rather than as part of a series, and neither presumes that the reader has prior information about the organization or the topic. However, fliers generally are meant to be read as a single unit, whereas brochures are more booklet-like. Here are some differences:

Fliers

- Fliers are meant to be read as single units.
- Fliers may be either poster-style sheets dominated by artwork and a few facts or editorial-style sheets with prominent textual information.
- Fliers are unfolded sheets designed to be posted or circulated.
- Fliers usually are time-specific, addressing a particular event to promote audience involvement or participation.
- Fliers are generally short-lived.
- Fliers are generally inexpensive to produce.
- Fliers primarily serve awareness and action objectives by presenting information.
- Fliers alternatively are called circulars, broadsides, bulletins, handbills fact sheets.

Box 12.5
How to . . . Create Readable and Functional Fliers

The key to effective fliers is visual appeal. Type should be pleasingly placed on the page and complement the artwork and other graphic elements. The layout should be clean and uncluttered. Several computer programs can help public relations writers design fliers, brochures, and newsletters. Nevertheless, the human touch is important in preparing well-designed materials because high-tech junk is still junk. Here are some guidelines for creating readable and functional fliers:

- Use a single family of type (Ariel, Times New Roman, Garamond, etc.).

- For emphasis, use variations within that type family (such as bold, italic, roman, condensed and extended) and use type of different sizes.

- Underlining can also provide emphasis as can all-capital letters (but be cautious, because it is difficult to read more than one or two words of all caps).

- Fliers often have type centered between the left and right margins; some are informally balanced for a more contemporary look.

- Paragraphs set flush left (with an even left margin and a ragged right margin) have a less traditional and more casual look than type that is set in full justification (straight left and right margins). Centered type is not appropriate for paragraphs.

- Avoid reversed type (white lettering on a dark background) for text information because it is difficult to read. However, reversed type can be effective for headlines.

- Use lines, boxes and dingbats (decorative marks) as well as tints, spot color or shading to separate sections of information, but don't overdo these elements.

- Use a single visually dominant item—headline, graphic or piece of art—rather than several that compete for the reader's attention.

Brochures

- Brochures are meant to be read as a series of panels.
- Brochures are likely to be editorial-style panels with accompanying artwork.
- Brochures are folded sheets designed to be circulated but not posted.
- Brochures are seldom time-specific. They are more likely to focus on organizations and programs rather than individual events.
- Brochures have a longer shelf life.
- Brochures are relatively expensive to produce.
- Brochures may serve awareness and action objectives, but also may address acceptance objectives by focusing on the interests and attitudes of readers.
- Brochures also are called leaflets, folders, booklets, pamphlets and tracts.

Box 12.6
How to . . . Design Brochures

Brochure design is a specialized art that involves much more than creating a flier. Public relations writers often need to call in designers to produce quality brochures. However, writers should be aware of the general guidelines for brochure design so their work can complement that of the designer.

- **Make the Cover Interesting.** The cover should attract favorable attention from potential readers. Generally, brochures emphasize the top third because the distribution may include placement in a display rack in which only the top third is visible.

- **Use Reader-Friendly Type.** Fonts and sizes should be readable. Most brochures use type that is between 10 and 12 points. Serif type (with fine cross strokes at the ends of letters, like the body type of this book) is generally easier to read in paragraphs. Sans-serif type (without the cross strokes) may be appropriate for bulleted information.

- **Use Easy-to-Read Text Formats.** Readable brochures combine short paragraphs with lists. Some material, such as narrative text, is best presented in paragraph form. Other material may be more appropriately presented as lists. Often, list items are preceded by hyphens, bullets, squares, asterisks or assorted graphic images called dingbats.

- **Set Text Flush Left.** A fully justified paragraph has a more formal look. For brochures, it is more appropriate for copy to be left-justified with a ragged right margin. This design has a more contemporary and informal appearance. Centered text does not work well with paragraph-length text.

- **Use Typographical Devices for Emphasis.** To emphasize words or phrases, use boldface and/or italic type, which has much reader appeal. Underlines also can be effective. Avoid printing words in all-capital letters because they are difficult to read. In any case, use emphatic devices sparingly; in a piece the size of a brochure, a little goes a long way.

- **Don't Be Afraid of White Space.** You may have a lot of information, but be careful about loading too much of it into a brochure. A crowded brochure gives the impression of being ponderous, which signals that reading it will be a chore. Instead, leave some white space—areas of the brochure without any words or pictures.

- **Consider Using Spot Color.** Using spot color—that is, a single color for highlights—costs much less than full-color printing; in something the size of a brochure, subtle understatement may be more effective. Spot color is particularly useful with tints, borders, and other graphic devices, and is sometimes used with headlines. Be wary about trying to print photographs in a color other than black because they might take on a washed-out look.

The key to writing for both is to focus on the facts without getting bogged down in unnecessary detail. As with other types of public relations writing, a planning sheet will help keep you on track by focusing on what you want to accomplish, who you are writing for, and the appropriate message strategy. Draft the message first, then add the graphic elements.

Writing for fliers and brochures calls for some planning. Because most fliers use a poster-style layout, the emphasis for the writer is more on selecting and placing information than on polishing the writing. Writers should identify the key publics and analyze their wants, interests, and needs. Then make sure the flier includes the information relevant to this group.

Writing brochures also calls for strategic planning. Identify the topic and subdivide or chunk it into sections, each of which might be presented as a page or panel in a brochure. Writing needs to be crisp and clean. Bullets and pull quotes sometimes can enhance the flow of information.

Box 12.7

It Happened to Me: Poster Production Problems

In working with fliers or brochures, you should always maintain control, especially during the production phase. On one occasion, when I was doing my two weeks' Naval Reserve duty in the public affairs office in San Francisco, a local artist brought us 400 beautifully produced, multicolored publicity posters that he had done gratis.

Essentially oversize fliers, they were to be distributed to publicize an open house of the Treasure Island base to benefit the Navy-Marine Corps Museum. The trouble was, the posters said it would benefit the Navy-*Army* museum.

Because the posters had been a gift by the artist, we didn't say anything. It was already too late to reprint them, but one sailor who was skilled in calligraphy offered to write "Marine Corps" 400 times on file-folder tabs of the same color to tape over the inaccuracy. So I sprang for pizza and soft drinks and four of us worked late into the night to revise the posters and get them distributed in time.

We vowed that, from then on, we would monitor the production process on anything and everything, every step of the way.

—WRW

Writing Newsletters

Newsletters are time-honored publications, historically among the oldest tools of public communication. Herodotus of Thurii, the first Greek historian, published a trade newsletter 24 centuries ago. Julius Caesar published a daily handwritten newsletter in Rome during the first century B.C. The Tang dynasty in eleventh century China circulated a newsletter, as did rulers in many of the medieval European city-states. The recognized forerunner of American newspapers, *Publick Occurrences Both Forreign and Domestick*, was a newsletter published in 1690. Many colonial publications were social and political advocacy newsletters that took up the cause for independence from Britain.

What defines a newsletter is not its size or paper stock but rather its function. A newsletter is an in-house publication, produced on behalf of an organization for the purpose of presenting its message to a particular public. It may be directed primarily toward a particular group of readers—internally to members, employees or volunteers; externally to customers, constituents, or fans. It may address a special-interest audience associated with a particular profession or industry such as stamp collectors, owners of 21-foot racing sailboats, financial investors or nuns. Or it may advocate for an environmental, political, social, religious or other particular issue.

Whatever the type, the purpose of newsletters parallels the three levels of the persuasion process: to increase awareness, to generate interest and support, and to foster a particular type of action. Newsletters are too expensive to publish without a clear understanding of their mission and objectives. That mission, to be effective, should focus on the newsletter's benefit to readers, and its contents are best determined by the interests of readers.

For example, a company with 350 employees may realize that it is losing money because of employee injuries and slower work patterns related to the use of new equipment. The company may view its employee newsletter as a convenient and cost-effective tool for disseminating training instructions and safety procedures for its new equipment.

In general, employees are interested in seeing more than policies and regulation in their newsletters. Articles likely to capture readers' interest are those describing ways to do their jobs better, the company's plans, competitors and the company's response to them, technological development within the industry, benefits and job security, and advancement information, as well as information about new policies and procedures. "Fluff" and personal notes about birthdays, vacations and the like generally are not appropriate for newsletters.

In the past, organizational newsletters were published top-down. They were one-way communication vehicles that began with information of interest to management. Today's effective organizational newsletters, however, are a more open communication medium in which the employee has a role greater than that of a passive receiver of information.

Newsletter Writing Style

Newsletter writing is concise and crisp with a style that is informal but not chatty. Although there is no standard length for newsletter articles, they often are between 300 and 500 words; some items are only a paragraph or two. Organizational magazines generally feature longer articles. Some newsletters include journalistic-type reporting in the form of news articles, briefs and features about people and programs related to the organization. Others have adopted a style featuring bulleted items in terse businesslike language that capsulizes information, referring readers to other sources for additional information.

Because most newsletters are sponsored by the leadership of particular organizations, writers should do everything possible to maintain credibility with their readers. One way is to edit out subservient references to organizational leadership, avoiding anything that appears trite, self-congratulatory or overtly promotional. Another way to maintain credibility with readers is to select quotes with care, using quotes with impact and relevance rather than those that are merely platitudes and clichés.

Writers and editors of newsletters should follow a stylebook for consistency. The *Associated Press Stylebook* is a good beginning point, although newsletters often modify it for their particular readers. For example, newsletters may capitalize job titles and department names even though the standard stylebook calls for lowercase. They also may use courtesy titles and abbreviations common within their industry or profession. Likewise, newsletters often use jargon commonly understood by their readers but not by the general public.

Writing for the Web

The World Wide Web presents public relations writers with many opportunities, particularly in nurturing relationships directly with their publics rather than indirectly through the news media. Most organizations have their own Web sites. However, organizational public relations involves more than a mere presence on the Web, and public relations practitioners will be particularly careful about the differences and peculiarities of writing for the Web.

Review the general advice on writing for the Web in Chapter 4, such as keeping the writing short and using active voice, alternatives to the inverted pyramid style, and the importance of using simple, legible text and keeping a simple background. Here are some other guidelines for Web-based writing for public relations purposes:

1. **Keep Information to a Single Screen.** If possible, format the information so it can be seen in a single screen, with links and connections, rather than a lengthy piece that the reader must scroll through. An exception to this is a link to a complete text of a news release or report.

2. **"Chunk" the Text.** Studies show that Web-based writing is more understandable when the text is "chunked," presented in short paragraphs. If longer passages are necessary, break them into several shorter sections that are easier on the eye.

3. **Provide links.** Similar to the benefits of chunking text, providing links can help readers pursue information at will. For example, some Web sites provide links to a photo gallery instead of imbedding pictures in the main pages, a practice which speeds up the loading for the main page. Other sites use small thumb-nail photos links to full-sized pictures. Links commonly lead interested readers to biographies, statistical and technical data, background or historical information, lists, and other detailed material related to but not necessary in the main story.

4. **Use Visual Elements.** It is important to display type in a user-friendly way. Consider frequent use of bullets, indents, italics, boldface, underlines and colored text. Also, be generous in the use of headlines, subheads and titles.

5. **Simple, Legible Text.** Keep the type simple, preferably a serif font with both capital and lowercase letters. Use black or dark lettering on a white or light background. Avoid text that is moving, blinking or zooming.

6. **Keep the Background Simple.** Don't overload your Web pages with fancy graphics or designs. Remember that some people have difficulty distinguishing background from text.

7. **Keep Photos and Artwork Simple.** If you are using several photographs, consider linking them to the Web page rather than actually placing them on the page. That way, readers can click on them if they wish to view the photos.

8. **Include Interactive Features.** If possible, build into your Web site an internal search engine and links to e-mail contacts for your organization. Other useful features include online registration, information requests, purchasing and donation tools, and online form submission.

Advocacy Writing

One of the most important roles of a public relations practitioner is that of an advocate, a counselor who helps promote an organization and its interests. Much like an attorney advocates for a client during a legal proceeding, a public relations counselor advocates for his or her organization—presenting information, interpreting facts, seeking to persuade in the court of public opinion. Consider these scenarios, all examples of public relations advocacy:

- A manufacturing company argues against a proposal to tighten federal import regulations.
- The directors of a maternity hospital pass a resolution favoring stricter provisions governing confidential adoption records.
- A church takes a public position favoring increased community assistance to refugees.
- A bus line explains its decision to cut bus routes from the inner city to suburban shopping centers and industrial parks.
- A political candidate expresses her views on stem-cell research.
- A university publicly asks banks to offer student loans at lower interest rates.

Every day, all kinds of organizations express their official viewpoints on matters of public or organizational interest. They may do so by making a public statement. They may involve the news media by inviting a reporter to interview the organization's spokesperson, issuing a news release, or writing a letter to the editor. Or they may go directly to their strategic publics by publicizing their viewpoint in a newsletter or presenting it in a direct-mail piece to donors, legislators, community leaders, or any number of other groups important to the organization and its cause.

All of these are possible methods for disseminating the viewpoint, but first comes the **position statement**, the document that outlines the position and arguments for it. Position statements vary greatly in the depth of their treatment of an issue. A position paper (sometimes called a **white paper**) may take several pages to express the collective opinion of a corporation or nonprofit organization. A **position paragraph** or **official statement**, in contrast, may be a concise message addressing a transitory or local issue. Regardless of length, position statements are important tools for public relations practitioners, who find that so much of their work involves clarifying and presenting the opinions of their organizations to various strategic publics.

Effective position statements are clear, logical and cohesive. Writers know that public communication is better at reinforcing attitudes than in changing them, and they often approach position statements as opportunities to maintain the support their organization already has on an issue. Additionally, public communication can help create new attitudes, so practitioners understand the importance of timely presentation of the organization's opinion. Effective writers also appreciate the value of presenting information from credible sources, giving both logical and emotional information and applying other lessons from studies of persuasive communication.

Writing a Position Statement

The following steps can help writers develop effective position statements:

1. **Plan.** Like other pieces of public relations writing, position statements require careful planning. Who are you writing for? What do you hope to accomplish? How will you evaluate the effectiveness of your writing?

2. **Identify the Issue.** Write a title and draft an opening paragraph that clearly states the issue being addressed by the position statement. Instead of sidestepping controversy, deal with it directly. If you are writing a position statement about the distribution of condoms as part of a safe-sex campaign, say so. Don't leave your readers guessing the topic.

3. **Give the Background.** Review what has already happened with the issue so your readers will have the same starting point. This background section may vary from a few sentences to several pages, depending on the complexity and visibility of the issue. Present this information clearly, simply and—above all—honestly. If you distort the background facts, you are building on a weak foundation that eventually will crumble.

4. **Note the Current Situation.** Having presented the background, bring the reader up to date. Tell what is currently happening. Because many issues warranting position statements are evolving, this section may need continual updating.

5. **Explain the Significance.** After detailing the issue, let the reader know exactly how it affects him or her personally and immediately. Refer to your planning sheet to ensure that you address the interests of each of your strategic publics. Honestly explain how the issue affects your strategic publics and any other key players. Your organization is one player. Another might be a beneficiary group on whose behalf you are writing. For example, a teachers' union might develop a position statement on behalf of students with learning disabilities. A human-rights group may speak out in defense of political prisoners. A mall may address an issue on behalf of its shoppers who rely on public transportation.

6. **Express Your Opinion.** This section is the heart of the position statement: Clearly and concisely state your organization's point of view on the issue. A good way to

begin is with a simple declarative sentence: *The Council on XYZ believes that . . .* Try to state your position in a single sentence.

7. **Support the Position.** Provide a logical argument in favor of your opinion. Report facts that bolster your stance.

8. **Refute the Opposition.** Remember that your readers do not live in a vacuum. If there is another side of the argument, they are likely to hear it. An effective position statement, therefore, acknowledges and refutes opposing viewpoints but with moderation and respect. Don't push undecided readers into the opposing camp by being overzealous or arrogant in your treatment of the other side.

9. **Suggest Solutions.** If an organization wants to take a stance on a matter of public interest, it owes its readers some reasonable suggestions. End your position statement with recommendations flowing from your stated opinion. Tell readers who agree with you how they might act on the issue: writing to legislators, supporting a proposal, joining a cause, and so on.

10. **Include a Bibliography.** Sometimes a formal or academic position paper concludes with a bibliography listing the various books and articles cited in the body of the paper. This is an optional element but one that can lend credibility to the facts being presented.

Powerful Tools

Organizational media allow the writer to control the packaging, timing and dissemination of the message, as well as its content—elements of a strategic plan that are important for public relations practitioners. Subsequent chapters discuss writing news releases and various advertising formats, but don't forget that the internal and organizational media can be among your most powerful tools as a public relations writer.

Use speeches to link personally and closely with your publics. Remember that fliers and brochures are time-honored tools precisely because they continue to be effective in helping an organization spread its message. Newsletters (in both printed and online versions) offer many opportunities for organizations to connect with their various publics. Add to these the new opportunities available through the Internet and you will realize that you have an impressive fleet of communication vehicles at your disposal.

Discussion Questions

The following are class discussion questions drawn from Chapter 12:

1. What are the functions of a public relations practitioner within an organization?

2. Differentiate between *advertising*, *marketing* and *integrated marketing communication*.

3. Differentiate between *publics*, *markets* and *audiences*.

4. One of the steps to successful speechwriting says, "Know the audience." What does this entail? What factors will you consider?

5. The introduction of a speech is analogous to the lead of a feature story. Why? What makes a speech effective? What elements can be in the conclusion of a speech?

6. Good speechwriting is similar to broadcast copywriting. In what ways?

7. What are the major differences between fliers and brochures? For what purposes are they used by businesses and organizations?

8. What are some of the guidelines for designing effective fliers and brochures?

9. What elements lead to effective newsletters?

10. What is a *position statement*? How should they be used by a public relations practitioner? What techniques can be used to make them more effective?

11. What are some guidelines for Web-based writing for public relations purposes?

CHAPTER EXERCISES

Exercise 12.1—Freewriting

Before you read the chapter, freewrite for five minutes on the following topic: "From what you already know and without studying further, how would you define public relations? What aspects of public relations interest you as a possible career?"

Set aside this definition and observation. After reading the chapter, compare your views with your informed understanding of public relations. ∎

Exercise 12.2—Radio Audience Profiles

Radio stations, especially those operating in the competitive atmosphere of a metropolitan area, usually conduct audience research that yields demographic information about listeners. Contact a station and obtain information about its listener profile. Then analyze how appropriate this particular station would be for the organization and key public in each of the following public relations campaigns:

1. A job-training program directing a message toward high school students in danger of dropping out or flunking out.

2. A museum of contemporary art directing a message toward high-end financial contributors.

3. A community soup kitchen directing a message toward volunteers.

4. A professional sports team directing a message toward potential season-ticket fans.

5. A research hospital directing a message toward senior citizens with early signs of Alzheimer's disease.

6. A manufacturer of electronic components for aircraft and guided-missile systems directing a message toward potential stockholders.

Exercise 12.3—Identifying Publics

Identify publics in each linkage category (consumers, producers, enablers and limiters) for your college or university. Be specific. For example, don't merely identify "students"; list the various categories and classifications of students.

Exercise 12.4—Freewriting

Think of a recent speech (lecture, talk, sermon) that you found particularly ineffective. Freewrite on the following topic: "Specifically, why do I believe this speech was ineffective for me?" Then think of a different speech that you found to be effective. Freewrite on the topic: "Specifically, why do I believe this speech was effective for me?" Discuss your reactions with others in class.

Exercise 12.5—Speech Outline

You are public relations director for your college or university. You have been asked to draft a speech for your dean of students to deliver at an orientation program for the parents of entering freshmen. This speech will deal with the safety and welfare of students.

As background, you are aware that the news media have reported two unfavorable incidents involving your institution—a 25 percent increase in burglaries involving cars parked on your campus and the attempted rape of a young woman visiting your campus three weeks ago. You also are aware that a national news magazine recently reported that both violent and nonviolent crime is up significantly on many campuses across the nation.

Draft the outline of the speech. Include four elements: introduction, main proposition, bullet points indicating the supporting information, and conclusion.

Exercise 12.6—Flier

Prepare a flier based on the following information. If you have access to a computer with desktop publishing capabilities, try to prepare a camera-ready flier. If not, type each element on the sheet and, in the left margin, indicate details about font and type sizes.

- Your client is the main library at your college or university.

- Your target public is incoming freshmen and transfer students.

- The library will sponsor a series of open sessions to acquaint new students with research resources of the library. The sessions will be held next week: Monday and Thursday from 8 to 9:30 a.m., Tuesday and Friday from 7 to 8:30 p.m., and Wednesday and Sunday from noon to 1:30 p.m.

- The sessions will be led by the senior research librarian, Bonnie Bookchecker (MS, Library Science).

- The sessions will acquaint students with traditional research tools such as books and periodicals, as well as with technological resources such as CD-ROMs and online computer searches.

- The sessions are titled, "Off to a Good Start: Library Research Capabilities."

- The sessions will be held in Room 102 of the library.

- Admission is free.

- Each participant will receive a packet of printed handouts.

- Following the presentation, library assistants will be available for guided tours of the library.

- The program is funded by the student government academic resources committee.

Exercise 12.7—Brochure

Select one of the following organizations:

- AIDS Community Services

- County General Hospital, Pediatrics Department

- Josh's Iaido Studio and Self-Defense Training Center

- Suburban Shade Retirement Center

Develop a brochure about the programs and services of this organization by completing the following steps:

1. Prepare a planning sheet.

2. Identify five to eight possible sections that would be appropriate for a brochure.

3. Design the cover and inside panels of the brochure.

4. Outline your copy and artwork for the inside panels of the brochure.

Exercise 12.8—Web Page

Review the information you prepared for the brochure in Exercise 12.7, then recast some of this information for a Web page. Indicate how the text would be written differently and explain how you would treat photos, links, and other visual elements.

Suggestions for Further Reading

General Public Relations

Ault, Philip H., Warren K. Agee, Glen T. Cameron, and Dennis L. Wilcox. *Public Relations: Strategies and Tactics,* 7th ed. (Boston: Allyn & Bacon, 2002).

Cutlip, Scott M., Alan H. Center, and Glenn M. Broom. *Effective Public Relations,* 9th ed. (Englewood Cliffs, N.J.: Prentice Hall, 2005).

Harris, Thomas L., and Patricia T. Whalen. *The Marketer's Guide to Public Relations in the 21st Century* (Mason, Ohio: South-Western, 2006).

Levinson, Jay. *Guerrilla Marketing for the New Millennium* (Avon, Mass.: Adams, 2005).

Levine, Michael. *Guerrilla PR Wired: Waging a Successful Publicity Campaign On-line, Offline and Anywhere in Between* (New York: McGraw-Hill, 2003).

Newsom, Doug., Judy V. Turk, and Dean Kruckenberg. *This is PR: The Realities of Public Relations,* 9th ed. (Belmont, Calif.: Wadsworth, 2006).

Seitel, Frasier P. *The Practice of Public Relations,* 10th ed. (New York: Prentice Hall, 2006).

Smith, Ronald D. *Strategic Planning for Public Relations,* 3rd ed. (New York: Routledge, 2009).

Wilcox, Dennis L., Glen T. Cameron, Philip H. Ault, and Warren K. Agee. *Public Relations: Strategies and Tactics,* 7th ed. (Boston: Allyn & Bacon, 2003).

Speechwriting

Carpenter, R.H., and W.D. Thompson. *Choosing Powerful Words: Eloquence That Works* (Boston: Allyn & Bacon, 1998).

Cook, Jeffrey S. *The Elements of Speechwriting and Public Speaking* (New York: Longman, 1996).

Detz, Joan. *How to Write and Give a Speech* (New York: St. Martin's Press, 1992).

Ehrlich, Henry. *Writing Effective Speeches* (New York: Paragon, 1992).

McCarthy, Edward H. *Speechwriting: A Professional Step-by-Step Guide for Executives* (Dayton, Ohio: The Executive Speaker, 1989).

Perlman, Alan M. *Writing Great Speeches: Professional Techniques You Can Use* (Boston: Allyn & Bacon, 1997).

Brochures and Newsletters

Abbott, Robert F. *A Manager's Guide to Newsletters: Communicating for Results* (Airdrie, Alberta, Canada: Word Engines Press, 2001).

Beach, Mark N. *Editing Your Newsletter: How to Produce an Effective Publication Using Traditional Tools and Computers*, 4th ed. (Portland, Ore.: Coast to Coast, 1995).

Bivins, Thomas H. *Fundamentals of Successful Newsletters: Everything You Need to Write, Design, and Publish More Effective Newsletters* (New York: McGraw-Hill, 1993).

Brooks, Pamela. *The Easy Step-by-Step Guide to Writing Newsletters and Articles* (Hayling Island, Hampshire, England: Rowmark, 2002).

Katz, Michael J. *E-Newsletters that Work: The Small Business Owner's Guide to Creating, Writing and Managing an Effective Electronic Newsletter* (Tinicum, Pa.: Xlibris, 2003).

Woodard, Cheryl. *Starting and Running a Successful Newsletter or Magazine,* 4th ed. (Berkeley, Calif.: NOLO, 2004).

Web and Online

Bly, Robert. *The Online Copywriter's Handbook: Everything You Need to Know to Write Electronic Copy that Sells,* 2nd ed. (New York: McGraw-Hill, 2003).

Guilford, Chuck. *Paradigm Online Writing Assistant* (Charleston, S.C.: BookSurge, 2006).

Hammerich, Irene., and Claire Harrison. *Developing Online Content: The Principles of Writing and Editing for the Web* (New York: Wiley & Sons, 2001).

Holtz, Shel. *Writing for the Wired World: The Communicator's Guide to Effective Online Content* (San Francisco: IABC, 1999).

Mill, David. *Content is King: Writing and Editing Online* (Woburn, Mass.: Butterworth-Heinemann, 2005).

Nielsen, Jakob J. *Designing Web Usability* (Indianapolis, Ind.: New Riders, 2000).

Porter, James., Patricia Sullivan, and Johndan Johnson-Eilola. *Professional Writing Online*, 2nd ed. (New York: Longman, 2003).

13

Public Relations Writing: News Media

Chapter Objectives

- To relate the concept of news to public relations writing
- To write effective news releases
- To explain the interdependence of journalists and public relations professionals
- To describe reasons journalists often rewrite news releases

---

The Quest for Publicity

In the past, public relations professionals devoted most of their time to the quest for publicity. Their mission was to obtain "ink" for their boss or client. This was logical because, until recently, the newspaper was tremendously influential in the lives of most Americans. Families generally subscribed to at least one daily local newspaper, and most cities had more than one paper. Most people also watched the evening news and listened to hourly reports on the radio, which also provided venues for public relations messages.

Times have changed. Today the news media present fewer opportunities for organizations to disseminate their messages. Newspapers give proportionately more space to advertising, television news is relegated to a few short time blocks two or three times a day (or to the same loops repeated continuously on 24-hour news channels), and many radio stations don't even have news reporters anymore. News articles are shorter; sound bites are briefer. Few cities have competing newspapers, and reporting staffs have been trimmed to save money for corporate owners. Additionally, the media's concept of news has changed, eliminating coverage of much of the routine activity of organizations. At the same time, as discussed in earlier chapters, the credibility of news-gathering organizations is falling as audiences become confused by the blurring of the traditional lines between entertainment and news programming, changing news standards, and trends toward sensationalism and superficial coverage.

Why, then, should a public relations writer prepare news-based reports? Because of the massive change within the news media and society's reaction to it, competition for time and space is keen. There are still many rewards from publicity, such as the credibility and reputation achieved through what public relations people call **third-party endorsements** (stories presented in the presumed unbiased voice of reporters and newscasters, rather than in the organization's own voice).

Organizations still try to find a role for the news media in their overall communication programs. To achieve this, public relations writers need sound news-writing abilities. At the same time, public relations practitioners take advantage of newer opportunities for providing news-based reports through emerging and alternative media or through internal media such as organizational Web sites.

News Value

News is an elusive concept, and in previous chapters you have looked at some of its characteristics. For the public relations writer, the definition of news has to be focused on the **gatekeeper**—the newspaper editor or reporter, the TV news director, the webmaster, or some other media person who decides what information to present to audiences. News is whatever the editor or news director says is news. The task of public relations writers is to anticipate the gatekeeper's interests by providing information with news value for media audiences. Thus, organizational messages must be exceptionally strong in their news value for the media gatekeeper to use them.

Newspaper and magazine readers, radio listeners and TV viewers want and expect information of significance to them that is local, timely, consequential and presented in a balanced manner. As a public relations writer, you will succeed to the extent that you focus on those interests rather than merely on what your organization wants to say. If you stay focused on providing media gatekeepers with genuine news, you will increase the probability of accomplishing your goal of presenting your message to their audiences.

Picture the relevant interests as overlapping circles. One circle represents the interest of the news media and its audience; another represents the interest of your organization; still another represents information of interest to your key publics. To the extent that the circles overlap, you are dealing with relevant and newsworthy information.

Finding Newsworthy News

Where does a public relations writer find information that interests the gatekeepers? Effective public relations practitioners use a systematic inventory to identify newsworthy activities within their organization.

One technique is to analyze your organization's activities in key areas: events, issues, trends, policies and governance, personnel, and community relationships. For example, the

---

Box 13.1

How to . . . 10 Ways to Make News

To make news, your organization must plan to do something newsworthy or show how its existing activities are newsworthy. Here are 10 ways organizations try to make news:

1. Give an award that draws attention to your organization and its mission.

2. Hold a contest that involves people in your organization.

3. Highlight personnel whose jobs or voluntary efforts contribute to your organization's mission.

4. Address a local need that coincides with your organization's objectives.

5. Issue a report from your organization that addresses an issue of public interest.

6. Launch a campaign that focuses on your organization's mission.

7. Make a speech that furthers your organization's goals.

8. Involve a celebrity to draw public attention to your organization's goals.

9. Tie into a public issue by linking your organization with an ongoing newsworthy matter of public concern.

10. Localize a report by highlighting the local implications of a general statement, policy, or research finding related to your organization's objectives.

---

public relations director for a health agency might focus on events such as weight-loss clinics, issues such as the link between exercise and mental alertness, trends such as the lowering age of women who begin smoking, policies such as new procedures for immunizing schoolchildren, personnel moves such as a new staff physician, and community relationships such as a partnership between the agency and the employee-services program of a large local corporation.

Another technique is to inventory activities according to the four categories of publics defined in the previous chapter: consumers, producers, enablers and limiters. Consider the example of a public school district. Consumers are students and parents, as well as colleges that eventually will educate the graduates and businesses who might hire them. Activities that involve consumer publics might include science fairs, school organizations, essay contests, scholarships and parent associations. Producers are teachers and staff, who generate newsworthy information about new faculty and in-service training. Enablers include school boards and state education departments, with activities involving elections, budgets, accreditation and standards. Limiters include other school districts, private schools and anti-tax groups, which may have raised an issue relevant to the public agenda, allowing your district to weigh in on an issue.

Writing News Releases

In 1758, King's College (now Columbia University) wrote the world's first news release, announcing its graduation ceremonies. Ever since, news releases have been the single most commonly used tool for media relations. Despite today's fragmentation of the mass media and the emergence of new opportunities with organizational and interactive media, news releases remain an important tool for the public relations writer. They provide an opportunity to help the writer's organization communicate its message to its various publics. An estimated 40 to 70 percent of material in the average daily newspaper has been linked to news releases, which provide journalists with both information and interview possibilities.

Simply stated, a **news release** is a news story supplied to the media by a public relations practitioner. It may announce an event or provide a follow-up report. It may present the organization's position on an issue or report significant progress within the organization.

Generations of public relations writers have used news releases. Despite changes within the media, news releases remain a basic tool in public relations. For that reason, the preparation and style of news releases merit detailed discussion.

Basic Elements of a News Release

Over the years, standard components have become identified with effective news releases, including categories of information that go in the heading, the text of the news release, and the footer (see Figure 13.1).

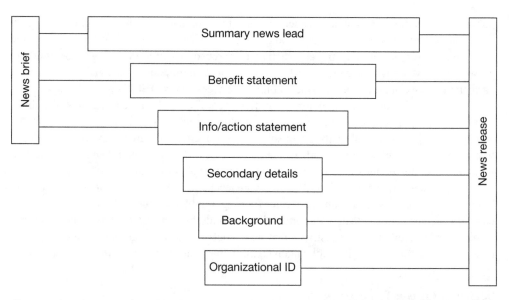

Figure 13.1 Components of a News Release and a News Brief. Note that the summary news lead, benefit statement, and info/action statement together form the news brief, which is the first part of a more comprehensive news release.

Heading Structure   At the top of the news release is the name and address of the sending organization along with the name and telephone number of the public relations contact person. An optional element in the news release heading is the **news flag** (which is simply the words *News* or *News Release* printed in large letters). With the current state of computer graphics, even the smallest organization with the tightest budget can produce an attractive and professional-looking letterhead for its news releases.

The top of the release also includes the **release date**, indicating when the release may be used. This usually is designated *For Immediate Release,* indicating the media are free to use the information as soon as they receive it. An alternative kind of release date—seldom used anymore—is an **embargo** which indicates a future release point, such as *For Release on or after Friday, May 15, at 6 a.m.*

Text Structure   The body of the news release may begin with a headline or summary. The first paragraph begins with a dateline if the release is to be distributed beyond the local area of the sending organization. The text of the release should be presented in short paragraphs in double-spaced, professional-looking type with standard indents and a ragged right margin. This format presents the look of a manuscript or a work-in-progress that invites an editor or news director to begin editing and adapting the release for media use.

Footer Structure   A visual signal indicates the conclusion of the text. This end mark may be written as a series of hatch marks, ####; the word *end* in capital letters with double parentheses, ((END)); or the traditional printing notation, -30-.

If the text continues onto a second page, the first page ends with a **more line** in double parentheses: ((more-more-more)). Then the second page begins with a **slug line** that recaps the headline or uses the name of the sending organization along with the page number.

An optional footer element is a note to editors and news directors. This message, not meant for publication, may be a note about special access for photographers, the availability of an interview, or a trademark notice.

Box 13.2

How to . . . Using Appropriate Terms

Get used to using appropriate terms. The proper term is *news release*, not *press release* and certainly not *handout*. Strictly speaking, radio and television reporters are not the press; along with print and online journalists, they all are members of the news media.

More importantly, a public relations writer's job is not that of being a press agent simply trying to get media mention for the client. Rather, the writer is working with and through the news media to communicate newsworthy information to an organization's publics among media audiences.

Box 13.3

Components of a News Release

News releases are rooted in common journalistic techniques, but they have some unique features that take them beyond basic news stories. Like most news stories, news releases use a summary lead and follow the inverted-pyramid style. The following components, which are also illustrated in Figure 13.1, can be found in most news releases:

- **Summary News Lead.** The summary lead gives primary information. This lead, usually one paragraph, highlights the basic facts and their significance to the audience.

- **Benefit Statement.** Following the lead, the benefit statement should clearly indicate the value to the audience. It tells what the audience might derive from the activity or issue being reported. This statement often is presented in the form of a quote. The benefit statement is one writing element added to the basic news reporting format of journalistic writing.

- **Action/Info Statement.** Rounding out the basic elements of a news release is an action/info statement that clearly indicates how the audience can become involved or where if can obtain additional information. The action statement is

presented as useful information rather than a directive. Like the benefit statement, the action/info statement is an addition to the basic news reporting format developed by print journalists.

- **Secondary Details.** Less important details follow, but these should be kept to a minimum. Detailed information seldom finds its way into print, and even more seldom is it used by radio or TV reporters.

- **Background Information.** Additional background information provides a context for the summary and benefit statement. This information sometimes gives relevant history or explains the environment of an issue.

- **Optional Organizational Identification.** Some writers add to their news releases a final paragraph that serves as organizational identification. This ID is a standard paragraph providing background on the organization releasing the information. Some writers present this information as a final paragraph in the release itself. Other writers present it as a note so editors and news directors will have background information about their organizations.

Types of News Releases

Broadly speaking, there are two types of news releases: those that announce something new and those that comment on something already in the news.

Announcement Release   The most common news releases are those that provide advance information about a planned organizational activity. These releases may describe upcoming events or personnel activities such as promotions. They may focus on progress within an organization or new programs being developed. Releases announcing new products are more likely to be used by specialized trade publications than by the general media.

Response Release   Response releases provide organizational comment on events, ideas or previous reports. They include new-information releases, which contain follow-up information

---

Box 13.4

How to . . . Personnel Appointment Release

Although news releases can't be written in fill-in-the-blank formats, they do offer a convenient pattern for presenting information. One of the most frequently written types of releases announces personnel appointments. Here is a logical format for this type of release:

1. Identify the person by name, stating the new position and attributing the announcement to an official of the company. Indicate when the appointment becomes effective.

2. Indicate the person's responsibilities and the role that position plays in the organization. Focus on

previously reported activities, and comment releases, which address messages to the organization's publics on matters of mutual interest. Response releases may tie into current events linked to the organization's mission. They also may provide follow-up publicity related to speeches given by organizational representatives. Releases dealing with an organization's response to bad news may be difficult to write because the issues can be very sensitive. Nevertheless, public relations practitioners have learned that getting on top of bad news with well-thought-out comment can minimize negative reaction and may actually provide an opportunity to present a positive message.

Building a Better News Release

Virtually all public relations practitioners use the same basic formats for writing news releases. Some, however, are more successful than others in creating effective releases. The secret lies in strategic thinking. Good releases have two elements: powerful quotes and local information.

Creating Powerful Quotes

A difference between journalists and public relations writers involves their use of direct quotations. Journalists are ethically bound to report only the actual words that come from a news source. Public relations writers, however, serve in the capacity of advisers who sometimes suggest comments for organizational news sources. The role of the public relations writer is not one of creating quotes out of thin air but rather of helping organizations package their message to provide effective, accurate comments for reporters. Public relations practitioners are qualified for this role because they are in a position to understand the wants, interests and needs of the organization, as well as the media and the media audiences, and because public relations practitioners presumably have excellent communication skills that can help organizations deliver strong and clear messages.

The key to writing effective quotes is to focus on the wants, interests and needs of your strategic publics and on the objectives of your organization in communicating with these publics. Think also of the concerns of the media gatekeeper, who is vigilant in barring pretentious and self-serving comments.

Additionally, follow a few simple guidelines:

- Think of the sound bite.
- Don't state the obvious.
- Say what you want to say with style.
- Above all, say something strategic that will propel you toward your objectives.

Of course the CEO is proud of her company's success, but an editor is likely to axe a say-nothing sentence like *"I'm very proud of my company's success," said CEO Matilda Bahzlaydi.* Rather, give Ms. Bahzlaydi an interesting and managerial way of expressing her pride: *"Our company's success means our people are working as a team and giving customers top-notch service, while still protecting the environment for everyone who lives around Centerville," said CEO Matilda Bahzlaydi. "That would make any CEO proud."*

Be aware that some editors prefer not to use direct quotes provided by news releases because they don't want to use the same quotes that their competitors have. Nevertheless, it's a good idea to make the quotes available because if they're not there, they can't be considered.

Localizing Releases

In several surveys, editors and news directors have identified the lack of a strong local angle as their main reason for rejecting news releases. Effective public relations writers know how

---

Box 13.5

How to . . . Too Much Localizing?

A public relations intern working at a hospital was told that all news release leads were to begin the same way: *Central Hospital of 123 Fourth Street announces that* . . . The intern recognized that a better way to write the news release would be to focus on the news rather than on the organization providing it.

She learned that the hospital was acting on the recommendation of a fund-raising consultant, who had accurately observed that the small hospital's location on a side street meant that many residents were unfamiliar with it. The consultant had recom-

mended that news releases emphasize the location and the community connection. The policy had a logical basis, although its application was rather arbitrary and ineffective, because most newspapers rewrite the release to remove the location from the lead and often from the entire story.

Knowing the motivation for the policy, the intern was able to write releases that included not only the introductory phrase but also substantive references to location and benefits to local residents.

Box 13.6

How to . . . That Story Looks Familiar!

How can you tell if you have a well-written news release? I knew it when I opened the afternoon newspaper and found my release published word for word with the byline of a newspaper's beat reporter.

The reporter soon called with an explanation. He had scanned my release into his computer to rewrite it but was called away from his desk. The editor noticed my release in the computer and, presuming it was the work of the reporter, slugged in the reporter's byline. The reporter said the editor reasoned that the story must have been the reporter's work because it was a balanced piece of newswriting.

There's a compliment in there someplace, I guess. —*RDS*

---

to enhance the likelihood that their releases will be used. They prepare several different versions of the same story, each tailored to the needs of the news media in a particular locality. The time it takes to prepare different localized versions of a release is time well spent. Often, the only difference is the lead and perhaps the benefit statement or quote; the rest of the release remains the same.

Rewriting the News Release

Public relations writers work hard to create effective news releases. Yet, more often than not, their work is rewritten when it gets into the hands of a journalist.

There are several reasons releases are rewritten. One reason is simply that news releases have developed a poor reputation. Reporters receive many badly written releases. Not from you, of course—but they get so many from uninformed amateurs or misguided promotionalists that reporters have gotten into the habit of rewriting all releases.

Rewriting news releases also may be a matter of policy. Some publications, especially larger ones in competitive markets, have policies against using news releases as they are received. Rewriting prevents the potential embarrassment of having exactly the same story as another publication.

Many public relations writers provide thorough reports and, eventually, the gatekeepers learn to trust the work of those writers. Editors and news directors often see their releases as a good starting place from which to delve further, to interview and investigate more. They may expand on a news release and prepare a more comprehensive report.

News Release Writing Style

With regard to the writing style of news releases, public relations writers take their cues from journalists. Good releases follow the rules and patterns of journalistic writing. Figure 13.2 illustrates a news release that an organization might send to its local newspaper. Notice that it is written in much the same way a journalist would write the story. The following paragraphs provide several reminders for writers of news releases.

The *Alternative Harmonica Ensemble* of Little Valley

123 Fourth Street
Little Valley XX 12345
(123) 456–7890

May 2, 2008

FOR IMMEDIATE RELEASE

Traditional Japanese Kabuki music performed by a 25-piece harmonica orchestra will highlight the spring concert of the Alternative Harmonica Ensemble of Little Valley. The free performances Friday, May 16, will mark the world premiere of Kabuki Harmonica.

Ensemble director Augustine Honer called the harmonica interpretations of the traditional Kabuki melodies "transforming" and "breathtaking."

"The emperor himself hasn't heard such beauty yet, but the lucky people of Little Valley will have the opportunity to enjoy this superb music," said Honer, a music teacher at Little Valley High School descended from the German inventor of the harmonica.

The concert, with performances at 3 p.m. and 7 p.m., also will feature Calypso music and classical Baroque chamber music performed on the harmonica. The "Harping Around the World" concert will take place at Mozart Auditorium in the Classical Arts Building on the campus of Little Valley Community College.

The Alternative Harmonica Ensemble began in 1989 as a group of players who had entertained informally at the Woodstock Concert. The tradition of a free public concert started in 1984, when the ensemble began receiving funding through the Little Valley Community Chest.

Contact for Additional Information. Bobbi McGee, Public Relations Coordinator

Figure 13.2 Sample News Release

Keep It Short

Short sentences. Short paragraphs. Short releases. Public relations writers try to keep news releases to one page, no more than two. If you are writing more than that, perhaps you should prepare a shorter release and then include additional materials with it, such as a secondary release, backgrounder or biographical narrative. For broadcast releases, 12 to 16 lines (about 45 seconds to a minute of copy) is generally the maximum you should write.

Use Simple Language

Keep word choices simple. Write *said* rather than striving for subjective alternatives such as *proclaimed, declared* and *observed.* Be careful when using objective variations such as *pointed out, added* and *replied* to make sure that the words reflect the appropriate context, such as *pointing out* additional faculty information or *replying* to a question. Avoid subjective superlatives such as *greatest* and *best,* and make sure that objective superlatives such as *first, unique* and *only* are actually true.

Attribute Matters of Opinion

News releases are vehicles for facts, not for the opinion or speculation of the writer. Opinion has a place in releases, but the opinion must be attributed to the person or organization holding it. For example, it may be the writer's opinion that a fund-raising event is a worthy cause. But a news release cannot simply state that, and any reputable editor would excise such a commentary. The release might instead quote the head of the fund-raising campaign or a recipient of the campaign-support services as calling it a worthy cause.

Write For, But Not To, the Audience

Don't tell the audience what to do. Effective news releases provide information of interest to the reader, listener and viewer, but they do so in an impersonal way, and they provide information but not directions. For example, if Toxico Industries is sending a truck into neighborhoods to collect hazardous household waste, the news release should indicate times, places and procedures for residents; it would not specifically direct or encourage them to have the waste materials ready for the collection. If directives and motivating statements are necessary, the writer would present them as quotes from an authoritative source.

Lead With the News

Begin with the newsworthy aspect of your story, not with minor details such as time or place. Don't put too much focus on the organization. Avoid leads that report topics but not significant information, such as a lead announcing *The trustees of Alma Mater University will meet Wednesday morning to discuss important business.* Readers don't learn much from this lead. Write a better lead by naming the items discussed, as in *The trustees of Alma Mater University will meet Wednesday morning to consider censuring the dean of academic affairs.* In short, begin with the news.

To present the main points quickly, the writer sometimes will delay specific information. For example, the lead paragraph may report *The president of Alma Mater University has received a top education award from Gov. Politico.* The governor's name would be used because it is well known; however, the lead would not identify the university president by name because he or she is not known beyond the campus. Neither would the lead provide specific details about the award or the presentation ceremony; this information would come in the following paragraph. The writing principles are the same for the delayed lead that was discussed in the newswriting chapters.

Use Passive Voice When Appropriate

It's true that active voice generally is stronger and more direct, but passive voice has a place. Public relations writers often use it for their leads, emphasizing the news rather than the newsmaker:

> Emphasis on the news: *Melvin Chick has been appointed executive director of the Center for the Enhancement of Poultry Farming.*

> Self-focused on the news maker: *The Center for the Enhancement of Poultry Farming has appointed Melvin Chick as executive director.*

Avoid Promotionalism

A news release is not an advertisement, and it is never appropriate to lace a release with "puff" terms such as *revolutionary* and *breakthrough.* Avoid overly polite and formal phrases such as *proud to announce.* Strive to keep the release balanced. A good release should not sound as if it were prepared by a cheerleader. Rather, it should read as if it were written by an objective news reporter.

These precepts, perhaps more than any others, separate the public relations professional from a flack. **Flack** is a disparaging term, referring to someone masquerading as a public relations writer while actually being little more than a con artist. (The journalistic parallel is **hack**, a poor and unprincipled writer pretending to be a reporter. Avoid using–or being–either.) In preparing news releases and other media information, public relations writers think about how a reporter covering this situation would prepare the story, then write as closely to that style as possible. Journalistic style enhances the likelihood of the release being used.

Consider the two following releases. The first is an embarrassment, most often sent by a publicist unschooled in public relations protocol. The second is more appropriate in its tone:

> *Oakwood Communications is proud to note the appointment of Dwilla Gwenwivver as assistant vice president in charge of new business development. The appointment was announced to Oakwood Communication's employees and clients by President and Chief Executive Officer Gary Shandstuffie.*

> *"I'm sure Ms. Gwenwivver will take us to even greater heights as we move toward becoming the premier full-service public relations agency in the county," said Shandstuffie.*

Oakwood Communications offers its growing list of clients a full range of professional services. This includes research and strategic planning, promotions and special events, and media relations.

Gwenwivver is a summa cum laude graduate of the School of Public Relations at Ivy Lee University.

Now, compare that version with this more professionally written version that emphasizes news value and presents significant information to readers in a more balanced, unpretentious manner:

Dwilla Gwenwivver, an honors graduate of Ivy Lee University, has been named assistant vice president for new business development by Oakwood Communications. The agency, the third-largest public relations agency in the county, offers a variety of public relations services. Gary Shandstuffie heads the agency.

Box 13.7

It Happened to Me: The Fate of Poorly-Written News Releases

The routine was the same every morning at the television station where I worked: The assignment editor would come into the newsroom with a glazed donut between his teeth and a Styrofoam cup of coffee balanced precariously on the stack of mail he'd picked up at the front desk.

He set the stack down on a table, then dragged a 25-gallon drum over to where he was working and then began to sort through the mail. There were separate piles for the news director, the sports director, the editorial writer and any that were addressed to individual reporters.

The rest he began quickly sorting through, saving some but pitching most into the adjacent drum. One day I asked what the rejects were. "Oh, those are P.R. releases. Most are a waste of paper and postage. I can tell by the return address," he said. "By the way, I'm going on vacation for the next two weeks, so you can do this while I'm gone."

The following Monday, I carried out the ritual, including glazed donut and coffee cup. One thing

would be different, however. I was going to read *all* those news releases. There had to be some gold among the dross, I thought.

Was I ever wrong! Most were poorly written, filled with puffery or self-promotion (especially from some of the local politicians). By the end of the two weeks I was pitching most of the releases into the nearby drum.

Not too long ago, the writer of this chapter asked a local city editor to share the unusable releases the paper received. He was kind enough to annotate them as to the reason why they weren't usable. Most were puff, not local, or not newsworthy. Lesson to PR writers: Remember that editors are busy people and that they don't have time for poorly-written, non-news news releases. If you know it's not news, don't put it in a news release. If you don't know whether it's news or not, look for a different job.

—WRW

Other Formats for News Coverage

In addition to the news release, the news media provide many other opportunities for organizations to communicate with their publics. To take advantage of those opportunities, effective public relations writers use a variety of writing tools: news briefs, fact sheets, factoids, feature releases, photo captions, events listings, media advisories, public advisories, story idea memos, news conference statements, interviews and opinion pieces. Here's a look at each.

News Brief

Increasingly, because the news media have less time and space available for reporting news, many busy public relations writers prepare information as both a **news brief** (just the summary lead and benefit statement) and as a full release. The news brief forces the public relations writer to carefully tell the organization's message in as few words as possible—focusing on a clear summary of the important information along with a concise indication of the impact of that information on the audience. By continuing the brief into a full-length release, the writer is able to present more detailed information of interest to trade publications, special-interest newspapers, community weeklies, and other media outlets seeking information beyond what is in the brief.

Fact Sheet

The easiest way to disseminate information to the news media is to use a **fact sheet**, which is a set of notes for a reporter, desk editor or assignment editor that addresses the obvious journalistic questions of who, what, when, where, why, how, with what effect, and so on. Fact sheets also can be prepared for non-journalistic audiences, such as consumers, donors, employees and others who need basic and unadorned information.

Fact sheets are useful in situations in which a public relations office coordinates the activities of decentralized sites, such as individual schools in a school district or local precincts within a city police force. With only a minimum of training needed, public relations staff and news sources in the decentralized locations may find it easier to prepare fact sheets than news releases and other print materials that call for greater time, effort and writing skill. By preparing fact sheets, you and the news sources can concentrate on the information rather than its packaging, especially if you know your news release will be extensively rewritten by a reporter or will form the basis of a broadcast news report.

Fact sheets generally are based on upcoming events. They announce activities of public interest. To write them, simply provide the basic facts of the event, along with brief background information and perhaps a relevant quote. Fact sheets often are written as brief paragraphs or, as in Figure 13.3, as a series of list items.

Factoid

Fact sheets focus on events; factoids are related to issues. A **factoid** is a brief presentation of background information, perhaps on technical or complex subjects. Using simple language,

The *Alternative Harmonica Ensemble* of Little Valley

123 Fourth Street
Little Valley XX 12345
(123) 456–7890

Who
The Alternative Harmonica Ensemble of Little Valley; a 25-member volunteer orchestra.

What
Annual spring concert. Theme: "Harping Around the World," featuring Calypso Harmonica and Baroque Harmonica, and the first-ever public performance of Kabuki Harmonica.

When
Friday, May 15. Performances at 3 p.m. and 7 p.m.

Where
Mozart Auditorium, Classical Arts Building, Little Valley Community College.

Why
The mission of the Alternative Harmonica Ensemble is (1) to provide opportunities for musicians to make music together, and (2) to educate the public about the beauty of harmonica music.

Benefits
The free concert will introduce people to harmonica music and to music of other cultures.

Quote
"Our new harmonica interpretations of the traditional Kabuki melodies are transforming. They're breathtaking. The emperor himself hasn't heard such beauty yet, but the lucky people of Little Valley will have the opportunity to enjoy this superb music." Ensemble director Augustine Honer.

Background on Alternative Harmonica Ensemble
AHE began in 1989 as a group of harmonica players who had entertained informally at the Woodstock Concert. It grew under the directorship of Augustine Honer, a music teacher at Little Valley High School and a descendent of Matthias Hohner, who invented the harmonica. The tradition of a free public concert started in 1984, when AHE began receiving funding through the Little Valley Community Chest.

Future Activities
AHE is seeking a grant from the United States Information Agency and from the Japanese Embassy to travel to Japan for a series of Kabuki Harmonica concerts.

<u>Contact for Additional Information.</u> Bobbi McGee, Public Relations Coordinator

Figure 13.3 Sample Fact Sheet

they define terms and explain complicated procedures. For example, a writer preparing a fact sheet or news release about the opening of a new hospital wing related to sports medicine also may prepare a factoid to provide a glossary of terms related to this area of health care—terms such as osteoarthritis, blood doping, arthroscopic surgery, shin splints, anaerobic threshold, swimmer's shoulder, and so on. The writer would give the factoid to reporters and others interested in understanding some of the complexities of sports medicine.

To write a factoid, prepare a list of terms and themes used in a specialized or technical way, then briefly and simply explain each item on the list. Figure 13.4 illustrates a sample factoid that could accompany the fact sheet in Figure 13.3.

Feature Release

In addition to releasing news items, public relations writers sometimes prepare feature articles. Three different styles of these are biographies, histories and service articles.

A **biography** provides background information about people important to an organization. The most basic format for a bio is a chronological narrative in which the writer presents relevant information. This is often presented in sections, related to categories such as current occupation, work experience, education, community activities, military service, and so on. Public relations writers try to have bios available for all key people relevant to their organizations. Biographical information is thus available to reporters, who may work relevant facts into their stories or perhaps develop a biographical sidebar. Military public affairs staffs, for example, prepare biographies of newly appointed ship, squadron and base commanding officers for use at change-of-command ceremonies. The biographies can be used for both external and internal publics and often are posted at organizational Web sites.

What the biography does for an individual, a **history** does for an organization. All businesses and nonprofit organizations have a past as well as a future. Written histories usually contain sections on the organization's founding, mission, progress through the years, current status, present priorities, and sometimes plans and expectations.

Public relations writers also sometimes prepare a **service article**, which is a how-to piece designed to teach readers how to accomplish something about which the organization has a particular expertise. For example, a retirement center may do a service article about nutrition for senior citizens, a bookstore may develop a service article about selecting books appropriate for beginning readers, or a tax preparation service may prepare an article of tax tips. In each instance, public relations writers identify an interest or need among their publics, research information within the organization relevant to that topic, and then write a service article to help readers satisfy that need or understand the issue. Often such articles are based on interviews of experts within the organization.

Photo Caption

Photographs can attract attention and tell a story quickly and with great impact, but every photograph needs a written message that explains in detail its visual message. These messages are called **captions** or **cutlines** (because printers used to call photos *cuts*). Captions often include a **dateline** (location and date of the photo) and a **legend** (title) or headline. Captions released

The *Alternative Harmonica Ensemble* of Little Valley

123 Fourth Street
Little Valley XX 12345
(123) 456–7890

BACKGROUND ON THE HARMONICA

Harmonica: A musical instrument of the woodwind family. It has metal reeds and is played by blowing or sucking air through blowholes for each reed. The most common version is the 10-hole diatonic harmonica.

Harp: Alternative name for a harmonica; commonly used by harmonica players.

Mouth Organ: Alternative name for a harmonica; commonly used by non-players.

Note: Individual musical tone.

Chord: A complementary blend of several related musical tones.

Riff: Pattern of notes that harmonizes with a chord pattern.

Blow: Blowing into the harmonica.

Draw: Sucking on the harmonica.

Bending: Twisting the sound of an individual note, usually making it lower, by changing the shape of your mouth.

Straight Harp: A basic style of playing by blowing or sucking air through one of the note holes in a harmonica, providing the sound of clear and distinct notes; accents the blow notes; used for playing melodies.

Cross Harp: An advanced style of playing that accents the draw notes; used for accompanying lead instruments or voices; most commonly used for playing blues and country music.

History: The original mouth organ was the *sheng*, which was developed in China in the 1000s B.C.E. It was adopted by the Japanese and called the *sho*, which was used as an orchestra instrument for gagaku music. In Europe, two similar instruments were patented in the 1820s: the *aura* or *mundaoline* in Germany and the *symphonium* in England. The 10-hole *diatonic harmonica* was first marketed by Matthias Hohner in 1877 to play German waltzes and polka music. More than 60 percent of the harmonicas were exported to America, where the instrument was popularized as an instrument for blues and country music.

Contact for Additional Information. Bobbi McGee, Public Relations Coordinator

Figure 13.4 Sample Factoid

LITTLE VALLEY, April 24—HARMONIOUS HARMONICAS: Augustine Honer rehearses Mitchell Jones, Elena Vega and Joshu Sumisu of the Alternative Harmonica Ensemble of Little Valley. The ensemble is preparing for its world premiere of a harmonica performance of traditional Kabuki music of Japan. The premiere will highlight the ensemble's free spring concert on May 15. (Photo by Nancy Nikkon)

<u>Contact for Additional Information.</u> Bobbi McGee, Public Relations Coordinator

Figure 13.5 Sample Photo Caption

The ***Alternative Harmonica Ensemble*** *of Little Valley*

123 Fourth Street
Little Valley XX 12345
(123) 456–7890

LISTING FOR EVENTS CALENDAR for Sunday, May 4
and Sunday, May 11

MUSIC: The Alternative Harmonica Ensemble of Little Valley will present a free spring concert Friday, May 15, at Mozart Auditorium, Classical Arts Building, Little Valley Community College. Performances at 3 p.m. and 7 p.m. Theme: "Harping Around the World" featuring world premiere of Kabuki Harmonica. Information: 456–7890.

<u>Contact for Additional Information.</u> Bobbi McGee, Public Relations Coordinator

Figure 13.6 Sample Events Listing

to the media also include a credit line identifying the photographer, although credit lines are seldom used when the photo is published.

Caption text generally is written in the present tense using active voice. It tells the basic facts of the action depicted in the photo. The text identifies every recognizable person pictured in the photo. Identification is smoothest when it explains who is doing what, although sometimes the identification is given by location, such as left to right or top to bottom. (Figure 13.5 is an example of a photo caption.)

Many photos are not published because the captions fail to provide newsworthy information. Good captions avoid overplaying the organization and instead focus on information of interest to media audiences.

Events Listing

Another information vehicle is the **events listing**, a daily or weekly calendar of upcoming events such as sports competitions, plays, concerts, lectures and open houses; these listings are found in most newspapers. Specialized magazines generally have events listings relevant to their readers. Most cable TV facilities and some radio and network TV stations list events of organizations within their broadcast area. Additionally, media websites often feature events listings

For the writer, preparing events listings is the ultimate fill-in-the-blank assignment, but it begins with a clear understanding of what you have to announce and the appropriate media for your announcement. Be sure you send the announcement to the person who handles calendar listings. Most listings are written according to simple formulas, and the best way to prepare them is to use the pattern found in the publication in which you want the announcement to appear. For newspapers, this pattern usually is similar to the one shown in Figure 13.6: category and title of the event; identification of presenter or sponsor; details about place, date, time and cost; and a telephone number for additional information.

Media Advisory

When public relations practitioners want to communicate directly with editors, news directors and reporters, they often write a **media advisory**, which is a brief message calling the journalist's attention to an upcoming activity of potential news interest. Whereas a news release provides a story about the event, an advisory simply tells the media that something newsworthy will take place. It may invite reporters to a news conference or to an interview session, or it may let photographers and videographers know about a photo opportunity.

Media advisories usually are written as memos from public relations practitioners to members of the media. As shown in Figure 13.7, they usually are addressed generically to editors and news directors.

Public Advisory

Organizations occasionally want to use the news media to communicate directly with audiences about matters of urgent public interest. For example, a law-enforcement agency may report a scam artist preying on elderly homeowners or a hospital may issue a warning about an outbreak of hepatitis. On these occasions, a public advisory is issued, in which the writer matter-of-factly provides the admonition on the agency's authority: *The Little Valley Police Department is warning residents that garages with open doors have been targeted in a recent string of burglaries.*

Public advisories are brief factual statements. They often include the name and number of someone to contact for further information.

The *Alternative Harmonica Ensemble* of Little Valley

123 Fourth Street
Little Valley XX 12345
(123) 456–7890

To: Editors and News Directors

From: Bobbi McGee, Public Relations Coordinator

Date: May 2, 2007

RE: MEDIA ADVISORY

The Alternative Harmonica Ensemble will open the final dress rehearsal of its spring concert to the media to provide you with advance material. The open rehearsal will be held at 7 p.m., Thursday, May 14, the evening prior to the public performance. The open rehearsal will be held at Mozart Auditorium, Classical Arts Building, Little Valley Community College. (Campus parking permits and maps are enclosed.) The auditorium is fully accessible for television camera gear.

Ensemble director Augustine Honer and members of the volunteer orchestra will be available for interviews at 6:30 p.m. and at 8:30 p.m.

Figure 13.7 Sample Media Advisory

Story Idea Memo

Rather than presenting information in advisories, public relations practitioners sometimes want to call the media's attention to possibilities for feature stories about something happening within an organization. The **story idea memo** offers the media an interview opportunity; it invites reporters to prepare feature stories about people or programs. This memo, like the sample in Figure 13.8, is similar to the query letter a freelancer would write to interest an editor in a story. The memo has a standard format: opening paragraph to pique the editor's interest, follow-up paragraph(s) to provide enough detail to signal that a good story is available. It might also include a final paragraph to specifically invite the editor to make contact.

The *Alternative Harmonica Ensemble* of *Little Valley*

123 Fourth Street
Little Valley XX 12345
(123) 456–7890

To: Editors and News Directors

From: Bobbi McGee, Public Relations Coordinator

Date: May 1, 200X

RE: INTERVIEW OPPORTUNITY

When Joshu Sumisu left his native Kyoto to become a pre-engineering student at Little Valley Community College, he thought he had left behind all hopes of enjoying his hobby listening to traditional Japanese Kabuki music. But here in Little Valley, he found that he not only can listen to Kabuki music, he also can perform it as a member of the Alternative Harmonica Ensemble.

Joshu had never even heard harmonica music before coming to Little Valley. But in his three years at the local college, he has mastered the woodwind instrument, similar to the "sho" of his native country. Joshu now plays lead harp with the ensemble.

Figure 13.8 Sample Story Idea Memo

Interview

Another important tool for public relations writers working through the news media is the interview. Review the basics of interviewing in Chapter 5 before you continue with this chapter, which looks at interviewing from the perspective of the public relations practitioner. In this case, an organizational spokesperson is the subject of an interview, fielding questions from reporters. Occasionally, public relations people are interviewed; more often they coach organizational leaders who are about to face the reporters.

Interviews, which have a strong base in writing, require planning. Who is your ultimate public beyond the reporter? What relationship do members of this public have with your organization, and what should they hear from you? What message can you give them that will help your organization strengthen its relationship with them? What are your objectives in communicating with them?

Anticipate questions a reporter might ask and write out brief responses to those questions. Then write a summary of the key message you want to leave with the reporter and ultimately with the reader, viewer and listener. Brush up on the topic and review helpful background material. Talk out loud to yourself, answering questions that might be asked of you. Or, if you are not the person being interviewed, coach the one who is by pitching questions that might come from a reporter. Better to ask the tough questions in advance, to be ready for the real interview.

Immediately before the interview, take a few moments to quiet yourself, focusing on the topic and putting aside distractions so you can devote your full consciousness to the interview. Remember that most interviews are not sparring matches with reporters but rather mutual attempts by a reporter and an interviewee to present a message of interest to readers, listeners or viewers.

During the interview, remember a few key strategies. Answer questions honestly, accurately and confidently; people will remember your attitude long after they have forgotten your specific message, and audiences appreciate candor and sincerity. Aim for brevity, remembering that sound bites for radio and TV are only a few seconds long. Be interesting and provide examples of how the topic affects the audience. Stick to the topics you have prepared; interviewees are likely to get into trouble when they ramble.

Keep restating your key point. Don't talk down to reporters or to your audience, but don't assume they know much about the topic. Respond to interview questions as fully as you can, but don't speculate or allow yourself to be pulled into areas you cannot handle. "I don't know, but I'll find out for you" or "We cannot comment on that at this time" are reasonable responses. "No comment" is no option without an explanation of why you cannot or will not comment. Distinguish between organizational policy and personal opinion, and note the difference between fact and opinion.

News Conference Statement

News conferences can be valuable opportunities for organizations to present their messages on important topics. But every reporter has a horror story, probably several, of time wasted at news conferences where everything was present except the news. Don't try to pass off a special event, a photo opportunity or a panel discussion as a news conference. Be wary of holding a news conference if your organization is not prepared to handle all the questions reporters will ask not only about this topic but about other, even unrelated, topics involving your organization.

On the other hand, don't be reluctant to arrange a news conference if your organization has news that is important, timely and appropriate for reporters to receive as a group rather than individually. If you do have a news conference, coach your spokesperson for a volley of follow-up questions.

Remember that reporters would rather not participate in group interviews if instead they can have a few minutes of one-on-one time with the newsmaker. If you decide to proceed with a news conference, prepare a planning sheet to focus yourself on the key publics: their wants, interests and needs, and the message you want to give them. Anticipate their questions as well as the questions of reporters. Then write a news statement that provides appropriate background about the issue and announces the new information. The news conference statement includes the same information as the news release, although the information is written more like the script for a speech.

Writing Opinion Pieces

Occasionally public relations writers take advantage of the opportunity in the news media to present the viewpoints of their organizations: brief opinion statements in news releases, news conferences and interviews. Opportunities for more formal presentation of organizational opinion include letters-to-the-editor columns and op-ed pages (so named because, traditionally, they are located opposite the editorial page in newspapers).

Letters to the Editor

Most publications take seriously their responsibility to provide a forum for readers by offering a letters column, but such columns are not required. Editors may reject any submitted letters and be selective about the ones they use. They also may edit letters chosen for publication. Despite this uncertainty, letters can be good vehicles for organizations wishing to provide their

---

Box 13.8

It Happened to Me: Sowing Seeds of Support

Public relations people know that the value of third-party endorsements especially applies to letters to the editor.

On several occasions involving controversial issues, I have seized the opportunity when someone volunteered that he or she agrees with my organization's position. I would ask the person to write the editor a short letter supporting my organization. The key is not to give out a form letter. Instead, I try to write down the name and address of the person on the newspaper who receives letters to the editor, and perhaps I add a few notes that the person might use in writing the letter.

—RDS

comments and viewpoints. Public relations writers should carefully consider if and how letters to the editor might fit into their overall media mix. Would a letter further their objectives to provide information about a new program, to offer affirmation to volunteers or reassurance to customers, or to encourage readers to support the organization and its cause?

In general, effective letters to the editor have a positive tone and clearly state the organization's opinion. They are brief, address just one issue, and indicate the signer's connection with the organization. Letters may be used to achieve various objectives, and public relations writers have come to recognize the value of each use. Following are some of the most common.

Letters to Gain Publicity   Letters to the editor may report information that was not reported by a newspaper or magazine but that the organization nevertheless considers important for readers. Such letters should not scold the publication for failing to report on the matter earlier; they should simply present the new information. Sometimes they can note that the organization was not included in the publication's coverage, as in the following remark: *The XYZ Co. is pleased to see the Daily Record take a lead in reporting on the problem of air pollution in Centerville. We applaud the achievements of local industry noted in the article, and we are happy to report that XYZ also is improving the air quality of area residents by . . .* Letters to the editor should have a positive tone. A company congratulating its employees for a certain business success and a school district applauding its students for lowering the dropout rate are examples of positive organizational publicity messages. However, there may be times when an organization wants to pass judgment, criticizing a government agency for failure to implement new regulations or complaining about lack of progress on a public issue.

Letters to Correct Misinformation   Letters to the editor may seek to remedy inaccurate information or inappropriate interpretation of facts in previously reported stories. When considering writing a letter to correct an error, public relations practitioners first should ask whether the issue warrants additional attention. Remember the adage about letting sleeping dogs lie; perhaps an issue is best left to fade away. If a correction seems appropriate, the writer should be prudent in addressing the issue. It is unlikely to improve the organization's overall media-relations program to begin a letter with an insult: *Dear Editor: The simpleton on your staff obviously can't take accurate notes, so it is no wonder he mistakenly reported that . . .* Instead, the writer might begin politely in an effort to soften the complaint and focus on re-presenting accurate information: *We appreciate the coverage you provided, and we have heard from many people who have told us they read your report. One point that needs to be clarified is that . . .* Or the letter might present a correction under the guise of offering updated information: *Your readers may be interested to know that the latest figures are . . .*

Letters to Advocate a Cause   Letters can be used to advocate a cause or draw attention to an issue. Public relations practitioners are constantly alert to activities and events that tie into issues of importance for them, especially when those issues already are on the public agenda. For example, an organization concerned about the issue of responsible drinking and safe driving might write a letter to the editor after a particularly tragic accident to encourage partygoers to have a designated driver. The purpose of such a letter, for example, might be to encourage voters to urge their elected officials to enact stricter laws against drivers with repeat offenses for drunken driving or to urge judges not to plea bargain repeat offenses down to simple traffic citations.

Box 13.9

It Happened to Me: Encouraging Tolerance

When I was working for a religious organization, I used the letters-to-the-editor column to help my organization jump into a local fray. The situation involved a widely reported desecration at a Jewish cemetery, and other letter writers were discussing the relative seriousness of the matter. I used the situation and the resulting community discussion as the launch point for my church to present a message encouraging tolerance and mutual respect, which was one of our key ongoing objectives. —*RDS*

Op-Ed Pieces

Guest editorials, sometimes called **op-ed pieces**, are opinion columns longer than letters. The public relations writer may prepare such a piece to appear under the name of the head of the organization.

Before writing opinion pieces, public relations practitioners generally contact the editorial page editor to find out two things: whether the topic would be considered interesting or important enough for the publication, and whether the newspaper or magazine would consider publishing an op-ed piece written on behalf of the practitioner's organization. Like letters to the editor, op-ed pieces are modifications of position statements. The writer should identify a relevant issue and plan a strategy to address the wants, interests and needs of the audience, as well as the objectives of the organization.

Public Relations Professionalism

The ideal relationship between journalists and public relations writers can be summed up in one word: **symbiosis**, nature's version of "You scratch my back and I'll scratch yours." This symbiotic relationship is based on the mutual and professional need that each has for the other.

The news media help public relations practitioners in three significant ways: by providing access to an audience, offering free access to media time and space, and enhancing credibility. Public relations practitioners help the media also in three ways: generating story ideas, providing information, and arranging interviews.

The basic reason that public relations writers need journalists is that editors and news directors provide the communication vehicles for bringing public relations messages to publics. Of course, the news media are not the only communication vehicles available to practitioners. Still, they are effective for reaching large numbers of people and they confer a certain credibility on an organization's message.

Journalists cannot know everything about everything, so they depend on public relations practitioners to provide background information, as well as to generate story ideas, arrange interviews, coordinate news conferences, present organizational comments and responses, and otherwise assist in reporting the news. **Information subsidy** is the name given to such material that public relations practitioners and organizational advocates provide to journalists.

The relationship of journalists and public relations writers is sometimes rocky. Occasionally, an organization's desire for privacy runs up against the media's need for information. Every once in a while, hot-tempered personalities on both sides rub nerves raw. Interestingly, some surveys have found that journalists say they are wary of public relations practitioners as a group, but they generally give high marks to individual practitioners they work with regularly, which shows that stereotypes often die under the light of personal familiarity.

Box 13.10

It Happened to Me: Nearly Submarined

I once read a guest op-ed column in the paper by the head of an anti-nuclear environmental group who declared that the incidence of cancer among sailors aboard nuclear submarines was far above normal levels for the general population. The writer charged that the Navy was involved in a massive cover-up to keep these facts from the public.

As a Navy public affairs officer, I knew that both assertions were nonsense, although I did not have hard data to refute the first charge. I clipped the article and sent it to the director of the regional Navy public affairs office with a note suggesting they have an expert reply.

I was pleased to notice a few weeks later that the paper printed a lengthy response article, authored by an admiral-physician with the Navy Bureau of Medicine. He used facts, figures and specifics to discount the charges, and ended his reply article by pointing out that there was no cover-up, simply because there were no adverse facts to keep from the public. The language was temperate and authoritative, a good example of effectively using a letter to the editor to correct misinformation.

—*WRW*

Sensitive Issues

A few concerns are not simple enough for dos and don'ts. Some common but sensitive issues include requesting to speak off the record, giving exclusive or advance information, making follow-up calls, and thanking journalists.

Off the Record   Be careful about setting limits on information you provide to reporters. It is best to consider that any information you provide may be reported freely. As explained in Chapter 6, *off the record* should mean that the information may not be used at all, whereas *background only* or *not for attribution* should suggest that the information may be used without reference to the source. However, each reporter may understand these limits differently, so if you must limit the use of your information, clearly negotiate the ground rules with the reporter before you provide the information or comment.

Box 13.11

How to . . . Maintaining Good Relationships with Journalists

To ensure the best possible relationship with journalists, here are some dos and don'ts for public relations writers:

Do

- Generate newsworthy activities for your organization and create valid opportunities to get your message out.

- Get to know the media gatekeepers and learn their particular needs and deadlines.

- Look at your organization with a reporter's eye, asking yourself whether the people outside your organization are likely to care about the information you provide.

- Be accessible to reporters gathering information for a story.

Don't

- Waste time on attention-getting gimmicks that usually don't work anyway.

- Beg for favors or rely on personal contacts to get a marginal story printed.

- Threaten to cancel your subscription if something isn't printed or if you are unhappy with the way something is reported.

- Say something is newsworthy or visually interesting when it isn't.

Also, remember that a journalist's loyalty is to the perceived public good, not to your organization. Ego could lead a reporter to publish a story rather than honor a promise to withhold information you have provided.

Exclusives and Advances Be wary about providing information to one journalist but not to others. Such an **exclusive** amounts to playing favorites, and this can have negative and far-reaching consequences. If a reporter at the morning newspaper believes your organization is favoring reporters at the evening paper, the morning reporter may become antagonistic toward your organization or ignore it altogether. Provide exclusives only if you have good reason to favor a particular publication or station. For instance, you might believe major coverage in one newspaper will be better than routine coverage in two papers.

Advances are stories provided to one news medium ahead of others, often to accommodate different schedules. For example, if you are planning a news conference for print and broadcast reporters, you might give the story to a reporter from a weekly business publication with several days' advance notice so readers of the weekly paper would get the story the day following your news conference. Note that there is a substantive difference between an advance given to a new medium that can report the information before its competitors, and an advance that more benignly gives early information to allow a slower-paced news venue such as a weekly newspaper to report the information at the same time as its media colleagues.

Follow-Up Calls Avoid making follow-up phone calls. When you send a news release, have faith that the postal service or the e-mail service is doing its job. However, if you have what you believe is indisputably significant information, it may be useful to alert a reporter in advance that a news release is coming.

Thanking Journalists   Use discretion about professional courtesies. Codes of public relations ethics prohibit practitioners from giving gifts of more than nominal value, and journalistic ethical codes prohibit reporters from accepting them.

If you want to send a thank-you letter to a reporter, consider the implications of what you say. Don't imply that the story was written as a personal favor. However, it is appropriate to let reporters and their superiors know that a story was appreciated, that the encounter between the news source and the journalist was pleasant and professional, and that the resulting story had a positive impact on the organization or on its strategic publics.

Winning the Competition for Coverage

Many opportunities exist for working through the news media to promote information and ideas about your business, organization or cause, but competition for print space and airtime has dramatically increased in recent years. There are more voices in the marketplace trying to be heard through the media, and they will use many of the techniques in this chapter to promote what's important to them. Although this competition eliminates any guarantees to using the media as informational vehicles, good writing and presentation will certainly increase your chances of making the paper or the evening news.

Of course, public relations success for your organization also spells career success for you as a public relations professional. Three things are necessary to be successful in public relations: continual development of your writing skills, attention to the conventions of news-style writing, and a keen appreciation for the news value of activities and issues associated with your organization and its clients.

Expertise in writing organizational messages in the style of journalists is a skill employers expect to find among candidates for media relations positions. Thus, you need to master writing news releases if you decide to pursue a career in public relations. Beyond this mastery, the ability to write in the related formats presented in this chapter will greatly increase your value to an employer (and, thus, your employability).

Discussion Questions

The following are class discussion questions drawn from Chapter 13:

1. Today, the news media present fewer opportunities for organizations to disseminate their messages. Why?

2. What are some ways to make news for your organization? Do you have any ethical concerns about doing any of these? Why?

3. The news release is the most commonly used tool for media relations. What is it, and how does it differ from a traditional news story? How do you write a successful news release?

4. One of the most frequently written types of news release deals with personnel appointments. What format do these take?

5. What role do public relations professionals have in creating quotes for their organization? What are some strategies for developing effective quotes?

6. Why are letters to the editor good vehicles for organizations wishing to provide their comments and viewpoints on issues that concern them? What are some considerations to be taken into account when writing letters to the editor?

7. Why is there a symbiotic relationship between journalists and public relations practitioners? What should public relations writers do to ensure the best possible relationship with journalists?

8. Why are news releases rewritten?

9. Three things are necessary to be successful in public relations. What are they?

CHAPTER EXERCISES

Exercise 13.1—Freewriting

Freewrite for five minutes on the following topic: "How much attention do you pay to news reports in newspapers, radio and TV? With this in mind, how important do you think publicity is to an organization such as your college or university?" Then discuss your thoughts with others in your class. ∎

Exercise 13.2—Fact Sheet, Factoid, and Events Listing

Assume that your academic department will hold an open house for high school juniors and seniors to acquaint them with your communication program. Prepare the following materials:

- Fact sheet to be distributed to invited schools

- Factoid explaining your program

- Events listing to be used on local cable crawl ∎

Exercise 13.3—Rewriting Leads

Each of the following leads has problems. Revise each to make it more appropriate for a news release and to conform to AP style.

1. The Eastern Cable Company is proud to appoint Clementina Gilbransohn as director of Service and Maintenance, where she will direct a staff of 27 repairmen and women dedicated to customer satisfaction.

2. WILLIE WEINER'S MITSUBISHI, known as the Friendliest Car Dealership in Town, invites everyone to his open house at the new showroom on Franklin Highway next Monday all day long from 9–9. Free refreshments.

3. On Monday, June 15, at 9 a.m., the Central High School Fighting Termites' starting lineup will begin a five-day basketball clinic for kids aged 6–10.

4. Ezekiel Xavier Jorgenson, president and chief executive officer of Jorg Enterprises, has appointed as his senior vice president for corporate communications Kateri Bonaventura-Chang.

5. The Department of Social Geography at Upland University will host a dozen urban planning specialists from Fiji, Guam, Tonga, Saipan, Tahiti, Bora Bora and Pogo Pogo, who are touring the United States to study examples of effective and innovative space usage by land-limited municipalities.

6. Upper Cheasboro Estates. August 25. The Nicholas Winslow Company, a longtime lock manufacturer located in this upscale community, announces that they have developed a revolutionary new security system for drivers to guarantee the security of their parked cars.

7. The Minier Theater will open "The Exotic Liaisons of Flopsy and Mopsy," an entertaining play to delight the entire family, at 2 p.m. Sunday, May 15. The two-act play, written by Tyler Tyrone, is a musical comedy performed with rap music accompanied by a string quartet.

Exercise 13.4—Announcement Release

Assume you are the assistant public affairs director for your college or university. Using information in the following fact sheet, write (1) a two-paragraph release brief for distribution to news media throughout your state, and (2) a full-page release for distribution to local news media. The releases will be sent from your public affairs office. The releases should serve the continuing objectives of promoting awareness of the contributions faculty make to the wider community, increasing positive attitudes about learning opportunities at your school, and recruiting quality students to your programs.

Who: Happy Baby Toy Co., manufacturer of toys for infants and toddlers. Carlo Geppetto is president.

What: Awarding a $350,000 grant to Dr. Benjamin Spot, a researcher and professor of child development at your college or university. The grant will fund Dr. Spot's study of the response of infants to colors and designs.

When: Yearlong award, effective on the last day of next month.

Where: Presentation ceremonies to be held during a reception at the home of the president of your college or university next Sunday at 3 p.m.

Why: Happy Baby Toy Co. supports continuing research into early childhood development.

Significance: First time the company has given a grant to a college professor. Previous grants went to clinical psychologists.

How: Dr. Spot will involve students in his "Infant Psychology" classes in research projects at local day-care centers and in private homes.

Benefit: Grant will enable students to be involved in applied research. Research findings will lead to better baby toys.

Background: Happy Baby is a 20-year-old toy company that seeks to apply current research into child development. Last year it introduced a new product line based on clinical research showing that babies are attracted more to brightly colored stripes than to solid colors. The company is headquartered in Ames, Iowa.

Quote: "Happy Baby is proud to be associated with behavioral scientists like Dr. Spot, who are working diligently to find new ways to stimulate young minds. And we are equally pleased that students will be involved in this important research. With the help of Dr. Spot and his students, Happy Baby will continue to provide quality infant toys."—Carlo Geppetto

---

Exercise 13.5—Responding to Criticism

You are public relations director for your college or university, which has just been publicly criticized by a famous alumnus, John T. Miller, who graduated 22 years ago with a degree in English. He now is CEO of Miller Associates, the largest financial investment firm in your area.

He also has been a major benefactor to your school, most recently having given $3 million 14 months ago to an expansion program for the library. He has served on the college advisory board, and two years ago was commencement speaker, receiving an honorary degree.

Miller was interviewed by a local daily newspaper about his rags-to-riches success story. During the interview, he commented on the high quality of education that he received at your school, but he also lamented that today's students are inferior to those when he was an undergraduate. He attributed this to the school's current financial crunch, which he said has led to "a noticeable lowering of admission standards because, frankly, they need the students and their money. These days, they're taking anybody with a pulse." He reminisced about the good old days "when kids went to college to become educated and make something of themselves. Now they just want to be handed a diploma without working for it."

You know Miller personally and you understand that he is generally supportive of your school and cares about its future. You know that he speaks quickly and bluntly, often using exaggeration and challenge as a way to provoke discussion.

Your vice president for enrollment management, Dr. Diana Holcombe, is calling for a news conference to refute what she considers unwarranted and damaging criticism. You decide that instead of a news conference, you will draft a news release in which the college can respond to the criticism. Your aim is to minimize internal anger of both staff and students, without turning the comment of one person into more of a public issue than it already is and ultimately without jeopardizing either enrollment or contributions.

Review the How To box "10 Ways to Make News" to develop some kind of action in response to this criticism. Then write a news release and include in it some quotes that you are suggesting for the V.P. Think strategically to develop a quote that can respond to the situation without further stirring up the problem. Also try to balance the interests of current and potential students, Miller, other alumni, and other constituents—all of whom are interested in your school's reputation.

Exercise 13.6—Photo Caption

Write a photo caption for the picture you took at the award ceremony for Dr. Spot to be sent to the local daily newspaper and any weeklies in your area. The picture shows Dr. Spot in the center of the photo accepting an oversize check with his name and $350,000 in big letters from your college or university president (left), while Gina Geppetto, on the right, granddaughter of the founder of Happy Baby Toy Co. and the supervisor of marketing, looks on. Give enough detail so that the picture could be run without an accompanying story.

Exercise 13.7—Follow-up Release

As a public relations writer for the Happy Baby Toy Co., prepare a follow-up news release for statewide distribution about testimony that company president Carlo Geppetto presented before a hearing of the Senate Consumer Affairs Committee (Subcommittee on Domestic Products) in Washington, D.C. Following is a partial text of this testimony:

> "The Happy Baby Toy Company welcomes congressional investigation into greater safety standards for children's toys, and we would wholeheartedly support a national system of reasonable, responsible standards on this subject. Too often, manufacturers with sub-standard quality control procedures use harmful materials to produce toys that, while they may be visually appealing to young children, do not meet the minimum standards of Happy Baby and other companies that have voluntarily adopted the Product Safety Standards of the American Association of Manufacturers of Infant and Children's Toys. The AAMICT standards provide a model for this committee as it reviews this issue.
>
> "Happy Baby stands ready to work with legislators and consumer groups to bring reasonable standards to the manufacturing and importation of toys for infants and young children who, after all, are our most precious yet most vulnerable national resource."

Exercise 13.8—*News Conference Statement*

Carlo Geppetto, president of the Happy Baby Toy Co., has asked you to advise him on responding to media inquiries about a crisis situation involving his company. One of the Happy Baby products is a crib toy that the state Consumer Protection Administration is recalling. In at least three cases, the toy came apart when babies sucked on it, causing them to be stained with an indelible green dye. No child has been seriously injured, though the ink stains are expected to remain for about three months. The defect has been eliminated in new models.

You are concerned about the company's reputation as a manufacturer of safe toys. You do not want to appear hard-hearted but neither do you want to admit to negligence. Draft a statement of about 60 to 100 words for Mr. Geppetto.

Exercise 13.9—*Local Releases*

As a public relations writer for your college or university's public affairs office, prepare a basic news release and four localized leads for distribution to the hometown newspapers of four members of a student research team working with Dr. Spot as part of the Happy Baby grant outlined in the memo included in Exercise 13.4. Include an appropriate quote you have prepared for Dr. Spot, praising the work of his students.

Background

During this semester, the students conducted a field experiment involving 130 infants aged three to six months. Their findings indicated that the infants spent 60 percent more time playing with toys that were red, orange or yellow than with toys that were green or blue. The research will be used by the Product Development Department of the Happy Baby Toy Co. The research also has been incorporated in Dr. Spot's article being published next month by the *Journal of Child Cognitive Development*. The students and their local newspapers include:

- Joshua Aaron Matthews of East Umbrella, Ark.; graduate of Umbrella–Spineytop Central High School; son of Joe Don Matthews and Priscilla Kowalczyk; *Umbrella Gazette*.

- Esmerelda Finsterlogan of Upper Chesapeake, Md.; graduate of St. Ludmilla's High School; daughter of Eulalia and the late Webley Finsterlogan; *Chesapeake Times-Press*.

- Jennifer Chang of Santa Francesca de Balboa, Calif.; graduate of Santa Francesca Honors Academy; daughter of Raymond and Prudence Chang; *Balboa Beach Bulletin*.

- You are the fourth member of the student research team.

Exercise 13.10—News Conference

Assume that the head of your academic department is preparing a news conference to announce that your college or university has been selected as one of the top three academic institutions in North America for communication education. The department head also will announce a program expansion and the hiring of two new faculty members. Prepare the following materials:

- Media advisory inviting reporters and photographers to the news conference

- News conference statement

- News release to be distributed at the news conference

- Anticipated questions reporters might ask

Suggestions for Further Reading

Bivins, Thomas. *Public Relations Writing: The Essentials of Style and Format,* 5th ed. (New York: McGraw-Hill, 2004).

Newsom, Doug, and Jim Haynes. *Public Relations Writing: Form and Style,* 8th ed. (Belmont, Calif.: Wadsworth, 2007).

Smith, Ronald D. *Becoming a Public Relations Writer,* 3rd ed. (New York: Routledge, 2008).

Thompson, William. *Targeting the Message: A Receiver-Centered Process for Public Relations Writing* (New York: Longman, 1996).

Treadwell, Donald., and Jill B. Treadwell. *Public Relations Writing: Principles in Practice* (Thousand Oaks Calif.: Sage, 2005).

Wilcox, Dennis. *Public Relations Writing and Media Techniques,* 5th ed. (Boston: Allyn & Bacon, 2004).

Zappala, Joseph, and Ann Carden. *Public Relations Worktext: A Writing and Planning Resource,* 2nd ed. (Mahwah, N.J.: Lawrence Erlbaum, 2004).

14

Advertising Copywriting

Chapter Objectives

- To explain the relationship between advertising and public relations
- To identify the various types of advertising available
- To present steps in writing effective print and broadcast advertisements
- To provide guidelines for effective copy for direct-mail appeal letters

What is Advertising?

The vehicles of advertising are all around us—from television commercials to roadway billboards, from pop-ups on the Internet to direct-mail requests for political contributions. Advertising is an element of both marketing and public relations, a tool of persuasive communication used by organizations trying to promote a product or service, cause or idea. Advertising relies heavily on research, not only marketing or consumer research, but also public opinion and attitude research.

Increasingly, advertising is associating itself with interactive technology that allows would-be consumers to access information-on-demand. It also associates itself with every vehicle of communication: television, film, newspaper, magazine, Internet and radio. An academic and professional discipline in its own right, advertising also draws insight and practice from disciplines such as psychology, sociology and anthropology, as well as communication-based disciplines such as public relations, journalism and marketing communication.

In recent years, the concept of integrated marketing communication has led to the coordinated interrelationship of various promotional and communication vehicles available to organizations. Thus, advertising often is one component in a wider strategic program that involves publicity, direct mail, interpersonal contacts, communication graphics and related vehicles that can carry an organization's message. Classically, advertising has distinguished itself from these related communication vehicles by several identifying criteria: ***Advertising*** *is paid placement of non-personal messages, often of a commercial nature and aimed toward informing and influencing a particular audience, presented by an identified sponsor (both profit-seeking and nonprofit entities), generally through mass media or various other media with large and usually anonymous audiences.*

Advertising offers benefits not only to businesses and nonprofit organizations but also to consumers and to society as a whole. For businesses, advertising provides a way to launch new products, increase the sale of existing brands, and maintain sales of mature brands. For other organizations, the parallel benefits are associated with fundraising, membership, promotion of events, and support of causes. For consumers, advertising provides the ability to learn about products and services that potentially can solve consumers' problems or satisfy their wants and needs. And for society at large, advertising plays a significant role in both local and global economies. It serves as a conduit for information about innovations and new technologies, and it has an influential role in fostering trends in fashion, art and entertainment, as well as politics, economics and social movements.

Advertising and associated forms of public relations call for a clear focus on persuasive communication, and they require writers who can draw on lessons from psychology and sociology to prepare promotional messages that will successfully encourage readers to buy, attend, join, contribute, vote for, or otherwise support the product, service, organization or cause being championed by the writer. Such promotional messages are all around us, so much so that they require writers to continually refocus their message strategy and refine their creative approach so they can be heard apart from all the competing messages.

The most obvious form of promotional writing is commercial advertising, which involves the use of purchased broadcast time or print space to promote a product, service, cause or organizational image. Advertising differs from public relations mainly in that it involves paid communication and that it more overtly tries to sell a product or promote a service or idea. Increasingly organizations and businesses are using advertising-like techniques on their Web sites and in their promotional materials, though strictly speaking, these are not paid commercial vehicles.

The two general types of advertising are product advertising and public relations advertising; each has subcategories.

Product Advertising

By far, the most frequent use of advertising media is to promote the sale of products or services. Cars, jeans, hamburgers, soft drinks—this is the stuff of consumer advertising. Product advertising can be of three types:

- **Local (Retail) Advertising.** Most local advertising is retail oriented. It presents a company's consumer message that advertises a sale or promotes merchandise or services. Retail advertising is specific in that it often includes dates, prices, locations, brands and models.

- **General (Brand) Advertising.** National advertising is more general than retail advertising. Its subjects are companies and brands. Whereas retail advertising may tell the consumer about a sale for a national-brand paint at the local mall, general advertising tells the consumer about the quality of paint, promoting the paint on a national level and complementing the retail advertising.
- **Business-to-Business Advertising.** The average consumer seldom sees business-to-business advertising, which companies place in trade, industrial and professional publications for other business people. For example, Super MegaMart might advertise its paint in a magazine read by people in the building trades. Makers of soap, shampoo and other amenities send their catalogs to boutique hotels and bed-and-breakfast inns.

Public Relations Advertising

Occurring less frequently than consumer advertising, public relations advertising takes on various forms and serves many different purposes related to the image of an organization and support for its messages, including institutional advertising, advocacy advertising, political advertising, and public-service advertising.

- **Institutional Advertising.** If an ad tells the merits of a national-brand paint, that's product advertising. But if the ad tells what Super MegaMart has done for the community, that's **institutional advertising**, also known as **image advertising**. It highlights the organization, not the product. The National Football League uses institutional advertising when it promotes its NFL Charities. Real-estate companies congratulate their agents and school districts applaud scholarship winners; both are examples of institutional advertising. Likewise, it is institutional advertising when beer companies and chain stores disseminate "Season's Greetings" ads.
- **Advocacy Advertising.** Closely related to institutional advertising, advocacy advertising (sometimes called **issue advertising**) focuses less on promoting an organization or a product and more on advocating for a cause or a goal important to the organization. Many organizations use such paid advertising to communicate about issues important to their mission. A department store ad about a consumer tax issue or proposed regulation of consumer goods would constitute issue advertising. A radio spot by the police union urging citizens to pressure City Hall against one-officer police cars also is advocacy advertising.
- **Political Advertising.** Generally, political advertising is advocacy advertising with a partisan rather than a public-service focus. Political advertising not only supports candidates, it also is used to advocate actions about a specific piece of legislation or policy. The University of Pennsylvania estimated that special interest groups spent $400 million in 2005 alone to influence Congress on a variety of public policy issues, from oil drilling in Alaska to tax cuts to prescription drugs. That's in addition to the millions spent on behalf of individual political candidates.
- **Public-Service Advertising.** When an organization advertises on behalf of someone else, it is engaging in public-service advertising. Nonprofit groups advertise to promote a benefit or advocate a cause such as health care, research, education or human services.

Sometimes the cost of this advertising is waived by a magazine, TV or radio station, or billboard company. The Advertising Council is a coalition of advertising agencies, corporations and media outlets that provides free advertising for nonprofit organizations on issues concerning health, education, the environment, religious values, community service and public safety. At other times, corporations may buy advertising on behalf of a worthwhile nonprofit organization or cause they wish to help.

Advertising Media

Each type or purpose of advertising noted above can be used in the various media, and each offers different opportunities for advertising writers. The print media offer a variety of advertising opportunities. Newspaper advertising generally focuses on specific products, often the promotion of sales and other imminent local buying opportunities; newspapers also offer

---

Box 14.1
How to . . . Develop a Visual Message

As a writer, you may not be responsible for taking advertising photos or designing the other artwork. But it may be your responsibility to develop the idea and then turn to an artist or graphic designer to carry it out. Here are some guidelines for developing the visual message for both print and broadcast ads:

Use simple images. Illustrations should be easily recognizable and not unduly complicated. A photograph of one person is likely to attract more readers than a crowd scene. Too much background detail tends to distract the reader from the main element.

Make instant connections. Advertising works on visual stereotypes because audiences need to make an instant connection through the visual message. For example, if you want to depict a tennis player, put him or her on a court wearing a white shirt and shorts and holding a racket.

Show the product. This guideline is so logical, it shouldn't have to be mentioned. Yet, some advertisements have failed to include the product. Bad move! The original Infiniti ad, for example, went "artsy" and didn't show the car. It didn't sell many cars either. Readers want to see the product being promoted, and they even need to "see" a service or an idea. Products can be shown in several ways: alone, in use, and in comparison with the competition.

Sell benefits, not ingredients. You don't care what chemicals go into your popular perfume or cologne. You probably wouldn't even want to know. But you do care how it makes you feel and how it appeals to others. Good advertisements tell the reader how the product or service will help them or make them feel.

Complement art with headlines. Some advertising copywriters say the headline is the single most important determinant of an ad's effectiveness. Headlines can be presented in various ways. Some present news: *Introducing a new way to diet.* Others play on emotions: *Little Marisa and her brothers go to bed hungry almost every night.* Some headlines ask intriguing questions: *Ever wonder why ArmoTech employees always seem to be happy?* Others promise the reader helpful information: *How to get a job before the ink dries on your diploma.*

Use copy that interests readers. The text copy in a print ad varies. Some copy describes the product or service. Some gives reasons for using the product. Ad copy may be humorous or emotional. It may feature personal testimonials from people who have used the product. In other copy, entertainers or athletes use their celebrity status to lend credibility to the product.

low-cost classified ads for employment and for selling everything from used cars to beagle puppies. General advertising is likely to be found in magazines, which promote product lines and corporate image. Advertising in directories (such as telephone books and organizational rosters) usually promotes the venue (location) where products or services are available.

Differences also exist among the broadcast media. Just as local newspapers do, radio primarily features local retail advertising directed toward a local audience. Television includes both general advertising of product lines and corporate image (network-wide commercials) and retail advertising (local commercials). Broadcast media also are used to present public-service messages.

Outdoor advertising, which usually feature corporate-identity advertising, includes billboards, posters and wallscapes. **Transit advertising** is associated with buses and trains, subways and airplanes. The term also includes vehicle wraps, truck sides and mobile billboards. Collectively, outdoor and transit advertising sometimes are linked under the umbrella term **out-of-home advertising**. OOH also includes venues such as movie-theater screenings, inflatables, skywriting, trade-show displays, point-of-sales displays, and table-top displays.

Direct-response advertising is another category, which includes media such as mail-order catalogs, TV infomercials, and direct mail.

A new advertising venue is **Internet advertising**, which uses emerging digital opportunities that include search-engine marketing, electronic mail, advertising-supported software, banner ads, and Internet-equipped cell phones. Some new formats such as **pop-ups** (also known as **interstitial ads**) can be annoying, so use them only if you are certain that your audience would appreciate the intrusive messages.

Writing Advertising Copy

The creative side of advertising offers many opportunities for wordsmiths who appreciate the power and subtlety of language. Advertising agencies call this the **creative department**, the folks who work with verbal and visual messages, who create the storyline that accompanies a strategy to gain attention, foster interest, build consumer desire for a product or service, and ultimately generate audience action. In "the business," that's called the AIDA model—attention, interest, desire, action. The creative department is the home of advertising copywriters, the people who write the slogans, develop the headlines, prepare the copy for print ads, and write the scripts for broadcast ads.

Writing for Print

Advertising messages can be primarily visual, primarily textual, or a combination of both. Billboards are an example of visual ads. Motorists have only seconds to view billboards, so artwork and logos are most often used to carry the message. **Advertorials** (similar to position statements) that look like newspaper editorials or articles are an example of ads that are primarily textual with little or no artwork. They play on the reader's attraction to the apparent news to be found in them.

Most advertising in magazines combines art and text. The art may be photographs and sketches, and advertising copywriters generally consider headlines as part of the visual message.

The textual part is the copy that takes some time to read. Advertisers know that if the art is not strong, nobody will bother to read the copy; likewise, if the copy is not compelling, nobody will be persuaded. So both aspects of an ad must work together.

The basic principles of advertising copywriting match those of public relations writing: Be brief, clear and easy to understand. Write about things that interest readers, and focus on benefits to them. Make sure the copy includes specific references and details. Make the writing believable and relevant to your audience. Following are more guidelines for writing advertising copy:

1. **Use one thought per ad.** Good advertisements focus on a single idea. Regardless of the size of the ad, the copy should promote just one idea. For example, an automobile ad might focus on the car's reliability, sportiness or affordability, but it's not likely to successfully accent all three. Rather, the advertiser would design a series of three different ads, each highlighting one of the major features.

2. **Make it memorable.** Writers want their words to stick in the reader's mind, like a haunting melody that just doesn't go away. Good advertising copywriters often create several drafts of an ad, carefully working over language until they create just the right combination of words that they think will stick with the reader.

3. **Use strong narration.** Storytelling is an effective form of communication, and good advertising copywriting often tells a story. Writers strive for dialogue that is natural. They use anecdotes and metaphors instead of simple definitions.

4. **Avoid generalizations.** Anyone can make claims and assertions, but provable facts are needed to convince a reader. Consider two universities offering professional training programs in public relations. One might advertise its *excellent placement record.* The other might report that *80 percent of our public relations graduates get jobs in the field.* Which is the better "sell"? Probably the one with the more specific selling point.

Writing for Broadcast

The guidelines above for effective print ads hold true for radio and television commercials, but such broadcast advertisements feature sounds and images that are active and dynamic. They move and make sounds, thus challenging the advertising copywriter to make effective use of the communication potential of radio, TV and digital media. Most of the guidelines for broadcast newswriting also apply to commercials. Here are a few more tips, specific to writing for broadcast and other electronic media.

1. Copy for broadcast commercials should be conversational. Dialogue must be natural and believable, so that the listener or viewer isn't left with the feeling, "Nobody really talks like that."

2. Scripts for broadcast commercials include two sound tracks: the main track (Audio A) with the primary dialogue or narration, and the secondary track (Audio B) with background music, sound effects and other sounds. In many cases, a commercial may have several different versions of Audio B. For example, a radio commercial for bar

soap may have different styles of music—rock, country and western, Caribbean, rap— to use on stations with particular audiences. It may even have different versions for Audio A, using different announcer voices or translating the commercial into different languages.

3. Some ads, particularly those for non-profit organizations with small budgets, often rely on personal testimonials or celebrity endorsements to present their messages without spending a lot of money on production. However research shows that endorsements are not the most persuasive technique.

4. Another money-saving technique is to use symbols. For example, you probably are familiar with the wooden match used in TV ads warning about forest fires or the eggs cooking in a frying pan that symbolize the effects of drug abuse on the brain.

The most basic broadcast ad is a straight-out sales pitch, voiced by an announcer. But you can do better than that. Add some sound effects, some music. Have the announcer introduce a testimonial from a typical consumer, or an endorsement from a celebrity spokesperson. Here are some creative strategies for preparing broadcast advertising copy:

- **Testimonials** are advertising pitches by people who use the product or service. Ethically and legally, these should be actual consumers and not paid actors pretending to be consumers.

- **Celebrity endorsements** use famous people to pitch the product, service or cause. The premise is that, because audiences like the celebrities, they therefore will be inclined to trust them when they endorse a product or organization.

- **Demonstrations** put the product or service to the test. Particularly useful in television, audiences can see the product in use. Advertisers should clearly indicate if the presentation is actual footage or a re-enactment.

- **Drama** is perhaps one of the most effective approaches to advertising. In just 30 seconds, creative writers and producers can create memorable and persuasive vignettes to sell products and services or to promote causes. This format has several categories: **Problem-solution** ads confront the audience with a problem and quickly resolve it, often by a hero figure. The **fantasy** ad relies on make-believe characters or real persons (perhaps historical figures) in unreal situations. **Animation** can be used for children and adults. **Humor** is another effective type of advertising, though it has a shorter run time than other types of advertising because humor quickly becomes old humor, which tends to be ineffective.

- **Reflective** or **mood pieces** provide another approach to advertising. These can be similar to the dramatic approach, but they rely less on action and more on an emotional mood setter, music, visuals and imagery.

- **Symbolization** has shown to be a powerful approach to advertising. In the hands of creative writers and producers, high-impact verbal or nonverbal symbols can carry a concept.

- **Sound** also can enhance advertising. Jingles and snippets of songs can be powerful ways to connect a product with a brand.

Box 14.2

How to . . . Develop Copywrite Appeals

Broadcast copy uses a variety of rhetoric treatments to gain audience attention. Consider the following:

- Claim statement. *Chickory Delight is America's best-loved coffee.*

- Rhetorical question. *Want to swim like an Olympic champion?*

- Suspense. *Only one local dealership sells the most popular car in America.*

- Humor. *Chickory Delight doesn't come from the hen house, but it tastes great with bacon and eggs.*

- Common problem. *It's difficult to find a nice restaurant without long lines and high prices.*

- Illustration of a problem. *The last time you took the family to a restaurant, you had to wait in line 45 minutes.*

- Reference to the audience. *You know what you want: Good food. Reasonable prices. And no waiting!*

- Provocative reference. *Bogus Beer—Our low alcohol content means you can drink as much as you want. And then drink some more!*

Be careful concerning legal limitations. Copyright law protects most music, and permission must be given. Check with the American Society of Composers, Authors and Publishers (ascap.com) for licensing and permission information. Similarly, don't try to incorporate copyrighted action or cartoon figures without permission from their corporate owners. Don't edit video clips from the news to make it look like the President is endorsing your product. Don't use a singer who imitates the voice of a famous vocalist. Do make sure you have permission every time you wish to use material produced by someone else.

What previously has been called a planning sheet for public relations writing, advertisers create a **copy platform**. The format for the copy platform, also called a **creative brief** or **creative strategy**, varies from one agency to another, but in general most include the following elements: a statement of goals and objectives, the advertising medium to be used (radio, television, print, and so on), indication of the target audience, statement of benefits, and overview of the competition.

Writing Direct-Mail Appeals

Appeal letters are used for everything from soliciting donations to selling products, from seeking members to promoting causes. How effective are direct-mail appeals? Some research shows that a mail appeal draws 10 times as many responses as newspaper advertisements and 100 times as many as television commercials. That's effective! The American Association of Fundraising Counsel reported in 2007 that more than $295 billion was contributed to charities in the previous year; more than 75 percent came from individuals and another 8 percent through personal wills and bequests. Most of these individual donors were responding to direct-mail pitches.

The difference between effective appeal letters and **junk mail** is the recipient's interest in the topic. Appropriate mailing lists are crucial. With such lists, organizations can take their message directly to the people who will be interested, thus optimizing resources, minimizing waste and generating the best results.

Effective appeal letters require top-quality writing. They need a personal tone and all the persuasive effectiveness you can pull together. Following are several suggestions regarding the standard elements found in the most successful appeal letters:

1. **Address the reader.** A letter sent to thousands of recipients hardly qualifies as personal correspondence, but mail that addresses the recipient by name is more likely to be read. Computer programs make it easy to generate thousands of individualized

---

Box 14.3
How to . . . Develop a Sample Copy Platform

Subject: Communication Department, Upstate University

Problem/Opportunity: Department has enrollment slightly below capacity, presenting an opportunity for expansion

Client Characteristics:
- Public-college tuition
- Only public program in the state recognized by the Accrediting Council for Education in Journalism and Mass Communications (ACEJMC)
- Strong reputation among media professionals
- Long-standing record of career success among graduates

Advertising Objective: To recruit 15 percent more incoming freshmen and 10 percent more transfer students than last year

Target Market:
- High school juniors and seniors interested in a career in journalism, public relations, broadcasting, or related profession
- Students in other colleges interested in profession-based career-oriented program
- Parents, guidance counselors and others who might influence education choices

Competition:
- Community College X: Technology-based program with only limited career potential
- College Y: Small private church-related college with high tuition and general communication program
- University Z: Large public institution with general communication program not rooted in professional practice and not focused on career development

Benefit Statement: The Communication Department at Upstate University offers the most affordable, most reputable and most career-focused communication program in the entire upstate area

Creative Theme: Your best choice to a professional career in communication

Selling Points:
- Low cost of state tuition
- Unique professional focus among alternative schools in upstate region
- Higher-than-average job placement record
- Demonstrable success of graduates
- Recognition by ACEJMC

letters in seconds. Be careful not to use gender-specific titles such as Mr., Ms., Miss or Mrs. unless you know for sure that these are accurate and preferred by the recipient. Also, review how your computer identifies names. The owner of the Town & Country Nursery would not spend much time reading a letter that addressed "Dear Town" or "Dear Mr. Nursery." And one of the authors of this text doesn't think much of a letter addressed to "Dear W."

2. **Use simple language.** Your writing should be simple, natural, concise, clear and powerful. It should be full of meaning and easy for the reader to understand. Here's an example from an appeal by a charity for food and medicine in a war-town part of the world then in the news: "As the whole world watches, seemingly unwilling to help, there's one way you can. Make a donation to Catholic Relief Services."

3. **Grab the reader immediately.** The opening of the letter must create instant interest. Introduce a provocative fact. Ask a pertinent question. Give a poignant example. Use a cogent anecdote. Report a paradox. Sometimes writers tie into current events that are fresh on the minds of their readers.

4. **Ask for help.** This is no time to be subtle. If you want a contribution, ask for it. If you are seeking new members, invite them. If you want people to write letters to the governor, ask (and give them the address). Experience with direct mail has shown that it is important to ask for help early and often, and to make it easy for people to respond. For years, Oxfam America used a fund-raising letter that stated clearly: "In our world of abundance, hunger is an unnecessary evil. And, today, you have the opportunity to do something about it."

5. **Set an appropriate tone.** Every letter should have its own feel or attitude. Some direct-mail appeals are folksy. Others are frenzied. Some are friendly invitations. The tone of each letter should be appropriate for the reader, the sending organization, and the person signing the letter.

6. **Explain the significance.** Appeal letters will succeed to the extent that they interest the reader. The writer's task is to explain the significance of a topic that the reader can reasonably be expected to care about.

7. **Show the benefit to the reader.** Few people care that your organization needs more money, more members or more support. Instead, most people want to know how contributions, memberships or other support can help them. You are not a beggar on a street corner asking for a handout—you are a professional writer advocating on behalf of your organization, offering something of value to the reader. Remember this! That something may be a chance to help find a cure for an illness that has affected a family member or to purchase a product that will help make the reader's life easier. It may simply be the opportunity to feel good about helping someone else. Whatever the benefit, give the reader a personal reason for supporting your organization or buying your product or service.

8. **Write for both the heart and the head.** People have different psychological make ups. Research suggests that some people are persuaded by factual and logical explanations, while others are more likely to be influenced by emotional appeals. Appeal letters can persuade both types of readers. Use facts, offer statistics, quote authoritative sources. But also humanize the issue, tell a story, and appeal to the emotions.

9. **Tell a story.** "Your tale, sir, would cure deafness," Miranda says in Shakespeare's "The Tempest." Our stories, too, can cure the deafness of an apathetic audience, if those stories are poignant and well told. Put a face on your message. Give a personal example. Sketch a verbal portrait of a person who has benefited from the organization's activities. Present a vignette about a program. In other words, find a way to make your message come alive for the reader. The Society for the Prevention of Cruelty to Animals in one large city used a letter with this vignette to tell about a dog it rescued: "The man looked nervously over his shoulder as he fumbled with the rope. He hoped no one saw him as he tied the young shepherd and a note to the fence. Her questioning eyes never left his face. She shivered from the arctic gust of wind that swept across the field next to the SPCA. Completing his chore, the man leapt into his car and sped off without a backward glance. Annie was her name. He could not afford to keep her any longer. Fear crept into her once-trusting eyes as she stood alone by the fence." The letter reports a happy ending: The SPCA cared for Annie and found a home for her as a mascot pet at a residence for handicapped children.

10. **Be passionate.** Write with a conviction and a fervor that can incite your reader to action. Be enthusiastic, even zealous. After all, if you don't seem to care, why should the reader? A few years ago, the Sierra Club sent out an unambiguous letter with this forceful beginning: "When extremist anti-environmental forces first swarmed into Congress, they believed they had a mandate to launch an all-out WAR against America's environment. They were wrong!"

11. **Don't exaggerate.** While being passionate, don't overstate the situation. Not every appeal involves a life-or-death matter. Don't risk your credibility with a short-term ploy, as did the boy who cried "Wolf!" so often that people stopped believing him. Instead, state the facts with honesty, candor and a proper perspective. The Humane Society points with pride to its victories but tries to keep things in perspective: "While our programs and activities have been successful in reducing animal cruelty, we are constantly faced with new problems of animal suffering that need immediate attention and drain our resources."

12. **Help the reader get involved.** Suggest several ways the reader can act on the persuasive message you give. If you are writing on behalf of a job-training program for school dropouts, for example, you may want to ask for money, volunteers, business sponsors, used equipment and supplies. Or itemize how financial contributions can help. In its plea for donations, Habitat for Humanity offers these options: "With a gift of only $20, you can help purchase a 50-pound box of nails to finish a Habitat house. Or, your gift of $35 could help purchase roofing materials. And a gift of $50 from you can help pay for a kitchen door."

13. **Feature credible testimonials.** Appeal letters often include statements of support from well-known and respected people, perhaps celebrities or previous beneficiaries of the program. Others are signed by honorary chairpersons. Local charities often enlist the assistance of sports figures, media personalities, and other hometown celebrities in appealing for community support.

14. **P.S.: End with a P.S.** Research shows that an effective conclusion for an appeal letter is a brief postscript, especially one that looks handwritten. In the postscript,

---

Box 14.4
Sample Fundraising Letter

The American Foundation for Suicide Prevention, which sponsors participatory fundraising activities, suggests that volunteers use letters such as this to generate support. Note that this letter follows the guidelines for effective fundraising letters. It makes an emotional impact with a personal story. It identifies the cause, establishes the credentials of the organization, and educates readers about that cause. It clearly makes the request, and its Web link makes it easy for people to respond.

Dear Patty,

I am preparing for something very important in my life, and I am asking for your moral, financial and emotional support.

My uncle, Jeff, took his own life 15 years ago when he was in college. It's not something that I have talked about often, but it is something that I have carried around in my heart for a long time.

I want to commemorate Jeff's life by participating in *Out of the Darkness Overnight*, an event that raises money for suicide-prevention programs. I will be among thousands of people walking 20 miles from sunset to sunrise to send a message of hope to the world.

No one talked to me about my uncle's suicide. That's why I'm walking in *Out of the Darkness Overnight*, to raise awareness and let people know it's okay to talk about suicide and mental illness. I want to do my part to prevent tragedies like Uncle Jeff's from happening in other families.

The American Foundation for Suicide Prevention is at the forefront of many research, education, prevention and survivor initiatives. Suicide is the 11th leading cause of death and the second leading cause of death among college students. Every year, more than 30,000 people in the United States die from suicide.

That's why I'm doing this. To do something bold about an issue that so few people talk about. I hope that you'll share this incredible journey with me by supporting me in my fundraising efforts. To help make a difference, you can go www.TheOvernight.org, click "Support a Participant," and look up my personal fundraising webpage to donate online. Please share this letter with other people who may want to lend their support as well.

Sincerely, Michelle

---

restate the main benefit to the reader and ask again for the contribution. Readers may skip over some sections of the letter, but they nearly always read a P.S. at the end. One example: "Doctors Without Borders teams are working around the clock to provide urgent medical care to thousands of children in Niger, Chad, and other treatment centers around the world. Please help us reach more children."

Exciting Careers for Writers with Vision

Public relations and advertising writers have many means at their disposal to communicate on behalf of their clients and organizations. Among effective practitioners, two qualities stand out. One is being able to develop strategies and make decisions for presenting the message;

the other is being an excellent writer. A public relations practitioner is called on to act as a journalist, business writer, copywriter, editorialist, speechwriter and editor, as well as a researcher and interviewer. An advertising copywriter likewise is a wordsmith who understands culture, psychology and current events. Demanding? Yes. Rewarding? Without a doubt!

The fields of public relations and advertising are exciting career choices for anyone interested in using his or her writing skills to advocate a cause, promote an idea, advance an organization, sell a product or support a political candidate or cause. With the right employer or client, it can be sheer satisfaction—one of those jobs that, even if you had all the money you'd ever dreamed of, you'd volunteer to do just because you care about the cause or like the product so much. Public relations and advertising can be careers that offer financial rewards and scores of job possibilities, as well as personal satisfaction associated with being creative, solving problems and contributing to society.

Discussion Questions

The following are class discussion questions drawn from Chapter 14:

1. How does *advertising* differ from *public relations*?

2. How does *consumer advertising* differ from *public relations advertising*?

3. What are some of the guidelines for developing an effective visual message for print and broadcast advertising?

4. What are some of the techniques used in writing successful appeal letters?

CHAPTER EXERCISES

Exercise 14.1—Print Advertisement

You have been asked to prepare a general (brand) advertisement for use in a national magazine. The full-page ad should promote one of the following commercial products:

- A new line of designer underwear

- A new CD by an up-and-coming music group

- Membership in a chain of health clubs

The advertisement should combine visual and textual messages. Plan the ad and write advertising copy according to the following steps:

1. Describe the art and write a headline for two versions of the advertisement: one showing the product in use, the other comparing the product to its competitors.

2. Indicate a specific audience for the advertisement, then write a text paragraph describing the benefits of the product to that audience.

3. For the same audience, write a text paragraph comparing the product to its competitors.

Exercise 14.2 — TV Script

You have been asked to script a 30-second TV public service advertisement (follow the writing format from the broadcast chapters: 16 lines of type on the right half of the page, with director's cues, including prospective visuals, on the left) for one of the following nonprofit organizations:

*   An environmental organization trying to improve water quality in state lakes and rivers

*   A summer camp for children with physical disabilities

*   A coalition of religious groups promoting spiritual values

Prepare three versions of the advertisement, including directions for video and both audio channels:

1. Write the script for a television or video advertisement featuring the personal testimonial of someone who articulates the message of the nonprofit organization.

2. Write the script for a television or video advertisement featuring dialogue between two people who present the organization's message.

3. Write the script for a television or video advertisement featuring the use of a symbol that presents the message of the organization.

Exercise 14.3 — Appeal Letter

Select a project or program sponsored by a nonprofit organization, then write the following paragraphs for an appeal letter:

*   An opening paragraph that quickly grabs the reader's interest

*   A specific and direct request for money

*   A benefit paragraph that explains how making the contribution will benefit the reader

- A story about one of the beneficiaries of the program

- A postscript of one or two sentences

Suggestions for Further Reading

Alsteil, Tom. *Advertising Strategy: Creative Tactics from the Outside/In* (Thousand Oaks, Calif.: Sage, 2005).

Bayan, Richard. *More Words That Sell* (New York: McGraw-Hill, 2003).

Bendinger, Bruce. *The Copy Workshop Workbook 2002*, 2nd ed. (Chicago: Copy Workshop, 2002).

Bly, Robert. W. *The Copywriter's Handbook: A Step-by-Step Guide to Writing Copy That Sells*, 3rd ed. (New York: Holt, 2006).

Burton, Philip Ward. *Advertising Copywriting* (New York: McGraw-Hill, 1999).

Drewniani, Bonnie L., and A. Jerome Jewler. *Creative Strategy in Advertising,* 9th ed. (Belmont, Calif.: Wadsworth, 2000).

Gabay, Jonathan T. *Teach Yourself Copywriting,* 3rd ed. (New York: McGraw-Hill, 2003).

Kranz, Jonathan. *Copywriting for Dummies* (Hoboken, N.J.: Wiley, 2005).

Parente, Donald. *Advertising Campaign Strategy: A Guide to Marketing Communication Plans,* 4th ed. (Cincinnati, Ohio: South-Western, 2004).

Sugarman, Joseph. *The AdWeek Copy Handbook: The Ultimate for Writing Powerful Advertising Copy from One of America's Top Copywriters* (New York: Wiley, 2006).

Veloso, Maria. *Web Copy That Sells: The Revolutionary Formula for Creating Killer Copy Every Time* (New York: American Marketing Association, 2004).

Afterword:
You and the Future

Welcome to the Information Age

The new interactive, multimedia, computer-generated CD-ROM, Internet–World Wide Web environment of the early 21st century is bringing about an even bigger revolution in human communication than did Johann Gutenberg's development of printing by movable type in the mid-15th century. The new communication technologies, in digital convergence through computer, TV and cell phone, are changing the way we live, work, access content and relate to one another. They will also change the way media writers do their jobs in the 21st century, if there even *are* media jobs in the present sense of the word 25 years from now.

Impact of Technology

Technology has always altered our patterns of communication. The printing press, which made possible the inexpensive mass production of written materials, went through increased stages of efficiency as hand-powered presses gave way to steam, then to electric and finally to today's high-tech marvels. News and information have increasingly traveled faster and faster, speeded by telegraph, telephone, wireless telegraph, radio and TV, then broadcasting in the satellite age. Now, the buzzwords are *interactive* and *multimedia,* technology applications that are increasingly determining the availability and distribution of communication messages.

Technology has also transformed communication among media professionals. The fax machine changed the nature of generating public relations news releases. E-mail accelerated information exchange and made the process less formal. Now, a new generation of **Personal Data Assistants (PDA's)**, handheld "smartphone" devices that provide state-of-the-art mobile communication and personal organization tools, have revolutionized the way communication professionals are able to do their jobs. One of the most popular has been the BlackBerry, a mobile phone with capabilities for e-mail and Web browsing that doubles as an electronic organizer and day planner that has become for many an indispensable business tool. Some of its more sophisticated models include a camera and media player, with "push" technology that sends e-mail to the device so that the user does not miss important messages. Cell phones have turned into picture-taking and video recording devices, such as the the iPhone, a camera phone and multimedia player, with text messaging, visual voicemail and Internet services such as e-mail, Web browsing, and local Wi-Fi connectivity. A multi-touch screen with a virtual keyboard and buttons makes it capable of spreading and receiving images across the Internet from almost any location.

The vision of an Information Superhighway only a few short years ago has turned into a cornucopia of nearly unlimited news, entertainment, financial services and personal communication in a multimedia mix of text, audio and video. Multimedia has become a mass-market commodity combining the computer, cable TV, and telephone into a single system. First appearing with only graphics, multimedia soon added audio, animation and video. Increasingly, the word "multimedia" is preceded by "interactive" because the consumer can become involved in developing content. Users not only can communicate information and ideas through text, but may also express emotions with sounds and images in real-time, interactive video delivered via the Web or a corporate intranet. Imagine what a creative public relations specialist can do with technologies like these!

Online journalists routinely use **hyperlinks**, elements that link to other documents or sources; click on the hyperlink for additional detail, they instruct readers. A news story about a newly-released report on global warming, for instance, has a link to the full report. It is a feature that readers have come to expect.

Hypertext, a word first coined in 1965, has the potential to revolutionize scholarship, analysis and education. Applications of hypertext include books that have a different ending for every reader and research papers that are electronically linked to hundreds of thousands of other works. The technology is important to journalists because, like other individualized services, it gives readers the power to customize their electronic "newspapers," selecting stories and information of interest or importance to them alone.

Hypermedia, an advance on hypertext, links not just words to other words but also words to images and sounds. It seems certain that investigative journalists of the future will be affected by this technology as more records and documents are placed on the Internet, capable of being stored on desktop computers with increased hard drive capacity. Their jobs will be easier because more information will be available. Their jobs will also become more difficult because of the necessity of wading through vast amounts of data.

Likewise, the definition of the broadcast journalist is changing, too, as newspapers depend on video pieces to complement traditional print stories. The role of the public relations professional is increasingly becoming that of an information specialist, managing data for a variety of internal and external publics.

Successful newspaper reporters, broadcast journalists, and public relations practitioners used to have one thing in common: outstanding writing ability. Now that skill is not enough. Communication specialists of the future will not only need strong writing skills, but also the mindset to master the information technologies of computing and the ability to adopt new skills to cope with this wondrous communication world of the 21st century. If you are not comfortable in front of a computer screen and don't know a modem from a mouse, you probably should either consider further computer training or other career options.

More Ways to Communicate Information

These technological developments are not abstract concepts for the communication professional of the 21st century. Instead, they are changing the way journalists, broadcasters, and public relations specialists do their jobs. Media practitioners are already tied to an invisible electronic tether, capable of being reached by sources or supervisors at all hours. A few years ago, the buzzword was "working 24/7." Now, with technology, the work time has expanded to 24/7/365. The resulting changes in communicating techniques are even more far-reaching than those that occurred when the telephone and typewriter were developed in the 19th century.

Some of these technologies involve improving the means of transmitting multimedia content. **Cellular digital-packet data (CDPD)** technology uses a cellular telephone network to transmit voice and data simultaneously by sending bursts of data during the tiny pauses in normal speech. Research into CDPD has resulted in a network that can cope with the intermingled text, sound, and graphics of multimedia. **Integrated Services Digital Network (ISDN)** technology uses telephone lines with specialized switching equipment to provide a combined voice and data communication capability. ISDN quality has improved since fiber-optic lines began to replace coaxial cable in the United States, and an international effort involving more than 100 nations is underway to tie world telephone systems to an ISDN link.

Asynchronous Transfer Mode (ATM) technology uses high-bandwidth, low-delay switching and multiplexing techniques to rapidly provide simultaneous transmission of voice, video and data signals. Analysts predict that this transmission method, coupled with increased use of broadband service for home computers, will give tomorrow's communication specialists worldwide access to information and instantaneous contact capability anywhere at any time. Yet another tool for tomorrow's communication specialists, especially those in public relations or marketing, is Web-based, or **LAN (local area network)**, teleconferencing. Software exists for point-to-point or multiple-point pickups and some provides "whiteboard" areas where participants can collaborate on various projects, such as slide presentations. One application is videoconferencing for marketing focus groups, increasingly used by public relations practitioners involved in integrated marketing communication. The presenter can control the pace and sequence of visuals and voice supports for pictures and graphics.

Even the personal computer may be on its way out. The trend is away from expensive hardware to a system where video is compressed at transmission and viewed with a browser plug-in. "Net boxes"—computer terminals that connect to the Internet or a service provider with a minimum of hardware and software—enable users to process e-mail, Web pages, word-processing programs and spreadsheets at a lower startup and maintenance cost. This technology will open new possibilities for media freelancers.

The End of Agenda Setting?

The linkage of Web sites and information content based on reader interest will make the agenda-setting function of the mass media increasingly consumer-driven, giving users the power to select what they want instead of receiving what today's editor thinks they need. These technologies are a mixed blessing for the public relations professional. While getting information to the mainstream media has been no guarantee that attitudes about a business, candidate or idea will be shaped by that information, the sender still had control of how the message was delivered to the gatekeeper. The first wave of mass computer technologies made it possible to reach selected publics or potential consumers. Now, the new technologies allow people to talk in chat groups or read blogs about a product or organization, and advocates or detractors can create Web pages filled with facts and information—not all of it necessarily true.

There has already been a problem of verifying material not gathered and checked by traditional journalists. For example, look at some of the rumors that spread (and persist) following the terrorist attacks of September 11, 2001. Although some of the wilder allegations were soon discredited, surveys found that because stories appeared on the Internet, many people said they believed that version of "news" due to the level of the credibility they placed in the new medium.

There was a hoax a few years ago that made the rounds of Internet chat rooms: Microsoft had bought out the Vatican and the Pope was going to be on the Microsoft board of directors, along with Bill Gates. That story continued for hours until Microsoft and the Vatican finally had to issue denials! The problem of verification, of course, has been present ever since mass-produced books began flooding Europe in the sixteenth and seventeenth centuries. There have always been fringe publications that shade or distort the truth (or tell the truth when no one else dares to). Internet users will have to become source-savvy about what's in cyberspace, just as print readers have done with books, magazines and pamphlets.

The Power of One: You

Engineers talk of a law of unintended consequences, which says that technological developments are at times used in ways the inventor had never imagined. For instance, increasingly user-friendly software has permitted ordinary people to easily and inexpensively create their own blogs and Web sites. Essentially, this means they can become publishers or broadcasters. These new online networks bear little resemblance to traditional mass media, with their top-down, hierarchical, "We'll tell you what we think you ought to know" frame of reference. Instead, they are horizontal, point-to-point, person-to-person. Access to the airwaves is closed except to licensees; the World Wide Web is open to all who have the ability to provide content. This development has already begun to blur the lines between public relations and journalism because it allows for the providing of material directly to consumers without the intervention and interpretation of reporters. And, where the traditional media audience is passive—audience members read, listen or watch—the new online world is interactive, with users able to challenge, amend or add content.

Further support for these trends comes from **push technology**, which automatically delivers specific types of information to PC desktops without the user browsing the Web to pull down sites of interest. The applications for public relations professionals include using push to deliver internal newsletter material to companies and to reach specialized external publics with controlled content and presentation.

Now information includes live audio and video, thanks to the concept of **streaming**, using real-time video and audio from the Internet without having to download prior to viewing or listening. Streaming has the potential to further revolutionize information retrieval and dissemination. Audio files can be sampled as they are downloaded—or be stopped, rewound or fast-forwarded—and users can choose from a variety of programs. Using this technology, events can be covered live, which means that freelance or independent broadcasters will be able to use stations broadcasting on the Web to reach new audiences or even start their own online radio stations, similar to today's home pages. For public relations, the technology allows companies to transmit daily radio programs to employees, stockholders or other publics, substituting audio clips for memos or inserting them in Web pages. With streaming technology, even the smallest of closed-system intranets can develop personal video, corporate TV or videoconferencing.

Now that the cost and size of satellite receiving dishes have dramatically decreased, interactive telecomputing is also being affected by **direct broadcast by satellite (DBS)**, in which rooftop receivers pick up satellite transmissions. If journalists do become freelancers, it should be possible for viewers to pick up a daily DBS report from a favorite correspondent, although a process needs to be developed for viewers to somehow compensate the reporter.

No Signposts on the Information Highway

This journey down the cyberspace information highway has led to some serious questions that will affect print and broadcast journalists, public relations practitioners, and society at large. For instance, how can we best use the astounding volume of information to which we will have access? Reporters commonly become bogged down in paperwork when researching a news story. That problem is being compounded with the increased availability of databases carrying enormous amounts of data. In the same vein, how can we avoid the proliferation of electronic garbage that clutters up networks and takes so much time to analyze? Just as we have junk mail, we already have junk messages in cyberspace, along with information we do not necessarily need or material that is detrimental to society.

If we take the view that most people will choose something other than news and information services, how do we deal with the social fragmentation that results from literally thousands of channels of communication? For all its faults, the limitation of television in the United States to only the three commercial networks for years produced a common agenda of news, public affairs and entertainment. Now, with the proliferation of channels, each targeting a narrow segment of the audience, TV is engaged in "narrowcasting." The Internet compounds this condition because isolated groups in society are increasingly talking only among themselves.

A related question is how we avoid having a nation and world of information haves and have-nots based on the ability to pay for technological services. If knowledge is indeed power, then lack of knowledge results in powerlessness. Ironically, the 21st century could be the one with the greatest potential for communication but with a majority of the population uninformed about basic information essential to their well-being, either because they do not have access to the technology, or because there are so many attractive, entertaining messages competing for attention.

Careers in Communication

Assuming that you want to be part of this exciting, challenging and fast-changing field of media writing, what career options are available? The good news is that there has been an explosion of opportunities in Internet-related media and alternative video programming spurred by cable and satellite TV. In the traditional media, however, the job market is increasingly competitive. Staffing cutbacks have resulted in a greater number of highly qualified people seeking to fill fewer news and editorial positions, often at reduced salaries. With a large pool of potential talent, pay and benefits have stagnated over the past several years and, although salary figures have climbed modestly, inflation-adjusted wages are still behind those of a few years ago. The economic downturn of late 2008 cannot help but to make the situation less advantageous for graduates entering the job market.

A 2007 survey of recent journalism and communication graduates reported by the Association for Education in Journalism and Mass Communication[1] showed little change in hiring patterns from the year before. Respondents reported almost the same level of job offers and interviews and were just as likely to land jobs, but often with better benefits. Most degree recipients reported at least one job interview, and three-quarters of them said they had a definite job offer upon graduation. Full-time employment was 63.3 percent of the graduates, about the same as the previous two years, as was part-time employment. Unemployment was slightly above the national average for the early-20s age group of recent college and university graduates and was several percentage points above the overall national unemployment average. Women fared slightly better than men in finding a job; racial and ethnic minorities were less successful than the general population.

While the median annual salary for 2007, $30,000, remained the same as the previous year, it essentially dropped $695 adjusted for inflation, a figure below that of five years earlier. More telling, the median salary in the communication field was more than $6,000 below that earned by liberal arts graduates. Salaries were below the median in daily newspapers ($28,000), weekly newspapers ($26,900), radio ($25,000), and television ($29,300). Exceeding the median were public relations and advertising ($32,000), cable TV ($30,500), specialized publications ($37,000), consumer magazines ($32,000) and the Web ($37,400).

More than half said they wrote and edited for the Web as part of their responsibilities, and 80 percent said they conducted research on the Internet, often on a daily basis. Web-related activities were most common for those in online publishing, specialized information outlets and public relations. The workload is intensive, however. A third of respondents said they spent more than 40 hours a week on the job. And while 42 percent of respondents said they were "very satisfied" with their jobs, one-fourth said they wished they'd chosen another career.

The AEJ report cautioned that the ongoing decline in the overall U.S. labor market in the first half of 2008 and continuing announcements of layoffs at large newspapers does not bode well for new graduates. An earlier *Editor and Publisher* survey[2] noted that while large and mid-size newspapers cut somewhat fewer jobs in 2006, "smaller papers are now beginning to slash." For every traditional editorial job lost, however, jobs were being added in online divisions, although Web-based advertising remains sluggish, not compensating for the loss of traditional newspaper revenue streams.

"May You Live in Interesting Times"

The Chinese toast "May you live in interesting times" has a double meaning. On one hand, it implies change and excitement; on the other, challenge. The years ahead should be exciting times of change for media professionals. Predictions are that news reporters of the future will become highly specialized "information agents"—independent entrepreneurs selling their knowledge-based wares directly to the public via the telecommunications network. Media outlets are becoming what is being termed "information distribution portals."

The newspaper industry is getting out of the printing business and into the knowledge and information business, where news arrives from many sources and goes out over even more channels, including the printed page, World Wide Web, computer bulletin boards, CD-ROM, and even DBS. This new technology has the potential to bring back long, interpretative news and features; in cyberspace, "length" no longer matters because the multimedia reader will be able to go as deeply into a story as he or she desires.

The TV news profession is already seeing the impact of changes in video technology, creating the paradox that field reporting techniques in some markets have returned to those of more than 30 years ago. With lightweight cameras and equipment, a "backpack journalist" can go out, set up a camera and a satellite dish, and then report a story and transmit it all without several members of a production crew tagging along. Computer editing stations, which allow reporters to type and edit copy as they screen the video, give reporters more control over how stories are produced. These advances present the reporter–producers with new challenges: They must know as much as their print counterparts and be capable of quickly covering virtually anything and everything.

Lightweight user-friendly video equipment capable of producing broadcast-compatible quality means that more pieces shot by independent and average-citizen viewers are making it onto the air, and onto the Internet. More than half of American adults (54 percent) had high-speed broadband connections at home at the end of 2007 and, a Pew Research Center survey found, nearly half (48 percent) visited YouTube or similar video-sharing Web sites on a regular basis. The survey also determined that 22 percent of Americans shoot their own videos and 14 percent post some parts of them online.[3] Another application, digital video in individual home pages is providing yet another source of information. Although traditional TV production jobs are dwindling due to automated studio technology, even greater opportunities are going to open up in an environment that has literally thousands of "broadcast" outlets.

Public relations practitioners, who are already looking at alternatives to traditional media to get messages to the public, are becoming management consultants whose primary task is to provide tailored and timely expertise by managing information. Relying on computer networks, personal communicators, videoconferencing, e-mail, and faxes, these consultants will be expected to sort through and make sense of large volumes of information, seizing opportunities and heading off problems.

Opportunities from New Technology

It seems clear that the unprecedented amount of information available will generate a critical need for talented people who can sift, shape and share it. The role of community journalism, for instance, may well increase because technology will permit micro as well as macro applications of news. However, future journalists will need to see news as a whole—text, audio, video, data—and organize the elements to best serve the user.

Canadian communication theorist Marshall McLuhan, who predicted that the electronic media, especially TV, would turn the world into a global village, noted that "linear" print media had fragmented society into a collection of individuals, each seeking dreams of personal fulfillment. Today, this computer-based electronic presence has the potential to bring us together into that global village or to fragment society far more than print was ever able to achieve. The Internet may either link us together as a shared community or create a host of smaller worldwide units that feed on isolation and intolerance.

We can't fully predict how the Internet and computer technologies will change society because so many computer-based applications are undergoing constant upgrading or development. Graduates in the communication field for the next few years will be entering a rapidly changing media landscape that blends new and traditional forms of communication, an environment in which sounds, images and information have become available whenever and wherever we like.[4] It's an exciting time, and if you have what it takes and want to be in a position to make your corner of the world a better place, to meet some fascinating people and work in a dynamic and rewarding profession, then journalism, broadcasting or public relations may be for you.

Suggestions for Further Reading

Careers in Media

Barnas, Frank, and Michael P. Savoie. *Careers in Media* (Boston: Allyn & Bacon, 2007).

Seguin, James. *Media Career Guide: Preparing for Jobs in the 21st Century*, 6th ed. (Boston: Bedford/St. Martins, 2008).

Impact of New Computer Technologies

Dizard, Jr., Wilson. *Meganet: How the Global Communications Network Will Connect Everyone on Earth* (Boulder, Colo.: Westview Press, 1998).

Edgerton, David. *The Shock of the Old: Technology and Global History Since 1900* (New York: Oxford University Press, 2006).

Gates, Bill. *The Road Ahead* (New York: Viking, 1995).

——. *Business @ The Speed of Thought: Using a Digital Nervous System* (New York: Warner Books, 1999).

Grant, August E., and Jennifer H. Meadows. *Communication Technology Update*, 10th ed. (Boston: Focal Press, 2006).

Hansen, Mark. *New Philosophy for New Media* (Cambridge: MIT Press, 2006).

Jenkins, Henry. *Convergence Culture: Where Old and New Media Collide* (New York: NYU Press, 2006).

——, and David Thorburn, Eds. *Democracy and New Media* (Cambridge, Mass: MIT Press, 2004).

Keen, Andrew. *The Cult of the Amateur: How Today's Internet is Killing Our Culture* (New York: Currency/Doubleday, 2007).

Lievrouw, Leah, and Sonia Livingstone, Eds. *Handbook of New Media* (Thousand Oaks, Calif.: Sage, 2006).

Negroponte, Nicholas. *Being Digital* (New York: Knopf, 1995).

Schuler, Douglas, and Peter Day, Eds. *Shaping the Network Society: The New Role of Civil Society in Cyberspace* (Cambridge, Mass.: MIT Press, 2004).

Notes

1. Tudor Vlad, Lee B. Becker, Megan Vogel, Stephanie Hanisak and Donna Wilcox, "2007 Annual Survey of Journalism and Mass Communication Graduates," August 2008, conducted by the Grady College of Journalism and Mass Communication at the University of Georgia, reported in *AEJMC News*, November 2008, pp. 1, 4–8, with the full survey online at www.grady.uga.edu/annualsurveys/ Graduate_Survey/Graduate_2007/grdrpt2007mergedb&wv1.pdf.

2. Jennifer Saba, "Job Cuts in 2006 Painful—But Fewer Than in 2005," *Editor and Publisher*, January 26, 2007, www.editorandpublisher.com/eandp/news/article_display.jsp?vnu_content_id=1003537810.

3. Lee Rainie, "Online Video Audience Surges," a report of the Pew Internet Project, January 9, 2008, http://pewresearch.org/pubs/682/online-video-audience-surges.

4. See "Key News Audiences Now Blend Online and Traditional Sources," "Audience Segments in a Changing News Environment," a survey by the Pew Research Center for People and the Press, August 21, 2008, at http://people-press.org/report/444/news-media.

Credits

Index